Publishing, Culture,
and Power in Early
Modern China

# Publishing, Culture, and Power in Early Modern China

KAI-WING CHOW

*Stanford University Press*
*Stanford, California*

Stanford University Press
Stanford, California

Printed and bound by CPI Group (UK) Ltd, Croydon, CR0 4YY

Library of Congress Cataloging-in-Publication Data

Chow, Kai-wing, 1951–

    Publishing, culture, and power in early modern China / Kai-wing Chow.
      p.   cm.
    Includes bibliographical references and index.
    ISBN 0-8047-3367-8 (alk. paper)—ISBN 978-0-8047-3368-7 (pbk. : alk. paper)
      1. Printing—China—History. 2. China—Civilization—960–1644. I. Title.
  z186.c5c56 2004
  070.5'0951—dc21        2003007586

Typeset by Integrated Composition Systems in 10/14 Sabon.

*In memory of my beloved teacher*
*Professor Kwang-ching Liu*

# Contents

*Figures*

# Tables

## A Note on Terms, Translations, and Usages

Romanization follows the standard pinyin system except in the following cases:

— For names of scholars who have published in English using different systems of Romanization: for example, Ying-shih Yu, instead of Yingshi Yu.

— Names of bureaucratic units in the central government are capitalized: for example, the Libu (Ministry of Rites).

— The term "Classics" is capitalized if it means Confucian Classics. Lowercase "classics" can mean Daoist or literary classics.

— Titles of books are translated in the text. Sources in the bibliography that serve as mere references are not translated; Chinese characters are provided in the Character List and Bibliography.

*Preface to the Paperback Edition*

This is a new paperback edition, with only a few errors corrected. More changes may be possible with another revision in the future. But for this new edition, it is most appropriate to take advantage of this paratext to address a major theoretical issue concerning the use of analytical concepts in this study.

Some reviewers of this book are confounded by the fact that I criticize Eurocentric approaches to Chinese history and yet the major concepts I use in the book are formulated by European scholars. This mistakenly perceived "contradiction" warrants a clarification. It is important to differentiate "Eurocentric" from "Eurogenic." The former refers to a way of representing and explaining social formation and history through European, or more precisely Western, perspective whereas the latter pertains to objects—both symbolic and material—originating in Europe. Unlike Eurocentric concepts and theories such as "print capitalism," "civil society," "individualism," and "modernity," the concepts of "field" and "paratext," for example, are not components of Western grand narratives of the unique development of institutional and intellectual systems that propelled Europe into the course of ultimate triumph and domination in the modern period.

Unlike the sociological theories of Max Weber and Anthony Giddens, or Jürgen Habermas' theory of the "public sphere," Pierre Bourdieu's major concepts such as "field," "habitus," and "symbolic capital" do not postulate any necessary connection—historical or theoretical—with theories of capitalism or modern nation-state. They are not formulated to explain and justify the presumably superior and unique practices of Modern Europe. In fact, his theory offers "a critique of modernity" (see Craig Calhoun, "Habitus, Field, and Capital: The Question of Historical Specificity," in Craig Calhoun, Edward LiPuma, and Moishe Postonel, eds., *Bourdieu: A Critical Perspective*, Chicago: University of Chicago Press, p.

62). Bourdieu is not interested in differentiating types of society. As evident in his early fieldwork in Kabylia and his later study of the French society, his analysis takes a specific "social world" as the target of study without postulating any universal course for and typology of social formation. He is concerned with the various procedures for creating differentiation in mental and social structures which allow dominant groups to reproduce modes of domination. Like those theories of Foucault, his theories focus on the analysis of the structure and procedures through which relations of domination in its multiple forms of practice are reproduced.

Despite his commitment to the study of practice as systematic knowledge (science), his concepts of "habitus," "symbolic capital," and "field" are developed to transcend the "knowledge" and culture produced by any specific society. He believes "that there are no *transhistoric laws of the relations between fields* [emphasis in original], [and] that we must investigate each historical case separately" (Pierre Bourdieu and Loïc J.D. Wacquant, *An Invitation to Reflexive Sociology*, Chicago: University of Chicago Press, 1992, p. 109). By avoiding the standard terminology deployed in Eurocentric theories, Bourdieu's theories offer ample opportunities for application in the study of non-European societies. His concepts have provided me with alternative tools to map the impact of printing on the production of culture and power in China in the sixteenth and seventeenth centuries.

The same can be said of Gerard Genette's concept of "paratext." There are indeed some paratexts in the European book that have no counterparts in the Chinese book—the watermark, the out-of-proportion initials, capital letters, and fantastic picture-in-letter initials, etc. But there are certainly numerous elements in the traditional Chinese book that qualify to be called paratexts—prefaces, postscripts, marginal and interlineal comments, method of packaging, paper, book cover, font sizes and colors, illustrations, title, name of author, editor, and publisher, etc. As I have demonstrated in this book, "paratext" can be used to analyze the profound impact of publishing on literary production and power relations in early modern China. The concept of "paratext" needs not implicate any Eurocentric grand theories of historical change or socio-economic and ideological configurations.

Michele Foucault and Michele de Certeau are among the most influential European scholars in furnishing new approaches and theories for the critique of theories and historiography of modernity and capitalism. There is no need to rehearse the criticism of the Enlightenment and the constraining apparatus and procedures of the modern state and society that infuse Foucault's works. The position of Michele de Certeau may warrant some words of explanation. Like Foucault, de Certeau is critical of the development of modern culture in Europe since the Enlightenment. The nation-state, capitalism, and their supporting institutions—writing, law, factory, city and discourses/knowledge—have re-organized practices, suppressing heterogeneous voices and non-standard practices. Unlike Foucault and Bourdieu, however, de Certeau's theories focus on the dominated people's "tactics" of resistance in everyday life—practices like reading, walking, and speaking.

In their analysis and criticism of the technology of power as well as their symbolic regimes in modern capitalist societies in Western Europe, these European scholars have fashioned various tools of analysis that dispute and undermine the assumptions and methods of social and historical analysis produced to explain the "rise of the West." They are Eurogenic theories challenging Eurocentric discourses and historiography. Their application in this study is meant to help clear the obstacles in our study of practices in early modern China, bypassing modernist theories of social and historical analysis, which have obscured and misrepresented the social and historical processes of China.

For this edition, I would like to thank my colleagues, friends, and students for their help in correcting mistakes: my mentor the late Professor Kwang-ching Liu, Tze-ki Hon, and Liangyu Fu; my students Yongtao Du, Lane Harris, Jing Jing Chang, Tonglu Li, Jie Cui, and Joshua Herr. Jing Jing and Lane are especially meticulous in ferreting out inconsistencies and errors.

Finally I would like to dedicate this new edition to my mentor, the late Professor Kwang-ching Liu, who, as he had always done for his students, kindly read the book and corrected some mistakes.

## Acknowledgments

There are many who have generously given their invaluable time to reading the manuscript in its various incarnations. I would like to thank in particular Lynn Struve, Evelyn S. Rawski, Cynthia Brokaw, Robert Hegel, and Tze-ki Hon, and my colleagues at the University of Illinois, Anne Burkus-Chasson and Janet Kelly, for their criticism and comments. There are many who have read different chapters and offered their comments and criticism. Oki Yashushi, Soren Egren, Jack Wills, and my colleagues Gary Xu, Rania Huntington, and Ueda Atsuko have generously offered their time and special knowledge.

I have also benefited from the comments and criticism from colleagues at various seminars and presentations: the Seminar of the History of the Book at Indiana University, the Mellon Dissertation Seminar at Washington University, the K. C. Liu Lecture Series at the University of California, Davis, and a presentation at the University of Hawaii. To Peter Lindenbaum, Lynn Struve, Robert Hegel, Susan Mann, and Daniel Kwok I express gratitude for providing me with great opportunities to test out my ideas. I am also indebted to Johan Hanselaer of Belgium who has kindly translated portions of his article on wages and prices in Antwerp in the sixteenth century.

From their insightful suggestions, criticism, and expertise I have learned to correct mistakes and make improvements. But I remain fully responsible for any mistake that remains in this book.

I must express gratitude to Patricia Ebrey and William Rowe, whose support and advice throughout my academic career hold special meaning. Their friendship and guidance in substantial ways facilitated the progress and completion of the project.

Many friends and librarians have provided assistance for the use and location of books. Qi Kechen and Zhou Shaoquan, Institute of History of the Academy of Social Sciences; Sue Small, School of African and Oriental Studies at the University of London; David Helliwell, Bodleian Library; Su Jing, who was formerly at the Center for Chinese Studies at the Central Library in Taibei. Other staffers at the center who had lent me valuable help include Zhang Lian and Liu Hsien-shu. Shen Jin at the Harvard-Yenching Library and Mi Chu Wiens at the Library of Congress helped me search for Ming imprints. At home, Karen Wei and her staff at the East Asian Collection of the University of Illinois Library have been forthcoming in their support throughout this endeavor. I am particularly indebted to Setsuko Noguchi for her dedication in locating titles for me.

This project originated with the plan to examine late-Ming culture through an in-depth investigation of the thought and life of Li Zhi. It gradually expanded beyond the study of Li Zhi's involvement in publishing to a comprehensive inquiry of the impact of print on late-Ming cultural practices. During its extended gestation and its various stages of mutation, this project has received generous support from various institutions and funding agencies. A grant from the Committee on Scholarly Communication with the People's Republic of China allowed me to conduct research on Ming editions in various libraries in Beijing and Shanghai. A fellowship from the Center for Chinese Studies in Taibei offered a great opportunity for me to examine the collection of late-Ming commentaries on the Four Books at the Center.

The writing of this book was facilitated by grants from various agencies. The Pacific Culture Foundation in Taibei and the Center for East Asian and Pacific Studies at the University of Illinois, Champaign-Urbana, have helped provide funding to support my writing. The Research Board and the Humanities Release Time Program at the University of Illinois have been generous with their support in grants. I am particularly grateful to George Yu, director of the Center for East Asian and Pacific Studies, for his unflagging support throughout the various stages of this project.

Thanks are also due to the National Archives of Japan for granting permission to reproduce copies of pages from four Ming imprints: *Sishu tiyi, Huang Ming bai fangjia wenda, Sishu qianbai nian yan,* and *Chen pi lieguo zhizhuan.* I am particularly grateful to Miss Yumiko Ohara at the service section of the Archival Affairs Division at the National Archives of Japan for her effective communication and professional assistance. Portions of Chapter 4 have been published in the June 1996 issue of *Late Imperial China*.

I would also like to thank Matt Stevens for his meticulous editing. His professionalism is highly salutary. I am truly appreciative of Muriel Bell and Judith Hibbard for their congeniality, advice, and help as editors of the Stanford University Press.

Finally, special thank must go to my wife, Teresa, and my daughters Roxanne and Lorraine, who have contributed substantially in many intangible ways to this project. Without their support and understanding, this project would not have seen the light of the day. This book is dedicated to my parents, whose sacrifice and unfailing love is the ultimate force that makes this book possible. While the sacrifice they made is hardly redeemed by the completion of this book, I hope we can all share the joy in seeing its final publication.

# Introduction: Printing, Eurocentrism, and the Study of the Social in Early Modern China

This is a study of print culture in early modern China.[1] It examines the impact of printing on cultural production. Woodblock impression and moveable type exerted a profound impact on Chinese society. More specifically, the expansion of commercial publishing in the sixteenth and seventeenth centuries impacted the production of literary culture by expanding the "literary public sphere" (*gong*).

This book is a part of my larger project on the role of printing in the production of an alternative literary culture—that of the *shishang* (literati-merchants-businessmen)—in this period.[2] The study of the profound impact of printing and commercial publishing on literary culture, centered on the examinations, reveals the extensive cultural transformation of China in the early modern period.

The impact of printing on literary production in early modern China was multiple. However, this study is concerned primarily with the effect of the growth of commercial publishing on cultural production and the negotiation between an expanding literary elite and the imperial state over the access to political power. First, the expansion of commercial publishing facilitated the growth of a class of literary professionals—writers, editors, compilers, commentators, critics, publishers, and proofreaders—which was but one form taken by the convergence of the careers of the literati (*shi*) and the merchants-businessmen (*shang*).[3] This study focuses on this specific group of *shishang* who engaged in the commercial production of literary culture.

Second, the expansion of the book market produced publicity for literary professionals whose authority came to rival and challenge the authority of the official examiners. This influence was not only over the reading of the Confucian classics but also over the style of prose writing. A new literary authority was created in the "literary public sphere" (*gong*), and new discursive space was opened up by virtue of the expansion of commercial publishing.

As part of the growth in commercial and industrial production, the boom in publishing vastly increased the number of literary genres, creating new and expanding reading publics whose interests were too diverse and heterogeneous for the imperial ideology to accommodate. Editors, critics, and writers were empowered by reputation generated in the market of commercial publishing. In the vastly expanded "paratextual" space of the book, representing personal as well as collective interests, they came to challenge the imperial authority in the field of cultural production.[4] The increase in book production provided the *shishang* with an expansive discursive space to negotiate, challenge, and subvert the authority of the officials in the examination field. They promoted models of literary excellence that were at odds with the official standard. Through editing critical anthologies of examination essays, they expressed dissatisfaction and criticism of the selection of examination candidates, and consequently intervened in the awarding of political offices through mobilizing public opinion of the examinees and the organizational power of professional critics.

Some of the impacts of print culture on literature and women in this period have been explored.[5] Many important changes outlined above, however, have remained unexplored, or more precisely, undetected. There are two main obstacles. One concerns what I call the "sinologistic" approach; the other is the linguistic veil in the literary representation of the

Chinese writers' own experience in this period. The metaphorical mode of representation had obscured much profound change in practice. As will be explained below, the sinologistic mode of history writing as a practice depends heavily on theories, concepts, and methodologies from social sciences that, until recently, have been predominantly developed from studies of European societies. Concepts and theories such as capitalism, the nation-state, Enlightenment, romanticism, individualism, rationality, modernity, the bourgeoisie, ritual, and lineage have been so interwoven into various versions of metanarratives about the "rise of Modern Europe" that scholars who use or avoid them in the study of Chinese history run the risk of activating their idiomatic uses authorized by different disciplines, and consequently misrepresenting practice in China, thereby reproducing Eurocentric narratives by default.[6] This mode of historical writing is common in the study of printing and culture in early modern China. This study is therefore positioned at the intersection of two historical discourses: the history of printing in China and the cultural history of the Ming-Qing transition—a critical juncture in the early modern period. The enormity of the problem presented by sinologistic history in the study of the impact of printing in China and the nature of change in the late Ming and early Qing can be best illustrated by an examination of the current view of the iconoclasm of Li Zhi (1527–1602).

*The Enigma of Chinese Iconoclasm*

"How small is the world! How immense are the books!" exclaimed Li Zhi in a four line poem entitled, "Pleasure of Reading."[7] Li Zhi was one of the best-selling authors in late-Ming China. A reader can justifiably interpret Li Zhi's words to mean that one can find a much bigger world or perhaps more worlds in the books—worlds that one may not experience first hand. They can be real and imagined—worlds of one's desires or worlds one dreads even in dreams. What did Li Zhi find in his vicarious journey across the landscape of the different worlds in the books? As a reader, he indulged himself in the joy of reading and critiquing poetry, novels, plays, and Buddhist scriptures. In the immense horizon unfolding before his eyes, he encountered people and events that moved him to tears. He read about things that made him laugh and spring to his feet to dance. He came upon words after his heart.[8] He found children whose pure, spontaneous, and authentic "child minds" (*tongxin*) could shame his contemporary literati and officials who were deeply infected with hypocrisy and depravity. He was dazzled by rebels who exuded admirable honesty and courage in killing ignoble and corrupt officials and sub-bureaucrats. He discovered the teaching of equality in the writings of Wang Yangming (1472–1528). He flouted conventional wisdom that enshrined the Confucian canon as the only repository of truth and the model of literary excellence.[9] For de Bary, "the tide of individualistic thought in the late Ming reached its height with Li Zhi."[10]

Li Zhi's personal discoveries, made in endless hours of reading in solitude, have never ceased to fascinate his readers. Scholars are enchanted by his iconoclasm toward Zhu Xi's Daoxue—the official orthodoxy. His suicide in 1602 has been hailed as an act of "martyrdom," a sacrifice for "his own conviction."[11] But what is the significance of Li's intellectual rebellion for China and for the world? How do we make sense of the worlds in print that revealed themselves to Li Zhi?

Li Zhi's "rebellious" cause did not involve a vision of a new social order. Li "was reared as a Confucian and died one," concluded the historian Ray Huang.[12] For Huang, not only are Li Zhi's "radical" ideas insignificant, everything that happened in that year and in fact throughout the Ming is of no consequence. Never mind Li Zhi's courageous tirade against hypocrisy of officials, his promotion of egalitarian ideas, and his "insatiable drive for personal emancipation," he "was never as self-assertive as Luther. He lacked even the self-confidence of Erasmus."[13] In the rebellion against tradition, Li Zhi paled in comparison to European intellectual giants. Indeed, as Huang explains, since childhood Li Zhi "was deeply imbued with traditional Chinese culture."[14] This "traditional Chinese culture" not only produced a "highly stylized society," hampering the development of the Ming empire, it rendered everything that happened in China "insignificant." In Huang's view,

> It no longer mattered whether the ruler was conscientious or irresponsible, whether his (the Wanli emperor, r. 1573–1619) chief counselor was enterprising or conformist, whether the generals were resourceful or incompetent, whether the civil officials were honest

or corrupt, or whether the leading thinkers were radical or conservative—in the end they all failed to reach fulfillment. Thus our story has a sad conclusion. The annals of the Year of the Pig must go in history as *a chronicle of failure* [my emphasis].[15]

The phrase "a chronicle of failure," chosen by Huang to conclude his popular book on the late Ming, succinctly bespeaks the theoretical problem in writing about the history of China. For Huang and many others, not only was 1587 a year of no significance, but the entire past of China could be condemned as "a chronicle of failure." Regardless of an effort to improve political conditions and a desire for ridding social injustice, like Li Zhi's tragic struggle, these endeavors were destined to fail to produce any significant radical change in China. Regardless of the magnitude and nature of change, they had no significance because China failed to make the leap over the unbridgeable divide between "tradition" and "modernity." It is in this "chronicle of failure" that "traditional Chinese culture" met its fate. And it is in this "chronicle of failure" that China joins other non-European societies as the Others of the West.[16]

## SINOLOGISTIC MODE OF HISTORICAL NARRATION

As a form of narrative, history writing can take any structure as its plot: success, failure, narrow focus, and open ended. History as a "chronicle of failure" is a common plot deployed in narratives of the pasts of non-European societies. "Failure" and its twin—"absences"—have come to characterize the knowledge of the past of the major non-Western areas—India, China, the Muslim Middle East, and Africa. Even one of the driving forces of postcolonial studies—the subaltern studies in its first phase—is no exception.[17] The heterogeneity and multiple temporalities inherent in all histories are conflated into chronicles of failure and absences—the fate of the Other in contrast with the success and plenitude of the Modern West.

Even as chronicles of failure, the pasts of non-Western societies take on different discursive forms. Ray Huang's book was written in a "sinologistic mode of history." To be differentiated from "sinological," the concept of "sinologistic" refers to a specific mode of historical narration that draws its narrative schemes from three different but intimately related discursive systems of time, space, and culture: historicism, Eurocentrism, and modernism.

Historicism overcomes all heterogeneous temporalities by reducing them to a single, homogenous, and universal scale of time that is both linear and progressive—the specific temporality of Western Europe. As Dipesh Chakrabarty has remarked: "Historicism is what made modernity or capitalism look not simply global but rather as something that became global over time, by originating in one place (Europe) and then spreading outside it."[18] Since the late nineteenth century, Chinese scholars and historians have begun rewriting China's history in a historicist or an "Enlightenment" mode.[19] In historicist narratives, China is given a place in History—a historical metanarrative—that puts China on a stage of human evolution that is condemned to be equivalent to the childhood of Western Europe. China will pass through the same stages at a slower pace. In historicist narrative, China acquired characteristics of primitiveness, underdevelopment, and absence.

Eurocentric narratives designated Western Europe as the agent blessed with the changes that have provided the driving forces to move humankind forward on a single path. In Eurocentric narratives, China is relegated to an insignificant space—the periphery of Europe. Only through gradual diffusion of its specific forms of practices (social, political, and economic formations) as well as symbolic systems (languages, ideological formation), the Others of Western Europe came to be drawn into the single destiny—modernity.[20]

Chinese society and culture in modernist narratives are often deemed lacking in specific forms of modern practice: economic formations (capitalism, stock companies, factories, and industrialization), political formation (nation-state, republican and representative forms of government), and social formation (bourgeoisie, working class, public sphere), and ideological formations (Enlightenment, individualism, and the ideas of progress, public, right, freedom of expression, science, and arts). Modernist narratives of the imperial history of China often register the need to receive from Europe a "cultural impact," or the seeds of change—modernization—without which China would be condemned to the eternal inertia of tradition or change that had no, or little, significance.

In the light of historicism, Eurocentrism, and modernism, China has acquired the civilizational characteristics of primitiveness and underdevelopment, marginality, and insignificance, as well as traditionalism and inertia. These characteristics lend a coherence to the concept of "traditional China."[21] It is easy to understand why Ray Huang was not impressed with Li Zhi's "radical" ideas. For Huang, Li was only less traditional and conformist than his contemporaries. He still stood on the other side of modernity, making gestures of change with no significance. Sinologistic narrative like Huang's reduces the heterogeneous past of China to a homogenous tradition and an ossified culture.

We will not be able to see anything beyond absence and deficiency if we continue to search through a Eurocentric lens, which in de Certeau's words, has redirected "the plurality of ways toward the single productive center."[22] This lens has blocked out lights that could have illuminated the otherwise complex and diachronic patterns of movement in the economic, social, political, and cultural landscapes of life-worlds in China before the nineteenth century. Sinologistic narrative simply is not capable of making intelligible any historical difference it does not recognize. In order to see the possible worlds found by Li Zhi in the books printed in ever larger number in the sixteenth and seventeenth centuries, we need to confront the history of Chinese printing, which has been written in the shadow of the general history of printing infused with heavy doses of historicism and Eurocentrism.

## A Technology of "No Significance": Chinese Woodblock Printing in Sinologistic Narratives

The invention of the movable type printing press in Europe in the mid-fifteenth century has been hailed as the key agent in bringing about or facilitating all major intellectual, political, and religious movements—the Renaissance, the scientific revolution, the Reformation, the Enlightenment, the French Revolution, and the diffusion of the modern nation-state. For historians of European printing, the triumph of modern Europe driven by these powerful forces of intellectual and cultural change was evidence for the superiority of the Gutenberg movable-type printing press as a technology of communication and an agent of progress. In contrast, and despite its invention and spread at least five centuries before in China and East Asia, the woodblock printing method was considered a primitive art, producing no revolutionary changes. This European exceptionalism can be found in standard European accounts that make reference to Chinese printing.[23]

In the now classic work *The Coming of the Book*, by Lucien Febvre and Henri-Jean Martin, the significance of woodblock printing is registered only as the "Chinese Precedent" that failed to advance to the modern stage. While acknowledging the invention of the movable type method in China, Febvre and Martin nonetheless insisted on its failure, which they attributed to the peculiar nature of the Chinese writing—its large number of characters, inferior ink technology, and the enormous capital needed to produce copper types.[24] Echoing the view of Febvre and Martin, Marshall McLuhan in his widely read book, *Gutenberg Galaxy: The Making of Typographical Man*, said: "Chinese ideogramic script proved a complete block against the development of print technology in their culture."[25] The lack of development in printing technology in China clearly refers to its presumed inability to advance the woodblock method to movable type printing. McLuhan thought of woodblock printing as an invention of no consequence, a logical corollary of the peculiar nature of the Chinese writing system.

Elizabeth Eisenstein makes reference to China's invention of movable type printing, but does so only to point out in the footnote that "discussion now centers on the advantages of an alphabetic as against an ideographic written language for full use of letterpress printing."[26] For Eisenstein, the "ideographic" nature of written Chinese language cannot make full use of letterpress printing.[27] The linguistic explanation is deeply rooted in the assumption that only phonetic languages are suitable for the development of the modern form of movable type printing.[28] Eisenstein's view is just another rehearsal of the standard, European view on the history of Chinese printing.[29]

Despite the fast-growing field of the history of the book in European and Anglo-American academia, the study of printing in China has remained largely in the shadow of studies employing the technological approach, which stress the function of printing in disseminating information and ideas. In fact, this approach is still influential in the study of printing in other East Asian countries, such as Japan.[30] Recently a fast expanding literature has been produced to explore the impact of publishing on different facets of Chinese society.[31] Within the purview of Chinese history, current scholarship has provided new information on, and important insight into, the involvement of literati in publishing as authors, editors, and publishers; the impact of publishing on women's culture; the specific manner in which printing created new reading publics; new types of religious texts; and sacred sites as well as commentaries on classical texts.[32] Nonetheless, the larger historical significance of the impact of printing on Chinese society has not been attempted from a comparative perspective on the history of printing.[33] A truly historical comparison of the impact of printing—both woodblock and movable type—can only begin with a confrontation with the dominant discourse of printing.

### Challenging the Gutenberg Discourse on European Printing

The Gutenberg press has taken on a significance of monstrous magnitude as a revolutionary means of communication in the metanarrative of the triumph of modern Europe. In his introduction to a special issue on printing in imperial China, the French historian Roger Chartier calls for a "strengthened dialogue between historians of China and Europe."[34] This dialogue, however, will not be conducted in earnest as long as European historians are not informed of the impact of printing in China and East Asia. As Henry D. Smith II has aptly pointed out, "The heights of sophistication and complexity that Chinese print culture had reached long before Gutenberg still remain difficult for European historians of the book to grasp."[35] Indeed, without a revisit from East Asia, the Gutenberg narrative will continue to diminish any attempt to understand the impact of printing in East Asia. It is therefore imperative to engage European historians with respect to the large issues in the study of the history of publishing in China.

Challenge to the Gutenberg narrative has already begun within the Anglophonic academe. Recent studies of the role of printing in modern Europe have moved away from the totalizing approach of Eurocentric historiography by raising new questions. Adrian Johns calls into question the master narrative of the agency of printing in the making of the culture of modern Europe—the so-called printing revolution. He situates its genealogy in the history of the struggle among printers over ownership of printing privileges.[36] It is time for historians working on areas outside Europe to interrogate this metanarrative that has enshrined Gutenberg as the technological agent of modernity in Europe. One of the ways that this can be achieved is to document the impact of woodblock printing in imperial China, to demonstrate, on the one hand, the complexity in the understanding of the difference between woodblock and movable type methods as means of multiplying and disseminating information during the sixteenth and seventeenth centuries, and on the other, the differential impact of printing on various aspects of society in early modern China. To do so is to underscore the need to investigate the specific historical context in which printing—both woodblock and movable type—brought about changes in practice in China and Europe.

## CONCEPTUALIZING THE SOCIAL IN EARLY MODERN CHINA

To avoid the pitfalls of the sinologistic mode of history is to run immediately into a problem similar to that encountered by colonial and postcolonial studies. How do we write about or, more precisely, conceptualize the social—the practice of early modern China—without using heavily loaded terms such as "bourgeoisie," "capitalism," "class struggles," "modernization," and "individualism"? Applying these concepts as universal categories of sociological analysis has obscured ruptures, erased historical specificity of practice, and reproduced chronicles of failure and absences in China in the sixteenth and seventeenth centuries. Indeed, as editors of a recent book on the relationship between the Chinese state and culture have aptly remarked, when taken as "universal and general processes,"

> Western theories centered on the formation of a sharp divide between state and civil society and between state power and personal autonomy . . . limit our capacity to conceptualize the political and cultural terrain upon which relations between state and various social groups were constructed in late imperial China.[37]

We need new ways to map the cultural terrain of early modern China, ways that allow us not only to view its historical specificities, but also enable us to reveal the specificity of the discourse on the rise of European modernity. A truly comparative study of cultures must be a study of heterologies. It must allow mutual questioning, giving no epistemological high ground to any culture.

## *Fields, Cultural Production, and the Civil Examinations*

To examine the impact of commercial publishing in the late Ming, I have borrowed analytical tools from many disciplines and fields of study, particularly literary and cultural studies. Pierre Bourdieu, Gerard Genette, Roger Chartier, and Michel de Certeau provide most of the analytical concepts for this study. Except Bourdieu's "field" and Genette's concept of "paratext," they will be introduced as the issues warrant in subsequent chapters. However, no theoretical works of these scholars are accepted in their entirety, much less as universal models for the study of practice.

Pierre Bourdieu's concept of "field" is most useful in analyzing the social as a site of practice and of its symbolic construction. Despite increasing interest in Bourdieu's theory of culture among American academicians, the concept of field receives the least attention.[38] The field is

> a network, or configuration of objective relations between positions. These positions are objectively defined, in their existence and in the determinations they impose upon their occupants, agents or institutions, by their present and potential situation (*situs*) in the structure of the distribution of species of power (or capital) whose possession commands access to the specific profits that are at stake in the field, as well as by their objective relation to other positions (domination, subordination, homology, and so on).[39]

The concept of field underscores the fact that social reality are practices constructed in relation to one another. "To think in terms of fields is to think relationally."[40] Human agents take positions in various fields of social action: "the field of power," "the field of cultural production," "the literary field," and "the field of economics." Fields are "fields of struggle" where agents compete for different types of capital—economic, cultural, linguistic. In advanced societies, access to "cultural capital" as noneconomic goods and services is important to the acquisition of economic capital.[41] Fields can multiply as new forces come to create new configurations of practice, hence the field of education, the field of arts, and the field of literary production.[42] The division of human practice into fields has the advantage of leaving open the specific structures of their relationship.

By taking various positions in these fields, human agents created social trajectories that traverse many fields.[43] As will be explained in Chapter 1, intensified commercialization resulted in the expansion of the *shishang* who took up positions in both the political and economic fields, significantly changing the relationship between the two fields. Notable was the opening up of the "cultural field" to agents working in the economic fields. Struggling examinees received remuneration from publishers and an expanding public of patrons for their literary labor expended as professional writers, critics, editors, and commentators. The increase in positions in the field of cultural production contributed to the rise of the authority of professional writers and critics who came to rival and challenge the imperial authority over interpretation of the Confucian canon and the standard of literary excellence. They became arbiters of taste in the field of cultural production, which intersected with another major field—"the examination field."

Unique to China in the sixteenth and seventeenth centuries was the examination field. The civil service examination itself was the center of the examination field, which included institutions such as the Ministry of Rites, the three levels of periodic examinations, the government school systems, educational intendants, and all the examinees. The civil service examination, through which political capital was distributed, was the arena where the quest for formal political power was conducted. The agents from various social classes—officials, literati, merchants, craftsmen, and peasants—struggled for access to and control of the field and the privilege to define the boundary of the field. The examination field is the site of resistance as well as domination involving the literate elites and the imperial government. It intersected with other fields of practice: the field of education, the literary field, the political field, and the economic field. This is one of the fields where the expansion of commercial publishing had made a great impact in the period under study.

*Paratexts, Discursive Space, and the Trajectory of the* Shishang

Another key concept of this study of cultural production is that of "paratexts" formulated by Gerald Genette. This concept helps to locate a major discursive space made public by the new literary culture of the *shishang*.

To draw attention to the intervening textual strategies in reading a text, Genette proposes to analyze the "paratext," which denotes parts of the physical medium of a text—title page, preface, postscript, fonts, spatial structure, comments, and intertextual references. In conventional study of the text, these surplus texts are often relegated to marginality. But as Genette points out, these marginalia are "thresholds of interpretation."

Genette divides paratexts into "peritexts" (inside the book) and "epitexts" (outside the book). It includes the "publisher's peritexts," including the format, series, cover, appendages, title page, typography, printings, paper, and binding. Other paratextual elements include the name of the author, title, intertext titles, prefaces, postscripts, epigraphs, illustrations, dedications, and notes.

Paratexts are protocols for reading. Many of them are not produced by authors. The publishers in their attempt to maximize sale would use a great variety of textual and nontextual devices to attract buyers. Because the theoretical examination of the practice of reading involves publishing, it is appropriate to study the various ways in which publishing contributed to the creation of paratexts whereby the editors, commentators, and the publishers sought to convey their messages to the reader. Therefore the study of the production, circulation, and consumption of literary texts requires the investigation of the role of publishing in these activities.[44] Precisely because the production of a text in a book form involves several contributors—the author or editor, the publisher or commentator, the proofreaders, the copyists—that paratext as "thresholds of interpretation" is "fundamentally heteronomous, auxiliary, and dedicated to the service of something other than itself, which constitutes its raison d'être."[45]

The concept of paratext also helps to overcome an obstacle in the study of the social in late-Ming China, namely, the suppression and erasure of change in the representations of practices by the educated elite themselves. It enables the tracing of the career trajectory of those *shishang* who were involved in commercial publishing. Collected works of Ming-Qing literati routinely and systematically suppressed or erased information through "poetic reductionism" and expurgation of writings containing explicit reference to economic undertakings. By "poetic reductionism" I mean the use of poetic expressions such as metaphors and allusions to insinuate one's economic activities. An expression like "*maiwen*" is a common allusion to selling one's literary labor. Except in cases where the literati clearly had chosen to remain in positions in the economic field, when a literatus was willing to mention such an undertaking, it was usually made with self-pity. But many did not even leave these kind of traces. This voluntary "forgetfulness" of economic undertakings makes it especially difficult to understand the specific conditions under which the literati interacted with the publishers, the process of proofreading, the organization of individual bookshops, and the distribution, transportation, and prices of books.

This problem notwithstanding, we can still document many literati's involvement in commercial publishing by evidence from paratext—prefaces, postscripts, commentaries, titles of contributors, and other genres of literary works. The overall conditions of the literati's involvement in commercial publishing can be gleaned from biographical information, writings of the literati, bibliographies, and, more importantly, paratext of extant Ming-edition books. In the collected works of many literati, some of the paratext of commercial books have been preserved for their literary value. Severed from the book, the economic context of the writing was lost. In light of the theory of paratext, we can be vigilant about the general practice of erasing information concerning careers in publishing.

The concept of paratext also facilitates the conceptualization of the impacts of printing on the formation of reading publics and on political practice in the sixteenth and seventeenth centuries. The boom of commercial publishing contributed to the expansion of discursive space in the book through an increase in paratext and books in new genres. Together with the elevation of the genres of fiction and plays as worthy literary undertakings, paratext offered the writers and publishers a vastly expanded space for comment, dissent, and even subversion of the imperial ideology as well as government policies.[46] This new discursive space expanded the "public" (*gong*) realm for the *shishang* and those who could read. Readers, writers, publishers, and critics came to constitute a community, a public connected by print.

## *SHISHANG* CULTURE AND THE EXPANSION
## OF THE *GONG* REALM

Scholars argue whether China had developed a "public sphere" before the nineteenth century comparable to what emerged in European societies in the modern period. This has been a subject of heated debate over the applicability of Jurgen Habermas's theory of the "public sphere." Both sides of the controversy expended much ink only to return to the question of how flexible one should be in defining the term "public sphere." To get around this debate requires the employment of the indigenous term "*gong*," which registers the difference from the "public sphere" and at the same time its similarity with the word "public," as in "reading public."

### Gong *and* Gonglun: *Literary Public Sphere and Public Opinion*

Contrary to common view, the term "*gong*" had long acquired meanings other than "official."[47] There are two meanings of "*gong*" that are relevant to our study. First, "*gong*" means "to make public" through printing a text or painting. Second, "*gong*" designates a space outside the family, the opposite of private or personal.

Books had been regarded as vehicles belonging to the *gong*, or the "public." As Ge Shihe remarked: "Books are public vehicles under the realm" (*shuji tianxia gongqi ye*).[48] In late-Ming usage, to make something *gong* was to print it for the reading public. Often the prefaces or colophons of books printed in the late Ming used the term *gong* in the sense of printing the book for the public. In a preface to an anthology of essays on statecraft, the editor referred to its publication as "*fu mu yi gong yu ren*" (carve it on wood for the public to see).[49] In a preface to an anthology of essays by famous writers of the Wei-Jin (220–420) periods, the compiler explained that he "wishes to publish it for those sharing the same interests" (*yuan gong tong hao*).[50] Another famous writer, Chen Jiru (1558–1639), decided to publish his collection of prose so that "the public could appreciate them" (*yi gong xinshang*).[51] In 1600, in his preface to Chen Jiru's *Dushu jing* (Mirror in reading), Shen Sichang explained his publication of the work in terms of "making it available to the public through print" (*ke er gong zhi*).[52] In another preface by Fan Mingtai, the publisher was praised for his effort to make the work public, "*gong er bu zhi*" (publish for public dissemination).[53] The publisher of an introductory guide to the understanding of the Four Books, published by Santaiguan, a commercial publishing house in Jianyang in 1607, explained the purpose of "publishing [the book] to make it public so that the world under the realm will know" the truth (*zi yi gong zhi, yi ling tianxia zhi*) Another compendium of commentaries on the Four Books refers to its publication as "*gong zhi hainei*" (to make public within the four seas) (see Figure 3.1).[54]

The above examples make it clear that by the late Ming, *gong* had acquired the meaning "to make public," and the method was through printing. It applied to both printing a text or a painting. I argue that the word "*gong*" signifies a public space shared by the literate population. Instead of adopting Habermas's term, "public sphere," I follow Chartier in using the term "literary public sphere," first, to distant my view from Habermas, and second, to underscore the centrality of print in constituting the public—a community of readers scattered over the immense geographical space of China and yet connected by means of their ability to read and access printed texts.[55] One can argue that there was no doubt a literary public in the late Ming whose membership was defined by literacy, access to printed materials, and mostly, but not exclusively, the male gender.

As the significance of *gong* changed with practice, the term "*gonglun*" had also undergone subtle change with the growth of commercial publishing in the late Ming. Hai Rui said that "public opinion originates in the schools" (*gonglun chu yu xuexiao*).[56] The "public opinion" in this statement does not require print and can be generated entirely in a community whose members knew and have direct contact with one another. As *gong* was used increasingly to mean "to publish," the term "*gonglun*" was extended to denote opinion articulated in print. The idea of consensus *gonglun* or *gongyi* circulated in print can be fully translated into the English concept of "public opinion" without compromising its usage in either language.

*Gonglun* was generated not only in print but also in public associations and places. The expansion of commercial and some government publishing beginning in the sixteenth century contributed to the expansion of a "literary public sphere" with different supporting institutions: literary societies (*wenshe*), paratext, poetics of the *xiaoshuo*, and the *dibao* (government gazette). All these institutions were either constituted of printed matter (paratext, poetics, *dibao*), or their operation depended heavily on publication (literary societies).

Chapter 1 discusses various aspects of book production: cost of paper, woodblocks, and carving. It addresses the issue of evaluating extant data on book prices and their economic significance in relation to income levels in the late Ming. I argue that books were cheaply produced and were sold at low prices. Chapter 2 discusses publisher's operations—methods of obtaining manuscripts, strategies in advertising their products, ways to secure supply of materials, methods of speeding up carving of blocks, and the distribution of books. The importance of commercial publishing is underscored in the discussion of the growing use of movable type printing, the rise of Suzhou as a cultural and publishing center, and the commercialization of Huizhou publishing. An underlying theme of this chapter is how the simplicity and operational flexibility of woodblock printing explained why inter alia woodblock printing appealed to Chinese publishers despite the growing use of movable type printing in this period. Chapter 3 seeks to explain the expansion of commercial publishing in terms of abundant supply of literary labor from examinees. I argue that the civil service examination, while holding up hope for a covetous career in the officialdom, kept the examinees in the elusive quest for the final metropolitan degree. The expenses incurred in regular trips to the provincial seats or the capital prompted talented candidates to sell their labor to patrons, many of whom were publishers.

Chapter 4 examines how commercially produced commentaries on the Four Books challenged the official interpretation and how the anthologies of commentaries contributed to an independent and "pluralistic" approach to the Confucian canon, challenging the imperial ideology and criticizing political abuses by the emperor in the commentaries. Chapter 5 traces the gradual shift of literary authority away from the political center to the commercial market populated by professional critics. It documents the growing importance of publishing, critiquing, and anthologizing writings in the generation of literary authority, which came to rival that of the examiners of the civil service examination. In this new light the Restoration Society was presented as an alliance of professional critics who first carved out their niches in the publishing market as public arbiters of literary excellence and subsequently sought to exert influence on the examiners by organized power. In the Conclusion, in addition to a brief review of the major points about the impact of commercial publishing on the examination field and the field of cultural production, I provide an elaborate discussion of the different conditions in which Chinese and European publishers operated.

# I
## Cost of Production and Book Prices

The simplicity of Chinese printing is what accounts for
the exceedingly large numbers of books in circulation here
and the ridiculously low prices at which they are sold.

MATTEO RICCI[1]

The cheapness with which books can be manufactured,
brings them within the reach of the poorest.

S. WELLS WILLIAMS[2]

Despite being separated by more than two hundred years, Matteo Ricci, a Jesuit missionary in the sixteenth century, and S. Wells Williams, a Protestant missionary in the mid-nineteenth century, were both struck by the low prices of books in China. It is clear they were comparing the prices of books in China with the market in parts of Europe. The scholarly community today, however, does not seem to take their words seriously, or does not understand what they meant. Based on very limited information on book prices, scholars opine that books were very expensive in late-Ming China and were "prized possessions" and, according to Arthur Smith, "a luxury of the rich" even in the late nineteenth century.[3] How do we understand and explain these apparently contradictory views of book prices in late imperial China? If books were so expensive, it would be difficult to explain the general view that there was a boom in commercial publishing in the late Ming. Whatever the extent and nature of commercial publishing, the high price of books would significantly restrict their distribution and impact on society.

Many questions arise from this apparent contradiction: Were books expensive in the late-Ming period? Did the cost of books preclude officials, merchants, and examinees from building small libraries? Could wage-earning laborers such as silk workers, woodcarvers, sailors, or entertainers afford books? The answers to these questions are important not only to the understanding of the nature and scope of the expansion of commercial publishing in China in the sixteenth and seventeenth centuries, but also to the question of why woodblock printing continued to be preferred by Chinese printers and was not replaced by the movable-type method despite its availability and in fact growing use in this period.[4]

*Printing before the Ming*

Despite the invention of woodblock printing in the Tang (618–907) period, printed works in the early Song (960–1279) were not commonly available.[5] Most students and scholars had to copy texts by hand. By 994, the Imperial Academy was allowing commercial publishers to reprint government editions of Classical and history texts. The government also published law codes and a large number of Buddhist and Daoist scriptures. Government publications were produced in offices in both the capital and the provinces. In addition, local government schools and the Imperial Academy in the capital published books for students. The Imperial Academy in the early decades since foundation had only four thousand blocks. By 1004, however, the number had increased to more than one hundred thousand blocks.[6] The Song (960–1279) government granted large number of books as gifts to officials, provincial government schools, private academies, and temples. Books included classics, history, Buddhist and Daoist scriptures, and medical texts.[7]

After the mid-eleventh century, it became increasingly easy to purchase printed books.[8] Printing shops were established throughout the empire, especially in greater number in Zhejiang, Sichuan, Fujian, Hubei, and Anhui.[9] After the ban on private publishing was lifted during the Shenzong reign (1068–77), books printed by commercial publishing houses in Fujian, Zhejiang, and Sichuan were available throughout China.[10] The number of printing shops was no more than thirty in the Northern Song (960–1126), but increased to more than two hundred in the Southern Song (1172–1279).[11] Printed materials had become an integral part of the imperial government and literary culture since the Song. Offices in the central government and provinces listed more than 2,482 titles as publications from the Song to the early Ming.[12] The distribution of central government and province publications is 18 to 82 percent. This distribution suggests perhaps more the ease with which the woodblock printing method was introduced in the provinces than the vigor of local government in book production.

A relatively large number of Song and Yuan (960–1368) editions have survived from the period between the 1550s and 1630s. In specific ways, this publishing boom beginning in the sixteenth century can be established by identifying new trends, new genres, and the growth in the number of publishers and publishing centers. Intensified commercialization and favorable government policy were the powerful driving forces behind the boom.

## Expansion of Publishing in the Ming

During the Song and the Yuan dynasties, prepublication permission from the government was required for the printing of personal writings. Until 1068, books were submitted to the Imperial Academy for approval prior to publication. The policy was not enforced during the Shenzong reign.[13] The Yuan government required submission of manuscripts for examination by the Secretariat (Zhongshu sheng). Only with its approval could books be published.[14] This requirement was not inherited by the Ming government. Unlike France and Britain in the sixteenth and seventeenth centuries, the Ming government did not have a censorship unit nor a specific set of statutes to police private publishing.[15] Nor was there a licensing system requiring registration of printers with the government. Anyone with adequate resources could become a publisher and was free to publish almost anything, including news, manuscripts, and government publications. Only a few types of publications were made the exclusive prerogative of the government, specifically calendars and books on astronomy as well as divination. But since the mid-Jiajing reign (1522–66), even these types of books were copied, printed, and widely disseminated. They had become a household item by the Wanli period (1573–1620).[16]

In the early Ming, books were printed by offices of both the local and central government.[17] Offices such as the Censorate (Ducha yuan), the Provincial Administration Commission (Buzheng si), Provincial Surveillance Commission (Ancha si), and the Hangzhou prefectural government were among the active producers of print materials. A major center of publishing since the Southern Song, Hangzhou in the early Ming continued to be an important center of government publishing. Many books published by local government offices in Hangzhou have survived.[18] Principalities were also active in publishing. Major institutions of education like the two Imperial Academies in Beijing and Nanjing published fewer books than the principalities.[19]

Commercial publishing in the first hundred years of the Ming dynasty did not see a significant change in its centers of production and output. According to Lu Rong, who was a native of the prosperous Suzhou area from the 1360s through the 1450s, books were mostly printed by the Imperial Academies. Commercial publishers did not produce books in large numbers or disseminate them widely.[20] However, as commercialization and urbanization intensified in the second half of the fifteenth century, commercial publishing shops began to proliferate, printing books in greater number and on a great variety of subjects.[21] In addition to the production by commercial publishers, publications by private groups such as families, lineages, and religious groups all contributed to the expansion of printing in the late Ming.[22]

Based on the collection of extant copies of Ming editions in the Beijing Library and Taiwan's Central Library, Joseph McDermott suggests that printed copies of text began to replace manuscript in the late fifteenth century; not until the sixteenth century did imprint culture supercede manuscript culture.[23] Commercial publishing began to expand in the last quarter of the fifteenth century, but it did not thrive until the sixteenth century, especially during the Wanli reign. Based on the limited number of extant editions, from 1368 through 1521, a period of one hundred and fifty-three years, the annual rate of book production was 8.1. For the ensuing fifty years, during the Jiajing and Longqing periods (1522–71), the rate was 14.0. And from the Wanli reign on through the end of the dynasty (1573–1644), a period of sixty-nine years, the rate was 19.1.[24]

The publishing boom was part of a commercial expansion that generated greater demand for paper, ink, woodblocks, and all materials for packaging books. By the sixteenth century all the major methods of publishing—including woodblock and movable type—were in use.[25] In the Ming there was a gradual increase in books printed by the movable type method.[26] There was no major technological breakthrough except in advances in woodcutting, multicolor printing, and the production of paper.²⁷ One major factor in the expansion of commercial publishing was the continued decline in the cost of book production as a result of the decline in the cost of paper production and the oversupply of labor resulting from population growth.

Unlike the upper-class British writers before the mid-seventeenth century, who "rarely committed their works directly to print," since the Song, if not earlier, Chinese literati had long accepted print as a legitimate and authentic form of preserving and disseminating their writings.²⁸ By the late Ming, the cost of printing had become so low that literati often published their writings. Books were one of the most widely available and affordable commodities. One poor scholar complained that he had so many books that he could never read all of them.²⁹ They were so common and inexpensive that some merchants opened shops to sell used books and used paper to be sold as wrapping paper.³⁰ In a hyperbolical statement, another scholar suggested that if the printing blocks were to be put on the fuel market, the price of firewood and charcoal would drop precipitously.³¹

*Collections, New Genres, and "Book-keeping"*

An indication of expansion in book production was the general increase in book collectors and the size of their collections. From the last quarter of the fifteenth century, there was a noted increase in the number of collectors in Jiangsu and Zhejiang, the most commercialized and urbanized Lower Yangtze area.³² Collectors with thirty thousand juan were not worthy of mention.³³ The well-known scholar and book collector Hu Yinglin (1551–1602) was only a poor provincial graduate (*juren*) but in a period of more than twenty years he was able to accumulate a collection of 42,384 juan by the time he died in 1602.³⁴ The same year, Xu Boxing completed a list of his own library collection, which included more than fifty-three thousand juan.³⁵ The wealthy Cheng family in Pujiang, Zhejiang, accumulated more than eighty thousand juan. Housed in the famous Jiguge (Pavilion Nourished from Antiquity) of the renowned publisher Mao Jin (1599–1659) was the enormous collection of eighty-four thousand juan. The collection in the lending library of Qi Chengye (1565–1628) in Shaoxing exceeded one hundred thousand juan.³⁶ Another collector, Wu De, also put together a collection of more than one hundred thousand juan.[37]

The expansion of commercial publishing both in scope and in volume resulted in greater division of labor and numerous refinements in the art of printing.[38] One factor of the expansion of printing in the late Ming is what one scholar calls "the triumph of popular print."[39] Popular demand for large-scale single prints appeared to have contributed to the expanded market for print culture. Single prints had become popular items of interior decoration. For both religious and aesthetic purposes, people took pleasure in displaying prints of Buddhist and Daoist deities, as well as popular deities such as door gods, the God of Longevity, the God of Happiness, and the God of Stipend.[40] Single prints of scenes from famous plays and novels also were common decorative pieces.[41]

A great number of books were printed to meet the various needs of the diversified *shishang* elites and growing urban population.[42] Different types of books were printed to prepare candidates for the three levels of the civil service examinations. The publication of new genres of examination aids after the mid-Wanli period attested to the expansion of commercial publishing. These included eight-legged essay exercises of members of literary societies and anthologies of essays by graduates with comments by professional critics. Genres were so numerous in the late Ming that a separate category (*shixue*) was assigned to them by the bibliophile Mou Yuanyi (1594–1640).[43] The large number of prefaces written for anthologies of examination essays had prompted Huang Zongxi to create a subcategory of *shiwen* (contemporary, or eight-legged essays) for the voluminous anthology of Ming essays. There was a total of eight *juan* of prefaces in his anthology.[44]

In addition to books published for the civil service examinations, publishers and printers produced books such as mountain gazetteers,[45] almanacs, encyclopedias, morality books,[46] manuals of mathematics,[47] medical manuals,[48] and maps.[49] Widely available were practical guides for writing letters, performing rituals, and choosing dates for all kinds of ceremonies, activities, and entertainment.[50] There were also guides for travelers, merchants,[51] connoisseurs,[52] and even books identifying methods of cheating commonly used by deceitful merchants and rogues.[53] Travelers visiting brothels in the big cities could obtain information from guide books such as *The Classic of Visiting Prostitutes* (*Piao jing*) or *The Pleasure of Women Shops* (*Xianqing nü si*).[54] Erotic albums and pornographic novels were also very popular. The popularity of erotic albums is evidenced by the increase in the refinement of color printing. Albums printed in the 1570s and 1580s were in four colors. Many published in 1606 to 1624 were printed in five colors.[55] Instructions for increasing sexual pleasure both in private chambers and brothels were included in popular almanacs like the *Wanbao quanshu* (Encyclopedia of myriad treasures).[56]

Conspicuous among the new genres that swelled the commercial book market was entertaining literature, a corollary of the expansion of *shishang* elites and urban population who had more leisure and resources at their disposal. Publication of plays and novels was hardly new in the late Ming. But new trends and practices developed to warrant a claim of a boom. Unlike the predominantly commercial editions published in Jianyang before the Wanli period, dramas were published by commercial houses as well as private writers and families in the Jiangnan region. Some publishing houses specialized in the production of plays.[57] Southern style drama, the *chuanqi* (stories of wonder), had many more scenes than the four-scene format of the Yuan *zaju* (variety plays). Growing interest and respect for the art of dramatic and musical performance among the *shishang* resulted in the increase in the number of playwrights and critics, as well as in the production of new works.

Illustrations of novels and plays had also moved in new directions by the late Ming.[58] Many Song and Yuan editions published in Jianyang had illustrations in the upper register of the page. The quality of illustrations was mostly crude, indicating the lack of involvement of artists. This changed in the Wanli period. Full-page illustrations of novels and plays became popular by the Wanli period, indicating that the market for richly illustrated books was expanding.[59] Visual images in increasing detail and artistic presentation became important supplements of printed texts.[60] The increase in the elaborate graphic details was evidence of the rapid advances in woodcutting techniques. Improvement in carving skills might have been facilitated by an improvement in tool design. A scholar of popular prints observed: "Illustration by the 1590s appears as a laboratory for experiment in the depiction on the blockprinted surface of the interior scene, landscape, scene of fantasy and combat, etc."[61]

Another genre was called *xiaopin*, or vignettes that include every genre of prose writings, excluding poetry. It resembles the genre of collected prose writings of a single writer with the emphasis on a wide range of topics, including prefaces, colophons, travel notes, life sketches, personal letters, maxims, biographical essays, and short treatises.[62] The emergence of *xiaopin* can be regarded as an attempt to valorize different aspects of life without privileging government service as the focus of literary production, a new sensibility characteristic of the *shishang*'s outlook.

The proliferation of genres of printed books rendered the existing cataloging method of *sibu* (four sections) inadequate, if not obsolete. A book collector, Qi Chengye, added the category of *congshu* (collectanea) because there were numerous collectanea, including items from different genres. They included both books from the Classics and history.[63] These collectanea contributed to the mixing and confusing of the genre boundaries.

Another development in bibliography was the inclusion of entertaining vernacular literature. The bibliography compiled by Xu Bo in 1602 included melodramas under the category of *chuanqi*.[64] The proliferation of new works on drama prompted the compilation of special catalogs. Songs in plays also received special treatment in separate bibliographies. The most famous were those compiled by Lü Tiancheng (1580–1618) and Qi Biaojia (1602–1645).[65] Interest in printing lyrics of songs was also strong enough to prompt Feng Menglong to compile and print an anthology of folk songs in the Suzhou dialect.[66]

The official catalog of the Hall of the Spring of Writing (*Wenyuange shu mu*) also set up a separate category for vernacular literature.[67] It should be noted that the *xiaoshuo* did not become a category for all novels. Most bibliographers still listed under *xiaoshuo* the conventional books that were notes and records of strange things.[68] Instead many were grouped together as a subcategory of history. In his *Baichuan shuzhi* (Bibliography of hundred rivers), Gao Ru entered conventional books on anecdotes and notes under the category *xiaoshuo*. Books that are novels by current classification are found in the subcategories of history. In his category of *yeshi* (unofficial history), Gao included works such as the *Water Margin* and the *Three Kingdoms*. Under the category of *waishi* (outer history), he listed melodramas such as the *Romance of the West Chamber* and the *Romance of the Lute* (*Pipa ji*).[69]

*Standardization and Differentiation*

Consequential to the expansion of commercial publishing in the sixteenth century was the development of two opposite tendencies most conspicuous in the paratext: standardization and differentiation. Trends of standardization were notable in the technological aspects of the production of the book: size, character style, type of paper. As Robert Hegel has demonstrated, patterns of uniformity are discernible in page size, number of characters per page, and number of characters for chapter titles in novels. Commercially and privately published dramas shared the same system of notation marks for reading, singing, and acting.[70] From the Wanli period onward, the "craftsman style" (*jiang ti*) quickly became the standard font for most publications. These scripts were distinguished by their standardized uniform strokes. They were designed for easy reading and to improve the cutting speed of carvers, reducing irregularities in width and length of the characters typical of calligraphic style. The almost-universal adoption of the craftsman style and the use of bamboo paper (*zhu zhi*) for most books from the Wanli period onward contributed significantly to the standardization of the material and formal aspects of the book, both of which could be attributed to publishers' attempts to minimize production costs.

However, trends of differentiation can be seen in complex strategies aiming at distinction. To compensate for the loss of personal style and aesthetic quality of calligraphy after the adoption of the craftsman style, prefaces and comments were often written in cursive-style facsimiles of the writers' own handwriting (see Figure 1.1).[71] This visual distinction produces an effect on the reader, underscoring the personal presence of the author.[72] This visual differentiation also endowed the preface and comments in calligraphic style with a sense of authenticity (*zhen*).[73] It served as a signature of the author and an imprimatur of excellence. In addition, it functioned as a reading protocol, visually and spatially separating the paratext from the text proper. Its aesthetic and personal quality put the preface on a higher ground where opinion would merit exceptional attention. The preface as a paratext precedes and exceeds the text proper in both spatial organization and significance. It costs more to produce because of the reputation of the author and the higher level of carving skill.

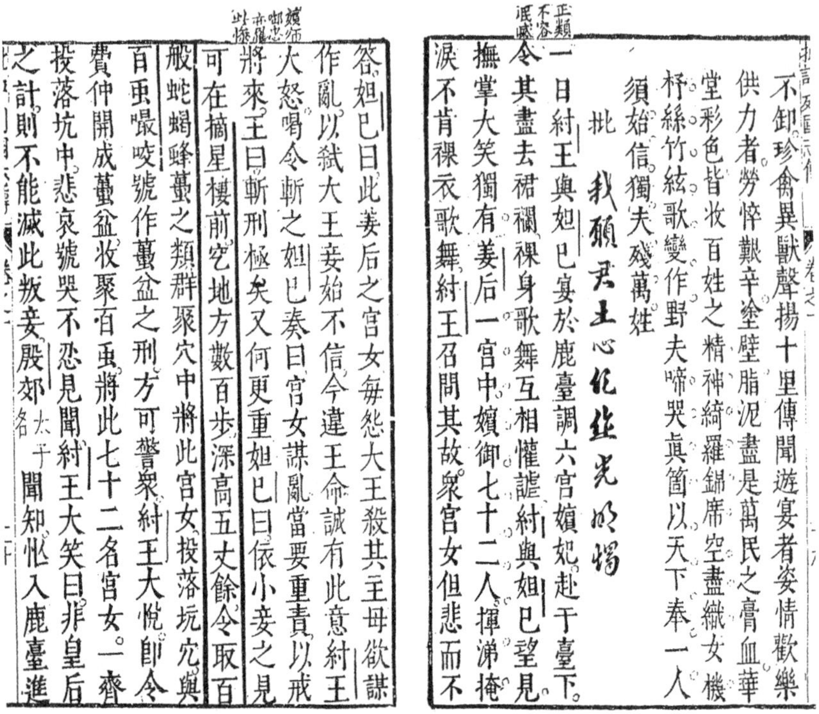

正類不容泯滅

不卸珍禽異獸聲揚十里傳聞遊宴者姿情歡樂
供力者勞悴艱辛塗壁脂泥盡是萬民之膏血華
堂彩色皆妝百姓之精神綺羅錦席空盡織女機
杼絲竹絃歌變作野夫啼哭真箇以天下奉一人
須始信獨夫殘萬姓
批 我願君王心化作光明燭
一日紂王與妲己宴於鹿臺調六宮嬪妃赴于臺下
令其盡去裙襴裸身歌舞互相懽謔紂與妲己望見
撫掌大笑獨有姜后一宮中嬪御七十二人揮涕掩
淚不肯裸衣歌舞紂王召問其故衆宮女但悲而不

嬪御忠烈此條

答妲己曰此姜后之宮女每怨大王殺其主母欲謀
作亂以弒大王妾始不信今違王命誠有此意紂王
大怒喝令斬之妲己奏曰宮女謀亂當要重責以戒
將來王曰斬刑極矣又何更重妲己曰依小妾之見
可在摘星樓前空地方數百步深高五丈餘令取百
般蛇蝎蜂蠆之類群聚穴中將此宮女投落坑穴與
百虫嚙咬號作蠆盆之刑方可警衆紂王大悅即令
費仲開成蠆盆收聚百虫將此七十二名宮女一齊
投落坑中悲哀號哭不忍見聞紂王大笑曰非皇后
之計則不能滅此叛妾殷郊太子聞知忙入鹿臺進

Figure 1.1: Folio from *Chen pi lieguo zhizhuan* showing: (1) the "craftsman style" of printing; (2) an end-of-paragraph comment employing a facsimile of the calligraphy of the commentator; (3) different modes of comment: in the top margin, after a paragraph and in between lines; and (4) different types of punctuation marks. Reproduced by permission of the National Archives of Japan.

But the overall cost did not appear to be substantial because the cost of the major material—paper—was low.

## PAPER IN MING SOCIETY

Cost of paper was much lower than that of woodblocks and labor in the sixteenth and seventeenth centuries. Chinese printers paid much less for paper than their European counterparts. Antwerp was a flourishing city that exported books to other European countries. Paper in Antwerp in the sixteenth century cost twenty to twenty-five stuivers per ream (five hundred sheets).[74] A painter and a card maker in Antwerp earned three stuivers a day. He needed to work seven to eight days to buy one ream of printing paper. In contrast, the cost for bamboo paper for printing in China was 0.02 tael per one hundred sheets. Five hundred sheets of paper cost 0.1 tael. A Chinese cutter needed to work two to three days to make enough money to buy five hundred sheets. Assuming the size of paper was relatively comparable, his European counterpart had to work six to eight days to buy five hundred sheets. The wage to paper cost ratio is 1:2.5 to 1:3.

From the fifteenth through the eighteenth century, most European printers depended on imported paper. In the mid-fifteenth century, only Italy and France produced enough paper for domestic consumption as well as export. Italy was the major supplier of paper for England, the Low Countries, Austria, and Germany.[75] Germany did not become self-sufficient in paper production until the mid-sixteenth century.[76] England still imported one-third of its paper for printing in 1713.[77] Before that date, most paper was imported.[78] Paper remained expensive because it was made with rag; the short supply of rag imposed constraints on the output of paper until it was replaced by straw in the 1860s.[79]

*The Paper Society*

In contrast, paper was an inexpensive and widely used industrial product in late-Ming China. It was an indispensable material in the daily life of urban residents.[80] As observed by Matteo Ricci, "The use of paper is much more common in China than elsewhere, and its methods of production more diversified."[81] In fact, the sixteenth century witnessed greater differentiation in quality and uses of paper products;[82] more than one hundred types of papers were produced.[83]

But in the early Ming, writing paper did not appear to be a cheap commodity. Writing paper was still saved for secondary uses. For example, written exercises and penmanship practice paper at the Imperial Academy was put to other uses. They were sent to the Ministry of Rites to be used as drafting paper by officials and to the Court of Imperial Entertainment (Guanglu si) for wrapping noodles. They were also used as fuel. But by the late fifteenth century, these exercise papers were no longer used.[84] Lu

Rong recalled that in the 1450s paper produced in government paper mills in Jiangxi was used by eunuchs to cover the wall, a practice considered inappropriate and wasteful. Even as late as the Wanli period, scholars used business accounting paper (*shisi zhangbu*) and litigation paper (*song zhuang zhi*) for copying purposes. When publishers like Mao Jin began using high-quality paper for copying books, others were following the same convention, avoiding used paper for copying books.[85] This could have been the result of emulating the example of Mao, but it might have been due to the further lowering of paper costs in the last decades of the Ming dynasty. The concern for wasting writing paper disappeared as paper supplies increased and costs diminished toward the end of the sixteenth century.

Like all commodities, paper was produced for a wide range of uses and customers: books, calligraphy, painting, correspondence, government announcements, folding fans, window papers, invitation cards, contracts, and lanterns. Printed ritual paper products for burning were in great demand.[86] Toilet paper was commonly used in Jiangnan cities such as Hangzhou and Suzhou.[87] The toilet paper produced in Hangzhou was famous for its softness.[88] Firecrackers were also made with paper.[89]

The demand and production of a great variety of paper products were evident in the local gazetteers of the Jiangnan region. Wuxian listed a great variety of paper products, including paper boxes, paper canopies, rolls of painting paper, door guardian posters (*men shen*), correspondence paper, and color papers.[90] Special types of paper like correspondence stationery were made to cater to the aesthetic taste of the gentry and merchants. A Shanghai man made special correspondence sheets with poems printed on them. They were in such great demand that he had more than twenty "family servant boys" (*jiatong*) filling orders, and still he was not able to meet the needs.[91] Li Yu (1610–80) made designer correspondence papers for sale in his bookstore.

Paper products for interior decoration ranged from hanging pictures to paper flowers. Printed and painted pictures were common decorative items in private homes, restaurants, and tea houses.[92] Fujian produced pictures made from paper threads woven into a great varieties of themes, including flowers, birds, and landscapes.[93] Paper flowers had become a popular item for interior decoration.[94] Almost every household in Suzhou had paper flowers as a regular decorative item.[95] There were also paper canopies (*zhizhang*) for beds.[96] Fujian produced a type of blanket made of paper.[97] The use of wallpaper was common and had become almost universal in the Jiangnan cities by the mid-seventeen century.[98] Residents in the cities had depended on paper communication for many important social occasions, including written invitation cards and letters or the hiring of tutors; money transactions required writing of some sort.[99]

Paper was also put to extraordinary use. It was used to make "paper armor" (*zhijia*). In 1645 when Manchu forces swept south, Chen Shiye's book collection—a total of several tens of thousand juan—was taken away and torn into pieces in order to make several thousand sets of armor.[100]

The imperial government itself was a big consumer of paper products. As early as the Yongle reign (1403–24), the Ming government established government paper mills in Jiangxi. There were numerous types of papers made for special purposes, including writing paper for the emperor (*yulan zhi*), official memorials (*biao zhi* or *zhouben zhi*), and public announcements (*pang zhi*).[101] Examination questions at government schools during annual examination, and examinations at the provincial and metropolitan examinations were all printed on "examination paper" (*shuajuan zhi*).[102] Students at the imperial academy were provided with submission paper (*chengwen zhi*), onto which examination answers were copied and then sent to the Ministry of Rites.[103] Because of its larger size, submission paper was sometimes used for pasting on windows of the Imperial Academy. It was procured from the Hu-Guang province.[104] Other government papers included paper for records and registrations (*zaoce zhi*), one of the several types of paper the imperial government consumed in huge quantity.[105]

*Production of Paper*

Paper in sixteenth-century China was produced in many provinces, especially Jiangxi, Fujian, Anhui, Zhejiang,[106] Guangdong, and Sichuan.[107] Since the Tang dynasty, the hilly areas in southern Anhui produced paper that came to be known as *xuanzhi*. Southern Anhui continued to be an important area of paper production in the Song through the Ming dynasty.[108] Fujian was famous for its bamboo paper (*zhu zhi* or *kou zhi*), which was produced throughout the entire province.[109] Because of its relatively low price, printing paper produced in Shunchang was in great demand by publishers in Jiangsu and Zhejiang. A large quantity of Shunchang paper was also exported.[110]

In the late sixteenth century Jiangxi produced more than twenty different types of paper.[111] Qianshan in Jiangxi was an important area for paper production. There were more than thirty paper production mills, each hiring one to two thousand workers.[112] Vats (*cao*) were operated by a production unit of four workers.[113] The smallest mill had more than 250 vats and the largest had five hundred vats. In 1600, in Shitang zhen, Jiangxi province, alone there were already forty to fifty thousand paper mill workers. This large number of workers would operate ten thousand to 12,500 vats. A vat would produce 8 *ba* of paper per day.[114] This means an output of eighty thousand to 96,400 *ba* in an industrial town in Jiangxi alone.

Paper was also produced in Youlong, to the northeast of Qianshan, in the western part of Zhejiang. Paper-mill workers came from Qianshan, and paper merchants came as far as Fujian.[115] The production of paper in the sixteenth century had become a transregional operation. Paper producers had to procure bamboo from other provinces. Fujian paper producers traveled as far as Jiangxi to secure an adequate supply of bamboo, renting hilly areas and hiring local peasants to plant bamboo.[116]

Technology improvements in paper making led to thinner and larger sheets.[117] Large-scale paper mills made extensive use of hydraulic and wind energy in their production.[118] Paper mills in Fujian and Shunchang, Jiangxi, used water-powered technology.[119]

Xie Zhaozhi (1567–1624) commented on different types of paper. The advantage of white *mianzi* (cotton paper) was its durability, but it was not good for writing because of its surface. Paper made in Huating was unable to hold ink; writing would become blurred and illegible. Paper from Sichuan was too expensive and not widely available. Korean-made cocoon paper was more widely available than Sichuan paper but had the same problem: it was easily attacked by bookworms over time. But the renowned painter Dong Qichang (1555–1636) was particularly fond of Korean paper for its snow-white color and mirrorlike surface.[120] The most inferior paper was bamboo paper (*lianqi zhi* and *maobian zhi*), which was produced in both Fujian and Jiangxi.[121] *Maobian* was a common type of paper for daily use.[122] It broke down immediately upon contact with water and was easily corrupted by bookworms. Bamboo paper was inferior but cheap. However, it provided a smooth service for the brush. Not only was it widely used in government office and printed books, it was also used for memorials, invitation letters, and cards.[123]

Of the different types of printing paper, the cotton paper (*mianzi*) from Yongfeng, Jiangxi, was the best and most expensive. Next came the correspondence paper (*jianzhi*) from Changshan. Shunchang paper from Fujian was even cheaper. The least expensive printing paper was the bamboo paper made in Fujian, but it was of very poor quality. By the mid-Wanli period, however, producers of bamboo paper in Fujian had made great improvements in its durability; publishers eventually chose to use bamboo paper over the relatively better quality Shunchang paper.[124] It was particularly good for printing, and Suzhou merchants were able to control its supply through prepayment.[125] Fujian merchants also found it more profitable to sell their paper in Suzhou.[126] Books printed after the mid-Wanli period were increasingly printed on better and cheaper bamboo papers. Despite his negative assessment of the quality of Fujian bamboo paper, Hu Yinglin (1551–1602) amassed a collection of twenty thousand books, 90 percent of which were printed on this type of paper.[127] After the 1620s few books were printed on white "cotton paper."[128] Almost all of the books published by the renowned publisher Mao Jin were printed on bamboo paper.[129]

COST OF BOOK PRODUCTION

Commodities and services in Jiangnan cities in the late Ming could be obtained at a wide range of prices. Books were not daily necessities like rice, salt, meat, or vegetables. They were, as they are in modern days, dispensable consumer goods. They came in a great range of prices because the book market and publishing industry had developed complex strategies targeting different income-level buyers. The price of newly printed books was determined significantly by the cost of paper, woodblocks, and carvers. In order to estimate the relative price of books in the late Ming, it would be useful to examine the proportion of these expenses.

*Table 1.1*

Prices of Woodblocks, ca. 1570s–80s

| NUMBER OF BLOCKS | TOTAL COST IN TAEL | PRICE PER BLOCK IN TAEL |
| --- | --- | --- |
| 3 *zhang* 5 *chi (chinese feet)* | 3 | 0.085/*chi (foot)* |
| 3 | 1.2 | 0.4 |
| 3 | 0.9 | 0.3 |
| 10 | 1 | 0.1 |
| 1 | 0.1 | 0.1 |
| 1 (pear) | 0.03 | 0.03 |

SOURCES: Shen Bang, pp. 138–42, 145; Hai Rui, pp. 41–42; Zhang Xiumin, *Zhongguo yinshuashi*, p. 534.

One of the most important materials in woodblock printing was wood planks. Different kinds of wood were used for printing blocks; the most common were jujube and pear. Even though we do not have itemized records of expenses in book production in Ming China, it is possible to establish a range of prices for different kinds of woodblocks. Table 1.1 shows a list of woodblock prices from the 1570s and 1580s. Since all data comes from Shen Bang's record of his tenure as the magistrate of Wanping county, it is safe to assume that the price differences arise from variations in size and type of wood. The more expensive wood that cost 0.1 to 0.4 tael per block was clearly of quality wood like jujube. Pear woodblock was much cheaper, at only 0.03 tael per block.

Publishers probably bought blocks in planks to reduce costs. However, pear blocks would cease to print clearly beyond twenty thousand copies.[130] But for most books, twenty thousand copies would be the limit of a large edition. Thus for most publishers and most books, pear woodblock would be adequate. Books published in Fujian were cheaper because they were printed from pear blocks. Fujian publishers also began to use cheaper wood like poplar (*baiyang*) for printing. Their example was later followed by Hangzhou publishers. Publishers in other places used different types of softwood to lower the cost of carving blocks.[131]

There is more data on prices of paper than on books. As shown in Table 1.2, the range of paper prices was even wider. The cheapest kind of paper

*Table 1.2*

Prices of Paper, 1550s–1650s

| TYPE OF PAPER | PRICE RANGE PER 100 SHEETS (IN TAEL) |
|---|---|
| Poster paper (*bang zhi*) | |
| Regular | 0.5–1.5 |
| Submission paper (*chengwen zhi*) | |
| Large | 0.25–0.4 |
| Medium | 0.2–0.4 |
| Regular | 0.4–0.66 |
| Memorial paper (*ben zhi*) | |
| Large red | 3.0 |
| Regular | 0.35–0.8 |
| Record paper (*zouce zhi*) | 0.08–0.18[a] |
| Printing paper | |
| "Cotton" paper (*mianzhi*) | 0.2 |
| Bamboo paper (*zhuzhi*) | |
| *Maobian* | 0.3–0.7 |
| *Lianqi zhi* | 0.065–0.14 |
| *Tailian zhi* | 0.09–0.1 |
| *Zhu zhi* (1640s–50s) | 0.026[b] |
| Noodle wrapping paper (*baomian zhi*) | 0.045 |

SOURCE: Shen Bang, pp. 138, 141, 145–46, 151; [a]Yuan Huang, *Baodi zhengshu*, 14.79a–80b; [b]Ye Mengzhu, *Yueshi bian*, juan 7.

appears to be the noodle wrapping paper (*baomian zhi*), which cost 0.045 tael per one hundred; the next cheapest was the government record paper (*zouce zhi*), which the government paid 0.08 to 0.18 tael per one hundred sheets. Paper used in memorials or reports submitted to the emperor was memorial paper (*zouben zhi* or *ben zhi*), which cost 0.35–0.8 per one hundred sheets. These types of paper and those listed in Table 1.2 were procured for government use. They were presumably of higher quality and hence more expensive than the kind of printing paper used by commercial publishers. The improved bamboo paper (*zhuzhi*) had become the most popular type of paper used by commercial publishers. The cost was 0.026 per one hundred sheets in the mid-seventeenth century.[132]

The decision to print or copy a text depended on the number of copies needed and on the relative cost of copying and printing. According to Weng Tongwen, the general cost ratio for a hand-copied manuscript and a printed book was ten to one.[133] The apparently extensive availability of clerks or copyists (*shushou*) in the late Ming was a major factor in choosing not to print one's text if the number of copies were small. It has been noted that there was an expansion of subbureaucracy in the late Ming. The number of copyists in local government offices had increased by tenfold by the 1620s.[134] Such an increase would have the effect of keeping the cost for hiring copyists low. The wage for copyists varied for the type of work and the location. Copyists in the Imperial Academy in Nanjing were paid an annual wage ranging from 1.2 to six taels.[135] These wage figures, however, are not comparable to modern wages. In addition to the monetary remuneration, workers were often provided with food, wine, tea, and sometimes housing and even clothing, depending on the type of labor rendered.

The cost for copying a twenty- to thirty-page essay was two to three *wen*, or approximately 0.02 to 0.03 tael.[136] Assuming two hundred characters per page for twenty pages, it would yield four thousand characters and a wage rate of 0.005 tael per one hundred characters copied.[137] Copyists with skills in different calligraphic styles would be paid more. Carvers (*kanzi jiang*) and printers (*shuayin jiang*) were among the 188 categories of specially skilled laborers.[138] An average carver could carve one hundred characters in one day, and a skilful carver would cut 150 characters.[139] For the labor of carving one hundred characters, some printing shops paid 0.03 tael, others paid twenty *wen*, or approximately 0.02 tael.[140] But some carvers might get as high as 0.05 tael per one hundred characters.[141]

It can be estimated that in the late Ming and early Qing periods in the Lower Yangtze area, the cost for carving one hundred characters ranged from 0.02 to 0.05 tael, depending on the level of skill and the size and style of the characters. A carver would make roughly 0.6 to 1.5 taels in thirty working days. This is close to what Mao Jin paid his carvers, 0.03 tael, which was on the high end of the wage scale for carvers.[142] The income of Chinese carvers compared unfavorably to that of printers in early modern Europe, who were highly skilled laborers and were among the highest paid workers. However, unlike European laborers, Chinese workers were not organized, an important factor in the low cost of book production in early modern imperial China.

Wages, like prices, varied by area. Hired laborers working along the Yellow River made less than their counterparts working in Jiangnan. Carvers working for publishers in Fujian made less than their counterparts in Nanjing, Suzhou, and Hangzhou. In the Jiajing reign, the cost for carving a 161-page book printed in Fujian was twenty-four taels. The average cost for each folio block (one side of a block) was only 0.15 tael. Assuming a four-hundred-character page, the cost for cutting one hundred characters would be 0.037 tael.[143]

The publication of the writings of Lin Zhao'en, the founder of the Religion of the Three Teachings in the 1620s, offers similar information on the cost of carving. From 1628 to 1630, followers of Lin, based at the shrine Zhongyi tang (mean-unity temple) in Nanjing, hired carvers to cut more than fifteen hundred blocks and over three thousand folio pages for the forty-juan *Complete Writings of Master Lin* (*Linzi quanshu*). The total cost for cutting the blocks was three hundred taels.[144] With fifteen hundred blocks carved on both sides for a total of three thousand folio blocks, each folio block, labor and materials included, would cost 0.1 tael, lower than the above mentioned books carved in the Jiajing period.

The page format is nineteen characters by nine columns and the characters were in the "craftsman style." Assuming a full page of characters with no space, each page has 171 characters. Assuming 0.02 tael for one hundred characters, a block page of 342 characters would cost 0.068 tael. Factoring in the cost of woodblocks, and assuming it was pear wood at 0.03 tael per block, the cost for materials and labor for producing one printing block was still under 0.1 tael. The average cost for carving one hundred characters was actually lower than 0.02 tael since there was obviously some bargaining between the publisher and the disciples in Nanjing for such a large project.

Thus the average total cost for producing one folio block (four hundred characters) was between 0.10 and 0.15 tael. Ten taels would be enough to produce a book with sixty-six to one hundred folio pages. This estimate comes very close to the cost of three hundred taels for producing *Complete Writings of Master Lin*. The book was not a commercial product, but obviously benefited from some discount by virtue of the scale of its production. The 0.01 tael-per-folio block cost may have come close to the level of production cost of commercial publishers. It is reasonable to speculate that in the early decades of the seventeenth century the cost of producing a printing block in average commercial books would not be more than 0.1 tael, including the wood block and labor.

Other factors might even drive the cost below 0.1 tael. Novels used simplified characters and few difficult words. This explains in part the lower cost of books printed in Jianyang, where many publishers used simplified characters. Thus, book production at the low-end scale was faster and less costly.

PRICES OF BOOKS

Despite scant data on the prices of books in the late Ming, it is nonetheless possible to speculate upon the prices of books among commodities and whether they were affordable goods for the gentry, merchants, and common people. The commodity economy of the late Ming is the proper context in which to assess the relative price of books. There is no question that books belonged to the category of consumer goods. They are dispensable. But the question is whether books were expensive within the category of consumer goods. Interpretation of the relatively limited information requires a proper perspective. For example, at bookstores in Fuzhou in the seventeenth century, a student from the Liuqiu islands bought eight books of multiple volumes for only two to three taels: a set of Four Books and Five Classics, each with commentary, an anthology of prose, and an anthology of poetry.[145] This information clearly suggests that common books such as the Four Books and Five Classics—the common examination texts—were sold under one tael. But were these books cheap?

*Books as Collectibles*

Most price data on books tends to pertain to collector's items. They were either rare editions or good editions for collectors and bibliographers. Wang Shizhen purchased a Song edition of the *History of the Former and Latter Han* (*Liang Han shu*) with a piece of landed property (*zhuang*). It was then bought by Qian Qianyi from a wealthy person from Huizhou for twelve hundred taels.[146] Early Ming editions of Zheng Qiao's *Tongzhi* and *Twenty-one Histories* were regarded as "inexpensive" when Xie Zhaozhi (1567–1624) bought them. But after a flood in Jianning, in Fujian, destroyed many book collections of big families, those two books became rare and could not be obtained even at a price of one hundred taels.[147] Books as expensive as these were rare items, and only wealthy Huizhou merchants or high officials such as Wang Shizhen and Qian Qianyi could afford to buy them. But they were not books newly published for the average reader. There is no reason to even include these prices in this study. However, a discussion of this kind of information is necessary in order to underscore the fact that books, like other objects of exchange in the highly commercialized economy of the late Ming, were one kind of commodity that could be used to accumulate surplus value in the market of connoisseurship, in which the *shishang* invested their money.

If one considers book prices in the context of the commodity economy of the late Ming, a book priced at twelve hundred taels is not expensive. There were teapots and cups made by renowned craftsmen in Suzhou that fetched two to three thousand taels.[148] These certainly were exceptional prices, beyond the reach of even reasonably wealthy people. But so were books priced at twelve hundred or one hundred taels. They were not books for reading but for putting away in the collector's bookshelf or for trading for profit by merchants of antiques and art collections.

This discussion serves to provide a historical perspective for interpreting the relative market value of books and the limited data on book prices. It is important to distinguish types of books when assessing data of book prices. Unfortunately, the scarce extant information on the price of books in the Ming is primarily that for collector items. The prices therefore should not be taken as representative of the average price of books that were produced and distributed for the general reading public. They should be viewed as the high-end books and often too high for ordinary books newly published in the late Ming.

Table 1.3 lists three sets of book prices that are based on Appendices 1–3. These sets of prices from the mid-sixteenth through the mid-seventeenth century provide a general range of book prices relative to other commodities in the Chinese economy, especially in the Jiangnan area.

*Table 1.3*

Range of Book Prices from Mid-Ming
through Early Qing (Appendices 1–3)

| PRICE RANGE | NUMBER OF BOOKS | | | |
| --- | --- | --- | --- | --- |
| | JGG | PYD | SJ | TOTAL |
| Under 1.0 tael | 29 | 4 | 11 | 44 |
| 1–3 taels | 45 | 8 | 9 | 62 |
| 4–6 taels | 17 | 4 | 1 | 22 |
| 7–10 taels | 7 | 2 | 0 | 9 |
| Above 10.0 taels | 12 | 3 | 0 | 15 |
| Total | 110 | 21 | 21 | 152 |

SOURCES: JGG, *Jiguge* (Appendix 1); PYD, *Pan Yunduan* (Appendix 2); SJ, *Shen Jin* (Appendix 3).

When Mao Yi (1640–1713), the son of the renowned publisher Mao Jin, planned to sell some of his collection of rare books to Pan Lei (1646–1708), he prepared a list of titles with prices.[149] The list has been preserved as "A catalog of rare books of the best collection of the Jiguge" (*Jiguge zhencang miben shumu*).[150] There are both hand-copied and printed books in the catalog, but Table 1.3 lists only the printed books (see JGG). Whether Mao Yi listed the prices at a discount or at current market price, we do not know. What is clear is that they were prices of rare and good quality books. Indeed, they were acquired as part of the library collection of his father, a commercial publisher. They were undoubtedly more valuable than average, newly printed books. Pan Lei himself was a book collector. All Song editions qualify to be included in the rare book category. Those printed in the Ming are probably not rare but simply ordinary books of reasonably good quality in terms of carving, printing, ink, and paper. It is safe to argue that the prices in Mao Yi's list were market prices because he indicated all instances of books priced below the market, whether current or at the time of acquisition.[151] It is reasonable to infer that other prices reflect the time of purchase or at least amount spent by Mao Jin or Mao Yi.

In Mao Yi's catalog, there are many hand-copied Song and Yuan editions. The price for many hand-copied books was under one tael; one was priced as low as 0.05 tael. Of the seventeen hand-copied Ming books, no single-volume (*ce*) book cost more than 0.4 tael. Only four books were priced above 1 tael, but they are all more than three volumes. The most expensive two—one in eight volumes, the other in ten volumes—were only 2.4 and two taels, respectively.[152]

Some observations can be made of Mao Yi's list of hand-copied books. As a general rule, the price of hand-copied books increased with the number of pages and hence the number of volumes. For single-volume, hand-copied books, which were more expensive than printed editions, the price was no more than 0.4 tael. It is reasonable to suggest that single-volume, printed books would be generally priced lowered than 0.4 tael. The late-Qing book connoisseur Ye Dehui believed Mao Yi's prices of Song and Yuan editions were low. He was comparing them with the value of those editions in his time, when Song-Yuan recensions were prized over Ming editions, which were by Ye's time dismissed as inferior in quality.[153] Even though they were not as expensive as they would be in the Qing, Mao Yi's editions in the late Ming were nonetheless collector's items. There is reason to believe that their prices were higher than newly printed books in the late Ming.

A list of books can be compiled from the account book of Pan Yunduan (1526–1601) of Shanghai (see PYD).[154] Pan and his father were officials. In 1576 he retired from government and returned to Shanghai to manage his famous Yu Garden (Yu yuan) and productive enterprises.[155] In his account book, he listed a number of books he possessed as collateral for loans. Twenty-one books have prices, and five more have pledges against other collector's items such as jade, painting, and other books. Except four, all were assessed with a value above one tael. The cheapest are three anthologies of essays by examinees (*mojuan*) for a total price of 0.6 tael, averaging 0.2 tael per book. The next highest priced book was an anthology of writings that cost only 0.25 tael. It is clear that single-volume books would be even less expensive.

It is important to put these prices in context. Obviously, these were relatively expensive books. Pan would not agree to lend money against cheap and poor-quality books. Therefore a book priced at 0.2 tael was not cheap compared with other books. Therefore, the books in Mao Yi's and Pan Yunduan's lists belong to the same category. Most are relatively good-quality books or valuable books worthy of the collector's or lender's money. They were relatively expensive books that book collectors, publishers, and wealthy *shishang* would purchase at an exceptionally high price, or accept as pledges for loans.

Shen Jin is a contemporary bibliographer. Over the years, Shen has come across several scores of prices stamped on rare books of Ming editions. It is safe to assume that these were bookstore prices. There are several points worthy of note in comparing Shen Jin's book prices with those in the other two lists (see SJ).

The highest price in Shen's list is 4.9 taels, which is the only price above 3 taels. It was probably comparable to the richly illustrated *Bencao gangmu* (A catalog of plants and herbs) by Li Shizhen.[156] The lowest priced book is an anthology of songs at 0.12 tael. There are eight books priced at 1–1.5 taels. The *Song Wen Wenshan quanji*, for example was a complete work of Wen Tianxiang in twenty-one juan.[157] It was printed in Hangzhou in a format of twenty-one characters by ten columns on paper measuring 21.3 by 14.4 centimeters, a size bigger than most Jianyang books and commercial examination aids. It was priced at only one tael.

There are two Jianyang books in Shen's list that cost three taels; one is the *Da Ming yitong zhi* (Comprehensive gazetteer of the Great Ming) in ninety juan, sixteen volumes, and the other is *Xinbian gujin shiwen leiju* (New classified compendium of events and writings from past and present), which has 170 juan in thirty-seven volumes. Both are multivolume books with illustrations. Jianyang books were notorious for their inferior quality and low price. The price of these two books was therefore not representative of average prices of cheap books printed in Jianyang.

More than half of the books in Shen's list were under one tael. We can therefore conclude that most books—except multivolume ones—aimed at the widest readership were priced below one tael. For example, the price of the book *Yuelu yin*, an anthology of arias from plays published in Hangzhou, is particularly significant. It is a book in four juan in a format of twenty-two characters by ten columns with seventy-one fine full-page illustrations. It was printed from 386 blocks.[158] But it has a price of only 0.8 tael! The price might lie at the middle or low end of the genre of vernacular plays and fiction.

Some imprints featured high-quality paper, superbly designed scenes, and well-spaced text. Many plays and novels published in Suzhou, Nanjing, and Hangzhou belong to this category. They were expensively priced at a range of one to three taels. They were published for the wealthy merchants, officials, and collectors. For example, a historical fiction *Chen Pi Lieguo zhizhuan* published by a Suzhou publisher, Gong Shaoshan, had a listed price of one tael. It has twelve juan with a 1615 preface and comments by the renowned Chen Jiru. This novel has 120 illustrations, although they are not as refined and exquisite as others.[159] The character size is large (twenty characters by ten lines) and evenly distributed on the page. It makes for easy reading with phrase and sentence markers. Personal names are identified by a straight line on the right. The interlineal comments attributed to Chen were in cursive style calligraphy. This is clearly a novel published in a format targeted at high-end book buyers. And it is priced at only one tael. Another similar example from Shen's list is a Suzhou imprint entitled *Xinke Zhong Bojing xiansheng piping Fengshen yanyi* (Installment of the gods with comments by Mr. Zhong Xing). Priced at two taels, this book is a fiction of twenty juan in twenty volumes.

Fiction published in Suzhou, Hangzhou, and Nanjing was clearly priced higher because of better material and aesthetic qualities. Books sold at 0.8 tael were not cheap for ordinary readers. But these were mostly illustrated books that cost more to produce because of extra expenses paid to famous critics for their comments. Nonentertaining books of regular length, without illustrations, would be priced lower than one tael. Many examination aids would fall into this category.

Indeed there were many inexpensive, low-quality books, which Xie Zhaozhi called "vulgar commercial editions" (*fangjian suben*) and "poor-quality collected writings" (*lanwu wenji*). For collectors, these were "non-books" of no value.[160] Examination aids, especially anthologies of model essays, were not regarded as collector's items. They were often deemed too common to be listed in bibliographies of collectors.[161] These books most likely would be priced under one tael.

A low-quality commentary on the Four Books published in Nanjing in 1615 was priced at only 0.5 tael.[162] The page size was twenty characters by nine columns, with characters big enough for easy reading. Another commentary on the Four Books published in the Chongzhen reign (1628–44) had a price of 0.3 tael.[163] It was published by the Changgeng guan publishing house, which had published at least one other commentary.[164] Judging from their exclusion by Huang Zongxi and a book merchant in their 1666 trip, examination aids had one of the lowest resale market values. These two commentaries sold for 0.5 and 0.3 tael, respectively, perhaps average prices that bookstores stamped on this type of book. They could very well be sold at a discount if the owners overstocked or the commentaries had no buyers. Lowering prices for speedy sale is a universal practice. Book merchants in the late Ming could not be an exception to this sale practice.[165]

However, 0.3 tael was clearly not the lowest price for printed matter. A 1628 almanac in thirty-seven juan published in Fujian was priced at 0.1 tael.[166] On the low end of printed matter, publishers produced libretto with lyrics of plays for audiences.[167] According to Shen Defu, popular songs were printed and sold throughout the empire.[168] These texts were more like pamphlets than books. They were widely available and inexpensive. They were not likely priced at the same level as fully illustrated novels and plays. If one tael was a high price for a newly published book targeted at the average reader, these small booklets consisting of several sheets could hardly garner prices higher than 0.1 tael. They could be purchased literally for pennies.

In fact, an anthology of songs published in Jianyang entitled *Xin diao wanqu changchun* (All-time popular myriad songs in new tune) was listed at a price of 0.12 tael.[169] The southern-style drama *Chuanqi* was much longer than the four-scene Yuan *zaju*. In actual performance, it was common to choose only several specific scenes. Audiences wanted to know the verses and lyrics of plays. Printed lyrics and texts of individual scenes were commonly available at restaurants, brothels, and private homes. It is reasonable to suggest that drama texts, especially those with single or few scenes, would cost less than 0.1 tael.[170]

One book published solely for record-keeping will further support the idea that single-volume books were relatively cheap to produce and sold at 0.1 tael or lower in the late Ming. In 1608 a group of gentry in Hangzhou donated money to build a shrine to express gratitude to a prefect for his great service to the community. The records of all donations, expenses, and supporters were published. Expenses disbursed for printing the couplets and the tablet inscriptions in the shrine, as well as the cost for printing 580 copies of the records, totaled 6.72 taels. The record is a single volume in twenty-four folio pages.[171] If the entire total went to the production of the 580 copies, each copy cost only 0.011 tael. This cost includes paper (twenty on cotton paper and 560 on bamboo paper), carving (wage and meal included), sixteen printing woodblocks, inks, and the labor for copying, printing, and binding. The record provides an itemized list of expenses: 2 taels for carvers (including wage and meals) and woodblocks, 0.24 tael for printing and binding twenty copies of "cotton paper," and 4.48 taels for printing and binding 560 copies on "bamboo paper." The 2 taels can be broken down further into expenses for blocks and wages for the carvers: 0.36 tael (twelve blocks at 0.03 tael) and 1.64 taels for carving twelve blocks, which yields a 0.14 tael per block. The average cost per printing side is 0.07 tael (carving on both sides, therefore 0.14 per side). This average cost for carving the block in Hangzhou in 1608 is still lower than the 0.15 tael of the above-mentioned book printed in Fujian in the Jiajing period.

With this limited information, one can calculate the ratio of producing printing blocks and the cost for paper, ink, and binding. The average cost for carving and woodblock is 0.003 tael (2 taels for 580 copies). The cost for bamboo paper per copy can be calculated at 0.008 tael (4.48 taels for 560 copies). The ratio of the cost of carving and woodblocks to the cost of paper, ink, and binding can be established to be roughly 1:3.

If produced in Jianyang, Suzhou, and Nanjing, a similar book of thirty-four pages in a single volume would cost even less than 0.011 tael per copy because commercial publishers could take advantage of the economy of scale. If it was a commercial product, and assuming a 100 percent profit, the book would be sold at 0.022 tael, a very low price. However, this price would not include transportation cost, which was usually included in the price stamped on the books by the booksellers. Even after transportation cost is added, a single volume book of fifty folio pages could still be sold at 0.1 tael or lower with a 100 percent profit (0.022 tael for twenty-four folio pages by 2). That the publisher deserved to make 100 percent profit is suggested in the colophon of an elegantly illustrated book *Lisao tu* (Illustrations of encountering sorrow) printed by Tang Fu, who listed the cost for carving the blocks, paper, and the labor of printing at 0.5 tael. The sale price of an unbound copy was 1 tael.[172]

That the cost of production of a book was 50 percent of its price suggests commercial publishing was a profitable undertaking. Commercial publishers selling their books at a range of 0.1 to 0.5 tael would still make a handsome profit.

Other printed booklets that cost under 0.022 tael were popular primers such as the "Trimetrical classic" (*Sanzi jing*), the "Thousand character essay" (*qianzi wen*), and the "Hundred surnames" (*Baijiaxing*). These texts ranged from one to three pages. Although there is no extant information on the prices of these publications, they could be bought by even the poorest families. They could not be more expensive than a calendar, which could be bought at 0.032 tael in 1588.[173] These three elementary texts comprised about two thousand characters, the typical vocabulary boys would acquire before they enrolled in schools that prepared them for the civil examinations.[174] Any family in the Jiangnan area, regardless of their wealth, could afford the elementary texts; there was also an abundant supply of inexpensive tutors.[175] The widely available elementary texts and examination aids helped spread literacy and expand the reading public in the late Ming.

The book was one of many forms a printed text could take. Single essays or even letters were printed and sold independently. Yu Shenxing (1545–1607), an official, wrote a letter to Qiu Shun, who was appointed to supervise the Wanli emperor's order to confiscate the properties of Zhang Juzheng after Zhang's death. Yu advised Qiu to be lenient toward Zhang's family. The letter was printed and sold by commercial publishers.[176] Wu Yingji, a critic of examination essays, was the editor of the *Number four edition of the Guobiao* (*Guobiao siji*), an anthology of the Restoration Society. He gained even more in popularity among the examinees while in Hangzhou, when he wrote an essay in the boat. Book merchants made handwritten copies of it for sale the next day. The demand was so great that it was printed to meet the need of buyers.[177] These kinds of printed leaflets were ubiquitous in the late Ming and could be produced by carvers in either bookstores or carver shops. They would be sold for pennies.

The above discussion provides some general observations about the price of books in China in the sixteenth and seventeenth centuries. Books were sold at a wide range of prices as reading publics multiplied and existing ones expanded. It can be safely assumed that a publisher would price his books under one tael, unless they were finely illustrated or multivolume books targeted at high-end readers. There were books in most genres that were priced under one tael. In general, the prices listed on books included a 100 percent profit for the publishers even though the actual price might be lower as a result of discount. Books were affordable not only to the gentry, merchants, and officials, but also to ordinary urban workers.

*Prices in the Late Ming*

What was the relative value of books in the late Ming? How much was 1 tael or 0.12 tael or 0.5 tael worth in the sixteenth century? Appendix 4 provides a wide range of prices of goods in the sixteenth and seventeenth centuries. With 0.12 tael, one could purchase six catties (three kilograms) of pork, or eight catties of beef or lamb, or five catties of carp, or three catties of peach or plum. But 0.12 tael was not enough to pay for one catty of spinach, which cost 0.15 tael, nor for a big goose priced at 0.2 tael. Furniture and household items were more expensive. One still could buy six knives, six regular porcelain soup bowls or two porcelain plates. For 0.5 tael one could buy a wool blanket, or a desk, or three regular chairs. In the commodity economy of the Lower Yangtze region, 0.5 tael or even one tael was hardly a large sum of money. An individual plant of jasmine (*moli*) in Suzhou could fetch a price of ten taels. It would cost three times more in Shandong.[178]

What is important to note is that commodities in the late Ming were often sold at a wide range of prices. The amount of 0.1 tael perhaps could fetch the cheapest, decent folding fan in Nanjing.[179] Fans with calligraphy by famous artists, however, cost from one to five taels.[180] A good fan could be pawned for 0.2 to 0.3 taels.[181] Umbrellas in the late Ming came in all sorts of designs and materials, from "all-purpose" to specially designed ones for rainy and sunny days. Their prices ranged from 0.13 to 1.5 taels.

Appendix 4 shows a list of prices of a wide range of goods. In the bond-servant market, for example, a teenage girl could fetch a much higher price than a boy. A teenage girl was sold to an owner of a brothel in the West Lake in Hangzhou for fifty taels.[182] A young maid could be had for six taels.[183] A teenage boy was sold as a bondservant for only three taels.[184] The payment for the service of a prostitute also varied greatly. Spending a night with a high-priced prostitute in Hangzhou might be as high as six, seven, or ten taels.[185] An expense of 0.3 to 0.5 tael was perhaps a relatively common price one had to pay for the service and entertainment of an average prostitute.[186] However, the price could be much lower. For example, women beggars-turned-prostitutes taking customers like laborers and even beggars in Beijing charged only 0.07 tael for their sexual service.[187]

## INCOME AND BOOK PRICES

Prices must be assessed in relation to levels of income. Scholars have argued that books were very expensive, and some argue that even officials such as magistrates could not afford to buy many books. Indeed, Qing scholars had complained about the ludicrously low stipend of the Ming officials. But one should not take the official stipend as the index of the actual level of income of Ming officials. The nominal monthly salary of a provincial official at 7 rank was only about one hundred taels, and those at 4 rank doubled to two hundred.[188] But the actual income far exceeded this amount. Hai Rui's reform proposal for Chun'an county provides a glimpse of the general sources of a magistrate. The magistrate in Chun'an would receive a ninety-tael stipend.[189] He was provided with a government residence. In addition, he received various allowances, including forty to fifty taels for new furniture.[190] Income from surcharges on regular taxes with fixed amounts was more than two hundred taels. Tariffs on salt passing through the county and salt sold in the county each year would produce more than 120 taels. With other miscellaneous charges, a magistrate of the Chun'an county in the Wanli reign received probably at least an income of five hundred taels.[191] These were not bribes received by the magistrate on his own initiative. They were well-established surcharges that were a legitimate part of the magistrate's entire income package. Even though they were not legalized incomes, they were regarded as income of the office of the magistrate. When officials insisted on maintaining integrity by refusing to finance their living expenses from these surcharges, they would be praised.[192]

Five hundred taels of income for a magistrate was certainly not a preposterous amount. The salary reform for officials during the Yongzhen and Qianlong reigns was designed to provide extra *yanglian* (nourishing integrity money). Thus officials could meet their personal expenses without resorting to embezzlement and fraud. The *yanglian* quota reforms suggests that five hundred taels for a magistrate in the Ming-Qing period was hardly a handsome remuneration. Magistrates in Fujian received a salary ranging from eight hundred to sixteen hundred taels; six hundred to one thousand taels in Anhui; eight hundred to sixteen hundred taels in Kiangsi; the lower level *yanglian* quota in Guizhou, four hundred to seven hundred taels; and four hundred to six hundred taels in Sizhuan.[193]

It is difficult, if not impossible, to obtain information about the extra-income of officials. There is fragmented and anecdotal information about compensations for any nonofficial services. Officials traveled free on the imperial postal service.[194] But on personal trips, many would travel on private boats because they were often offered "boat-ride money" (*zuo-cang qian*) from merchants. In return, officials provided the boat with a tax exemption as it passed through custom stations.[195] The amount could be several dozens of taels.[196]

"Selling one's writings" (*maiwen*) was a common way for gentry and officials to augment their income. Biographical essays or tomb inscriptions, or any other genre of writing from a renowned writer, even by a friend, would require monetary remuneration (*runbi*). There was other nonofficial income that officials often received from other officials as gifts. The most common was the greeting gift called *shupo* (book-wrapping cloth). The amount increased to thirty or forty taels in the early 1600s.[197]

There were probably many other sources of extra income that were not registered. With several hundred taels as net income, and with housing and daily expenses provided by the magistrate office, a magistrate could easily afford a book priced at one to three taels.

Students preparing for all levels of the civil service examination constituted one of the largest reading publics in the sixteenth and seventeenth centuries.[198] They needed to buy a great variety of examination aids. The quest for success at the metropolitan examination was expensive and psychologically excruciating (see Chapter 2). They needed to maintain a certain level of income in order to purchase books.

A private tutor, with only a *shengyuan* degree with stipend, could earn more than forty taels a year in addition to other compensations, including meals and gifts during festivals and holidays.[199] However, Wei Dazhong, a young man in his early twenties in 1598, worked as a private tutor with the status of government student but took home only ten taels. He still managed to save three to four taels for books.[200] He would be able to buy at least eight to twelve books sold at 0.3 to 0.5 tael. Most tutors and examinees with higher degrees could earn extra income by providing a wide range of services such as writing letters, calligraphy, commemorative essays, and epitaphs. For higher-degree holders, income from writing fees varied from a fraction of a tael to hundreds of taels. A professional critic working for a bookstore could make one hundred taels.[201]

It was a common practice for literati and officials to receive money for writing an essay or poem or calligraphy.[202] According to Ye Sheng (1420–1474), officials in the Hanlin Academy would be offered 0.5 to one tael for writing a short piece of prose in the 1460s.[203] Most officials would pay a huge sum to get an epitaph, tomb inscription, or a mourning poem for their deceased family member.[204] When the famous writer Zhong Xing (1574–1625) died, his son requested a biographical essay from his good friend Tan Yuanchun (1585–1637), another writer from Hubei. He sent the request with money. Tan agreed to write the essay but returned the money, not because he would not accept money for his literary service, but because he wanted to honor his best friend.[205] He assuredly accepted money for writings he undertook for other patrons.

Not only officials and their descendants sought the services of famous writers. Wealthy merchants were no less generous in paying for biographical essays or epitaphs for parents and grandparents. Merchants of Huizhou were famous for their handsome rewards for tomb inscriptions and biographies. Li Weizhen (1547–1626) openly accepted payment for his literary services.[206] Officials who were reputable writers like Wang Shizhen and Wang Daokun would not need to render their services indiscriminately but would not consider it a breach of decorum to receive remuneration for writings they undertook on request.

There were professional writers who depended entirely on their brush and literary skill for a living. Beginning in 1580, the renowned playwright Zhang Fengyi (1527–1613) posted at the door of his house a list of fees for various literary services. For either poems or verses in the (*kaishu*) style, written on a folding fan, the fee was 0.1 tael. For eight verses in cursive (*xingshu*) style, the fee was 0.03 tael.[207] A professional writer who often traveled to Suzhou to write tomb inscriptions, birthday greetings, and elegies, wrote several pieces a day, each fetching a price from 0.1 to one tael.[208] The residence of the famed Chen Jiru was always crowded with people requesting prefaces, biographical essays, calligraphy, poems, and commemorative essays.[209] He was given ten taels to write a preface for a work by Wang Shizhen.[210]

The use of writing skill for extra income was commonly reflected in literary works. In the *Golden Lotus*, Ximen Qing paid a *juren* degree holder 0.5 tael for writing calligraphy on a pair of handkerchiefs.[211] A self-styled "famed literatus" (*mingshi*) was offered eight taels for an epitaph.[212] Xu Wei (1521–1593), a renowned playwright and writer, received 220 taels for writing a commemorative essay. This undoubtedly was a rare case.[213]

Professional writers and painters could live off their literary and artistic skills in the late Ming and early Qing. Chen Hongshou (1599–1652), the renowned but "poor" painter supported a family of twenty members by selling his paintings. He printed copies of portraits of Lord Guan and made playing cards of characters from the *Romance of the Water Margin* and other historical figures.[214] He might also have been involved in collecting and selling works of other painters. An amount of twenty to thirty taels appears to be the scale of transaction he was capable of undertaking.[215] He often exchanged paintings for monetary gifts from his friends.[216] One tael was an amount he often received from friends. He once paid one tael for a painting and gave it to his friend Mouqi.[217] His paintings were in great demand, so much so that countless professional painters specialized in emulating his style, selling their own paintings under his name.[218]

A professional writer (*shanren*) who rendered literary service to families in Suzhou was hired to write tomb inscriptions and commemorative essays for occasions like anniversaries, birthdays, and auspicious events. He charged his customers mostly from 0.1 or 0.2 to one tael.[219] Li Yu, the well-known publisher-cum-writer, referred one of his friends to a Wu *shanren* residing in Suzhou who supported his parents and himself by selling his paintings.[220] For professional writers and painters, books priced at one tael or lower would hardly be considered unaffordable. The *shishang* who had a higher level of income would find books of average length and quality very affordable and often inexpensive. Books priced under a tael would be very affordable for the educated elite. But were books still too expensive for the majority of low-income residents of towns and cities?

## Wage Level and Book Price

Adequate information does not exist to permit a full reconstruction of the structure and complete range of various levels of skills and their corresponding wages. But some general observations can be made. First, the pay level of carvers supports the point that production costs for printing blocks would not make books expensive in the late Ming; and second, wages of most workers included sufficient income to buy inexpensive books.

Table 1.4 shows the wages for different types of work. A navigator made 1.6 taels per month in the Zhenjiang area in 1597, and a sailor whose level of skill was lower made 1.2–1.3 taels per month.[221] The work of the navigator and sailor involved much higher risk than did the carver's, even though all three provided specially skilled labor.

During the Wanli period, a silk worker made 0.04 tael a day.[222] In the mid-Wanli period, a private building worker made 0.033 tael a day, 0.003 more than those paid by the Ministry of Public Works.[223] The monthly pay of a silk worker was 1.2 taels and 0.99 for a building worker. Bear in mind that the "wage" was not the entire compensation the worker normally received for services rendered. If practice of compensation for labor in other professions was standard, wages often came with other fringe benefits, such as meals and accommodation. Sometimes the employers even included clothing and gifts during important festivals.[224] But this wage refers to the money amount paid to the workers. It was only part of a remuneration package. Often, other allowances for special categories

*Table 1.4*

Monthly Wages in the Late Ming

| TYPES OF WORK | WAGES (IN TAEL) |
| --- | --- |
| Postal officer | 7.5 |
| Navigator | 1.6 |
| Theatrical player | 1.5–15 |
| Hired laborer (in Jiangnan) | 1.5 [a] |
| Construction worker (Beijing) | 1.5 [a] |
| Clerk | 1.2–7.5 [a] |
| Sailor | 1.2–1.3 |
| Silk worker | 1.2 |
| Porcelain worker | 1.05 [a] |
| Construction worker | 0.99 |
| Hired laborer (by the Yellow River) | 0.9 [a] |
| Carver | 0.9–1.5 |
| Hired laborer | 0.8 |
| Hired courier/transporter (Henan) | 0.6 [a] |

SOURCE: [a]Huang Miantang, p. 369. All wages, except those of the laborer by the Yellow River, were from the Wanli period.

were included, such as travel expenses, wine, and tools.[225] It seems safe to conclude that the range of carvers' pay falls within the range of other skilled workers. But they did not receive exceptionally high pay for their skill. Thus their skill cost no more than the labor unit cost for other consumption goods like silk cloth.

For no-risk nonskilled labor, the pay was much lower. In 1597 a boatman (*shuifu*), a worker responsible for supplying water to the Imperial Academy, earned 0.8 tael per month.[226] Hai Rui recommended that officers of the postal station receive 0.25 tael per day and clerks 0.05 in order to provide sufficient income and discourage the solicitation of bribes.[227] The monthly incomes were 7.5 taels for the postal station officer and 1.5 taels for the clerks; the annual incomes were about ninety taels and eighteen taels, respectively. But these recommended higher salaries in fact did not reflect the actual income level of the clerks and runners. Through fraud and extortion, the clerks and runners were able to increase their actual level of earning substantially. Corruption of the subbureaucrats had often been cited as a major source of the financial burden on the people and of the inordinate increase in expenses of local government.[228]

Theatrical performers appeared to earn high income. Some of them received 0.5 tael a day for simply waiting to be called for a performance.[229] If they were hired for a period of thirty days, they would earn fifteen taels. There were of course idle days for many performers. People rendering various services often were rewarded with tips. In the fiction *Jin Ping Mei*, Ximeng Qing routinely gave 0.3 to 0.5 tael to entertainers, servants, and messengers. And higher amounts from one to five taels were not uncommon.[230]

Women from *shishang* families could definitely afford to buy books in the late Ming. Even working women and entertainers could afford to buy inexpensive books. Women of well-to-do families often hired beauty specialists called *chadaipo* (old maid assistant in hair dress and adornments) to help improve their appearance. These women beauty specialists could make 0.2 to 0.3 tael in a matter of one to two hours.[231] Storytellers and actors were among those who benefited from consumerism and growing demand for entertainment across the social spectrum in the cities and towns. In Nanjing, the famous storyteller Liu Jingting charged one tael for covering one chapter of a novel like the *Water Margin*.[232] The famous actor Peng Tianxi often charged several scores of tael for his performance. He traveled to cities like Shaoxing, Hangzhou, and Shanyin. He was able to save several tens of thousands of taels.[233] There is no question that these fees were on the highest side of the scale. Less talented entertainers would be rewarded in accordance to the demand conditions of the market.

A carver who made 0.05 tael a day for carving one hundred characters would need to work twenty days to earn one tael if he wanted to buy a copy of the *Xinbian shiwen leiju hanmo daquan* printed in Jianyang. It should be noted that it is a book of 120 juan, a relatively voluminous book. But he only needed to work one day to earn enough to buy two small books from Pan Yundaun's list, and these were rare Song editions.

For the lowest paid laborer and the highest paid postal officer, a book selling at one tael would be very expensive. But a postal officer, navigator, sailor, silk worker, clerk, and carver could all buy a one-tael book with the savings of one month. But to buy a commentary on the Four Books at 0.3 tael for their sons would only require them to work ten days or less. Building a moderate-size library was beyond their means. If they bought poor-quality books, they could manage to acquire five or six books a year at a price under 0.5 tael each. If we factor in the earnings of the wife and children, books were not inaccessible to the "lower classes" from the family's viewpoint.[234]

In *Jin Ping Mei*, ordinary doses of medicine would cost 0.3 tael, and the fee for a doctor's home visit to examine a woman was three taels.[235] A prescription of medicine from the best doctors in Suzhou was five taels.[236] There must have been doctors whose services were worth much less. But it is reasonable to suggest that for literary professionals such as the average doctor, a book priced at one tael would be expensive but still very affordable.

That the value of one tael was not substantial in the late Ming in economic terms is also reflected in its insignificance in religious terms. In late-Ming religious practice, "morality books" (*shanshu*) translated monetary value into religious credits. In his attempt to encourage good deeds, Lü Kun transferred religious methods of salvation to administrative methods for promoting good order. In a scale easily understood by the common people, Lü Kun differentiated three levels of good deeds. Those who contributed two to three taels to help the poor cover their expenses in weddings and funerals would earn a "great good deed." Those who donated more than one and less than two taels would be accorded a "medium good deed." Those who offered less than 0.5 tael to help would be rewarded with a "small good deed."[237] One tael could only purchase two small good deeds and one medium good deed but not enough to acquire a great good deed! Commodities priced at one tael were clearly not cheap but nor were they too expensive to be out of the reach of low-income families.

It is safe to conclude that the price of books in the Ming was not high compared to other commodities. Besides, books were one of the two types of commodities exempted from commercial taxes.[238] While books were exempted from taxes, paper was not.[239] In China in the sixteenth and seventeenth centuries most people could afford to buy books that were produced for readers with different level of income. They might still be expensive for the poorest, but they were certainly not a privilege reserved only for the rich. This situation was similar in Europe, but with the general decline in real wages in the sixteenth century, books would be much more expensive for the European poor in the cities.[240] It is reasonable to suggest that there were numerous books that were produced for the widest possible readership, and the generally low prices of these books were based on the cost of their production. If one under financial constraints wanted to buy a book priced at 0.2 tael, one only had to forgo a new chair, goose, or folding fan. The above discussion on book prices substantiates Matteo Ricci's observation that books were sold at "ridiculously low prices" in late sixteenth century China.

2

# The Chinese Book and Late-Ming Publishing

The myth about printing technology in imperial China is that despite the invention of movable-type printing, China failed to make the complete transition from woodblock printing. It therefore lacked the agent of change that propelled Europe into modernity.[1] While woodblock printing had its disadvantages compared to movable-type printing, it had many economic and production advantages. Whether woodblock or movable type, printing as a technology of reproducing text lent itself to commercialization in China as much as in Europe.

The myth that woodblock and movable-type printing were two very different technologies is widely accepted by scholars of book history. It is often presented in a historicist narrative, treating the two as successive phases of the evolution of the same technology. The very brief discussion of Chinese printing in the classic history of printing by Lucien Febvre and Henri-Jean Martin deserves some discussion.

In this classic work on the history of the European book, woodblock printing is called "a precedent" or the "infancy" of movable-type printing, which eventually emerged to be the only "normal" or "standard" method of printing. M. R. Guignmard, author of the section on Chinese printing, attempts to explain in *cultural* and *linguistic terms* why movable-type printing failed in China. Guignmard emphasizes the enormous cost and technical difficulties of reproducing Chinese character types. First, the huge number of Chinese characters required capital investment beyond the reach of private printers. The only example given was the voluminous project of *Gujin tushu jicheng* (Collection of books from the past and present), a sort of "encyclopedia of books" commissioned by the Kangxi emperor in 1720.[2] The authors take pains to point out that it was printed with ten thousand copper-engraved (rather than cast) characters.[3] The problem of the huge number of Chinese characters was somewhat solved with the creation of a system of 214 radicals, which allows for the organization and location of characters. But the cost problem was too great to be overcome. For the authors,

> No individual could have financed such an enterprise, or engaged such a work force, or kept such a vast number of characters in a usable order. Further, the fluid quality of the ink used in China hardly lent itself to printing in metal; and lastly, the book was unattractive on *aesthetic and sentimental* [emphasis mine] grounds, since it deprived the reader of the pleasure of fine calligraphy and of the style of such a calligrapher working in *harmony* [emphasis mine] with his text. Woodblock engraving and block-printing, by contrast, make possible a faithful reflection of the calligrapher's style. Only in the twentieth century was movable type again adopted and then only for newspaper and popular editions. . . . While publication in China was often subsidized by private individuals who *insisted* on traditional wood-block method.[4]

The author underscores the economic, linguistic, technical, and cultural obstacles to the development of movable type and Chinese printers' *insistence* on employing woodblock printing. These reasons are not entirely wrong but exaggerated. Most make sense in comparison with the advantages of movable-type printing. But Guignmard has only considered the disadvantages of woodblock printing from the point of view of the movable-type method. Movable-type printing has its own disadvantages in comparison with the woodblock method. Furthermore, the author is not informed about the history of Chinese printing technology, especially the variety of movable types made from different materials: copper, tin, lead, porcelain, and wood. The movable-type method was not able to re-place woodblock printing as the dominant technology due to certain ad-vantages of woodblock printing and specific conditions in early modern China. The explanation lies in the economics of printing technology in Ming–Qing China.

## Advantages of Woodblock Printing

Since the invention of movable-type characters by Bi Sheng in the mid-1040s, printers have experimented with several different types of materi-als: wood, pottery, copper, and tin.[5] Movable-type printing continued to be practiced and refined even though it did not become the common method of reproduction. By the Ming there were two types of printing technology available to Chinese publishers: woodblock and movable type. The publisher's choice would be determined by his financial situation and business plan, not by a cultural or exclusively aesthetic disposition.

The woodblock method offered many paratextual, technological, and economic advantages to the publisher: flexibility in page layout de-sign, flexibility in production, a low level of investment, minimal skill, and great mobility. The conventional explanation for the failure of the development of movable-type printing in China exaggerates the impor-tance of aesthetics. Xylography allowed easy incorporation of graphic—calligraphic or paratextual—elements in the text without complicating the printing process. Technically, carvers and printers did not need to make the distinction between producing characters or iconic designs. Pub-lishers could insert illustrations, punctuation and accentuation marks, or chose single, double, or even triple register layouts as commonly adopted in many Jianyang imprints. Commentaries could be inserted in many dif-ferent modes: interlineal, in the top register, or with different calligraphic styles.[6] But the biggest advantages for commercial publishers remained in block printing's technological simplicity and flexibility in levels of invest-ment. Figure 1.1 shows one folio page layout of *Chen pi lieguo zhizhuan* (Romance of the contending states with comments by Chen Jiru) *(see page 28)*. Comments are inserted in three modes: outside the top border, in-terlinearly, and as a concluding comment at the end of a paragraph. Other iconic elements include punctuation marks (hollow period), accentuation marks (continuous hollow periods), and right lines marking personal names.

Chinese woodblock printing can be characterized as "atomistic" in contrast with the movable-type method, which is "organic." It centered on the individual carver, and each carver could operate as an independent printing unit.

The most important skill required for the production of a Chinese book was the carving of blocks. The carvers needed only a set of carving knives and tools. Printing from the blocks was relatively simple, and it was not difficult for a carver to master the skill of printing and sewing the pages together.[7] If the carver was literate, he could compose and write the print form of the book. In this case, a book could be produced by one person—from copying the text to the block to printing copies and finally stitching up the pages.

In terms of technology, there was no difference in the production of books by a private scholar and a commercial publisher. The only difference was in the time required for carving and printing and in the quantity of copies. Commercial publishers, private scholars, bookstore owners, and private academies all faced the primary task of finding a carver and the necessary materials of woodblock, paper, and ink.

The simplicity of block printing, based on the "self-sufficiency" of the carver, gave rise to a number of economic advantages. First, in contrast to European publishing in the sixteenth and seventeenth centuries, a Chinese woodblock publisher did not have to invest in a printing press and sets of metal types. The initial investment could vary considerably depending on his level of resources and business plan. In mid-eighteenth-century England, for example, one needed several hundred pounds to set up a printing house, and the capital often came from family members and close friends or acquaintances.[8] The operation of a movable-type printing house required a greater concentration of laborers in the printing shop. The movable-type publishing had a great disadvantage compared with xylography in terms of the level of investment and the cost of operation.

Because paper remained the most expensive material of the European book, a higher number of copies required greater capital investment in the operation. The cost for typesetting also forced European publishers to print enough copies to lower the overhead cost of each imprint. The investment could not be covered until the books were sold. Paper was one of the most expensive components of book production, thus a large inventory tied up the capital of a publisher.[9] In order to ensure that the books would be sold, the method of subscription was developed.[10]

The production process in a European printing shop was more structured and rigid than the individual carver's in China. A European printing unit was "intensive" and "organic" in the sense that it was organized around the printing press and the division of labor between the four workers, each with his own special skill. A typical European printing shop included a metal worker to cast types, a woodcutter to cut blocks for illustrations and other iconic elements, a bookbinder, and a printer. It is important to note that contrary to conventional view, block printing was not completely replaced after the invention of the printing press by Gutenberg in the 1450s; it was integrated into the process of book production. European printing shops continued to employ woodcutters to make illustrations throughout most of the sixteenth and seventeenth centuries. Woodcuts were used extensively by printers in Frankfurt and Antwerp.[11]

The Chinese publisher's largest investment was in block carving. He could print a small number of copies if he did not have enough money to buy paper, or if the anticipated sale in the short term was small. As demonstrated below, Chinese publishers could even carve blocks by installments for voluminous works if they did not have sufficient money. With the profit from the sale of the first part of the book, they could continue printing the rest of the work. Unlike his European counterpart, the Chinese publisher faced less risk of having his capital frozen in unsold copies.[12] This flexibility not only allowed publishers to begin business operations with limited resources, but also made publishing a less risky business.

Carvers, bookshop owners, and any *shishang* with limited resources would find block printing attractive if they decided to venture into the publishing business. With the general presence of carver shops and bookstores in the cities, independent and itinerant carvers always found publishing a widely available option. In Beijing, Nanjing, Hangzhou, and Suzhou, carvers could find jobs in carver shops (*kezi dian*) and bookstores.[13] Owners of carver shops and bookstores themselves could easily publish books if they had the capital. Carver shops and bookstores also offered the services of professional critics who could help to produce manuscripts for publication.[14]

In Kong Shangren's famous play *Peach Blossom Fan* (*Taohua shan*), the bookseller Cai Yisuo hired famous writers Chen Zhenhui and Wu Yingqi to compile anthologies of examination essays.[15] Both Chen and Wu were reputable critics.[16] As Kong Shangren explained, the characters were real people. Indeed, Cai Yishuo was a Nanjing bookstore owner whose bookstore was located at the Shuixi gate of Nanjing. He hired examinees like Wu and Chen to edit and comment on examination essays. Wu Yingqi was a member of the Restoration Society.[17] Critics could also become publishers themselves by hiring carvers to print their work. A story in the *Rulin waishi* offered an account of the publication of a critical anthology by three critics. After completing the selection and comments, they hired seven to eight carvers to work on the project. It took them about five months to complete it.[18]

Not unlike seventeenth-century Europe, booksellers and publishers in China were not entirely distinct professions. Often "the majority of them carr[ied] out both jobs at the same time."[19] It was not uncommon to find European woodblock cutters who were also booksellers and printers.[20] The simple methods of woodblock printing made it even easier for Chinese booksellers and publishers to undertake both jobs in the late Ming.

### Between Private and Commercial Publishing

With woodblock printing the boundary between private and commercial publishing was easily crossed. One could pay carvers to have one's work carved and printed if one had the money to pay for all the expenses. Since at least the Song period, woodcarvers were itinerant workers.[21] In the late Ming numerous woodcarvers operated as individual printers, hiring themselves out to private scholars, publishers, owners of carving shops, or anyone who could pay for their service. The case of Tang Shunzhi (1507–60) and the mode of his publishing operation is a good example of how woodblock printing obscured the line between private and commercial publishing.

Born to an eminent family in Wujin, Kiangsu, Tang attained the highest *jinshi* degree in his twenties in 1529. A man of many talents with a reputation in statecraft learning, he was the leading exponent of the Tang-Song prose style in the mid-sixteenth century.[22] He had compiled, edited, and commented on many anthologies of prose essays.[23]

Tang's publishing activities were more likely prompted by his quest for literary achievements and a secondary attempt to make commercial gain. He hired independent carvers such as Hu Mao, who worked for different publishers and served as a go-between for publishers and *shishang* like himself. Hu was from Youlong, Zhejiang, a region famous for its book merchants and carvers. Hu's father and uncles were all involved in the book trade and publishing business. As one of his patrons, Tang Shunzhi worked closely with Hu on editing manuscripts for publication.[24] Hu was particularly talented in designing textual layout of the page (similar to composition of the page in the European book). Tang admired Hu's ability in editing and page formatting by cutting up or combining sentences, paragraphs, and chapters.[25] Indeed, spacing was an important aspect of preparing the copy of the manuscript for pasting over the blocks.

Tang's relationship with his carvers and publishers was multiple. In some cases, Tang was the publisher paying for the expenses.[26] In other cases, he was only the author or editor, and the publication expenses came from an official or the carver-cum-publisher like Hu. It was not uncommon to find a high official to pay for the publishing cost. Tang had edited *An Anthology of Essays* (*Wenbian*), which was printed in 1556 with expenses provided by a magistrate.[27] Another voluminous work on history compiled by Tang was published by a censor in chief, Hu Zongxian.[28] An anthology of essays on government policy compiled by Tang with comments was published by a bookstore owner in Nanjing who might have been a relative of Hu Mao.[29]

## Flexibility of Woodblock Printing

The production schedule of woodblock publishing was extremely flexible. Playwright Mei Dingzuo (1549–1615) hired carvers to make blocks for his books. One of his works was delayed because he was out of money. On another occasion, the carver had to take leave; production of the work did not resume until the next year when he returned.[30] Mei appears to have published his own books with his own money.[31] He was a typical literatus-publisher, a specific configuration of the *shishang* elite.

Zang Maoxun (1550–1620) had a similar experience. He published many books, and his strategy for dealing with shortages of capital followed the same pattern. After publishing part of the work, he used the money from the sale of the first part to pay for the carving of blocks for the remaining parts.[32] Zang was strongly interested in Yuan drama and was committed to publishing a series of one hundred Yuan dramas. For lack of money, he first published only fifty titles. He apparently printed only a small number of copies for the first impression. In a letter to Huang Ruheng (1558–1626), he apologized for not being able to send a copy with his previous letter. Later he made another impression with newly published titles. He sent one copy to Huang and asked him to promote it to Huang's friends, but he was still not able to finish printing all of the titles in the series for lack of money to pay for carving blocks. He sent his bond-servant to the capital to sell copies. He was determined to publish the entire series by using profits from the sale of copies of the already published titles.[33]

Books could be produced by successive printing of parts, chapters, and even individual essays or poems. Blocks carved to print essays, poetry, biographical essays, notices of celebration of birthdays, and funeral and other occasions written by a literati could be kept by his family.[34] Printing a collection of that person's writings would be relatively easy. His family or descendants could speedily put those blocks together and carve additional blocks for writings not yet printed.

## Scale of Publishing and Commercial Expansion

Because each carver could operate as an independent unit, the scale of woodblock publishing could vary from one person to an infinite number of workers working as a large team. The Qizizhai publishing house of Gu Qilun (1515–87) in Wuxi was a medium-sized publisher. For a twenty-juan book published in 1574, ten block cutters and six copyists had been hired for the production.[35]

Because of the atomistic nature of woodblock printing, the scale of production could be expanded easily. The speed of production increased by employing more carvers and printers as supplies allowed. Carvers could work for commercial as well as private publishers.[36] An expansion in scale in private or commercial publishing employing woodblock printing would require only obtaining the services of additional carvers.

Compared to the European movable-type printing that centered on the printing press, woodblock printing was therefore more mobile and diffused, allowing carvers to work either as independent and itinerant printers or as a component of a large publishing house.[37] If there was a shortage of carvers in the community, expansion of scale and increase in the speed of block carving still could be accomplished by enlisting the service of additional carvers from other cities. The woodblocks for a text could be carved by different carvers scattered in different carver shops located in a number of cities.[38] In this case, a supervisor would be needed to coordinate and supervise the quality and accuracy of the carving. Agents served as printing supervisors (*dukan*) responsible for monitoring the progress of the printing of books at different carver shops (see Chapter 3).

Gu Qijing (1515–1569) of Wuxi, who was also a self-styled "mountain man" (*shanren*), published an anthology of poetry in 1556.[39] The blocks for the nineteen-juan work were carved at eleven different places with names like "pavilion," "chamber," "study," and "cabin" (*shi*).[40] This could be understood as two modes of operation. Gu could have brought with him the same group of carvers as he moved from one place to another, or different groups of carvers produced blocks more or less at the same time. The fact is that carving of blocks for a book could be done by different carvers even if they were geographically scattered.

Because the speed of production depended primarily on the number of carvers, the time of production could be cut in half with the doubling of the work force. The anthology published by Gu included rare information about the number and names of copyists, carvers, proofreaders, and the duration of the book's production. It lists three copyists, twenty-four carvers, and three binders.[41] The ratio of copyists, carvers, and binders was 1:8:1, although it does not provide a basis for predicting a corresponding change when the number of one group changes. In each juan, there are names of proofreaders.[42] The carving and printing of the anthology took six months to complete. With the same work force, a book of about ten juan in six *ce* could be produced in three months, and a book in three juan in two *ce* could be finished in just one month. Gu's operation represents the more commercial type of book production. Unless there was a sudden boom in publishing in any given period in a particular city resulting in a shortage of carvers in the short term, the speed of production could always be increased. Speed in woodblock printing was a function of the availability of carvers and capital.

The total production time in commercial and government publishing was shorter with more block cutters and laborers. Table 2.1 shows a list of selected books published in the sixteenth century. The book entitled *Huang Ming shuchao* (Copies of memorials of the Ming dynasty) was published in 1584 by a group of government officials headed by a censor. It was produced with the largest number of cutters, 101. Compared to another anthology of memorials entitled *Huang Ming choushu leichao* (Classified anthology of memorials of the Ming dynasty) and published four years later by a commercial publisher, Wang Shaoquan, who employed only sixty-six block cutters, the production time was likely almost 40 percent shorter. *Daozong liushu* (Six Daoist texts) was published by government officials in 1576. Forty-five block cutters were employed in the production, which was not a huge group compared to that used to produce *Huang Ming shuchao*. But other books produced by government offices did not necessarily use a large number of block cutters. Two books published in 1552 and 1558 hired only nine and eight block cutters, respectively.

Despite the relative simple operation and low level of investment, publishing multivolume works was not an enterprise that one could undertake without adequate resources. Private scholars who wanted to publish voluminous works but did not want to publish them in installments would find it necessary to solicit contributions from friends. Wu Zhenyuan of Taichang compiled a two hundred-juan book. He did not have enough money to publish it by himself. He solicited contributions from Dong Qichang, Chen Jiru, Yao Ximeng, and other friends.[43] It is not clear if this was a joint business venture or simply friends lending a helping hand.

In sum, there were many advantages of woodblock printing in early modern China. The ubiquitous presence of carver shops and the flexible woodblock methods provided easy and inexpensive access to printing

*Table 2.1*

Number of Carvers by Government and Commercial Publications

| TITLE | YEAR | JUAN | CUTTERS | TYPES |
|---|---|---|---|---|
| *Huang Ming shuyi jilei* | 1552 | 37 | 9 | G |
| *Qin-Han shushu* | 1558 | 18 | 8 | G |
| *Shisan jing zhushu* | 1568 | 335 | 202 | G |
| *Daozong liushu* | 1576 | 36 | 45 | G |
| *Huang Ming shuchao* | 1584 | 70 | 101 | G |
| *Huang Ming choushu leichao* | 1588 | 61 | 66 | C |
| *Guoya* | 1573 | 21 | 10 | C |
| *Shiji pinglin* | 1576 | 131 | 41 | C |
| *Huang Ming Jingshi wen bian* | 1638 | 504 | ? | C |

* SOURCE: Shen Jin, *MGHF*, in the order of the list, pp. 2, 161, 156, 583, 100, 162, 161; Chen Zilong, *Huang Ming Jingshi wen bian*. G = government publication; C = commercial publication.

technology. In contrast to movable-type printing, woodblock printing allowed speedy entry to and exit from commercial publishing, one of the flourishing but extremely competitive industries in the sixteenth and seventeenth centuries. These advantages notwithstanding, movable-type printing received unprecedented attention, and many publishers in the late Ming experimented with and developed movable type made from different materials.

*Growing Use of Movable-Type Printing in Late Imperial China*

The unique characteristics of Chinese scripts and woodblock printing allowed Chinese book production to expand in the late Ming without creating great pressure to shift entirely to movable printing. It is true that the large number of distinctive scripts discouraged publishers with limited resources from adopting the movable-type method. The advantages of movable-type printing, however, did not fail to attract the attention of commercial publishers with greater resources.

Since the mid-1400s many large printing houses in Wuxi, Suzhou, Nanjing, and Fujian used movable scripts to print voluminous works. As early as 1465, the Hua family in Wuxi began casting copper-tin types for their publishing business. They were followed by the An family in the mid-sixteenth century.[44] Publishers in Wuxi, Suzhou, Changzhou, Nanjing, Zhejiang, Jianning, and Jianyang in Fujian, had also published books using copper-tin movable scripts.[45] Publishers in Changzhou experimented with lead movable scripts.[46] The high cost of making metal types prompted publishers to experiment with wooden movable scripts. By the Wanli reign (1573–1619), there was a growing number of publishers who began using wooden movable types.[47] This method was used by publishers in Hangzhou, Suzhou, Nanjing, Fuzhou, and even in Sichuan and Yunnan. There are at least one hundred extant books from the Ming that were published by wooden movable types, printed mostly during the Wanli period.[48] The increase in the use of wooden movable-type methods since the Wanli period is evidence of the desire to speed up production as commercial publishing expanded.

In the Qing period (1644–1911), the wooden movable-type method continued to spread. During the Qianlong reign (1736–95), Zhou Yongnian proposed using wooden movable type to print a "Confucian Library" (Rucang). The Qianlong emperor accepted a proposal to create wooden movable types to print books. More than 134 books were printed with wooden types at the printing office of the "Wuying dian" (Hall of military eminence). The number of imprints from this office ranged from five copies to three hundred.[49] These edition sizes were still relatively small and could not have justified their printing had they been commercial productions.

The wooden-type method was preferred when small numbers of copies were needed. It was suitable for printing genealogies that were primarily produced for exclusive circulation among kin members. Genealogies of lineages in the Jiangsu and Zhejiang provinces in the Qing period were produced more by the wooden movable-type method than by the woodblock method.[50] There were itinerant printers of genealogies who traveled from village to village. They normally carried twenty thousand types made of pear wood; they would carve new types on the spot when needed.[51] Because genealogies were not printed for profit, and the text concerned primarily personal names and their relationship, quality and bigger size of characters were preferred. These conditions made wooden types more suitable for printing genealogies. There is no question that using wooden movable type to print a small number of copies of genealogy was more economical than carving blocks. The need to update the information in the genealogy also justified the use of a cheaper method.[52] Some publishers in Changzhou began carving bigger wooden types especially for printing genealogies. The wooden types of Changzhou publishers were of such superior quality that lineages in other provinces took their genealogies to Changzhou for printing.[53] The extensive use of movable type in the Qing period is evident in the large number of extant copies. There are more than twenty-five hundred titles printed from movable types made of various materials; imprints from wooden types constitute the majority.[54]

## The Speed of Printing

Scholars of books and printing often considered the invention of the press as a modern technology simply because of the presumed ease of typesetting and the superior capacity to turn out a larger volume of print than woodblock printing.[55] However, when Matteo Ricci came to China in the late sixteenth century he was surprised by how fast Chinese carvers cut the blocks. "Chinese printers are so skilled in engraving these blocks, that no more time is consumed in making one of them than would be required by one of our printers in setting up a form of type and making the necessary corrections."[56] This observation by Ricci informs any comparison of the advantages of movable-type printing and woodblock printing.

Ricci might have exaggerated the speed of the Chinese carvers. It is not possible to compare the composition of one printing form to the carving of one block. A skilful carver cutting 150 characters a day could come close to the speed observed by Ricci when the text was written in the vernacular and contained simplified characters. A block with an average folio of full text (twenty-one characters by eighteen columns) would yield 378 characters, which would require a skilful carver to work overtime for at least two days. Under normal circumstances, carving blocks took longer than composing a form.

Nonetheless, composition was a very time-consuming part of movable-type printing.[57] A compositor in Rome or Frankfurt was generally expected to complete one to three forms each day.[58] It can be assumed that the lowest number applies to a form containing four pages of text. A finished form still needed proofreading and correction before going to the press.[59]

The most time-consuming part of woodblock printing was the carving of blocks. Printing was fast by comparison. According to Matteo Ricci's observations, a skilful printer could turn out as many as fifteen hundred copies from a block in one day.[60] The speed of a printing press in mid-sixteenth-century Europe varied. In Frankfurt, it could print on both sides of a ream of paper in a day, amounting to 960 to one thousand impressions.[61] In Lyon, Paris, Rome, Frankfurt, and London in the late sixteenth century, a pressman was expected to print between 2,650 and 3,350 impressions per day. But one needs to be cautious when considering these figures. These may not be the actual production speed. Robert Ponder, a pressman at Cambridge University in 1700, was considered "noteworthy" in his performance as he printed sixty-one hundred sheets in a single week. The printing speed of around one thousand sheets per day was perhaps the actual production rate. The Frankfurt pressman and Ponder had to perform at their top speed to attain the one-thousand-sheet mark.[62]

The European printing press did indeed have some advantages over the Chinese method of block printing. But the printing press in Europe down to the mid-eighteenth century was still largely the same as the hand press used to print the Gutenberg Bible.[63] Whether the speed advantages of the printing press could be utilized to the full depended on many factors: book demand, which in turn depended on cost of production, and the sociopolitical conditions under which European publishers operated. Before the nineteenth century, the speed advantages enjoyed by the printing press were offset somewhat by the relative higher cost of European paper and the various religious and political constraints.

As noted above, woodblock printing was integrated into printing after the printing press was invented in Europe.[64] In fact, the aesthetic use of paratextual elements such as initials, borders, and illustrations could have minimized the advantages of the hand press over block printing. The typesetter could not complete his form without initials, illustrations, and borders cut by the woodcutter. For those who chose to use copperplates for illustration, production would be stalled because the engraving took longer to produce and the printing process required special handling. The greatest disadvantage of copperplates was that they could not print side by side with the letter-type press.[65] The much higher cost of copperplates forced publishers to continue to use woodcuts for illustrations in order to keep cost low and book prices competitive.[66] Throughout the sixteenth, seventeenth, and eighteenth centuries, European publishers continued to use woodcuts for initials, illustrations, and borders.[67]

The above discussion aims to make a few points about printing in the sixteenth and seventeenth century and to answer the question of why movable-type printing did not replace woodblock printing in China. First, both woodblock and movable-type printing methods were used extensively in China since the sixteenth century, both contributing and attesting to the boom of commercial publishing. Second, the availability and growing use of metal and wooden-type printing did not result in the decline of woodblock printing. Woodblock printing continued to be the dominant technology because of the economic advantages derived from its simplicity and flexibility. Adventure into woodblock publishing as a commercial enterprise was not a high-risk decision because it did not require a substantial investment in casting metal types. Third, despite the dominance of woodblock printing, a growing number of publishers experimented with different materials for movable types. Despite a relatively higher level of investment in casting metal types, there was no shortage of commercial publishers who had enough resources to establish printing shops using metal movable types. Guignmard's suggestion—that only with the resources of the government were Chinese printers able to undertake copper movable-type printing—proves to be injudicious. It is nonetheless true that metal movable types were costly to make, thus wooden types emerged as the most popular choice during the Wanli period. The skill of woodblock carving could be applied easily to the carving of individual wooden types. Besides, the technology of casting metal types was far less accessible to publishers than hiring carvers.

THE BUSINESS OF PUBLISHING

This flexibility of scale notwithstanding, there were nonetheless advantages in assembling a group of carvers in one place. Chinese publishers with resources were able to take advantage of the economy of scale. Although a book could be published by one literate carver, there were ad-

vantages in the division of labor. Commercial publishers had to hire copyists, editors, proofreaders, carvers, and printers to work in their "work-
shops." Information on the organization and operation of commercial
publishing houses is scant. The information left behind by the commercial publisher Mao Jin reveals how commercial publishers operated in the
late Ming.

### Mao Jin: The Jiguge Publishing House

Mao Jin was a native of Changshu who began as an owner of a number
of pawnshops, several thousand *qing* of land, and two thousand bond-
servants. He sold all of his pawnshops and land perhaps because of the
decreasing profit margin of his pawnshop business and the growing pressure on land resulting from surcharges and tax collection frauds. He invested his money in a huge publishing business. Printing books clearly
yielded a higher return than did pawnshops or land investment. Mao's
business operation bears witness to the fact that late-Ming *shishang* not
only invested in monetary enterprises such as pawnshops and cash crop
production, but also in industries such as commercial publishing.

Mao Jin acquired several buildings to provide accommodation for his
writers and workers. Jiguge was the name of the main building where
copyists, editors, and proofreaders labored as a team. Behind the Jiguge
were nine buildings housing Mao's library of more than eighty-four thousand juan. Carvers and printers were housed in different buildings in the
same workshop complex.

Jiguge published a wide range of books, including Classics, histories,
anthologies of poetry, prose, songs, and novels. Mao Jin also participated
in printing some of the titles in the "Buddhist Treasury of Jingshan" (Jingshan cang).[68] He hired thirty "renowned scholars" (*mingshi*) to work on
each of the Thirteen Classics and the Seventeen Dynastic Histories. He
had twenty printers and a large but unknown number of carvers to help
him publish his books.[69] Based on the carver-printer ratio 2:1 to 2.6:1 in
government offices listed in the *Compendium of Statutes of the Ming Dynasty* (*Da Ming huidian*),[70] Mao had to employ at least forty to fifty
carvers. His publishing house would have well over one hundred workers
living in his workshop complex.

In a little more than forty years of operation from the late Ming to the early Qing, Jiguge published more than six hundred titles.[71] Mao took great pains to collect "good imprints" and hand-copied books of the Song and Yuan periods. His role in preserving and printing Song-Yuan books was unsurpassed. He published numerous new editions. But like other publishers, he also bought incomplete text blocks (carved blocks) and carved new ones to complete a set for printing new editions.[72]

## Advertising and Packaging

Marketing books had long been an important concern of publishers. Bookstores were the logical place to distribute and advertise forthcoming books.[73] But posting lists of new books in bookstores would not have the direct effect of bringing the information to the fingertips of the target buyers. One common strategy employed by Ming publishers was to include titles of forthcoming books in the paratext of the book. In 1591 Yu Xiangdou, a prolific publisher from the famous printing center Jianyang, in Fujian, published a book with an advertisement listing a number of published and forthcoming books, which were "published exclusively for examination."[74] A Nanjing publishing house, Jukuilou, published a commentary on the Four Books by a popular critic from Fujian, Guo Wei. At the end of the list of references is a list of fifty-five commentaries on the Four Books that were authored by Guo (see Figure 2.1).[75] At the end of his "Reading Guidelines" for the *Sishu zhujia bian*, Zhang Zilie, a commentary critic, listed sixteen forthcoming books by himself. They ranged from poetry, history, the Four Books, and collected writings of other scholars. He also told the reader that his other two books, *Shigui bian* (Critique of models of poetry) and *Zihui bian* (Critique of the collection of characters), were selling well.[76] In a commentary on the Four Books by Wu Dang published in 1644, a list of "forthcoming books" (*sichu shumu*) was attached to the commentator's preface.[77] An expanded anthology of lyrics originally compiled by the renowned lyric critic Shen Jing (1553–1610) was published in the 1650s. On its title page are listed five forthcoming titles.[78]

In addition to conventional methods of advertisement, publishers and authors began experimenting with new forms of advertisement. Some authors would print the preface and title page of a forthcoming book for distribution even before the woodblocks for the rest of the book were

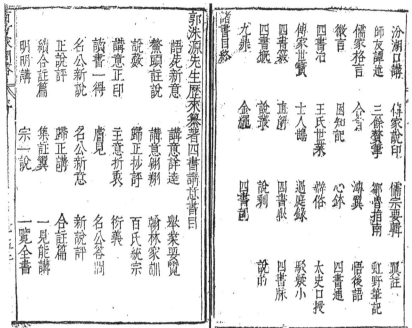

Figure 2.1: The last page of the bibliography of the *Huang Ming bai fangjia wenta* (Questions and answers by a hundred specialists of the Ming dynasty) by Guo Zhuyuan, followed by a list of other examination aids published by Guo. Three books on this page include "reputable master" (*minggong*) on their page. Reproduced by permission of the National Archives of Japan.

completely carved. Fang Yingxiang, a critic himself, once wrote a letter to a critic whom he had hired to edit and comment on examination essays. He explained that the title page and the preface for the book had been printed and circulated in the two capitals. The text actually had not been carved, and Fang was concerned that the readers or potential buyers were losing patience and could dismiss the advertisement as a hoax.[79]

The boom in commercial publishing contributed to the new "packaging" of the book. Publishers presented the book in new ways that brought about changes in discursive practices. One of the important changes was the growing importance attached to illustrations. Books printed with illustrations in the upper portion of pages and text in the lower portion dated back to the Song. Full page illustration began in the Yuan but did not become a popular format, especially in novels and dramas, until the sixteenth century.[80]

Books as commodities were packaged differently in order to appeal to targeted customers. As Robert Hegel has demonstrated convincingly, the publishing industry in the late Ming had developed very sophisticated strategies in differentiating targeted buyers.[81] Fujian books were cheaper not only because publishers used cheaper paper or less experienced carvers and copyists, but because they seldom used protective folding covers (*han*) or various types of expensive silk material (*ling, jin, juan*) for the folding covers. Fujian editions were packaged for ordinary to low-end readers, not for collection. They were sold without covers. Books published in Suzhou used better quality paper and many were sold with decorative and protective folding covers.[82] Various packaging methods contributed to the differential pricing of books in the late Ming.

## Manuscript Acquisition

There were many conventional avenues through which publishers could obtain texts. To carve new blocks from existing printed works was one of the easiest and most economical ways. The purchase of printing blocks was also a common means of acquisition. The most expensive method of issuing a new printed edition was to carve new blocks. This source for new books by well-known literati was not available to all publishers because it depended significantly on the publisher's personal connection network with the literati. Publishers could always pirate existing books.[83]

But with the profitable prospect of publishing new writings of famous men of letters, publishers began using their publications to solicit manuscripts and writings.[84] The anthology *Ming wen qi shang* (Appreciation of original writings by Ming writers) exemplifies the common solicitation method used by publishers. It was compiled by Chen Renxi in about 1623. Shen Guoyuan, a Suzhou publisher listed as proofreader (*jiao*), included "methods of soliciting writings" (*zheng shu fa*) that provided information on compensation for submission of materials for publication.

> Solicited works included collected writings by "renowned writers" (*minggong*) in print that were scarcely available locally. They could

be sent by mail or by special delivery. Travel and copying expenses were to be duly reimbursed. The copy would not be marked on or smeared. It would be returned when the copying was finished. The sender could also exchange his own copy for printed works in the publisher's stock. For unpublished manuscripts (*zhuzuo*) of "renowned writers," the publisher would pay the cost of delivery and copying. The collected writings of "renowned writers," whether printed or unpublished, completed or fragmented, short or long, would be accepted and compensated handsomely. Those who were interested could either mail or bring the texts to a Mr. Chen Long-shan at the Youyou tang bookshop in Suzhou.[85]

Another prolific publisher in Hangzhou, Lu Yunlong, also included instructions for submission of works for publication. In an anthology of poetry printed in the 1630s, he included an advertisement soliciting writings from the readers. The types of texts solicited were imperial edicts and orders (*gao chi*), memorials regarding government affairs, letters and writings by famous literati, biographical essays of famous persons, and strange happenings. Senders were instructed to mail texts to a Mr. Lu at a bookshop in Hangzhou.[86] Deng Hanyi (1617–89) of Yangzhou, a publisher of anthologies of verse by women, announced his plan to publish sequels in his anthology and listed five addresses for manuscript submissions. He reminded the readers that mail was the most convenient method.[87]

Other types of manuscripts required different methods of solicitation and contracting with the authors. Many publishers took a more aggressive approach to finding manuscripts for anthologies of examination essays with critical comments. Publishers competed in publishing these anthologies as soon as the triennial metropolitan examination concluded in the spring. Many publishers went to Beijing, Nanjing, and other prefectural cities during the examination period in order to hire candidates-cum-critics to work on selecting and critiquing the examinations. Xu Fenpeng, for example, had literary renown even though he was still struggling to pass the *juren* degree examination. Publishers sought his service without success. One publisher succeeded only when he pursued Xu when he was taking the provincial examination.[88] A wide range of books was published with Xu as author, editor, or commentator (see Chapter 3).

In the 1620s Ai Nanying had attained empirewide acclaim as a critic of examination essays while he was still struggling to pass the metropolitan examination. Publishers from Suzhou were anxious to hire him to produce anthologies of examination essays with his comments (see Chapter 3). The practice by publishers of seeking out writers clearly indicated the market value of a literary reputation. Wu Yingji was another editor of examination essays who began his professional career as a critic of examination essays in 1634. He was hired by a Suzhou publisher who went to Beijing to solicit his service.[89] The fictional writer Ma Er in *Rulin waishi* was originally a critic residing in Hangzhou. He was hired by a Nanjing publisher to anthologize examination essays.[90] Although the novel was written in the 1740s, the practice was a continuation from the seventeenth century.

## BOOK TRADE AND DISTRIBUTION

While the geographical distribution of commercial publishers can be documented, empirical data on the geographical distribution of books hardly existed. We have only fragmented information on book distribution and circulation in the late Ming.[91] As commodities, however, books roughly followed trade routes and government postal stations. Several cases suggest that there were book dealers or merchants engaged in long-distance trade who were involved in the distribution of books throughout the empire in the late Ming.

The printing and distribution of the *Huang Ming jingshi wen bian* (An anthology of statecraft writings of the Ming dynasty) is a good example. The publication was planned and organized by Chen Zilong (1608–47), Song Zhengbi, and Xu Fuyuan (1599–1665), all natives of Songjiang. The voluminous book when first published in 1638 had 504 juan, including writings and memorials on statecraft by 429 authors. It was published by Chen's Studio Pinglutang, which was not a commercial publishing house.[92]

According to Chen Zilong, the compilation and copying process took about nine months and the carving took a little more than one year to complete.[93] The project began in the spring of 1638, and carving was completed at the end of the year. Although the book was published by Chen's studio, the distribution and marketing was done by a book dealer involved in long-distance distribution. There is little information to indicate how the project was negotiated between Chen, Song, and Xu on the one hand and the book dealer on the other. Clearly there was some formal agreement regarding the deadline for the editors to deliver the printed copies to the merchant, who had a scheduled date of departure.[94]

There were booksellers who traveled long distances. When a register of the Donglin Academy was published in the south, merchants transported several scores of the book to Beijing.[95] In the novel *Rulin waishi*, a publisher in Hangzhou hired Kang Chaoren to comment on examination essays. Kang needed to finish them in less than twenty days because the books needed to be ready for transportation by merchants traveling to Shandong and Henan.[96] Examination anthologies were among the most marketable books and were sold locally and in other Jiangnan cities such as Suzhou and Nanjing. But publishers in Hangzhou, Suzhou, and Nanjing also distributed their books to far away provinces where commercial publishers were less numerous.

In the two capitals and in big cities like Suzhou, Hangzhou, and many provincial government seats, there were numerous bookstores. Peddlers of books were even more numerous than bookshops. In Beijing, Nanjing, and provincial government, booksellers traveled to stage exhibits in accordance with schedules of the civil service examination.[97] In addition, books could be put up for sale in shops, restaurants, or places that attracted visitors. Books were traded during major festivals, at fairs, and at places where parades and religious rites would be held. The polymath Yang Shen (1488–1561) went to a lantern festival and bought two books of good quality. The renowned painter Chen Hongshou saw a book he wanted to buy during a New Year lantern festival.[98]

Books were widely available in the Lower Yangtze area and the two capitals, where there was a higher concentration of educated elite. But in remote provinces like Guangdong and Guizhou, a lower level of cultural integration and economic prosperity created a lower demand for books. For example, sets of classical works rarely reached areas like Guizhou.[99] When Zhu Yunming was serving as magistrate in a Guangdong county, he found it difficult to locate a copy of the voluminous *Annotated Thirteen Classics (Shisan jing zhushu)*.[100] But in Yu cheng in Yunnan, merchants from other provinces came to trade during periodic markets. When Xu Hongzu (1586–1641) traveled there in 1638, he found that examination model essays and primers published in his home county of Jiangyin were for sale in the market. It is clear that in a remote province like Yunnan, there was still demand for examination model essays, which were distributed by long-distance book dealers.[101]

While publishers might not be able to control the distribution of their books, they could in general determine how their books circulated. When Zhang Zilie traveled to Jianyang in the 1650s, he saw numerous commentaries on the Four Books that were falsely attributed to famous scholars.[102] Zhang himself was active in Nanjing, where he published examination aids. He realized that the commentaries he saw in Jianyang were not distributed to the Jiangnan cities where most of the famous masters resided. This could have been the result of a distribution strategy adopted by Fujian publishers, who in order to avoid legal problems excluded Nanjing and other Jiangnan cities from their routes of distribution.

Lineages engaging in trade were one of the major networks of book production and distribution.[103] In some places, the whole village was engaged in book trade.[104] In the Lower Yangtze region, books were often distributed by mobile bookshops called "book boats" (*shuchuan*). Book traders from Huzhou were particularly notable for their book boats. These mobile bookstores could have started as early as the Song.[105] These book merchants traveled in their boats loaded with books. Their boats frequented Songjiang, Hangzhou, and Dantu, trading in both new and old books.[106] They plied along the waterways, reaching remote villages to sell and buy books from rural residents.[107] These mobile bookstores came to the doors of wealthy *shishang* residing along the waterways.[108] Some book merchants in boats would allow customers to borrow books probably for a fee.[109]

Beijing was one of the largest centers of book trade because of its high concentration of officials and literati. According to Yang Shen, a scholar and book collector, Beijing had a high concentration of bookstores.[110] Wang Shizhen often visited the small book merchants who displayed their books in hall spaces rented from the Ciren temple, a Buddhist monastery in Beijing.[111] Book merchants carried both new and old books. Rare editions were often obtained in these bookstores at the Ciren temple.[112] The large book market in Beijing attracted booksellers from all over the empire. The playwright and publisher, Zang Maoxun, published his own books and sent his servant all the way to Beijing to market them.[113]

Suzhou was one of the centers of book trade and publishing that were connected by river to other Jiangnan cities.[114] Many book merchants from Zhejiang went to Suzhou by boat.[115] Li Rihua was well known for his tasteful collections of paintings, calligraphy, and books. A Suzhou book merchant who traveled with his books in a boat was a frequent visitor of Li's home in Jiaxing prefecture. He traded not only in books but also in calligraphy and paintings.[116] Because the renowned publisher Mao Jin (1599–1659) was willing to pay high prices for rare editions, merchants in book boats often visited his publishing house Jiguge in great number.[117] Book traders on boats were also a major conduit for the distribution of Mao Jin's books.

Private scholars who published their own works distributed their books through personal connections and servants. As we have seen above, Zang Maoxun, for example, published his own works and marketed them directly through servants. He published an anthology of Yuan lyrics (*Yuanqu xuan*), which his servant took to Nanjing for sale.[118] It was not clear how his servant marketed the books. It was likely that his servant visited bookstore owners in Nanjing and sold them at wholesale prices. Books published by private scholars were also deposited (*jimai*) in bookstores for sale.

*Publishing Centers*

In the Ming, there were at least six publishing centers: Jianyang in Fujian, Suzhou, Nanjing, Huizhou, Huzhou, and Hangzhou.[119] Publishers in these centers produced a wide range of books. While most published Classics, histories, collected writings, and books related to civil examinations, they pursued different strategies in the production of certain categories of books.

Jianyang was no doubt the largest publishing center in terms of volumes and variety—from Classics, histories, novels, plays, and examination aids to medical manuals and almanacs. There were more than one hundred publishers in Jianyang.[120] In general, Jianyang books were cheaper because of the lower quality of paper and printing.[121] Jianyang publishers appeared to be major printers of books for primary pedagogy. Inexpensive Classics packaged for children were widely circulated throughout the empire. Even children in cities that were centers of book trade and publishing would use pedagogical books from Jianyang.[122]

Books as major commodities in the late Ming were also produced to target different buyers. Inexpensive examination aids from Jianyang publishers cost very little money while exquisite illustrated novels and plays could cost a lot more. Books printed in Jianyang and other areas in Fujian were notorious for their inferior quality and printing mistakes. There was almost a consensus on the inferior quality among scholars and book collectors.[123] Zhou Lianggong spoke of the mistakes in a Fujian edition of Yang Shen's popular *Danyuan conglu* as being as numerous as falling leaves.[124] But the low price of Jianyang books compensated for their inferior quality.

Since the Southern Song, Jianyang publishers had been able to specialize in publishing specific categories of books without concern for competition. Many publishers before the mid-sixteenth century appeared to be able to operate without dependence on the biggest market of examinees. The publisher Cundetang in Jianyang began publishing at least in the 1430s, specializing in medical books. Books published by the Cundetang before 1511 were exclusively medical books, but those published in the Wanli period were clearly directed at examinees.[125] This shift in categories might have been the result of the growth in demand for more examination aids, or increased competition in medical books.

The Anchengtang in Jianyang was a well-established publishing house that published from 1503 until 1611. Of the forty-eight books listed in *Mingdai benke zonglu* (A comprehensive catalog of Ming imprints, *MDBKZL*), there are books on the Classics, histories, medical manuals, calendars, and anthologies of poetry and writings.[126] The Mingde shutang in Jianyang published from the early 1500s until 1532. Three of their six books were on medical knowledge; they also published the *Book of History* and the history text *Guoyu*.[127]

In contrast, another Jianyang publishing house, Zixinzhai, began operation in the late Jiajing period under several publishers who were most likely kinsmen or even family members. Between 1551 and 1627, they published primarily examination aids on the Four Books, histories, and anthologies of writings.[128] The Shuangfengtang in Jianyang, mostly active from the 1590s through the 1630s, had twenty book listed in *MDBKZL*, publishing a wide range of books from practical guides, medical manuals, literary anthologies, novels, almanacs, and examination aids for history and philology.[129] Despite some publications for examinees, neither the Zixintang nor the Shuangfengtang published anthologies of examination essays with critical comments, which had been emerging since the 1590s as a very profitable subgenre of examination aids.

Some publishing houses in Jianyang began publishing plays. Shijiantang of Xiao Tenghong published at least six plays, two of which were accompanied by comments attributed to the famous Chen Jiru. His son, Shaoqu, expanded the categories into examination aids and popular practical manuals. But of the eleven books published by the son, only two were dramas.[130]

Hangzhou had been an extremely important publishing center during the Song period.[131] But its importance was overshadowed by Jianyang and Nanjing in the Ming. According to Hu Yinglin, the best books were published in Suzhou, followed by Nanjing and then by Hangzhou.[132] Despite its reputation for publishing excellent books in the Song period, Hangzhou by the late Ming was no longer the leading city.[133] Publishers from other cities in Zhejiang and Jiangsu produced books that rivaled the quality of Hangzhou books. In Wuxing county of Huzhou prefecture in Zhejiang, the Lings and the Mins were commercial publishers that published a wide range of books. The Lings were famous for their excellent editions of novels and plays such as the *Water Margin* and the *Lute* (*Pipa ji*). They were however criticized for turning out poorly edited books in other categories.[134]

Following Jianyang, Nanjing had the second largest number of publishing houses in late-Ming China. As the Southern capital, Nanjing was a center of politics, culture, and commerce, with a population of close to one million by the late sixteenth century.[135] The government roads in Nanjing in the early Ming were wide enough for nine carriages. But population and commercial growth had narrowed the roads as shops lined both sides of the streets.[136] Large number of examinees came to the city during the civil service examination. The Southern Imperial Academy was also located in the capital. Provincial degree holders who did not pass the metropolitan examination entered the Imperial Academy in Beijing. In the sixteenth century increasing numbers of *juren* chose to go to the Southern Imperial Academy in Nanjing. But fewer and fewer stayed at the academy for the full period. Many just stayed for three months and returned home. As examination dates approached, many students at the Imperial Academy returned to Nanjing to take the examinations. The high concentration of literati helped to create great demand for books and helped Nanjing become a major center of publishing and book trade.

Nanjing had become a popular residence for many professional writers.[137] After retiring from government in 1616, the renowned writer Zhong Xing left his home town of Jingling, Hubei, for Nanjing, where he supported his family by providing literary services.[138] Mei Dingzuo was considering where to eke out his living as a professional writer. He considered moving to Nanjing but was concerned about the much lower level of remuneration for literary service as compared to Beijing.[139] Li Yu, the writer-cum-publisher moved his publishing house from Hangzhou to Nanjing for the obvious reason that it was a major publishing center with a high concentration of literati who were both producers and consumers of books.

By the late sixteenth century, Nanjing was known for both its excellent publishing houses and as a center of book trade.[140] The Cheng'en temple at Sanshan street was a book trade center. Books published outside Nanjing were transported first to the Cheng'en temple, where book merchants from other provinces gathered.[141] Whereas inexpensive books published in Jianyang were sold throughout the empire, books of better editions could be found in Nanjing and Suzhou.[142] Cai Yisuo, the book merchant in the drama *Peach Blossom Fan*, boasted that his bookshop was the largest in Nanjing, with books from all over the empire.[143] Cai in fact was a real bookshop owner in the Sanshan street in Nanjing. The fictional Cai's statement was hardly an exaggeration when applied to Nanjing as a center of book trade.

Nanjing was more than a book trade center. Bookshop owners could easily enter the business of publishing due to the simplicity of technological requirements and the low level of capital investment. The availability of skilled laborers in literary production in Nanjing also contributed to the development of Nanjing as a publishing center in the late Ming.

Nanjing may have superceded Jianyang as the largest publishing center in late-Ming China, perhaps not in terms of the volume of sale but in the number of publishers. A recent study identifies more than 180 publishers in Nanjing, and most of them were active in the late Ming.[144] The emergence of Nanjing as one of the largest book trade centers also prompted publishers from other centers such as Jianyang to set up branches or joint enterprises. There were books of similar editions published in Jianyang and Nanjing.[145] It is possible that some Nanjing publishers were branch publishing shops set up in Nanjing by Fujian publishers.

As the second capital visited regularly by examinees, Nanjing offered one of the largest markets for examination aids. Examinees were the common targeted readers for most publishers. Specialized publishers such as the Guangyutang in Nanjing published primarily for examinees.[146] Many publishers in Nanjing could afford to produce for a small clientele of wealthy buyers. Hu Zhengyan operated a publishing house in Nanjing called Shizhuzhai, which published at least twenty books between 1627 and 1644. Among its special books were high-quality prints of paintings and correspondence stationary. It did not publish any anthologies of examination essays, nor any books for examinees.[147] Hu's publishing house clearly targeted the high-brow literati.

Publishers in Nanjing in the Wanli period published a large number of plays, exceeding those printed in Jianyang.[148] The Wenlinge of Tang Liyao in Nanjing published mostly dramas from the 1580s to the 1620s. Twenty-two of the thirty books listed in *MDBKZL* are drama. It did not publish classics, history, or any examination aids.[149] The Shidetang of Tang Fuchun in Nanjing also specialized in publishing plays and novels. Of the sixteen books listed in *MDBKZL*, eleven were dramas, and only one on examination essays.[150] But some publishers preferred to target the largest readership—the examinees. Li Chao's Jukuilou in Nanjing did not publish any books on drama. It published three books prepared primarily for examinees.[151]

Li Yu's printing house, the famous Jieziyuan (Mustard seed garden), was located right inside the "Book street." Li Yu not only published dramas and novels, but also printed stationery. The widely acclaimed Jieziyuan letter-writing papers were his products.[152] He published manuals on how to enjoy life in a material sense, a typical value of the *shishang*. His *Liweng ouji* includes designs, suggestions, and instructions for a wide range of topics regarding one's living environment, including interior design, architecture, and garden design. All these subjects were of great interest to the new ideal of the "urban recluse," a literary expression for a *shishang*.

Li Yu's experience was indicative of some general trends in the movement of publishers. Li began his publishing in Hangzhou. He later moved to Nanjing. The relative "decline" of Hangzhou as a leading printing center was a result of the rise of new publishing centers such as Suzhou and Nanjing. Publishers left Hangzhou, while others opened branch shops in other thriving towns and cities. For example, in the novel *Rulin waishi*, a Hangzhou publisher, Wenhanlou, opened a branch in Jiaxing.[153] Jiaxing was a new important publishing center in the late Ming.

## Suzhou as a Cultural and Publishing Center

The emergence of Suzhou as a major publishing center was a part of the story of its rise as the most important cultural center in late-Ming China. Literary and artistic products from Suzhou became models for the entire empire. Suzhou by the mid-sixteenth century, if not earlier, was the most important commercial city in the whole Ming empire. Unlike in Nanjing, where there was still an important presence of official institutions, Suzhou's importance and prosperity derived primarily from its centrality in the commercial sector of the Ming economy. It was the hub of all major trades in rice, silk, cotton cloth, and lumber, as well as commodities like paper, books, tea, and porcelain.[154] It was a center of finance, manufacturing, distribution, and marketing for consumer and luxurious goods. There were merchants from all over the empire: Huizhou, Shandong, Shanxi, Shensi, Henan, Guangdong, Jiangxi, Hunan, Hubei, and Zhejiang.[155] Many had built *huiguan*, or "merchant associations," in Suzhou city.[156]

Suzhou in the late Ming was a city of migrants and sojourners, attracting both the wealthy and the poor. Large number of Huizhou merchants settled in Suzhou. Residents of Suzhou had cultivated a sense of pride in the glamorous city and regarded people elsewhere as uncouth.[157]

As late as the 1510s, clothing fashions were still set in Beijing.[158] By the Wanli period, however, fashion was set in the south, especially Suzhou. Suzhou designers had acquired an empirewide reputation for their elegance and taste. Commodities made in Suzhou were regarded as fashionable. Fans, hats, shoes, and dresses made in Suzhou were trendy.[159] Suzhou hairstyles and clothing attire were popular, especially among members of the imperial family in Beijing.[160] Fans made in Suzhou were particularly notable for their calligraphy and paintings.[161] Suzhou interior design had become the model for emulation. Wall paintings were common decorative items, and flowers were indispensable objects of display in Suzhou homes.[162] Even local products from other regions would mimic the style of Suzhou commodities. For example, Guangzhou (Canton) was famous for its tin and iron works. But craftsmen had to adopt the Suzhou style even though they were the only makers of tin products.[163] In Beijing, Suzhou chefs were particularly preferred by those who held banquets.[164]

Special terms such as *suyi* (idea of Suzhou) and *suyang* (model of Suzhou) were used to designate things and styles of speaking of the Suzhou people. There were different anecdotal origins of the terms, but they later became synonyms of anything rare, unconventional, new, and fashionable. A new style of seating was called *suzuo*; it placed the host and guests facing each other in east-west directions.[165] A special style of hair knot was called *suji*.[166] The term *suyi* even became a popular catchphrase among members of the imperial family.[167] Northerners were particularly anxious to emulate the lifestyle of Suzhou.[168]

Some things did not originate in Suzhou but gained popularity throughout the empire by way of their popularity in Suzhou. A card game called "*yezi*" (leaves) was popular among residents of Suzhou, from gentry to women and children. It later became a popular game of the whole empire.[169] Many printers of the *yezi* cards hired painters to draw heroes of the *Romance of the Water Margin*. The famous painter Chen Hongshou had painted a set of heroes on the cards, which were printed and circulated widely.[170]

Suzhou had emerged as the taste-setting center of culture, whereas Beijing was the center of the political field. The authority over the standard or definition of literary excellence had gradually shifted from the political field to the field of cultural production centered in Suzhou and Nanjing—the Nanzhili region. Suzhou was also a city that boasted the largest number of critics involved in publishing critical anthologies of examination essays (see Chapter 5).

Suzhou publishers were particularly aggressive in competing against their counterparts. The publication of the famous novel *Jin Ping Mei* (Golden lotus) offered a glimpse of the aggressiveness and efficiency of Suzhou publishers. The manuscript of *Jin Ping Mei* had been circulated among the literati for many years in the early 1600s before it was finally printed. In 1606, when Shen Defu wrote to Yuan Hongdao inquiring about the manuscript, Yuan had only a few chapters and intimated that Liu Yanbo of Macheng had a complete copy. Three years later when they met again in Beijing, Shen was able to make a copy of the complete version from Yuan's copy. Shen showed it to the famous professional editor and publisher Feng Menglong, who urged a commercial publisher to buy the manuscript even at a high price. Shen was approached by publishers but refused to sell it for fear that the novel and its pornographic details might have a negative impact on public morality. However, within a year or two, the novel was published in Suzhou in 1613.[171] This episode testifies to the willingness of Suzhou publishers to undertake risky projects and their embrace of fiction and plays, the new literature of the *shishang* elites. Suzhou publishing will be discussed further in later chapters.

## Commercialization of Huizhou Publishing

Huizhou in Anhui had long attained a reputation for its stationery, especially ink stick and ink slab production. Since the Song, books had been published in Huizhou. It was not a major publishing center down to the mid-sixteenth century. Before the Wanli period, publishing in Huizhou remained primarily private. Unlike Jianyang and Nanjing publishers, few publishers in Huizhou produced for an empirewide book market.[172] The strong tradition of *Daoxue* learning and the importance of lineage helped natives of Huizhou perpetuate their dominance in commerce and trade throughout the empire. With wealth from commercial and industrial operations, Huizhou families supported education and the quest for entry into the imperial government through the civil examinations.

Ironically, before the mid-Wanli period, publishing in Huizhou appeared to have a very strong local orientation—the lack of an interest in publishing entertaining literature for an empirewide readership. Extant Ming imprints of novels and dramas that were published in Huizhou before the Wanli period are rare. In contrast, Huizhou was most notable for its large number of genealogies published before the seventeenth century.[173] There were publishers that did not publish any books on drama. As is well known, Huizhou *shishang* families had a strong tradition in combining careers in the economic and political fields. Despite widespread involvement of Huizhou natives in commerce and trade, local publishers served more private, scholarly, and communal needs by printing Classics, histories, collected writings of individual scholars, medical texts, local gazetteers, genealogies, memorials, and didactic books.[174] Wu Mianxue from Huizhou (his publishing house was in Suzhou) operated a publishing house mostly active in the Wanli reign. He published at least six medical books but only the *Xingli daquan* (Complete collection of works on nature and principles) and Sima Qian's *Shiji* (Historian's records) were for examinees.[175] Wu Mianxue as a publisher continued the Huizhou tradition of publishing for the conventional readers. He hardly published any novels, plays, or any commercial publications aimed at ordinary readers. But since the Wanli period, many publishers from Huizhou moved in new directions. Huizhou grew in reputation throughout the empire as a center for producing quality imprints, especially prominent in illustrated novels and dramas.[176]

Huizhou had become an important publishing center in the late Ming. The "rise" of Huizhou as a publishing center can be understood as part of two trends in commercial publishing: first, the increase in demand for entertaining literature like fiction and plays; second, the growth of iconic commentary on the text. Full-page illustrations were increasingly included in fiction and plays published in the Wanli period. The participation of artists in designing story scenes required precise execution by skilful carvers. This demand was met by the exceptional skill of Huizhou ink carvers who had been carving elegant and elaborate images on ink sticks. The successful adaptation of the carving skill of ink-stick cutters to woodblock cutting, and the collaboration between artists and craftsmen, lifted the artistic quality of woodblock illustration to a higher level.[177]

Following the example of many Huizhou merchants, many carvers began moving to big cities like Suzhou, Nanjing, and Hangzhou. The Huang lineage from Huizhou began to participate in the carving of illustrations for fiction, plays, and songs. Notable examples were the fiction and plays published by Huizhou publishing houses: the Huancuitang of Wang Tingna and the Huanhuxuan of Wang Guanghua.[178] The publication of novels and plays expanded the generic scope of the publications of publishers and carvers from Huizhou. The movement of carvers from Huizhou to cities in the Lower Yangtze signals the increase in the supply of carvers—a transfer of skilled labor from publishing patronized by private families, lineages, and local government offices to commercial publishing serving an increasingly diversified and expanding reading public.

The expansion of commercial publishing in the late Ming presupposes a corresponding increase in the supply of literary workers: calligraphers, copyists, compilers, editors, and proofreaders. This literary working force was readily provided with the superfluous number of examinees seeking to pass the examinations.

# 3
## Commodification of Writing, Examinations, and Publishing

THE EXAMINATION FIELD AND CULTURAL
PRODUCTION IN MING CHINA

In structuring practices in the economic, political, and cultural fields in early modern China, no one single institution was more important than the civil service examination. A study of the social structure of Ming China must focus on the major institutions and structures that governed the access to and distribution of political capital. As Benjamin Elman has cogently argued, the civil service examination was a key institution in reproducing the social, political, and cultural order.[1] This perception masks significant changes in practices in the economic field, which in various ways transformed the process of cultural production. The boom of commercial publishing created positions in the economic field that came to restructure the field of cultural production.

The adoption of the civil service examination system by the Ming government continued a pattern of structuring practices in the production and distribution of political capital. Local elites were allowed to compete in the "field of examination" for political offices. Education practices and the general curriculum, institutions like government schools and to a considerable extent private academies, were structured to prepare students to compete at the various levels of civil examination. Local elite families since the Song had made heavy investment in education in order to gain specific symbolic capital—reading and writing literary skills—which they hoped would perpetuate, if not increase, their social status. Marriage alliances were formed among political elites in order to maintain their ability to compete favorably in the examination field.[2] In brief, the examination field was the major arena for legitimate and formal struggle for ascendance in the social hierarchy of Ming China. The acquisition of political capital in the form of examination degrees and bureaucratic offices was determined by one's success in the examination field.

The civil service examination was therefore the most important institution in structuring practices in cultural production in Ming-Qing China until 1905. It was the axis around which the "examination field," the "educational field," the "linguistic field," and the "literary field" were structured. There are preliminary qualifications one had to acquire before one was allowed to compete in the civil service examination. Early education of children was designed to prepare them to compete in the examination field. Local elite families sought to invest in pedagogical resources such as teaching materials, books, and instructors who taught their children how to read and write classical Chinese. Since the ultimate goal was to attain office in the imperial government, students aimed to master both the written and the spoken official language.

The civil service examination not only structured educational practices, it structured the economy of linguistic exchange, reproducing the power relation among the users of linguistic systems by privileging the "language of the official" (*guanhua*), what Bourdieu calls the "legitimate language," and relegating local dialects to the status of illegitimate languages.[3] Success in the examination field depended upon the successful acquisition of "linguistic capital"—classical Chinese and the official spoken language. By linking the acquisition of competence in reproducing the legitimate language and writing with the struggle for political capital, the civil service examination reproduced the power relation between the users of literary and phonological systems. Dialects were relegated to secondary status. As I will examine in later chapters, the growth of the market for vernacular fictions and drama came to challenge and negotiate the definition of what constituted the legitimate language. While the overwhelming majority of the holders of examination degrees and political offices were bilingual, their mother tongues were "inferior" and "illegitimate" in comparison to the official language and classical Chinese.

Through the reproduction of linguistic competence of the legitimate language, examinees also reproduced the linguistic habitus that privileged classical Chinese over the vernaculars.[4] But a large number of examinees were denied access to political offices, despite having acquired the linguistic and cultural competence. As a result of repeated failure, many converted their linguistic capital into economic capital by selling literary skill to the publishers and readers. The expanded market of commercial publishing came to absorb the surplus linguistic capital, rewarding literati who were willing to exchange their literary skill for economic capital rather than political capital. The commercial publishing market, however, was still structured around the civil service examination because the examinees constituted the largest reading public. Nonetheless, new reading publics, which were not directly linked to the civil service examination, invigorated the growth in demand for new genres such as fiction and drama. These new genres were not subject to the same codes that regulated the production of the legitimate language and literary style. The subsequent ascendance of these new genres in the hierarchy of genres contributed to redefining literary taste through incorporating vernacular and dialectical linguistic styles into the official language. The justification of the value of these new genres and linguistic styles was the product of the new practice of position-taking by supernumerary examinees in the economic field. By selling their cultural capital in the market of literary production for nonexaminees, the literati came to produce new literary taste and alternative standards for literary excellence. While discourse had been produced to legitimize the new genres and literary styles, the practice of selling cultural capital to publishers in exchange for economic remuneration was still largely suppressed by the desire to identify with the ultimate social group—the officials—and by the anxiety to deny the failure to take up positions in the political field. This disavowal of the position-taking in the economic field by the literati presents difficulties in the study of their involvement in commercial publishing.

## The Humiliating and Expensive Ordeal

The history of the late-Ming literati's involvement in publishing has yet to be written. This "nonhistory," or the "other" history, cannot be studied independently of their "recorded" or objectivated history—their long and bitter struggle to gain entry into the officialdom. Memory in the "other" history was one that the literati themselves had no interest in keeping, whereas their desire and anxiety in the "objectivated" history were retained with great care in their literary traces. Their desire to identify with their failed expectations was so intense that their words had buried their adventures deep in the wilderness of the market of letter, an "other land" where many found food for thought and for their family. But it was a place they were anxious to leave behind, a place whose landscape they did not care to map out. A place their habitus did not prepare them to recognize. In brief, these "secondary" adventures have yet to be narrated into history. To rechart the "other" history of the literati in the late Ming is crucial to the understanding of the profound impact commercial publishing had made on literary production in the sixteenth and seventeenth centuries. A reconstruction of these "other" histories of the late-Ming literati reveals the history of commercial publishing and the modes that involved the literati.

The civil service examination has been regarded as a major institution of the imperial government for the reproduction of the social, cultural, and political order.[5] There is no question that this imperial institution had been crucial in fashioning an educated elite who through participation was involved in reproducing the political and the ideological order of the imperial regime.[6] This political use of the examination system, however, hardly exhausts the complexity of the politics of recruitment in Ming-Qing China. Elite families were aware that the examination system was the major avenue through which political symbols and power were distributed. It is therefore necessary to recognize that the examination system was also the same arena where the educated elite struggled against and resisted the authority of the imperial state concerning the distribution of political power. Furthermore, it was also the place where seeds of discontent with the regime were planted.[7] The majority of candidates had to spend decades fighting over the extremely small quota of graduates.[8]

After 1450, the metropolitan examination success rate of provincial candidates was between 7.5 and 10 percent. The second half of the sixteenth century saw a further decline in the success rate from 7.1 percent in 1549 to 6.4 percent in 1601.⁹ The extremely low rate of success and the competitiveness of the examination kept the majority of the examinees from obtaining the ultimate metropolitan degree.¹⁰ Sustained effort in preparing for the examination created a great financial burden for the majority of the examinees. The boom of commercial publishing created new positions in the economic field for many talented literati. The positions they came to occupy as editors, compilers, writers, and proofreaders in the publishing market generated the needed income to support their continued quest for the elusive metropolitan degree. By selling their literary talent in the market of writing, they could continue to sharpen their skills and keep alive their dream.

The examination process was a protracted ordeal for the candidates and their families. Most who finally succeeded in passing the metropolitan examination had to wait ten to thirty years before they could earn the highest degree. The majority never made it beyond the *shenyuan* degree. The examination process provided a common arena in which candidates from all over the empire could experience the state. That experience, however, was anything but pleasant. Dejected and yet irate, the professional painter Chen Hongshou (1599–1652) confessed that after every examination he could not stop himself from cursing.¹¹ Chen's emotional condition was typical of the examinees.

Ai Nanying, a renowned critic from Kiangxi, neatly recounted the humiliating treatment given to the candidates at the examination halls. Ai voiced his grievances in a preface for the anthology of his own examination essays. Candidates had to be searched before they were admitted into the examination sheds. While waiting for their names to be called outside the hall, they had to untie their clothes and expose their legs. In winter they suffered from bitter cold and in summer they had to bear the heat; they were not allowed to use fans. Guards searched everyone from head to toe. Once they were admitted, candidates would not dare stretch or talk to one another. Otherwise they would be penalized and would have their examination papers stamped with a red sign (*zhuqian*), which would lower their grades by one. Guards watched candidates from two watchtowers on the east and west ends of the hall. Although there was provision for tea, no one dared request it for fear of getting a red stamp for doing so. Examinees also refrained from going to the restroom.[12]

When it rained during the examination, the conditions got worse. Not only were the candidates soaked, they often had to bear with flooding.[13] Ai Nanying's preface accurately expressed the frustration, physical suffering, agony, anxiety, humiliation, and resentment shared by all of the candidates. It so touched the heart of every candidate that the preface itself was widely read and praised.[14]

The journey to officialdom was expensive and incapacitating. Candidates with moderate means had to support themselves by taking up tutoring or other side jobs.[15] Even after an examinee passed the lowest level examination and became a student at a county or prefectural school, he received very little support from the school. By the mid-Wanli period, the land endowment of government schools had suffered great loss through mismanagement and frauds. The proceeds simply did not benefit the students. In addition, students suffered from widespread corruption among subbureaucrats and government instructors. Students were often extorted by clerks and runners. Since the 1450s, government school instructors were drawn mostly from old-aged examinees who were "presented scholars" (*gongsheng*). Their lowly origin in the academic hierarchy hardly commanded respect from the students.[16] Corrupt instructors concocted demands for fees and gifts for officials.[17]

Many examinees in their quest for the highest degree had incurred a large debt from merchants, creditors, and publishers.[18] The most expensive activity of the students were the trips to the provincial capital and Beijing to take the triennial examinations. On their way to the examination halls, they incurred huge expenses for transportation and accommodation. Except for those who lived close enough to the examination halls in the county, prefecture, and the two capitals, all the examinees had to make special trips that lasted from days to months, depending on the distance and the level of examination. For example, a trip that took fifteen days would require five taels.[19] During the examination periods, they had to rent places to stay.[20]

Provincial examinations and metropolitan examinations were held in cities that had much higher living costs, particularly in Beijing and Nanjing. Renting houses in examination cities was a profitable business. For example, officials in Beijing purchased estates to rent out to candidates.[21] During provincial examination in Hangzhou in the Wanli period, several examinees rented a house together for twenty taels. A rich examinee might rent one for himself and pay fifteen taels.[22] Many rented a room in temples.

Few could make the trip without borrowing from creditors, except those from wealthy families. Students from poor families often had to take loans from pawnshops. The demand for reduction of interest rates by the students was one of many issues that brought local officials, merchants, and the gentry into conflict.[23] Examinees suffered even more when an examination was postponed. In 1616, when the emperor's formal approval for the examination did not arrive on time, more than three hundred examinees had to return home to get more money and did not return in time to take the examinations.[24]

Those fortunate ones who graduated at the provincial and metropolitan examination often found themselves deep in debt. Shen Shouzheng (1572–1623), the author of many popular, commercially produced commentaries, continued to incur many debts even after he obtained his *juren* degree in 1603. He supported himself by compiling and editing examination aids for publishers.[25] The financial situation of the examinees did not improve, even after they passed the metropolitan examination. New graduates had to pay numerous expenses. When news of success was reported, the fortunate candidates had to come up with extra money to reward the reporters (*baoren*). The amount in the Wanli period had reached such an outrageous level that some attributed it as one of the factors for official corruption. Wu Yingji argued that since the examination result was carried by the *Government Gazette* (*Dibao*), banning reporting by commercial messengers would save examinees at the provincial and metropolitan levels several hundred taels.[26]

Wang Shizhen recalled that when he became a metropolitan graduate in 1548, the expenses incurred from giving gifts and throwing banquets for fellow graduates and examiners ranged from one hundred to three hundred taels. This did not include money spent on clothing and travel. By the 1580s, the same activities cost six hundred to seven hundred taels, and no one could avoid taking loans.[27] After Chen Jitai, the famous critic from Jiangxi, finally passed the metropolitan examination in Beijing in 1634, he had no money to entertain examiners and fellows graduates. He had to write home to urge his family to borrow money for him. His expenses amounted to four hundred to five hundred taels.[28]

New graduates of the metropolitan examination often had to wait for a long time for appointments. During the wait, they had to spend huge sums of money on gifts and bribes in order to receive good positions. It had become a common practice to take loans from pawnshops.[29] Some metropolitan graduates without immediate official appointments would have to continue to serve as tutors while waiting for openings.[30] It would not be unnatural for new metropolitan graduates such as Shen Shouzheng and Chen Jitai to repay their debt by continuing their service to publishers as commentary critics or editors.

This brief account of the expenses incurred in pursuing degrees at the provincial and metropolitan examination provides a context for understanding why many examinees worked for patrons and publishers while they were preparing to take the next examination. The names of famous literary figures appearing on commercially published books should not be routinely dismissed as marketing tricks by commercial publishers. Many "reputable masters" had to repay their debts by working for publishers. There are indeed extant late-Ming imprints that list top-ranked metropolitan graduates as authors, editors, compilers and critics.

### Publishing and the Symbolic Capital of the Literati

The boom in commercial publishing in the late Ming could not have taken place without the growing involvement of the literati.[31] The expansion took place as the literati class grew in size and as the average length of time for the successful candidates to obtain the highest degree increased.[32] Many literati, while continuing to prepare for the next examination, took up writing, editing, compiling, or even publishing as viable means of living. The excessive number of literati that the bureaucracy failed to absorb found careers in the economic field.

Expansion of commercial publishing created new opportunities for many talented but unsuccessful examinees. Publishing was one of the careers that allowed them to convert their literary skill into marketable labor. Despite their intention of entering the officialdom, these "men of culture [*wenren*] were only minimally involved in government, or not at all; arts were more than a pastime or entertainment."[33] In other words, they were *shi* as well as *shang*, engaged in both the quest for an official career while taking up positions in the economic field as literary workers and businessmen. This two-career track constituted a distinctive mode of commodification of knowledge and writing. It rendered the literary production of a writer a mode of activity rather than a well-defined, job-specific role of a position in the economic field. The literary profession was therefore a mode of action that late-Ming literati could enter and exit as often and as much as they wanted and needed to; it was not a "professional career" they could pursue in total separation from their quest for entry into the imperial government. The distinction between amateur and professional modes of literary production therefore was blurred and irrelevant because of the lack of institutional and discursive boundaries. This ambiguity and flexibility were inherent in the newly configured career trajectory of the *shishang*.

Of the various *shang* careers, publishing, writing, editing, and compiling had obvious advantages over others. As Elman has rightly stressed, acquiring a classical education required special literary and linguistic skills.[34] The examinees' training in calligraphy, classical learning, historical knowledge, and poetic and prose skills made publishing most feasible and desirable as an alternative to government service and private tutoring. Publishing offered a second advantage. By working on literary materials, the literati could continue to take examinations without having to learn a different trade anew. This body of specialized knowledge itself became a commodity in the publishing market on the one hand, and it continued to be an asset for the pursuit of political office on the other.

For many, the writing, compiling, and editing of books on subjects such as the Classics, history, prose, and poems coincided with their own preparation for the examination. For example, the playwright Zhang Fengyi (1527–1613) published his own examination aids.[35] Other notable examples include the publishers Yu Xiangdou and Min Qiji.[36] The famed publisher-cum-writer Feng Menglong (1574–1646) did not even pass the prefectural examination and was only given the "presented scholar" status at the age of fifty-seven. He chose *Spring and Autumn Annals* for the required examination on one of the Five Classics. He had authored two works on the *Spring and Autumn Annals* targeted at examinees. These books no doubt had been prepared for his own examination on the subject.

Another example was Zhang Pu, the famous leader of the Restoration Society, whose Classic of specialization was the *Book of Changes*. In addition to the regular anthologies of essays on the Four Books, he compiled an anthology of examination essays on the *Book of Changes* for a publisher. He wrote letters to his friends to solicit essays on the Classics.[37] The examples of Zhang and Feng clearly show the attraction of publishing jobs for examinees.[38] The other obvious advantage would be access to the libraries of the publishers.

This new alternative career, however, was a mixed blessing for the examinees. The unprecedented expansion of the publishing industry benefited as well as hindered their careers. On the one hand, commercial printing created new career opportunities. On the other hand, expansion of education opportunities and widely available inexpensive books of all sorts made the civil service examination ever more competitive for the literati.[39]

Commercial publishers did not recruit their literary workers only from the examinees; they also obtained assistance from retired and former officials, many of whom resigned or cashiered as a result of defeat in political struggle. Tu Long, a native of Qingpu, Zhejiang, became a *jinshi* in 1589 and was cashiered nine years later. He depended on "selling writings" for a living for more than twenty years.[40] Tu depended more on a small circle of wealthy patrons. He had published several books, at least one of which was funded by a friend.[41] Tu's experience was similar to Zhang Fengyi.

Unlike most of his contemporaries, however, Zhang Fengyi had no qualm in hiding the commercial nature of his literary labor. Beginning in 1580, Zhang posted the prices for different types of literary commissions.[42] He published a commentary on the literary anthology by Xiao Tong with money contributions from his friends.[43] While Tu Long's work was not for profit making, Zhang's anthology was meant to be a commercial undertaking. In both cases, the cost of book production was provided by friends, but the Zhang Fengyi's published books were intended to be sold as a source of his income.

Zang Maoxun (1550–1620), a native of Changxing, Zhejiang, became interested in drama. He passed the metropolitan examination in 1580. In 1583 he was appointed an instructor at the Imperial Academy.[44] But two years later, he was criticized for his improper public conduct and his involvement with a student at the academy.[45] He was cashiered and returned to his home by Lake Tai. From then on, his family depended on income from weaving by his wife and maids.[46] He began selling his literary labor, writing essays for patrons and publishing books.[47]

Chinese writers in the sixteenth century and later in the seventeenth century eked out a living in a way comparable to their French counterparts in the sixteenth and seventeenth centuries. Throughout these two centuries, the majority of writers in Europe depended on a combination of patronage and "selling prefaces and dedications." Many European authors also sought to try out as publishers. Authors who received large sums from publishers remained few. A few cases of large payments occurred at the end of the seventeenth century.[48] The impact of commercial publishing on the economic conditions of men of letters in China was quite similar in France and England. European scholars depended on patronage, selling writings in the form of prefaces, letters, and commemorative essays.[49] In general, the old order of the literary world in England and in France was still in place throughout most of the eighteenth century, as it was in China in the sixteenth and seventeenth centuries.

### Self-Representation and "Forgetting" in the Economic Field

The merging of the career trajectories of the literati and merchants in practice was not accompanied by a corresponding discourse that articulated and valorized a *shishang* identity. The absence of such an identity was a result, first, of the desire of the *shishang* to identify with the *shi*, not the *shang*; and second, of their voluntary suppression, or "forgetting," of the positions they had taken in the economic field.

In his theoretical analysis of the practice of cultural production, Bourdieu distinguishes two histories: "To understand the practices of writers and artists, and not least their products, entails understanding that they are the product of the meeting of two histories: the history of the positions they occupy and the history of their dispositions."[50] The late-Ming writers themselves had left ample evidence about their dispositions, their social desires and aspirations. They had taken great care in preserving writings about their aspiration to positions in the political field. Those writers were known in particular for their courageous battle against corrupt officials and eunuchs as well as for their heroic resistance to the Manchu conquest. However, they left very little information about positions they took in the economic field. If they did, they were laconic and metaphorical, allusive and often apologetic. Few were emphatic in providing an accurate and detailed record of their undesirable sojourn, which all would be anxious to end with a stroke of luck at the metropolitan examination.

Numerous literati who once depended on publishing for their income chose to leave their trajectory in the economic field in oblivion after their eventual entrance into the officialdom. There are several strategies of forgetting: the exclusion of prefaces, postscripts, and correspondence with publishers from one's "collected writings" (*wenji*). Hardly any collection of personal writings, either by the person himself or by his descendants, is comprehensive. Often we find prefaces explaining the common practice of including only those regarded as "important," which simply means worthy of "memory."[51]

In these literary traces of one's personal or family memory, information about involvement in commercial publishing, if preserved at all, was scant and often allusive. But such information needs to be scrutinized carefully. Through compilation, the writings of a writer were taken out of their commodity context and reinscribed with a new significance in the anthology as evidence of literary achievement. With the removal of prefaces from their commodity phase and their reinsertion into the writer's personal collection of writings, the memory of positions in the economic field was erased and suppressed.

The subjective tendency to "forget" their involvement in commercial publishing has rendered it difficult to document the impact of commercial publishing on the literati. The systematic suppression and "distortion" of the economic aspect of their literary activities presents a slanted representation of the literati, indicating that little had changed in terms of the literati's commitment to the pursuit of literary excellence, political office, and moral cultivation. Penetrating the veil of the literary and moral language requires the combined use of bibliographies and research on extant copies of Ming edition books. This task is formidable given the enormous number of books published and the large number of extant copies of Ming books. The common practice by commercial publishers of attributing books to famous writers has planted a general doubt on researchers on Ming books. Scholars often display suspicion and are distrustful of the names of famous writers listed in books.[52] Even though this incredulity is justified and useful in cautioning against hasty correlations of works with specific authors, it can be an obstacle to retracing the career trajectories of numerous late-Ming literati in the economic field. In this study, no such incredulity is taken for granted. Each case is treated with care based on available intertextual evidence.

Chen Jiru was perhaps the most popular literary figure in the Lower Yangtze region in the late sixteenth and early seventeenth centuries. No one perhaps authorized more prefaces. Extant books published in the late Ming often featured a preface bearing his name. Prefaces attributed to him could be found in a wide spectrum of genres, from examination aids to philosophical works.[53] While prefaces included in Chen's own collected essays are small compared to the prefaces found in extant late-Ming recensions, one should not dismiss all that were not found in Chen's own work as forgeries. To verify all prefaces is indeed a formidable task. One needs to remember that an author, his friends, or descendants did not publish everything by said author. When they were involved in the publication, authors differentiated their writings before publishing them. There were writings that were considered by the author himself as inferior, frivolous, worthless, or potentially dangerous. These writings would not be included in publication. However, his friends or descendants might or might not make such a differentiation. When Shen Shouzhen's descendants published his collected writings, they publicly solicited Shen's writings that had not been included in earlier printed editions. Prefaces and postscripts that were included in the printed edition amounted to less than 10–20 percent of Shen's total writings.[54] While the publisher or family members of an author solicited some writings, even more writings were excised from the collection of that individual author. The point is that the absence of prefaces in personal collections of writings does not justify automatic discrediting of prefaces found in extant Ming books produced by commercial publishers.

Writing prefaces for publishers after all constituted a legitimate sale of literary labor (*maiwen*) on the publishing market. Evidence suggests that Chen Jiru did write many prefaces for publishers who offered him the right "price of letter."[55] By his own account, he was a professional writer who lived entirely on remuneration for his literary services.[56] To a considerable extent, his dependence on literary service was comparable to that of Samuel Johnson (1709–1784) in the eighteenth century, who was the first to live entirely off his pen in England.[57]

Fame often brought patrons who requested literary pieces from professional writers such as Chen and his good friend Dong Qichang. In a play by Li Yu, Li referred to the dilemma of Chen and Dong, whose fame had attracted admirers from afar. There were so many patrons and customers seeking to possess a piece of their writing and painting that they were not able to meet their requests on time. They had to hire other writers to do their work.[58] In fact, Chen Jiru did assemble a group of friends who would write biographical essays and tomb inscriptions in his name. When his friends handed him their writings, he would make changes to improve on them. If his friends could not produce in time, he would write them himself.[59] In the play, Li Yu had concocted a conversation between Dong and Chen. Chen explained that his situation was different from that of Dong for he did not have choice regarding whom to write for. He was a professional writer who sold his literary skill for a living. His writing was not produced as gifts but as commodities. He would not refuse to write for a publisher if he was offered a reasonable fee.

Tang Xianzu, the famous playwright, was only a magistrate when he withdrew from government in 1598 at the age of forty-eight. Thereafter he depended on writing and tutoring for income.[60] Despite his exasperation of mundane types of writings, he depended on his patrons for support. His patrons sought biographical essays of "village folks," "little scholars," and prefaces to examination essays.[61] It is important to note that Tang emphasized prefaces to examination essays as a major type of his writing for patrons.[62] This supports the authenticity of the many prefaces by famous writers such as Tang and Chen Jiru that appeared in anthologies of examination essays or other genres of writings.

## Shanren *and Cultural Production*

The voluntary suppression of information about writers' careers in the market of cultural goods in their personal writings however did not succeed in erasing their profound role in helping restructure the field of cultural production by exchanging their linguistic capital for monetary reward. Despite their effort in forgetting and misrepresenting their secondary affairs with the publishers and patrons, traces of their trajectory could still be documented. A discussion of the term "*shanren*" will help us understand the discursive tension between the literati's aspiration and the practical need to engage in pecuniary endeavor on the one hand, and the practical convergence of the literary and economic undertakings of many *shishang* writers on the other.

The expansion of commercial publishing could not have been possible without a corresponding increase in the involvement of the educated elite in the process of book production. Their linguistic capital could be sold in the market of cultural products either through providing service to individual patrons or to publishers.

Chinese writing symbols had long evolved into an art form. Calligraphy had become common, and for the upper classes it was an indispensable decorative item. Calligraphy could be written in couplets, on fans, and as poetry on paintings. Merchants also needed attractive calligraphy for banners and signboards for their stores. Calligraphy on a hanging scroll had become a standard decorative fixture in *shishang* homes. By the mid-sixteenth century, the practice of writing a tomb inscription had spread to the lower classes. According to Tang Shunzhi, everyone, even as poor and lowly as the butcher and peddler, would have a tombstone inscription written for him.[63] Such a practice required literary labor, which was readily provided by the large number of examinees and professional writers. The request for a piece of writing from writers, whether famous or not, often came with monetary remuneration.[64]

A new career, no matter how vaguely it was defined institutionally, began to emerge in the sixteenth century. It was a type of skilled labor that specialized in the production of literary work, especially poetry, prose essays, calligraphy, painting, novels, and dramas. It also included specialization in government affairs and litigation. A range of names came into use indicating a difference in attitude, rather than in the nature of the service rendered by the writers. The cluster of names for professional writers ranged from the highly desirable *minggong* (famous master), to the less desirable *shanren* (mountain man). In between was the relatively positive term "author" (*zuojia*).

The term "*shanren*" as a social identity in the late Ming was ambiguous. It was both a positive and negative title for the literati. It could be a self-styled title fondly adopted by literary figures. The high official and renowned writer Wang Shizhen called himself *Yuyang shanren* (Mountain man of Suzhou). On the other hand, a *shanren* could be a professional who lived off his literary skills. *Shanren* often were versatile in literary skills, which were used to entertain their patrons.[65] Despite many professional writers' preference for the identity of *shanren*, the term retained negative attributes that implied vulgar taste.[66] For conventional literati, the term "*shanren*" could also be used in the negative sense when it was applied exclusively to those who had stopped taking the civil service examination and lived entirely on income from selling their writings. This complete break with the official career path and the commercial exchange of literary skill gave the term a lingering negative connotation. *Shanren* as professional writers were often a target of ridicule. There is a popular song saying that the *shanren* did not reside in the mountain, but on the contrary frequented government offices.[67] The less talented *shanren* were often stationed in temples of the earth god (*tudi gong*), where people would come to ask for literary services such as letter writing, essays, or poetry. They were primarily the "literary proletariat," who were poor and always looking for jobs in tutoring, medical services (*xingyi*), and divination.[68]

What is significant, however, is the fact that *shanren* was no longer a term referring to a person living in the mountain, nor to someone withdrawn from the political arena. A *shanren* was someone who could write poetry, letters, and other literary works, including calligraphy and painting. It is this very ambiguity—the poetic aspiration and the pecuniary labor—that allowed the term "*shanren*" to attain popularity in this period. *Shanren* had become a respectable title for a new career and was even considered a marketable status. The title of *shanren* indicates nothing of the actual space where the *shanren* worked. It indicated a disavowal of the purely economic nature of their operation as professional writers who moved in urban rather than bucolic areas. Some publishers simply used *shanren* rather than the personal name of an author on the cover of a book.[69] The title had attained such respect that professional writers simply used the title in their work.[70] An anthology of writings by "reputable masters" included the writings by 327 authors, among whom were eighteen writers listed with the title *shanren*.[71] The blind writer Tang Ruxun gave his own writings the title of *Youyang shanren bianfeng ji*.[72]

Tang Ruxun, a native of Songjiang in Jiangsu, is an interesting case of the literati experience of a *shanren*. He became blind at the age of five but was talented at writings, especially poetry. Like others, he took part in the examinations without passing the metropolitan examination. Despite his blindness and repeated failure in earning higher degrees, Tang had achieved a reputation as an expert in producing examination aids and as an insightful critic of poetry.[73] In 1600 Tang finished writing a history of poetry; he sold it to Gu Zhengyi for thirty taels. Gu then published it as *Gushi shishi* under his own name. It was lamented that his price was too low for such an original work.[74] Tang's enterprise was significant in a number of ways. His literary labor was given a price and was bought by a customer. Tang sold his ownership as well as his authorship, not just the manuscript itself.

In 1609 Tang, Zhong Xing, and other examinees founded the Yechengshe (Society of the beautiful city) to prepare for the examination. By that time, Tang's published essays were already highly regarded among examinees.[75] As a critic, Tang had edited and commented on several anthologies of Tang poetry. In 1615 he compiled a *Tang shi jie* (Understanding Tang poetry) in fifty juan, which was probably funded by local officals.[76] In 1623 he completed another anthology of Tang poetry, which was actually a collection of reprints of other writers' anthologies.[77] This was apparently a work commissioned by a commercial publisher. Eventually seeing no hope in success at the examinations, he decided to participate in compiling a history of the Imperial Academy in return for an appointment as assistant prefect in Fengyang.[78]

As a literatus seeking a career in the imperial government, Tang found it profitable to render his services to publishers. He was involved in publishing both for economic and professional reasons. No doubt income from literary labor contributed significantly to his sustained quest for entry into officialdom. His status as a *shanren*, a professional mode that he intended to be temporary, turned out to occupy the longest segment of his career trajectory.

In addition to being producers of literary works, some *shanren* were specialists in connoisseurship of antiques and art works. Because of their knowledge, they were not gullible when it came to assessing antiques and artworks.[79] Li Rihua, a connoisseur in books, calligraphy, and painting, had streams of brokers bringing him art objects, including painting, calligraphy, wine cups, ink, bronze vessels, and musical instruments.[80] Being a connoisseur himself, Li was able to identify forgeries, which were common among those brought to him by the brokers.[81] But the less informed had to depend on the expertise of the *shanren*.

*Shanren* were often patronized by wealthy merchants and high officials for their special knowledge, literary skill, and wit. The most prominent *shanren*, Wang Zhideng (1535–1612), served as secretary of officials. Some even rendered assistance in litigation.[82] Even eunuchs had to hire *shanren* for their literary skill. One eunuch in Beijing actually entrusted a defense in a legal case to a *shanren*.[83]

*Shanren* does not refer to professional writers of a particular genre. It refers in general to literati who "write in order to live" (*maiwen wei huo*). They were professional writers, not unlike those in eighteenth-century France.[84] There were playwrights who also assumed the title *shanren*. *Shanren* were also involved in writing and commenting on dramas. Many dramas reviewed by Qi Biaojia were authored by *shanren*.[85] The renowned Xu Wei referred to himself as *shanren*.[86] He befriended other *shanren*.[87] Xu was a good friend of a *shanren* Wang Yin, who served with Xu as the secretarial staff of Hu Zongxian (1511–65), the notable governor of Zhejiang in charge of fighting the Japanese pirates in the 1560s.[88] Xu wrote memorials for Hu and other officials.[89] In addition to serving officials as secretary, Xu also made his literary talents available to a wider clientele. Among the literary works Xu sold were books, paintings, and calligraphy.[90] However, he was extremely selective in rendering his service when he was not in need of money.

Xu Wei's experience shows that the patrons of *shanren* could be a few, or even one, at a given time, or they could be simply the general public.

During the Wanli period, Lu Yingyang (1542–1627), a renowned *shanren* in Songjiang, Jiangsu, lived on writing poetry and calligraphy. His poetry was in great demand.[91] No *shanren* was endowed with greater talents than Chen Jiru, also a native of Suzhou. In 1586, before he was thirty years old, he burned his Confucian cap and gown.[92] He lived off tutoring at a shrine devoted to Lu Shiheng and Lu Shilong. He restored the shrine and created a floral garden there. With the gift of flowers from Wang Xi-jue, he was able to make a reputation in cultivating and selling flowers.[93] He made a living tutoring, selling his own calligraphy and paintings, and writing books.[94] He often received requests to write tomb inscriptions (*beiwen*) from patrons from near and far.[95] His paintings were common decorations in restaurants and teahouses. They reached remote towns and villages, and were popular even among leaders of indigenous peoples in the frontier.[96] In addition to his literary reputation, Chen was held in high regard as a leader in the Suzhou area. He was deeply involved in local politics. He was often requested to author important documents for local events.[97] He was appointed as the chief compiler for the gazetteer of Songjiang.[98]

Some professional artists specialized in painting but also designed illustrations for publishers. Ding Yunpeng (1547–after 1620), a native of Huizhou, was a professional painter who also produced illustrations for books.[99] It is evident that Ding received a good education but failed to obtain a degree beyond the *shengyuan* level.[100] He collaborated with other artists in the production of exquisite illustrated books, including the *Bogu tu lu* (Comprehensive album of images of antiquity), published by a Nanjing publisher around 1600. Ding was a prominent artist in the designs of ink sticks and had contributed to the two major catalogues of ink sticks published by two Huizhou manufacturers—Fang Yulu (active ca. 1580–1620) and Cheng Dayue (1541–1616).[101]

Chen Hongshou, a famous painter, had only a student status at the Imperial Academy. In addition to being a tutor, he was primarily a professional painter and calligrapher.[102] He began selling his own paintings as a teenager.[103] Poverty had kept him busy writing and painting.[104] Some of his paintings were also mass produced in printed form. Chen printed a painting of Guan Yu, the God of War, a popular "hero" whose image was among the most common in the late Ming.[105] He had painted at least two sets of playing cards: one set of forty characters from the *Water Margin* and the other called *Investigation of Antiquity* (*Pogu yezi*).[106] Chen, like Ding Yunpeng, was hired to illustrate the popular play *Xixiang ji* (Romance of the western chamber).[107] His painting was so popular that falsifying his painting became a special career for numerous professional painters.[108] His paintings were collected even by rulers in Korea and Japan.[109] Among Chen's friends were many who also depended on editing, publishing, and selling calligraphy and painting. He was a friend of Huang Ruheng (1558–1626), another reputable master from Hangzhou.[110]

These writers, painters, and publishers, who had no qualm calling themselves *shanren,* offer us a few glimpses of their careers in the economic field. The growing acceptance of the career in the economic field by literati like Zhang Fengyi, Chen Jiru, and Chen Hongshou was significant only against the fact that the majority who had similarly labored hard and long in the market of cultural goods chose to forget their secondary careers by either not preserving their literary products or misrepresenting them as pure literary achievements. Despite the profound impact of commercialization on the field of literary production, the field was still linked to the center of the political field by the examinations that held out a promise of possible entry into the imperial bureaucracy. And the habitus of the literati to reproduce the experience and the representation of the trajectory of a scholar has obscured their often longer career in the economic field. We need to rediscover the *shanren* trajectory of the literati who in practice had a career in writing, editing, and publishing.

## PARATEXT AND THE PRODUCTION OF CREDIBILITY, PUBLICITY, AND NETWORKS

In order to recover the forgotten positions in commercial publishing, it is imperative to examine the new practice in which paratext had been put to use in the sixteenth and seventeenth centuries. Gerald Genette analyzed paratext for its relationship with the text and interpretation thereof. He said little of how the paratext functions in the context of social relations, especially outside the socioeconomic context of Europe.

Paratext, especially the preface, postscript, and comments, was put to several uses in book publishing in the sixteenth and seventeenth centuries in China. Publishers inserted prefaces by famous authors to lend credibility to their books. Writing prefaces became an important source of income for the *shishang* involved in cultural production. Preface writing required the circulation of manuscripts through the mail, increasing communication and networking among the *shishang* (writers). Authors of prefaces also served as peer reviewers of publications. Preface writing was an economic, marketing, communal, and professional act.

## Prefaces for Sale

Writing prefaces was nothing new in the late Ming. But the proliferation of new genres and in the number of texts meant the growing importance of preface writing as a source of income and as a means for social networking, creating publicity for writers and generating patronage. While patronage through personal networks was still important, writers could depend increasingly on the reputation driven by the expanding commercial publishing market.

Preface writing was one of the most acceptable ways for *shishang* writers to earn a living. The growth in the number of prefaces can also be viewed as evidence of the literati's growing dependence on publishers as patrons. Monetary remuneration for writing prefaces was often represented as a "gift" (*kuang*[a]). Chen Jiru, for example, often received *kuang*[a] with requests for his writing.[111] Evidence of a commercial origin can still be found in writings marked with the word "*dai*" (on behalf of) in personal collections. The growth in the number of prefaces in both privately and commercially published books meant greater demand for literary services, which would allow a greater number of writers to live off their literary skills. Chen and the many others discussed in this study were but the most notable in this period. Prefaces were therefore means of exchange, commodities in the market of literary production in the late Ming.

## Reputable Masters and the Credibility of Books

Reputation was a symbolic capital that could be converted into economic capital. As Gerard Genette has argued, giving the name of a person as the author of a book is no small matter.[112] Signing the name of the "author" or "editor" or "critic" is one of the most important strategies for distinguishing a book from others when marketing books to readers with too many choices. Putting the name of the author on the book was no longer just a way of identifying the creator of a text. It was an extremely valuable tool to help the reader recognize the worth of the book. A book with a "famous or reputable master" (*minggong*) as its author, editor, critic, or compiler guaranteed quality.

Official titles of authors had long been used to sell books. Publishers came to deem prefaces by "reputable masters" (*minggong*) or "reputable writers" (*mingjia*) as more useful in attracting buyers.[113] Three commentaries on the Four Books, either edited or compiled by the prolific writer Guo Wei, advertise their authorship as being "*minggong*" (see Figure 2.1, page 74). A *minggong* or *mingjia* was a writer with a reputation. To identify the author as a "reputable master" was to create credibility for the author. The identification was deployed in the paratext like the title of the book or the author, or in the editorial principles (see Figure 3.1).[114] At a time when there was no established forum or procedures for reviewing books, the evaluation and accrediting of books became a problem for both the buyer and the publisher. As Adrian Johns has aptly remarked, "Printers and booksellers were manufacturers of credit."[115] The credibility of a printed book could be generated by the reputation of the author. The credibility endowed by the presence of a reputable master could be deployed in a great number of ways. The reputable master could be listed as a proofreader, a compiler, or an editor.

The addition of paratexts helped locate the text and its author in the literary as well as social hierarchy. The name of the preface writer immediately helped the reader assess the relative value of the text before proceeding to the main text. In times when there were no special textual mechanisms for reviewing books, the credibility and advertising power of the preface was even more important.

Preface writing provided writers with renumeration, connections, as well as publicity. Given the importance of packaging one's book with prefaces by "reputable masters," finding the right person became an integral part of the production of the book. Adding paratexts like prefaces was therefore no small matter for both the author and the publisher.

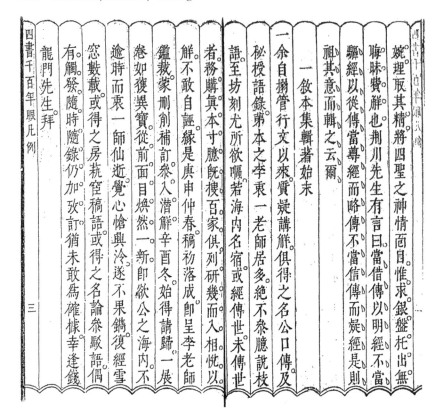

Figure 3.1: "Editorial principles" (*fanli*) in *Sishu qianbai nian yan*, a commentary on the Four Books. The phrase "*gong zhi hainei*" appears in the editorial principles. The compiler assures his readers that the various expositions he included came from the "reputable masters." Reproduced by permission of the National Archives of Japan.

## Prefaces and the Network of Writers

Reputable masters themselves also sought prefaces from friends and other well-known writers. When Chen Jiru published his own works, he requested prefaces from his friends. Li Rihua contributed a preface to his *Guan miji* (Expanded edition of secret books).[116] In 1603 his good friend Wang Heng, the son of Wang Xijue, wrote a preface for his *Yimin zhuan* (Biographies of recluses).[117] Chen wrote a preface for his best friend Dong Qichang's anthology of examination essays.[118] Tang Xianzu had written prefaces for his friends Tan Yuanchun, Huang Ruheng, Qiu Zhaolin, and Li Tingji, whose names often appeared in late-Ming imprints as authors of prefaces, anthologies, and commentaries.[119] When Mei Dingzuo completed his voluminous *Lidai wenji* (Anthology of writings of all periods) in 1611, he wrote to Tang to tell him of his plan to go to Nanjing to show him the work so that Tang could write a preface for it.[120]

The famous critic Zhong Xing had written a preface for the writings of Huang Ruheng, a critic from Hangzhou.[121] When Zhong was in Nanjing, he was sought out by numerous examinees who wanted him to evaluate their examination essays.[122] One of his friends passed the provincial examination; before taking the metropolitan examination in Beijing in the following spring, the friend mailed his examination essays to Zhong for review and requested a preface.[123]

The writing and inclusion of prefaces by reputable writers was something many budding writers or examinees took very seriously. A young poet from Suzhou sought to solicit a preface from Zhong Xing. He knew Chen Jiru was a friend of Zhong's. Before he visited Zhong, he requested a letter of recommendation from Chen. Upon seeing Chen's letter, Zhong was happy to grant him his wish.[124] The Suzhou poet sought Zhong Xing primarily because Zhong was a reputable poet and critic of poetry. Prefaces were not to be written merely by someone with a reputation. They needed to be written by those who were recognized as authorities in the specific genres. The evaluation or credibility had to come from the experts.

This is equally true in other categories like commentaries on the Four Books. The reputation of established critics and writers was used by neophytes and less well-known writers to enhance the attraction of their anthologies. The popular commentary by Gu Menglin, entitled *Sishu shuoyue* (Concise exposition on the Four Books), had prefaces by Zhang Pu and Yang Yi. Both Zhang and Yang were members of the Restoration Society. In 1638, Gu mailed the manuscript to Yang Yi, who after reading it wrote a preface. The carving of the book was completed two years later.[125] It is common to find a large number of prefaces written for examination essays by friends and students in the collected works of critics. During the 1620s and 1630s Zhang Pu, Chen Jitai, Ai Nanying, and Zhong Xing were the most prominent examples.[126]

The increase in the number of prefaces was facilitated by the mail service. Manuscripts were often sent by mail to the preface writers for review. In 1608, when Shen Jing finished reading and commenting on a new edition of *The Romance of the Western Chamber* edited by Wang Qide, he mailed the manuscript back to Wang.[127] The extant edition by Wang, *Xin jiaozhu guben Xixiang ji* (newly edited old edition of the *Romance of the Western Chamber* with annotations), lists Shen as the commentator and carries a preface dated 1614.[128]

The increased functions of prefaces in late-Ming publishing was a major cause in the proliferation of prefaces in a book. It was quite common to find books printed in the Jiajing period (1522–66) with two or three prefaces. The number grew to three or more in books printed in the late Wanli and Chongzhen (1628–43) periods.[129] A commentary on the Four Books has eight prefaces.[130] In 1606, when Cheng Dayue published his catalog of design, *Chengshi moyuan* (Ink garden of Mr. Cheng), he solicited prefaces from such luminaries as Wang Xijue, Shen Shixing, Dong Qichang, Jiao Hong, Tu Long, Guan Zhidao, and even Matteo Ricci. The catalog had a total of eighteen prefaces![131] The trend of including large number of prefaces continued into the last decades of the Ming dynasty. A novel published in the 1620s has as many as fifteen prefaces![132]

Repelled by this trend, Xu Fenpeng, a prolific writer from Jiangxi who published books by publishers in Jianyang and Nanjing, decided not to solicit prefaces from "reputable masters" and insisted on writing them for his own books.[133] Xu, however, was the exception to the rule. Most authors and editors would solicit a preface from relatively well-known writer if they wanted their book to sell well. The famous critic of examination essays, Ai Nanying, had written prefaces for more than one hundred anthologies of examination essays, testifying to the "marketability" of his reputation as a critic and to the credibility his prefaces lent to the books, as well as to his position in the market of literary production as a *shishang* writer.[134]

"Reputable masters" were primarily men who derived their reputation from their published writings, products of labor exchanged in the market of literary culture. When Li Yu referred to the typical work of the *wenren* (literati), he compared their criticism with the weaving work of women.

"The hand of the *wenren* never stops writing criticism and the embroidery maids hardly cease embellishing with the needle."[135] Writing prefaces, editing, commenting, and compiling were the proper labor of a "professional" writer.

## Titles of Authors and Equality in Literary Reputation

The titles of the author and contributors helped to market a book. It had been a common practice to include the titles of government office of the author with the book title. Many titles carried the actual ranking of metropolitan graduates such as *chuangyuan* (highest graduate at the metropolitan examination) or "grand historians" (*taishi*). This strategy continued to be widely used by publishers, especially for examination aids.[136] After all, the ultimate goal of the examinees remained: success at the metropolitan examination. Gradually, however, publishers came to use a different strategy to market their books.

Publishers in the late Ming increasingly used either the title *fu* (Mr.) or *xiansheng* (elder), or sometimes simply the name of the listed contributor without any designation or title (see, for example, Figure 3.2). These titles were given to authors, editors, and compilers. Those with reputations were referred to as "reputable masters," even though many were holders of the highest degree or high official rank. This practice can be considered as evidence of the growing autonomy of the literary field. Accumulated political capital of a writer would not necessarily lend credibility to a book. The fading of political authority over literary matters is evident in the application of titles that did not replicate the hierarchy of the political field.

Tang Binyin (b. 1568) became a *jinshi* in 1595 and rose to become the director of the Imperial Academy in Nanjing. Yu Yingqiu, who operated the Jinshengju (Residence of approaching the sages), published two books in the 1610s that listed Tang Binyin as the author. He was simply referred to as "Mr. Tang" from Xuancheng, Jiangxi.[137]

The famous anthology of writings on statecraft, *Huang Ming jinshi wenbian* (Anthology of writings on statecraft of the Ming dynasty), compiled by Chen Zilong, Xu Fuyuan, and Song Zhengbi, is another typical example of the exaltation of literary reputation over official status. The anthology was printed in 1638, a year after Chen became a *jinshi*. But on

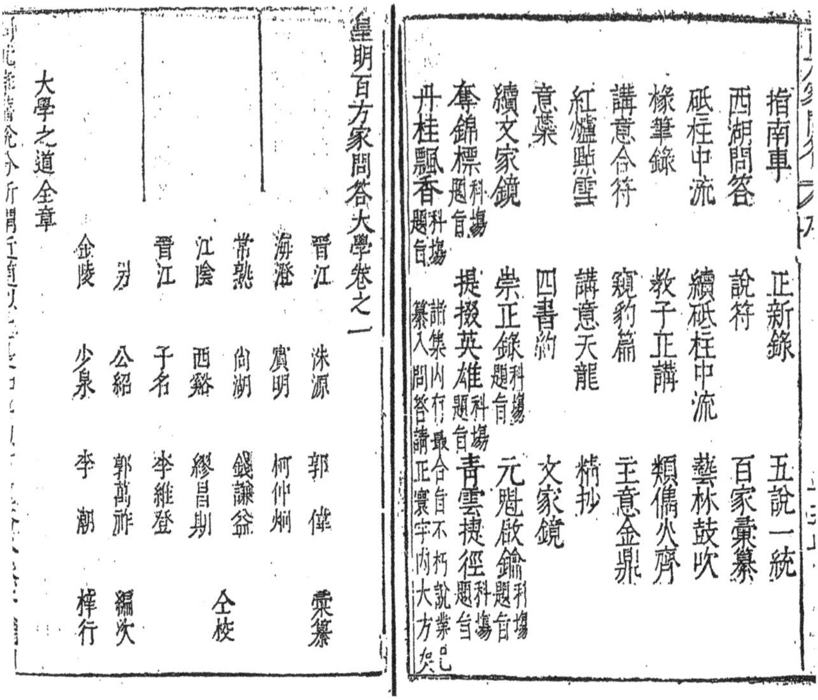
指南車 正新錄 五說一統
西湖問答 說符 百家彙纂
砥柱中流 續砥柱中流 藝林鼓吹
椽筆錄 教子正講 類儁火齊
講意合符 窺豹篇 主意金鼎
紅爐點雪 講意天能 精抄
意槩 四書約 文家鏡
續文家鏡 崇正錄題科旨場 元魁啟鑰題科旨場
奪錦標題科旨場 提掇英雄題科旨場 青雲捷徑題科旨場
丹桂飄香題科旨場 諸集內有最合旨不朽說業已纂入問答請正寰宇內大方矣

皇明百方家問答大學卷之一
晉江 洙源 郭偉 彙纂
海澄 賓明 柯仲炯
常熟 尚湖 錢謙益 仝校
江陰 西谿 繆昌期
晉江 子名 李維登
男 公紹 郭尚祚 編次
金陵 少泉 李潮 梓行
大學之道全章

Figure 3.2: Folio from *Huang Ming bai fangjia wenta* (Questions and answers by a hundred specialists of the Ming dynasty) by Guo Zhuyuan. On the right is the last page of references that the editor purportedly consulted in compiling the book. On the left is the first page of the commentary listing the contributors. Guo Wei, the prolific professional editor of commentaries is listed as the chief editor (*huizuan*), followed by four proofreaders, including the famous Qian Qianyi and Miao Changqi. Guo's son is listed as a compiler and Li Chao as the Nanjing publisher. All are listed by their own names with their respective native county or city. Reproduced by permission of the National Archives of Japan.

the cover he was simply listed by his personal name as the commentator and editor. Chen was one of the leaders of the Restoration Society and was a well-known critic of examination essays (see Chapter 5 for a discussion of his involvement in commercial publishing). On the cover, in addition to Chen, two persons were listed on the top margin as proofreaders. One of them was the famous Chen Jiru and the other was Fang

Yuxiu. Chen Jiru, an elderly friend of Chen Zilong, was listed with his style name, Meigong.[138] In this particular case, Chen Jiru was involved in some capacity in shaping the selection of essays since he was widely respected in the Suzhou literary circles in which the Restoration was based.

The reputable master was not a personal teacher, friend, or mentor, but someone who appeared everywhere in print, in a variety of capacities as a contributor to a book. The reputable master was someone who was an arbiter and impersonator of literary excellence. He was a judge of books. He was enlisted as a contributor by publishers. His presence was an indication of quality and authority. This strategy helped redefine the meaning of "reputable master." If someone had a reputable name but was not "publicized" in the print world, that reputation remained restricted to the local community in which he operated. A reputable master was an author known to his readers through the wide circulation of books. His name was portable and exchanged as part of the commodity—the book in the market. "Reputable masters" were signposts amid the sea of books that flooded the reading publics in the late Ming.

When publishers solicited manuscripts or writings, they referred to writers with reputations as *minggong*. In the early 1620s, a Suzhou publisher, the Youyoutang, published an anthology of writings by Ming authors entitled *Ming wen qi shang* (Appreciation of original writings of the Ming dynasty). It featured an advertisement soliciting unpublished manuscripts and collected writings, or works published with limited circulation by "reputable masters."[139] Another anthology of vignettes written by Ming writers published in the early 1630s advertised a number of upcoming compilations. The publisher welcomed the submission of writings, poems, memorials, and plays by "reputable masters," recluses, and ladies.[140] Some publishers simply included the term in the title of their books.[141]

"Reputable master" was not an official title, nor a social appellation with a clear institutional affiliation or semantic stability. Since the reputation of the writer was derived from his literary skill, his achievement in other areas of experience, including his success in the officialdom, was irrelevant. The manifest expression of this purely literary identity was the adoption of the title *"fu"* by both writers and publishers. Authors, editors, or commentators were preceded by their native place rather than by their official title regardless of how illustrious their official achievement might have been. Such was the common practice in commercial publishing in the Wanli period. In 1590, one of the major publishing houses in Nanjing, the Ten Thousand Scrolls Studio (Wanjuan lou) of Zhou Rijiao, published an anthology of essays by members of the Hanlin Academy; it listed the names of Wang Xijue and Shen Yiguan. Both were high officials eventually attaining the highest positions as members of the Secretariat.[142] When the book was published, Wang had already been a grand secretary for several years. Even though Shen did not enter the Grand Secretariat until 1594, he had risen to the position of the vice president of the Ministry of Personnel in 1584.[143] In the anthology, both were simply listed as "*fu.*" Most informed readers would surely know their high positions in the imperial government. But in the book, they were listed under the same title as other contributors who had far less or none of their achievement in the political field. This practice suggests that political status was no longer the most desirable qualification of an author or editor. Success in politics was incidental to literary excellence. It was the "reputable master's" literary skills, talents, and guidance in the form of comments and criticism that would bring success in the publishing world.

There were a number of authors whose names (*ming*) themselves had become evidence of excellence and quality. Many of these authors were not officials when their reputation was established and subsequently came to occupy insignificant positions in the political field. Thus the authority they commanded was not derivative of their political position but of their personal success in the commercial publishing world. The names of Li Tingji, Qiu Zhaolin, Chen Jiru, Zhang Nai, and Zhong Xing were often included as compiler, editor, or reader.[144]

Perhaps no writer surpasses Chen Jiru in publicity in the late Ming. More than fifty titles listed him either as author, editor, compiler, commentator, or reader.[145] Chen had never been an official. The official titles of writers who had success in the political field were not always chosen by publishers to market their books. Li Tingji from Fujian earned his *jinshi* in 1583 and became a high official, rising to the top of his career as president of the Ministry of Rites with a concurrent appointment as grand secretary in 1607.[146] He established his literary excellence by placing first in both the provincial and the metropolitan examinations. Many books continued to refer to him as a "grand historian."[147] But there are many titles that refer to him simply as "Mr. Li" from Wenling.[148] Li had authored several works for publishers from Jianyang. His native place connection clearly explained his relationship with publishers from Fujian. Two books published by the Shuangfengtang carried his name as the compiler. One listed him as "grand historian" and the other simply listed him as "Mr. Li."[149]

Li was apparently an honest official and had attained a reputation of integrity. According to Tang Xianzu, he was very "poor."[150] To be sure, he certainly did not participate in the acceptable practices of corruption. Selling one's literary product was an important way to stay honest at a time when extensive corruption had swept throughout the entire officialdom in the late Ming.

## Proofreaders and Publicity

Another paratextual strategy used to enhance the importance of the work was the inclusion of a large number of popular authors as editors and proofreaders. In many cases, the list runs to more than one hundred. For example, a commentary on the Four Books, the *Sishu shuosheng* (Residual meanings of the Four Books), prefaced in 1615, provides a list of fifty-two proofreaders (*jiaoyue*) with county identifications.[151] In the 1620s a Nanjing publisher, Wanjuantang (Studio of ten thousand juan), published a three-color commentary on the Four Books, listing Ai Nanying, Luo Wanzu, Chen Jitai, Zhang Shichun, and Xu Fenpeng as proofreaders, all well-known critics of examination essays during the 1620s and 1630s.[152] The well-known publisher, scholar, critic, and novelist Feng Menglong published in 1625 an examination aid on the *Spring and Autumn Annals*, entitled *Linjing zhiyue*, for examinees preparing for examinations on the Classic.[153] Of the 103 persons listed as proofreaders, thirteen were his students and ninety were probably friends and members of the same literary societies.[154] The famous commentator Gu Menglin, a leading figure in the Restoration Society, had written several popular works for the civil service examination. In the *Sishu shuoyue* (Concise exposition of the Four Books) published in 1640, fifty-three persons were listed as proofreaders. Another equally popular examination aid by Gu was the *Shijing shuoyue* (Concise exposition of the *Book of Odes*), published in 1642; there was a list of 106 persons grouped under two categories: teachers and friends who reviewed (*jianding*) the work, and disciples who proofread the work.[155]

The expansion of the list of proofreaders clearly suggests the strategic use of the paratextual space for publicity. The individuals whose names appeared in long lists of proofreaders might not all actually read the manuscript before publication. The growth of this practice, however, was hardly the exclusive result of the marketing strategy of publishers. After all, adding scores of names with no actual contribution to the book would likely increase the cost of production. The increase in the number of proofreaders might well be the result of the demand by those individuals for publicity. Being listed as a proofreader is a public statement of one's involvement in endorsing the high quality of a book; it also publicizes membership in the emerging community of critics. The commentary on the Four Books published by a Nanjing publisher mentioned above is a typical example. The publicity of an examinee would increase as his name appeared as proofreader in many other books. This publicity would increase the chance of success at the examinations.

## Publishers and Supervisors

While many literati were content to work as editors, compilers, proofreaders, and critics for publishers, others ventured into publishing. The technology and the business environment of publishing offered them an enticing alternative career. The experience of Zang Maoxun is indicative of the ease with which one could enter publishing. After only four years in the government, Zang was cashiered as a result of a scandal of homosexuality. He turned his interest in poetry into business. Zang compiled anthologies of poetry. He published *Gushi suo* (Repository of ancient poetry) in fifty-six juan in about 1590; he compiled a different anthology, *Tangshi suo* (Repository of Tang poetry), in 1606.[156] When he published an anthology entitled *Shisuo* (Repository of poetry) in Nanjing in 1603 or 1604,[157] Zang hired a "supervisor of cutting" (*duke*), Xu Zhi, to assemble and supervise a team of woodblock cutters.[158] The major work published by Zang was the anthology of Yuan songs. In 1615 he published half of the Yuan songs that he edited. The next year, he published the other half.[159] Zang paid carvers to produce the blocks, and he sent his own servant to Beijing to market the books because they could be sold at higher prices than in Nanjing and Suzhou.[160]

The manner in which Zang published his books was a very common practice in the late Ming. Anyone interested in putting a manuscript in print could hire cutters to carve the blocks. There were cutters in certain quarters of big cities like Beijing, Suzhou, and Nanjing. For small works, one cutter would be adequate. If time was a factor, more cutters could be hired to complete the carving. Hiring carvers for larger works required coordination and supervision. This would be true particularly if cutters operated independently of a publishing house. In this case, a supervisor coordinated and monitored the cutters' progress. Zang Maoxun probably did not have a publishing workshop with permanent cutters working as regular employees. Thus when he published a book, he hired a "supervisor of cutting" to recruit cutters and to monitor the progress of the printing.

The title of "supervisor of cutting" or "printing supervisor" was initially used in publishing when the official in charge of the printing project was also commissioned as supervisor. It was therefore a managing position that might not require knowledge of carving and printing.[161] He could also be the chief carver of a team of carvers. A completed collection of Wang Yangming's writings was published by a Zhili censor from Jiangxi who served concurrently as the provincial education commissioner during the Longqing reign (1567–72). Three officials were listed as "printing supervisors." They were the assistant prefect of Yingtian prefecture, the magistrate of Shanyuan county, and the magistrate of Jiangning.[162] These officials were given supervisory responsibilities simply because the printing was being done in Nanjing. Similarly, a county gazetteer printed in the Tianqi reign (1621–27) was completed under the supervision of Tang Shaoyao, who was listed as the "*dukan*," which was a variant term for "*duke*." The other variant is "*duzi*."[163] Noteworthy is the fact that no official title was given for Tang. The gazetteer was published under official supervision. A commercial publishing agent was hired to oversee the official publication.

Supervisors or managers served as agents of publishing and were responsible for putting together a team of woodcutters for a project. In fact, the same Xu Zhi who supervised the publication of Zang Maoxun's

*Shisuo* was listed as publishing supervisor for another work. In one of the books published by the Huizhou publisher Wu Mianxue, Xu Zhi of Nanjing was also listed as "supervisor of cutting" (*duke*).[164] Wu had published many more books than Zang and was clearly a commercial publisher.[165] Despite Wu's large number of published titles, he still hired Xu Zhi to supervise the publishing. Perhaps Wu needed to travel between Nanjing and Huizhou. He thus needed to hire a person to oversee publishing in Nanjing.[166] Xu Zhi was listed as "printing supervisor" for several books published in the period between 1571 and 1603.[167]

A book published by Feng Menglong listed a "printing supervisor" from Youlong.[168] Youlong was famous for its population's involvement in book trade and production. The supervisor was perhaps the chief cutter of a group that he assembled in Youlong. He was not the owner of a publishing house with its own workshop and regular cutters. But he had great connections with cutters and was responsible for recruiting and monitoring their works for a client or publisher in another city.

But printing in the late Ming had not developed to the point where publishing and printing became separate professions. Some publishers were knowledgeable enough about block cutting to serve as the printing supervisor. The well-known publisher Zhou Rijiao of Nanjing listed himself as a "*dukan*" in some of the books he published. In an anthology of writings by members of the Hanlin Academy, Zhou listed a number of *minggong*, including Wang Xijue as the chief compiler and Jiao Hong as the contributing reader. Zhou listed himself as the printing supervisor.[169] The author of one of the prefaces referred to Zhou as the "printer" (*ziren*).[170] Another Nanjing publisher, Tang Guoda, was listed as "printing supervisor" (*duzi*) for an anthology of exercises by members of the Hanlin Academy.[171]

The discussion above is not meant to argue that an entirely new position in commercial printing developed as indicated by the titles of "supervisor of printing" (*duke, duzi, dukan*). It is rather to highlight that publishing teams in the late Ming were flexible and complex. Books could be published by a team scattered in different places: manuscripts could be compiled by the editor, prefaces were solicited from renowned writers; editors and publishers could communicate by mail over changes and problems of corrections; different parts of the manuscript and full-page illustrations, if there were any, could be cut by carvers from different shops and locations; a shortage of capital could be resolved by cutting blocks in installments. Blocks could be sold, replaced in part by new blocks, and reissued under the new owners of the blocks.[172] The flexibility and simplicity of publishing operations rendered it relatively easy and attractive for literati to venture into publishing as a secondary career.

## THE VARIETY OF *SHISHANG* PUBLISHERS AND WRITERS

Literati who decided to try their luck in commercial publishing did not have to make tough choices. The specific combination of scale of operation, strategy of selection and marketing, as well as the range of genres of books varied with the resources, personal interests, and marketing choices of the individual publisher. The dramatic increase and expansion of reading publics allowed publishers to choose their niches. Like most Jianyang publishers, they could target examinees and the general reading publics. Or they could publish lavishly illustrated books on fiction and plays, or medical texts for high-end buyers and medical professionals. Many of these *shishang* publishers themselves were writers; some specialized in drama, others in poetry and commentaries of the Four Books. As publishers and writers, most tended to establish their names in one or two genres, while a few were able to attain reputations in many genres.

### A *Publisher of* Shi *Culture: Chen Renxi*

Despite the convergence of the trajectories of the *shi* and *shang*, some *shishang* publishers chose to publish books only for orthodox readers. They avoided vernacular novels and drama and other genres not related to the conventional concerns for the Classics, histories, statecraft, and the civil examination.

Chen Renxi (1580–1634), a native of Changzhou, was a good example of a *shishang* engaged in commercial publishing. His personal writings are representative of the *shishang's* tendency to suppress their economic involvement, revealing only their *shi* identity and activities. His involvement in commercial publishing is revealed in extant Ming imprints bearing his name as publisher and contributor. Further evidence can be ascertained in the prefaces he wrote for them. They were preserved in his collection of writings entitled *Wumengyuan ji* (Collection from the garden of no dream), which he himself edited and completed in 1633.[173] But even in these prefaces, no hints were given to his role in the production of the books, much less dates, locations, and details about the actual process of production.[174]

Chen was hardly known among intellectual historians, nor was he known in standard political history of the late-Ming period. Like the majority of the *jinshi* who had struggled more than twenty years before passing the metropolitan examination, Chen eventually became a *jinshi* in 1622 after twenty-five years of being a *juren*.[175] But in 1627 he was deprived of his official status for his protest against Wei Zhongxian's attempt to confer on himself the title of a duke (*gong*).[176]

Chen was heavily involved in publishing while he was still a *juren*. In nineteen years, he had authored, edited, commented, and published at least forty-four works.[177] Chen operated a publishing business under two names: Yuefantang (Studio of pleasure in sails) and Qishangzhai (Studio for the appreciation of masterful books). He published at least fifteen books, and most of his books that could be dated were published between 1618 and the 1630s.[178]

His books were of high quality and were targeted at the highly educated and conventional buyers; many were anthologies of prose. It should be noted that all books published before 1628 were primarily anthologies of essays in classical Chinese, which were unmistakably commercial in their appeal.

Chen did not abandon publishing after he became an official, and his publishing strategy remained the same: targeting examinees who were interested in improving their writing skills.[179] His own interest in statecraft prompted him to publish a voluminous anthology of essays entitled *Jingshi ba bian leizuan* (Collection of statecraft writings in eight chapters).[180] He might have been collecting materials before he was cashiered. His major works on statecraft were all published after he was expelled from officialdom in 1627.

Chen did not operate only as a publisher. He edited books for other commercial publishers while he was publishing his own books. Perhaps because of inadequate capital, he gave some of his manuscripts to other commercial publishers. One of his major works on government, *Zizhi tongjian daquan* (Complete concordance on the Mirror of Government, preface 1629), was published by a Suzhou publisher, Dahuantang.[181] His interest in publishing statecraft books appeared to be closely connected to his successful entrance into officialdom and his subsequent unpleasantly brief career in the political field.

Throughout his publishing career of at least nineteen years, Chen never published a drama or a novel. Nor did he publish any practical guides. In terms of his career trajectory, he was a *shishang*, but in outlook and identity, he was a staunch *shi*, indicative of the incongruity between the history of his dispositions and the history of economic positions he had occupied. However, as a commercial publisher, Chen had to make some profit. In 1633, he published an anthology of "model examination essays" (*chengwen*) and the next year a commentary on the Four Books entitled *Sishu beikao* (Full annotations of the Four Books).[182] It is not surprising that he published the *Books to be Hidden* and its sequel by Li Zhi. Printing the works of best-selling authors like Li Zhi and examination aids was the fundamental strategy that almost all commercial publishers had to fall back on for survival.

## Publishers of Entertaining Culture: Feng Menglong

In contrast to Chen Renxi, there were commercial publishers who were receptive to the growing demand for vernacular novels and drama. Notable examples are many publishing houses in Nanjing: the Fuchuntang and Shidetang of Tang Fuchun,[183] Wenlinge of Tang Liyao,[184] and Chen Dailai's Jizhizhai.[185] Suzhou publishers such as Feng Menglong (1574–1646) and Ling Mengchu (1580–1644) were responsive to the expanding market for fiction and plays. Neither become an official until very late in life, but they were successful in their publishing careers.

A friend of Chen Renxi, Feng Menglong was a writer, playwright, and publisher whose operation appeared to be much bigger than Chen's in both scale and range. The publishing record of Feng Menglong and Ling Mengchu attests to the specialization in the areas of literary expertise and diversity in late-Ming publishing. Feng is known today more for his contribution to vernacular novels and drama. But his interests in commenting upon and editing literary works like short stories and dramas were in fact intimately tied to his publishing business.[186]

Like all ambitious and talented young men, Feng Menglong sought to pursue an official career. He belabored assiduously but, like the majority, had little luck in success for more than forty years. Finally, he was chosen as a "presented student" (*gongsheng*) in 1630 and was appointed magistrate of Shouning county in Fujian. He was over sixty years old when he took up his first administrative position. He stayed in the magistrate office for four years before returning to Suzhou, giving up his official career. Despite his final momentary entrance into the officialdom, he spent most of his life working as a tutor, professional writer, and publisher.

Following the example of most commercial publishers, Feng published several examination aids, including a commentary on the Four Books and a general history text.[187] Feng had requested a preface from Chen Renxi for his commentary.[188] While preparing himself for the examination, Feng took up tutoring in a Tian family in Macheng, Hubei. For his teaching and preparation for the examination, he compiled notes on the *Spring and Autumn Annals*, which he later published in 1620 and again with another version five years later.[189]

The range of books that he authored and published clearly distinguished Feng Menglong from Chen Renxi. Even though he published books for examinees, his publishing career clearly belonged to the more radical form of entrepreneurial publishing. Feng was part of the new generation of writer-publishers who approached the publication of novels and drama as a serious undertaking. Feng was the famous author of the popular books *Jingshi tongyan* (Vernacular words for exhorting the world)[190] and *Jingu qiguan* (Great episodes from all times).[191] In addition to vernacular novels, Feng's Moganzhai publishing house had published many southern-style dramas.[192] Despite their different publishing strategies, both Chen Renxi and Feng Menglong shared a typical trajectory of careers in both the economic and the political fields. Both had a long career in publishing but a disheartened moratorium on the imperial bureaucracy.

## Shishang *Publishers as Patrons: Xu Zichang*

Another category of publishers was men of wealth, who engaged in publishing more as patrons of literary culture as the means of establishing their places in literary circles. They were well-connected and often secured help from renowned writers and scholars. They published very selectively and mostly for the upper literary circles.

Xu Zichang (1578–1623) from Changzhou, Nanzhili, specialized in more restrictive categories. Xu's father has accumulated great wealth. Xu took the metropolitan examination four times without success, and at the age of thirty purchased an official position. He stayed in his office for only a short time before deciding to withdraw from government.[193] Like all wealthy *shishang*, he built a big mansion with a designer garden, which became a major attraction for literati who visited Fuli, Changzhou.[194]

Xu operated a Feiyuxuan publishing house. The books he published were targeted at the highly educated. He hired many scholars to compile and edit texts for publication.[195] Ye Zhou was a professional writer who lived on his literary skills, hiring himself out to patrons and publishers. He wrote books for publishers who published them as Li Zhi's works. Xu Zichang hired Ye to compile a book and published it under his own name.[196]

His friends were among the most famous scholars and artists, including Chen Jiru, Dong Qichang, Zhong Xing, Jiao Hong, Tu Long, and Wen Zhenmeng.[197] Xu's granddaughter married the grandson of Chen Jiru.[198] The network of scholars and writers he befriended provided him with ideas and helping hands in his publishing.

Chen's literary renown and his close connection to Xu rendered him an important source of guidance in Xu's publishing agenda. Chen suggested that Xu publish the works by the Tang poet Lu Guimeng, a native of Jiangsu. Chen also expressed his admiration for the poetry exchanged between Lu and Pi Rixiu.[199] Xu published both the collected works by Pi and the poetic exchange between Pi and Lu in 1608 and 1620.[200] Xu's son Yuangong, whose daughter married Chen Jiru's grandson, was also involved in publishing. With Chen Jiru, he edited *Dushu hou* (After reading) by the renowned writer Wang Shizhen.[201]

As a publisher, Xu distinguished himself from those who published a wide variety of genres. The books clearly showed a narrow focus on the highly educated community. Xu published collected works of literary figures such as Li Bai and Du Fu. His publication of the voluminous *Taiping guangji* (Comprehensive record of great peace) no doubt was meant to establish himself as a great patron of literary publications. Unlike most commercial publishers, he did not publish any texts especially written for students preparing for the civil service examination. Not dependent on the profitable sale of books, Xu could afford not to publish examination aids and instead published books with no market potential.

His interest in writing and in soliciting writers for dramatic scripts reflected his personal interest in drama rather than a commercial strategy. He supported private theatrical troupes that often staged plays to entertain friends in his immense "Plum residential complex" (Meihua shui).[202]

Another publisher who published selectively was Wang Tingna (1569?–1628), whose wealth and motive for operating a publishing house was similar to that of Xu Zichang. Publishing was a form of patronage and a means of cultivating relationships among the literati. Wang was famous for his contribution to the writing and publishing of plays. Wang, an adopted son of a wealthy Huizhou merchant, inherited a fortune. Like many wealthy contemporaries, he spent lavishly in building a complex residential property with lake and garden, the Huancuitang, which was also the name of his publishing house.[203] He published at least twenty-one books, almost half of them plays and songs. None of his publications was aimed at examinees.[204] He himself authored at least eight plays.

## Critics, Writers, and Publishers: Sun Kuang and Zhong Xing

The literary market provided support for former officials. Among scholars from Zhejiang who had written comments on texts in various genres in the late Ming, perhaps no one was more prolific than Sun Kuang (1543–1612). Qian Daxin, the renowned polymath in the eighteenth century, singled out Sun and Zhong Xing as two of the most popular writers of comments in the late Ming. Qian criticized Sun for his lack of rigor and competence in dashing off insolent comments on the Classics.[205] Sun was among a few who had left extensive evidence in his own letters regarding his involvement in commenting on various texts. Sun's writings offer a rare glimpse of late Ming writers who worked with coeditors and publishers during the process of producing the manuscript for publication.

Sun Kuang, better known in the literary world by his courteous name (*zi*), Yuefeng, was an official who reached a high position. He was already a renowned critic of examination aids and drama during his official career. While still in his early forties, he retired from his position of minister of War in 1609. He had written comments on and edited many books. His correspondence with his nephews, Lü Tiancheng and Lü Yusheng, who were famous playwrights and publishers, reveals with rare details the manner in which late-Ming literati participated and cooperated in publishing.

Sun was one of the most informed publishers in his times. His interest in new imprints was clearly prompted by a commercial publisher's goal of "hunting for" (*liequ*) profit. He watched the publishing market closely in order to determine what to publish. He corresponded frequently with his nephew Lü Yusheng, exchanging views on the selection of books for publication and information about the availability of extant editions of specific texts.[206] Lü Yusheng sought Sun's opinion as he worked with two other scholars on a new commentary on the *Rites of the Zhou*. His brother Tiancheng, while preparing for the civil examination, discussed with Sun his plan to publish a historical work on the Jin standard history.[207]

Sun Kuang, however, was not only a publisher with an eye for profit. His selection of texts for publication was guided by some intellectual orientation. He was particularly interested in seeing Classical exegeses by Han scholars published in Nanjing and Jiangxi.[208] His interest in Han works resulted in the publication of *Taixuan jing* (Classic of the great mystery) by Yang Xiong.[209] In making suggestions to Lü, Sun mentioned his preference for the publication of the *Thirteen Classics*. Lü, however, had his own agenda. He was interested in publishing a comprehensive anthology of Tang poetry.[210] He had a great plan. In his letter to Sun Kuang, Lü Yusheng mentioned that Wang Shizhen and another scholar already had an agreement to collaborate on commenting and punctuating the poetry of Du Fu. But they never got to complete the project.[211] Lü therefore wanted to enlist the help of Wang Shizhen to comment on the poetry of Du Fu since he was already interested in such a project. Sun, however, suggested that it was impractical to expect Wang to agree to such a task given Wang's carefree personality and his old age.[212]

Lü's attempt to seek help from such a towering figure in the literary field was not unique in his times. In fact, collaboration among scholars and writers appeared to be increasingly common in the late-Ming period. Sun Kuang edited an anthology of writings by Ming writers entitled *Jin wenxuan* (Selections of contemporary writings), which was published in 1603.[213] What is particularly revealing is the exchange between Sun and two other editors: Tang Hezheng, son of Tang Shunzhi, and Yu Yin, a native of Jin county, Zhejiang. As chief editor, Sun discussed and reviewed the selections and comments through mail. Sun and Yu commented on each other's selections. Sun conceded that he was not as good in commenting on poetry and invited Yu to take responsibility of the selection and writing comments.[214] But Yu and Sun failed to agree on the selection.[215] They did not even agree on the cut-off date for inclusion. Sun wanted to begin with those writers after the Hongzhi reign (1488–1505). Tang and Yu argued that the anthology was a major undertaking that needed to include writers from the beginning of the dynasty.[216]

The anthology was published around 1603, six years before Sun Kuang retired from office.[217] As explained in the preface by Tang Hezheng, who was listed as one of the editors, those writings that both Yu and Sun agreed upon were included in the "proper section" (*zhengbian*) of the anthology. Those that Sun had selected but had been disapproved by Yu were included in the "sequel" (*xubian*). The "proper" section in seven juans preceded the "sequel" section, which included five juans. Sun is listed as the person who made the selection (*xuan*), and Yu and Tang are listed as the persons who edited (*ding*[b]) it.[218]

It should be noted that the collaboration between Sun and Yu was undertaken in the field of literary production, and the relationship between the two editors was governed by conventions of the publishing market. Even though Sun was an influential official, in his dealing with Yu he conducted himself exclusively as an editor. The publisher's decision to include those chosen by both in the "proper" section and those disapproved by Yu in the "sequel" section also suggested the publisher's conscious appropriation of the differences between editors; he turned that practice into powerful evidence for the quality and authority of the anthology whose "proper" section was based on the consensus of the expertise of the editors.

What is remarkable about Tang's preface is the evidence of increasing use of paratextual space to inform the reader how the text came to be written and printed, removing any veneer of immutability that the reader may attribute to the text. Second, Tang's preface attested to the rising status of editors in judgment over literary excellence. The strategy of dividing the selection into "proper" and "sequel" serves to promote the idea that those selected in the "proper" section represent the truly excellent writings; the "sequel" conveys clearly to the reader that there is room for disagreement and differences.

Zhong Xing (1574–1625) was among the writers whose experience was similar to Sun Kuang's, but with a much lower level of achievement in the political field. He never rose beyond a minor official position but was a best-selling critic of poetry. While heavily involved in publishing, Zhong Xing was not a publisher. He enjoyed wide reputation as a critic, especially of poetry. There are at least thirty-seven titles published in the late Ming bearing the name of Zhong Xing as author, editor, or compiler.[219]

Because of his reputation, Zhong often received requests from publishers for his writings and works.[220] Zhong Xing appeared to have a good working relationship with his good friend Tan Yuanchun, also from Hubei and a renowned critic. Both befriended the celebrated Yuan Hongdao. Zhong proofread the manuscript of the complete works of Yuan, and Tan brought the manuscript to a Hangzhou publisher.[221] In 1614, Zhong Xing and Tan had a collaborative literary project on an anthology of poetry.[222] Their working relationship was much more congenial than that between Sun Kuang and Yu Yin. The anthology *Gu shigui* (Models of ancient poetry) was completed around 1617 and was published in three-colors by Wuxing publisher Min Qiji, who specialized in producing multicolor books.[223] Comments by Zhong and Tan were differentiated by different colors. It became a bestseller. Zhong also initiated literary projects all by himself. He was a great admirer of Su Shi. He undertook to edit an anthology of Su's writings, which he completed in 1620.[224] After he left Beijing in 1616, he settled in Nanjing. During the next two years, he immersed himself in reading and taking notes on the twenty-one dynastic histories. It was his endeavor to learn more about statecraft. The notes were published as *Shihuai* (The memory of history) in seventeen juan.[225]

It was common for literati to publish a few books under their own names. Zhong Xing, who published most of his books with commercial publishers, had published a Buddhist text and a commentary on Sima Qian's *Shiji* (The historian's records).[226] Several members of the Restoration Society had published books with their own publishing houses. Chen Zilong, a critic and leader of the Restoration Society, was not known as a commercial publisher. But he had published several books under the name of Pinglutang, including an anthology of Ming poetry, military strategies, and the voluminous work on statecraft essays, *Huang Ming jingshi wenbian* (An anthology of writings on statecraft of the Ming dynasty). He also published Xu Guangqi's complete work on agriculture and government (*Nongzheng quanshu*).[227] Gu Menglin, who had written several very popular commentaries on the Classics, operated the Zhilianju publishing house, which published the popular *Sishu shuoyue* (Concise exposition on the Four Books) that he authored.[228] It also reprinted a book with Chen Jiru as the compiler.[229]

The involvement of the educated elite, be they examinees or officials, in commercial publishing was indeed common. Moreover, collaboration among writers was facilitated by the extensive use of correspondence. The increase in the number of roles, including editor, compiler, reader, and reviewer, in the paratext of late-Ming books was an accurate reflection of the increase in the involvement of literati in publishing, and to a greater degree, of the cooperation among writers in selecting, commenting, and publishing new books.

### Xu Fenpeng: A Forgotten Best-Selling Author

Most of the above writers were not only famous in their times, they have since received scholarly attention in literary or political history of the Ming period. In contrast, there were many who enjoyed great reputation in the late Ming and have passed into oblivion. One of them is Xu Fenpeng, a native of Linchuan, Jiangxi. He was a prolific writer and publisher. His works were popular in the late Ming and yet reference to him is nonexistent in almost any genre of history. However, there are still numerous extant Ming imprints bearing his name as author, editor, commentator, and publisher that permit his rescue from the fading pages of Ming editions.

Based on information in extant Ming books, Xu was a popular writer with a reputation beyond his home area. He was an active producer of literary culture from the 1590s through the 1620s. Xu apparently was writing books to supplement his income from tutoring.[230] His reputation as a writer was such that he was able to publish his books with commercial publishers outside Jiangxi. Working for different publishers in Fujian and Nanjing, he had compiled, edited, and wrote commentaries on the Classics,[231] drama, novels,[232] as well as almanacs.[233] He worked with Fujian publishers such as the famous Santaiguan.[234] Unlike many literati whose collection of personal writings were published privately, Xu's completed works were published in 1608, by a Nanjing publishing house, Guangqitang. Before that year, he had already published at least twelve books.[235]

Like other writers, Xu Fenpeng occasionally financed his own publications. His commentary on *The Western Chamber* was issued under his own name, suggesting his own financing of the publication. Other publications were clearly produced by commercial publishers. He wrote a commentary on the *Book of Songs* for examinees for a Nanjing publisher.[236]

Xu criticized the common practice of including prefaces by reputable masters to accentuate the value of the book. He insisted on writing prefaces for his own books. He asked, "Why can one be a reputable master oneself and leave his name to posterity?"[237] Most of the books he edited do not include prefaces by reputable masters.[238] Xu's reason for using his own prefaces is obvious in light of the preface's function as the most effective way to increase the writer's visibility in print. While it was in the interest of the publisher to include many prefaces by reputable masters as a marketing strategy, the writers themselves might find it offensive to be dependent on the authority of other writers. His refusal to publicize other writers' names in the paratext of his books could have been the cause of his fleeting fame.

The obscurity of Xu Fenpeng is startling when one considers the large number of extant books from the late Ming that still bear his name. This lack of intertextual reference to Xu, and his absence in the expanding paratextual space, greatly reduced his visibility in the conventional history of literary culture of the period. It was the extant books that help to salvage him from eternal obscurity. But no doubt numerous others whose books in fewer number have been lost completely to history with the perishing of the physical evidence of their involvement in publishing.

## Best-Selling Authors: Li Zhi, Jiao Hong, and Yuan Hongdao

Li Zhi, Jiao Hong (1541–1620), and Yuan Hongdao (1568–1610) were the best-selling authors par excellence in the late Ming. The role of Li Zhi in late-Ming publishing has been dubious. Attention given to his radical ideas has overshadowed the important issue of his involvement in publishing. It is common knowledge that many books published in the late sixteenth and early seventeenth centuries listed him as author and commentator. And it is often assumed that most of the works were falsely attributed to him by commercial publishers. Li Zhi or his alias, Li Zhuowu, had become household names, and publishers everywhere found the names useful in selling their books. His books were very popular in Nanjing.[239] Apart from *Fenshu* (Book to be burnt) and *Chutan ji* (Collection from the first pond), *Li Zhuowu piping zhongyi Shuihu quanzhuan* (Li Zhuowu's comments on the romance of loyalists in *The Water Margin*) has generated much controversy over authenticity of the critic.

After withdrawal from government office in 1580, Li Zhi had lived almost as a recluse with the support of a small group of friends and patrons. As Ray Huang points out, he depended on the very "gentry-official class he condemned."[240] Given his vehement assault on the hypocrisy of his times, it must have been a soul-wrenching dilemma to depend on those he criticized.[241] Against this background, there is reason to suggest that his involvement in commercial publishing through commenting on novels, drama, and literary texts was more the result of need than a pure thirst for knowledge and wisdom.

In 1591 Li Zhi wrote a letter to Jiao Hong requesting a copy of the *Romance of the Water Margin*. One of his attending monks, Wunian, was interested in it.[242] But Li Zhi himself had become enamored with the novel after Jiao Hong sent it to him. In the summer of 1592, when Yuan Zongdao went to see Li Zhi in Wuchang, Li was instructing his servant, a monk, Changzhi, to copy a manuscript that was a collection of Li's comments on the *Water Margin*.[243] The manuscript with Li's comments was brought to Yuan Wuya, a publisher in Suzhou by Li Zhi's disciple. Yuan and his friend Feng Menglong both were enchanted by Li's comments. Even though the extant edition had been changed by the editorial hand of Ye Zhou and Yuan Wuya, there is little question that Li Zhi commented on the fiction; Yuan Wuya hired Ye to edit and add comments before printing it.[244]

The controversy over the authenticity of the commentary is just another example of the danger of applying contemporary notions of authorship to texts of this period. While scholars in general agree that Li Zhi
did comment on the novel *Water Margin*, they are not in accord regarding the degree and level of Li's contribution in the two major editions by
Rongyutang and Yuan Wuya.[245] But it should be noted that Li would receive remuneration for the manuscript he sent to the publisher regardless
of who it was.

It is clear from letters he wrote to friends that Li Zhi did not simply
enjoy reading and commenting on books. He did it in order to publish
them. He read, selected, compiled, and commented on a wide range of
texts, from Confucian texts like the *Mencius*, the Four Books, and the
*Book of Changes* to Buddhist and popular morality texts like the *Ganying pian* (Treatise of retribution).[246] There is reason to suggest that Li Zhi
depended in part on critiquing and commenting on fictions and literary
work for publishers in order to either repay patrons and friends, or to supplement his income. When he was in Longtan, he had written comments
on *Mencius*, *Pipa ji* (Romance of the lute), *Xixiang ji* (Romance of the
western chamber), and many other literary works.[247] He even published
model essays on the Four Books for the civil service examination.[248]

Li Zhi was a great admirer of Su Shi. But he disagreed with Su Shi's exposition on *Laozi*. He wrote his own interpretation and sent it to Jiao
Hong. He thought that his treatise should only be read by a few and
should not be printed. But he deferred to Jiao's decision as to whether it
should be printed.[249] It might be true that Li Zhi took no active role in
overseeing how and which of his works would be published. Nonetheless,
he undertook writing and commenting with full knowledge and intention
that they would eventually find their way to print. The deference to Jiao's
decision to print the work could well be an expression of formal humil-
ity. Jiao Hong did publish two collected works by Su Shi that Li Zhi had
commented on in 1599.[250] Li's interest in Su Shi was deeper than a mere
appreciation of the poet's literary achievement. He decided to compile a
chronological biography of Su and promised to bring the manuscript to
a publisher in Nanjing.[251]

Albeit living away from big cities like Suzhou, Nanjing, and Hangzhou,
Li was intimately connected to his friends and publishers by messengers

and mail. The place where Li Zhi led a deceptively reclusive life was but one point in the intricate and well-connected node of communication and patronage in late-Ming China. The communication system included the official postal system and merchant and religious communication networks.[252] In fact, traffic arising from religious needs provided one of the major communication avenues for late-Ming writers.[253] Buddhist monks traveled extensively in the late Ming, giving rise to a relatively regular communicating system called "*sengyou*" (monk mail).[254] In different areas there were major monasteries where letters were sent and delivered by monks. One such "communication center" in Suzhou was the Wanglu (Kingly road) cloister.[255] Li Zhi and Yuan Hongdao depended on "monk mail" for their communication with friends and publishers.[256]

In addition to his friends who visited him, Li Zhi had at least two monks—Wunian and Changjue—working as his messengers. Similar to the commentary on Laozi he sent to Jiao Hong, Li Zhi did not always give clear instructions to the monks as to which of his works could be published. Since he did not deal with the publisher directly except his friend Jiao Hong, it was left to the liaison or the messenger, the monks, to make the decision. A case in point is his collection of notes entitled *Hushang yulu* (Records of conversations on the lake). Wunian copied it and took it to Nanjing to print without Li Zhi's prior instruction. According to Li Zhi's letter to Jiao Hong, he did not instruct Wunian to have it published.[257] It would not be impossible that Wunian made the decision in order to obtain adequate income to support Li and himself.[258] It could also be a breakdown in communication between the two. Either way, income from publishing appears to be an important source of support for Li's reclusive mode of life. Li did not just write and comment on books. He intended to print them for economic, intellectual, and personal reasons.[259]

Li Zhi's friendship with Jiao Hong provided him with the necessary liaison for commercial publishers. Jiao Hong, living in Nanjing, had himself published at least ten books, including Li's *Cangshu* (A book to be hidden) and *Xu Cangshu* (Sequel to the book to be hidden).[260] Li often asked Jiao to help him make changes to manuscripts, as if the latter was an editor for his books.[261]

Even though Jiao published books himself, he also sent his own works to other publishers. Jiao appeared to have a close working relationship with a Hangzhou publisher, Yu Xiangyun. Both of his major works were published by Yu.[262] No doubt Jiao had help to find publishers for Li Zhi's works when he himself chose not to publish them.

The literary activities of Li Zhi and, for that matter, all literati from the sixteenth and seventeenth centuries, must be analyzed in terms of their economic context. The meaning of their products was readily obscured and misrepresented by the producers. There is no question that Li Zhi had very interesting things to say about his times and the texts he read. His pungent criticism of pedantry and hypocrisy, flashes of brilliance and wit, and his maverick spirit no doubt explains the popularity of books with his name printed on them. Whatever laurel one would put on his head, he was a producer of printed commodities in his time. He was known in his time not as a "radical thinker" nor an "anti-traditionalist" individualist. He was a "reputable master," a best-selling author whose books were popular and read widely. He was known as an author throughout the empire, and books with his name were a sign of credibility and a promise of novelty.

Yuan Hongdao was another best-selling author.[263] Among the few friends of Li Zhi, Yuan was one who shared his strong interest in Buddhism. Yuan was also well known for his unconventional ideas, especially on prose writing. He was one of the three Yuan brothers who are regarded as the leaders of the Gong'an school of prose.

Compared to the majority, he was very successful in his quest for entry into the officialdom. Yuan Hongdao was appointed magistrate of Wuxian county in 1595. During his first year of tenure, he complained endlessly to his friends and promised to request release of his appointment the following year.[264] He was anxious to return to writing and learning.

Yuan Hongdao appeared to have good working relationship with Yuan Wuya, owner of the publishing house Zhongshutang in Suzhou. It is no accident that the *Li Zhuowa piping zhongyi Shuihu quanzhuan* (Li Zhi's comments on the *Water margin*) was published by him.[265] He also published all of Yuan Hongdao's writings from 1602 through 1608.[266] Like Li Zhi, Yuan Hongdao conducted correspondence with Yuan Wuya mostly through traveling monks.[267]

As a reputable master, Yuan Hongdao also worked with other publishers. He was invited to compile and edit an anthology of examination essays.[268] He once wrote a letter to a Mr. Yang, expressing his discontent with the changes made to the essays he had edited. He asked him to reprint them in accordance with the original draft (*yuangao*) and made no further changes. He also evaluated and commented on (*dianding*) the examination exercises of Mr. Yang's son, as requested.[269]

Yuan Hongdao's reputation also prompted a commercial publisher to attribute falsely to him a book entitled *Kuangyan* (Impetuous remarks). Yuan's brother Zhongdao found out and wrote to Yuan Wuya, who was working with Zhongdao to publish Hongdao's poetry. Zhongdao promised Wuya that together with him he would settle the matter when he went to Suzhou. Zhongdao planned to pursue the publisher and possibly bring him to court.[270]

Ironically, the book was authored by a Sheng Tingyan, a poor literatus in Hangzhou. During his illness, he jotted down some of his thoughts to idle away his time. Mysteriously, without his knowledge, they were published as *Kuangyan* under Yuan Hongdao's name. It was Zhou Yinglin, a commercial publisher, who published them as part of Yuan Hongdao's collected writings. Sheng later went to rectify the situation with the publisher and had the book excised from Yuan's book. However, other publishers reprinted the title without correcting the problem.[271]

## Printed Publicity and Textual Transgressions: Forgery, Piracy, and the Right to Print

The reputation of renowned writers and critics such as Sun Kuang, Zhong Xing, Li Zhi, and Yuan Hongdao was a form of printed publicity, which was a symbolic capital that publishers could easily appropriate. Appropriation of printed publicity took two common forms: forgery and piracy. To understand the complex issues involved in the practice of forgery, one has to look beyond the issue of authentic authorship and take into account the role of publishers in the production of books. Assigning an author to a book is one of many strategies the author and publisher can choose to maximize the book's appeal and sale. There is more than one way to "sign" a book. According to Gerald Genette, depending on the use to which the book is put, the name of the author can appear in three basic forms: *onymity*, *pseudonymity*, and *anonymity*. When the author signs his or her name, it is onymity. When a false, fictional, or borrowed name is assigned, it is pseudonymity. When the author or publisher decides to leave the book unsigned, the mode of authorship is anonymity.[272]

For Genette, pseudonymity includes both borrowed and invented names. Perhaps we can reserve pseudonymity for invented names and coin a new term for the mode of signing someone else's name. The name of an already well-known writer is not fictional. It is the misapplication of a name to a book. This false relationship between the author and the text can be given a different name, *misonymity*, a name misplaced. This distinction between misonymity and pseudonymity is useful because they serve different functions for the publisher.

When a certain writer attained a high reputation, his name would be used as evidence of credibility and a marker of excellence. While pseudonymity and anonymity are modes often used to shun legal responsibility, misonymity was the result of marketing strategy. The actual author of the book was inconsequential to the sale of the book. Misonymity is an appropriation by a publisher of the printed publicity of a literary celebrity.

Books had been falsely attributed to persons for a great variety of reasons. "Forgery of a kind is as old as textual authority," as the Renaissance scholar Anthony Grafton has observed.[273] Forgers often committed their crime in order to secure patronage or to defend or advance an expository position.[274] In the case of late-Ming China, however, transgressions of misonymity were commonly committed by publishers as a marketing strategy.

It should be noted that when forgeries were discovered, there were ways to rectify the situation. Feng Menglong, in *Zhinang* (Repository of wisdom), juan 28, recorded the extensive problem of piracy in publishing. Publishing in Suzhou was a very profitable business, but all publishers had to deal with the problem of piracy. Publisher Yu Shanzhang adopted a strategy of advanced warning in order to prevent his book from being pirated. Before he published the book *Tang leihan* (Anthology of writings in categories), he filed a case with the magistrate office, making a false report that copies of his new book had been stolen. A reward was posted for the thief of the books. No one dared to pirate the book, which sold out and made him a great profit.[275]

Tang Dazhen, the son-in-law of Chen Jiru, published the writings of Chen. They were pirated by a Suzhou publisher. Tang filed a case with local government at both the county and the prefectural levels. The authorities succeeded in tracing the publisher, punishing him, and destroying his woodblocks. In order to prevent piracy and discourage potential attempts, Tang included the incident in his "editorial principles" of a new collection of Chen Jiru's prose. In the last principle, Tang solicited afterword and laudatory essays for Chen's volume. Those who were interested were advised to mail it to his publishing house, Jianluju in Hangzhou.[276]

Despite the rampant piracy in commercial publishing in the late Ming, persistent publishers with adequate connections were able to prevent and stop pirated editions. Lin Chao'en, the founder of the Religion of Union of the Three Teachings (*Sanyi jiao*) had attracted a large following from every walk of life.[277] Shrines were built to honor him after his death. His followers assiduously promoted his teachings by holding meetings and publishing his writings. In 1627, Yan Jiugao, an owner of a bookstore, hired Pan Jiuhua to write a novel based on the story of Lin Chao'en. The novel, *Sanjiao kaimi yanyi* (Romance of the three teachings exposing delusions and returning to truth), was a satire, poking fun of Lin and his teachings. Lin's followers were enraged and filed a complaint with the local authorities. Yan appealed to his friends, who were students at the Imperial Academy, to mediate and finally agreed to destroy the woodblocks of the novel.[278] Although this case was not related to the piracy of books, it offers us an example of how the publication of a book could be traced and stopped.[279]

Li Yu, the well-known playwright and publisher, encountered the problem of piracy when he operated his publishing house in Nanjing. Many of his books were the target of pirated editions. When he learned that publishers in Suzhou were planning to pirate his newly published book, he went to notify the censor of the Suzhou and Songjiang circuits (Su-Song dao) and urged him to issue public notice against pirating his book. Unfortunately, while those Suzhou publishers eventually abandoned their plans, he received news from his family that publishers in Hangzhou had already completed a pirated edition, and the books were available for sale. Since he was preoccupied with other business in Suzhou, he sent his son-in-law to file a case against the publisher in Hangzhou before he could personally go there to settle the case.[280]

A few observations can be made of the above cases regarding the prob-

lem of forgery and the ability of late-Ming publishers to deal with pirating. Piracy was common, and some publishers in Hangzhou and Suzhou
sought to pirate books by popular authors such as Chen Jiru and Li Yu.
The above cases are significant in several ways. First, Chen Jiru's reputation is marketable and Chen and his son-in-law were able to track down
and punish publishers who pirated his books. Pirating books was a risky
business. Those who committed the crime were not left unpunished. False
attribution of his name was not the only problem; Chen would not allow
publishers to attribute prefaces to him because both his writings and name
were commodities. Since he was a professional writer, a request from a
publisher for his service would be just a normal commission from a patron. Publishers would not have to worry about legal problems if they just
paid him the fee for a preface. The case of Li Yu is interesting because it
reveals that commercial espionage was obviously a common practice.
Suzhou and Hangzhou publishers had found a way to obtain a copy of
the text and was able to carve the blocks while Li Yu's own book was still
in production. It clearly reveals the competitive nature of commercial
publishing and the effectiveness of publishers in production. That the disciples of Lin Chao'en were able to force the publisher to destroy the
blocks of the novel was indicative of the fact that commercial publishing
could not operate in complete secrecy.

Even though local government officials appeared to be responsive to
complaints of piracy, publishers themselves often had to file the case
themselves. Unlike in prerevolutionary France, where books were published by licensed publishers, local officials in late-Ming China did not
have knowledge of pirated books because publishers were not required to
submit books for review before publication was approved. Only with the
publishers' complaints would pirated editions be identified, traced, and
confiscated.[281]

European and Chinese publishers in the sixteenth and seventeenth centuries had to protect their financial investments, whether they called it
"copyright" or simply the idea of owning the right to carve woodblocks
for a text. This idea is clearly articulated in the phrase *"fanke bijiu"* (recarving the blocks will be brought to trial) which appeared in many
books. The publisher was recognized as having a sort of "right" to print
a specific text because he had paid to acquire the manuscript and carve

the blocks. The Chinese term *banquan* (right of the blocks) is used today as a translation for the concept of copyright. It is an appropriate term for the practice and belief that the "right to print" involves both the right to carve the blocks and the right to make copies from them. The right to carve the blocks includes the rights to reproduce the original text, which the publisher bought from the author or editor or his hired literati. The punishment for piracy involved therefore the destruction of the blocks (*huiban*), which the pirating publisher did not have the right to carve because he did not own the original text. Officials destroyed the blocks of a publisher who pirated a book in order to protect the economic investment of the publisher of the original text. This stands in great contrast to the early history of copyright in Europe, which "was a history of control before it became a history of the individual's right to own what she or he created in words."[282]

The European concepts of authorship and copyright were intimately linked to the monarchist states' attempt to control through the licensing system of the authority that was transmitted through print.[283] Unlike their counterparts in France and Britain, Chinese publishers in the sixteenth and seventeenth centuries did not have to apply for permission or to pay dues to the government in order to publish works. In his preface to the writings of Li Zhi, Yuan Zongdao recounted that after Li Zhi was arrested, his books were banned for only a short while. A few years later his books became best-sellers again.[284] Without a licensing system or regulatory practices of guilds of printers, the imperial government would not be able to enforce a ban on books or control piracy and forgery.

The problem of forgery of late-Ming books became even more complicated when one considers the role of contributors. One salient trend in late-Ming book publishing is the appearance of a large number of role-specific titles assigned to the major contributors to the book. New terms proliferated to differentiate the new roles of contributors to the paratextual aspect of the book. There were various specific roles of the editor: "edit" (*zuan*), "finalize"(*ding$^a$*), "correct"(*ding$^b$*), and "cut"(*shan*); and their combination with the role of compiler: (*zuanji, zuanding, ji*); the proofreader: "read" (*yue, jian, can*), "read and finalize" (*jianding*), "proofread" (*jiao, jiaoyue*), or "proofread and finalized"(*jiaoding, canding$^a$, canding$^b$*). There are also a large number of variants of terms that specify the roles of editors who punctuated and underlined the important passages (*dian*, *dianding*). The various roles of a commentator include: "compile and comment" (*jiping*), "critique" and "comment" (*pi*ᵃ, *ping*, *piping*); and its combination with proofreading: "comment and proofread" (*pingyue*).

Even though these titles may not serve any practical purpose in differentiating the division of labor among the contributors, the increase in the titles and the number of names of contributing literati suggest a change in attitude toward print publicity. Those who participated in book production in the capacity of editor, proofreader, and compiler were interested in having their names published with the book. In other cases, when the publishers arbitrarily and falsely included names of "reputable masters," they did so to impress the readers, despite the extra cost of carving the blocks or paying the individual.

The impact of the proliferation of these titles on the readers is difficult to assess. The inclusion of these role-titles of editors and proofreaders, authentic and otherwise, could have contributed to a heightened sense of the need for guidance in reading. Or at least, the publishers and writers sought to convey the idea that their guidance or intervention was necessary in illuminating the meaning of a text. These paratextual elements served to create an authority for the editors and commentators, who held the key to the understanding of the text.

To conclude this chapter, I would like to make several observations on the impact of the boom in commercial publishing in the sixteenth and seventeenth centuries. First, the impact of commercialization accelerated the process of commodification of knowledge and literary production, resulting in a significant reconfiguration of the relationship between the economic field and the political field. Positions in the commercial publishing sector of the economic field multiplied to provide literati, examinees or otherwise, with an economic foundation to pursue a double career as a *shishang* writer or publisher. Commercial publishing had expanded to the extent that it allowed the literati to shift from a narrow and personal patronage network to an extensive and impersonal patronage network based on commercial publishing houses in Fujian, Nanjing, Suzhou, Hangzhou, and other emerging publishing centers. A much larger number of patrons now provided the needed economic support, especially for examinees and literati who had abandoned government service as a career. Patrons could be officials, wealthy merchants, publishers, and ordinary people who would pay for their literary labor.

Second, the diversification of the reading public was evidenced by the increasing specialization in literary criticism. The importance of literary excellence was no longer confined to the genres of poetry and prose. There were new genres that required competence in literary skills that conventional training in poetry and prose could not provide. There were specialized fields within the domain of literary production in which literati with a wide array of talents could make a reputation. Some were distinguished by poetry and poetry criticism. Zhong Xing headed the list in the field of poetry. In contrast, he was not an authority in commentary on the Four Books. Excelling in the field of Classical exposition were writers such as Huang Ruheng and Xu Fenpeng. In the area of criticism of the examination essays, most well-known were Chen Jitai and Ai Nanying. In plays, Tang Xianzu, Shen Jing, Wang Deji, and Zang Maoxun were among the better known playwrights and critics, although not critics of examination essays. Even though many traverse more than one genre, the publishers and the writers themselves had expected the readers to find certain names as commentators or preface writers in specific genres of books. There were writer-cum-publisher types of literati like Feng Menglong, Ling Mengchu, and Li Yu who clearly had genuine interests in writing, editing, and publishing vernacular short stories and drama.

Specialization within the field of literary production was firmly established in practice, if not in discourse. The commonly accepted criteria of "practitioner" (*danghang*) and "authenticity" (*bense*) imposed limits on what one could produce in the field of literary production. Few could move comfortably across the expanding spectrum of literary genres. A writer could not possibly be competent in all the genres. The commodification of knowledge and literary production required specialization and division of labor. This division was fueled by the explosion of new works and the need to establish criteria in assessing the relative qualities of the works. The skills of the critics were not the same as those with which a writer created a novel or a play, even though the two were closely related. However, despite this trend of growing specialization in literary production, there were professional writers whose name could be found across genres. The names of Chen Jiru, Zhong Xing, Li Zhi, Sun Kuang, and Jiao Hong could be found in books across the spectrum.

Third, a set of practices involving the manufacturing and illegal appropriation of credibility grew as a result of the expansion of commercial publishing: print publicity, plagiarism, forgery, piracy, and the idea of a Chinese publisher's "copyright." Chinese publishers and writers unequivocally demonstrated a conscious belief in protecting their ownership of literary labor and investment by various publishing and legal strategies. The notion of "copyright" found its Chinese equivalent in the phrase *"fanke bijiu"* (those recarving the blocks will be bought to trial). That publishers were able to bring forgers and publishers committing piracy to justice attests to the existence of a consensus among literary producers and officials that the intellectual labor and economic investment incurred in the production of an original text for print deserved legal protection from unlawful reproduction of duplicating blocks. An implied recognition of originality in the creation and production of text clearly informed the consensus and the practice of prohibiting and prosecuting piracy in the publishing world. Whether rendered as a "right" or a "privilege," *fanke bijiu* is an equivalent of the English term "copyright" in terms of the right to print.

The final observation is that commercialization of the literary field produced different impacts on the representational strategies of the Chinese writers and European writers in the period under study. The expansion of the career trajectory of many literati into the publishing industry only brought about significant, but not radical, rupture in the reproduction of habitus. The growing frustration and dependence on the literary market for economic support for their quest for political offices did result in the spread of hostility toward, and the complete alienation from, the imperial government. The institutional openness of the officialdom, however, continued to keep many from forsaking their expensive pursuit. Despite the presence of this strong tension between the habitus and the practice of the literati's *shishang* career, it was not strong enough to endow the literary field with the level of autonomy witnessed in Europe since the eighteenth century.

The lack of a strong assertion of a distinctive career identity as entirely separate from that of an official was responsible for the continued practice of misrepresenting their career history to the extent that its trajectory in the economic field was left obscured or unrecorded. There was at least one identity that could have been used for that purpose, namely, "mountain man" (*shanren*). But the lingering semantic ambiguity and ambivalence in which the title was used by Chinese writers and publishers bespeaks the apprehension and unpleasant experience of the *shishang* literary producers. Their experience with the expansion of commercial publishing was not consciously empowering and positive. It was registered with ambivalence, uncertainty, and a longing to forget and retreat to the political field.

Thus the impact of the boom in commercial publishing was subtle and yet profound. It was subtle because the language remained poetic and metaphoric through change in practice. The growth in critical language continued to cover the transformed nature of literary production. The exaltation of literary skills and the rhetoric of aesthetics continued to shroud the growing dependence of the literati on a changing system of patronage. Those who eventually made it into the officialdom desired to "forget" their positions in the economic fields. Even if the products of their literary labor were included in their personal collected works, they were stripped of the economic origins as they were represented as works of literary achievements.

The impact of commercial publishing was too profound and extensive to be forgotten and erased completely. The traces of thought buried in misrepresented literary conventions reveal economic information under the inquisitive lens. Commodification of writing and knowledge expanded and transformed patronage. Many now could find jobs tutoring, ghostwriting, editing, compiling, producing all sorts of writings, and selling calligraphy, poetry, and paintings. Their positions were located in the economic field even though their destination was projected into the political field, which appeared to be deceivingly close at hand and yet practically an impossibility for the majority of the candidates. For those who continued to entertain hope of entering the officialdom, positions in the economic field became critical in sustaining their efforts. Most died in those positions with their hope of entering the officialdom enshrined in their literary traces.

The relationship between political practice and cultural production in late-Ming China cannot be adequately studied in terms of the concepts derived from modern European experiences. In Europe the emergence of professional writing as a career depended on the book market because income transpired in a specific social structure where professional writers were excluded from the path of political careers. Professional writers such as Rousseau, Voltaire, Diderot, and many French writers held no public offices. They could only take up positions in the economic field. Excluded from the political field, they voiced their opinion and criticism of the government through printed words. Their literary skills were restricted to the realm of private production of writings that might involve criticism of the government. Commenting and criticizing the monarchy was the only way they could articulate their opinion on politics. Institutional structure whereby their literary skills could be translated into symbolic capital in the political field was almost nonexistent. The famed British writer Samuel Johnson could serve as a ghostwriter for his clients, which included priests and lawyers. But there was no institutional avenue through which he could gain entry into the officialdom.[285] Writers took positions outside politics and in areas that would hardly lead to political offices. The structural exclusion of writers from political offices contributed to the emergence of a conscious attempt to justify and defend their authority and privilege to comment on and criticize social and political issues.

In contrast, in the case of late-Ming China, literary skills were crucial symbolic capital that could be translated into political power if one chose to take the civil examinations through the metropolitan level. It could also be translated into economic value through selling one's literary products in the literary market. The possession of literary skills in the late Ming allowed the literati the options of concentrating on a political career, or on a writing career, or in many cases a career that traversed both the economic and the political fields. The fact that the gate of officialdom was open despite a small graduation quota at every examination kept many from abandoning completely their attempt to seek success at the examinations. To a considerable extent, one can argue that the boom in commercial publishing in the late Ming allowed more candidates to keep their hopes alive of obtaining an official career despite their continual subjugation to the humiliating and expensive ordeal. It is precisely the presence of this two-track career structure that diffused the tension and antagonism between the literati and the imperial government, allowing the absorption of more literati in the pursuit of political offices.

The discrepancy between practice—two tracks and literati's representational preference of the political track—needs to be considered when comparing the rhetoric of the European professional writers and the Chinese literati's writing on publishing. For European writers, to glorify the impact of publishing, the freedom of expression, and freedom of the press is to claim a different but legitimate social space for criticizing the government. The worth of the writers themselves, the value of their writing, received no justification in the rhetoric of cultural production dominated by the church and monarchy in the medieval period. The discursive space needed to be opened, justified, and defended. In contrast, there was no such need in late-Ming China. Unlike in eighteenth-century France, expansion of commercial publishing in China in the sixteenth and seventeenth centuries did not produce a growing group of discontented, antagonistically critical, and increasingly secular producers of print. If printing did not precipitate radical social and political change in late imperial China, it was not because China failed to develop the movable-type method, nor because woodblock printing was a primitive technology. The impact of commercial publishing in early modern China was profound in its own unique fashion.

# 4

## Paratext: Commentaries, Ideology, and Politics

Since the late Qing, the civil service examination had been universally condemned for its stress on conformity to formalists and ideological standards set by the imperial government. Consequently all those who went through the system were trained in rote learning and indoctrinated with the official ideology. Benjamin Elman has argued cogently that the civil service examination was a "masterpiece of social, political, and cultural production," linking the imperial state, the gentry, and the Confucian orthodoxy into a strong whole from the Song until 1905.[1] The social, cultural, and political functions of the civil service examination system can hardly be exaggerated. Benjamin Elman goes as far as calling the examination compounds a "cultural prison."[2] This view underscores the overdetermining power of the civil service examination in domesticating the Chinese literary elites, treating them as docile conformists of the imperial system.[3]

There are two problems with this approach. First, it exaggerates the ideological coherence and the indoctrinating power of the civil service examination. This view fails to recognize the various ways the literati could resist and even subvert the official ideology. Such a view comes close to the theoretical position of Michel Foucault, who attributes hegemonic power to the institutions and discourses of the dominant ruling group, treating the dominated classes as passive victims.[4] By emphasizing that the civil examination system was an instrument of the imperial government, Elman is attributing a homogeneity to the effect of the civil service examination that neglects the dynamics of the interaction and negotiation between the imperial government and the examinees from various social backgrounds.[5] There are many factors that need to be considered. One concerns the control over the interpretation of the Confucian canon, which in turn had a direct impact on the learning process of the examinees. Publishing played a significant role in the battle between the imperial government and the examinees in controlling the interpretation of the Confucian canons.

Power can only be exercised with the participation of the weak in institutions and practices formally controlled by the ruling group. We have to look beyond the simple institutional and formal controls imposed by the imperial court to discover how the civil service examination was in fact an arena where no one single group could establish absolute dominance. There were other factors—social, economic, and technological—that were part of the matrix in which the drama of power struggle unfolded. In the late Ming, one of the important factors that changed the rules of the game in the examination arena was commercial publishing.

Commercial publishing shaped the practice of examinees in their preparation for the civil service examination. The function of the civil service examination as a means of ideological control was significantly undermined in the late Ming when many forces—commercial expansion, monetized economy, and the increase in eunuchs' institutional interference with bureaucratic operation—were battering the Cheng-Zhu orthodoxy, the legitimacy of the imperial state, and the hegemony of the gentry.[6] The expansion of commercial printing during the sixteenth and early seventeenth centuries had contributed to the unlocking of the relationship between the imperial state, the gentry elite, and the Cheng-Zhu Confucian orthodoxy. Expansion in commercial printing had contributed to the creation of an intellectual milieu that encouraged open and pluralistic interpretations of the Confucian canon in the civil service examination.

## Publishing, Paratexts, and Reading as Resistance

Michel de Certeau criticizes such Foucaultian analysis that privileges the dominant group and posits a discursive hegemony over the dominated. He argues that Foucault has selected and thus isolated certain discourses that privilege the dominant. But for him, "It is in any case impossible to reduce the functioning of a society to a dominant type of procedure."[7] He criticizes Foucault for imputing "coherence" to the practices he selected for analysis. That "coherence" for de Certeau is simply a priori. He argues, "It remains to be asked how we should consider other, equally infinitesimal, procedures, which have not been 'privileged' by history but are nevertheless active in innumerable ways in the openings of established technological networks."[8]

The boom in commercial publishing provided expanded avenues for the examinees and the *shishang* to negotiate, resist, and appropriate the imperial ideology. According to de Certeau, one of the tactics used by the weak in modern society is reading, one of the most powerful operations in everyday life practice. Referring to reading as an operation of "poaching," de Certeau points to the shifting relationship between the creativity of the reader and the institutional control by the dominant society: "The creativity of the reader grows as the institution that controlled it declines."[9] While de Certeau rightly underscores the tension between the reader's creativity and the ruling elite's institutional control, his analysis omits the constraining effects of reading protocols embedded in textual structures that the author, editor, and publisher employed to present the text in its printed form. It is hardly possible to read a text independently of its paratextual, generic, discursive, and political contexts.[10] An analysis of reading that leaves the construction of meaning entirely to the reader, without considering the important roles of reading protocols deployed in textual structures of the material form of the text, is oblivious to the complexity of the act of reading and the need to understand the role of the medium in which the text materializes. Giving full autonomy to the reader in constructing meaning of the text is no less mistaken than granting the text or discourse the same autonomy.

*Discursive Strategies: Paratext, Anthology, and Commentary*

The protocols of reading were provided by the publishers and the critics through mostly paratext. The expansion of paratext in the form of an increase in the number of prefaces, reading guides, references, and commentaries, and in the length of the appellation of the contributor and the length of title of the book, expanded the semantic field of the book, creating more points of intervention in the process of reading. The proliferation of commentaries and compendia of commentaries in the late Ming resulted in the vast expansion of the semantic field of the Four Books. Commentators offering dissenting exegesis came to challenge the officially sanctioned ones.

Commentary, as both peritext and epitext, came to influence the reading process. The authority was wrenched away from the imperial state via specific discursive strategies. Evidence of this can be found in an analysis of the material form of text and the formal structures that intervene in the creation of meaning by the reader. These textual structures can be included as the tactics of the author, the editor, the illustration artist, and the publisher. In other words, an analysis of publishing and the textual structures of the book is crucial to the understanding of the perimeters within which the reader could create his personal reading of a printed text. The manipulation of the textual structures of the book permits the employment of discursive strategies that set up the pattern of passage for the gaze of the reader. Since de Certeau's analysis of reading as an act of resistance by the weak still treats the text in its nonmaterial form, it does not include an analysis of the text in its material medium. To adequately examine the various roles of the material form of a printed text—the book in our case—we need to draw from the insights of literary criticism and textual (bibliography) studies.

Any analysis of the act and history of reading has to begin with a "materialized text," a text inscribed on a material medium, be it paper, film, microfilm, or the latest cyberspace. Each type of material imposes specific ways in which the text is presented to the reader or viewer. D. F. McKenzie has insisted that a text cannot be understood independently of its material form.[11] The notion of a nonmaterial text obscures the enormous role played by the formal structures of a printed text in the construction of meaning. The format of the book, its page layout, division of the text, and the symbolic conventions, are intentions of the author and the editor inscribed on the text to guide, or for that matter, to control the way the reader constructs meaning.

The textual and nontextual aspects of the printed book play specific roles in shaping the ways in which the reader makes sense of the text. For Genette the formal structures, both textual and nontextual, that constitute a book are crucial to the interpretation of a materialized text. Indeed, to find a text free of common trappings (cover, title page, the name of the author, the title, preface, notes, and epigraphs) is impossible. For Genette, "A text without a paratext does not exist and never has existed."[12] In his words, "The paratext is what enables a text to become a book and to be offered as such to its readers and, more generally, to the public."[13] A text can exist in personal memory and be recited in public. But it is private and impalpable. An immaterial text requires performance, be it oral or textual, before it can be rendered public. In contrast, the book, in our case, the printed book, as a materialized text is public in the sense of being inscribed on a portable material medium capable of being exchanged. Paratext is what endows a text with a public or objectivated existence.

The function of the paratext in any act of reading is crucial because it is the "threshold" where the reader look for information that will invite or discourage further reading.[14] The main reason why paratext is considered the threshold of interpretation is that a paratextual element can communicate a piece of information, make known the author's view of the nature of the book, and command how the reader should read the text.[15] In brief, "The paratext in all its forms is a discourse that is fundamentally heteronomous, auxiliary, and dedicated to the service of something other than itself that constitute the raison d'être."[16]

The paratext, the threshold of interpretation, is the newly expanded space where commentators on the Four Books brought to the public their nonconforming readings and political critiques. In light of de Certeau's analysis of the "tactics of practice," the paratext—different levels of commentary (*zhu, shu, jie*), preface, "editorial principles" (*fanli*)—contributed to the promotion of an open attitude toward the interpretation of the Confucian Classics.[17] To understand how various tactics were used and the conditions that made possible the use of those tactics, one must examine the various issues involving the production of meaning centered on the printed book.

## The "Semantic Field of the Book" and the "Circuit of Communication"

Recent studies in literary theory, cultural studies, and the history of the book have drawn attention to the various roles played by the author, publisher, printer, bookseller, bibliographer, and the reader in the production of meaning in the process of reading. These agents bearing different relationships with the book constitute an ensemble, a system in which the book is produced, packaged, distributed, ordered, read, and used.

Robert Darnton refers to this ensemble of persons as constituting "the circuit of communication."[18] But to underscore the communication aspect of this circuit is to privilege communication over other equally, if not more important, aspects of this circuit. This characterization of the circuit is not so much wrong as it is narrow in regard to the issue of how meanings can be produced. The metaphor of a circuit evokes the idea of fixed patterns of routes for messages to travel. Even though signals can take many routes, they are fixed. In contrast, the notion of "field" is not associated with regularity and pattern. It is compatible with forces, institutions, and agents in multiple ways of interaction. It favors a multiplicity of meanings, ambiguities, and productions of new meanings by users of the book. The points in the circuit function like relays that transmit the same message until they reach the reader. But in view of the complexity in the production of meanings this metaphor of "circuit" fails to register the numerous ways in which a sign—textual and iconic—can be encoded and recoded during the process of meaning production.

I propose to conceptualize these points of book production, materialization, distribution, generic classification, and reading as a "semantic field of the book." At every point the meaning transmitted can be passed on to the next relay either unchanged or in an altered mode. But it can also be resisted, modified, subverted, and negotiated. This notion of "field" corresponds better with the heteronomous nature of the discourse conveyed in the paratextual elements, which allow conflicting, competing, and heterogeneous signification to exist, presenting to the reader a great variety of ways in which meaning can be constructed.[19]

Even though the readers are travelers, moving "across lands belonging to someone else, like nomads poaching their way across fields they did not write," there are landmarks, existing trails, man-made structures that facilitate or hinder their movement.[20] There are specific sets of mechanisms at each point that will allow the agent to intervene in the production of meaning. It is impossible to freeze the meaning of a text because total control of the production of meaning at all the points cannot be achieved. These specific sets of mechanisms can be used to compare the role of publishing in Chinese and European history, thereby revealing the different impacts of printing in a comparative perspective without using a modernist viewpoint that privileges technology as the driving force in the dissemination of knowledge and ideas.

The production of meaning or the meaning of a materialized text can be generated when the author produces the manuscript; it continues with the modification and packaging by adding paratexts by the editor and publisher, and culminates with the bookseller, bibliographer, and buyer and reader of the book. At each of these points, meaning can be changed, added, and suppressed. It is therefore not only about how meaning is transmitted but how it is inscribed by means of textual devices and paratexts. Therefore, these points are not relays where the signal is transmitted but rather points where meanings can be produced, negotiated, or suppressed, and even subverted.

Darnton's notion of "circuit of communication" is still useful because it can be used to designate *an effect* produced in the "semantic field of the book" through mechanisms of control internal and external to the system—censorship, licensing system, control of book trade, and hermeneutical devices such as reading protocols embedded in the paratextual elements of preface, commentary, and generic classification. Censorship, reading protocols, and paratexts are means whereby government, authors, and critics employ to produce an effect of the circuit of communication, that is, a pattern of fixed route signals that can be transmitted to the targeted recipient—the reader. This effect of "circuit of communication," however, can never be total. Its efficacy depends on how effectively all the points of intervention are controlled. But commercial publishing rendered it increasingly difficult for any single agent, including the government, to turn the semantic field of the book into a communication circuit.

Any government seeking to disseminate an ideology through printed books will strive to turn the semantic field of the book into a "communication circuit" that will suppress and eliminate different readings. As de Certeau has aptly remarked, "Textual circuit: applied political pressure (censorship), it would turn more into a communication circuit for the government, erasing or suppressing resistance and modification of the meanings."[21] The methods used by a government to freeze meanings can be positive and negative. Positive methods involve the employment of mechanisms to reward and encourage the faithful reproduction of the official ideology. Contests, awards, and honors are used to uphold models of conformity. Negative mechanisms often involve various forms of censorship and policing of the semantic field of the book, keeping vigilance over publishers, writers, booksellers, and public forms of reading.

In Ming China, the imperial state depended primarily on positive mechanisms for the reproduction of the official ideology—the Cheng-Zhu orthodoxy. Private academies were free to adopt their curricula.[22] Through the civil service examination, the Ming government distributed degrees to reward aspirants who reproduced official readings of the Confucian Classics in accordance with Zhu Xi's commentaries.[23] Differences and challenges were discouraged and erased as disparate expositions were rejected. To write and publish a commentary different from that of Zhu Xi's was a public act of disagreement.

## Commentary and Anthology as Paratext

A commentary is a derivative text. It can be a peritext as part of a book or an epitext with a separate material embodiment in another book. As a threshold of interpretation, a commentary intervenes in the production of meaning by filling gaps, illuminating obscure text, reconciling contradictions, highlighting muted points, and opening new directions of exposition as well as creating conflicts in the semantic field of the book. A commentary provides a system of protocols for reading. More commentaries written on the same text may mean more systems of protocols, resulting in the expansion of the semantic field of the book and the increase in the number of points for intervening in the reading process. Failure to control the publication and circulation of commentaries that offer alternative readings would undermine the imperial government's effort to maintain its ideological readings of the Classics. The boom of commercial publishing in the Wanli reign resulted in the proliferation of nonconforming commentaries on the Four Books and the Five Classics.

In the late-Ming commentaries were published as both peritext and epitext. While there were commentaries published with the text of the Four Books, a new genre of commentary did not include the Classical text. Only titles of chapters and sections were identified. This genre of commentaries is tantamount to a form of anthology, a further detachment of the comments from both the commentarial and the canonical contexts. As an epitext, an anthology of commentaries pushes the canon away from the center position it occupied by locating the selected comments as the text of a new book. The canonical text became a physically and visually marginal part of the commentary, existing in skeletal form with flesh provided by the commentary. Such reversal of the center-periphery relation, or text and paratext, was made possible by the publication of anthologized commentaries.

The physical separation of commentary from the text of the Four Books attested to the growing authority of the commentators, whose comments and selection of comments came to constitute the very threshold for interpreting the canon. Examinees striving to excel viewed these commentaries as their keys to success. These commentaries sow the seeds of deviance and can be investigated to document resistance to official discourse.

An investigation of the commentaries and anthologies of commentaries on the Four Books reveals the hitherto unexamined "tactics" of the literati and the publishers in their resistance and subversion of imperial control over literary production. These commentaries were published in large number by mostly commercial publishers in roughly the last half century of the Ming dynasty. They represent the objectification or actualization of the various readings of the Four Books and the Classics by examinees and scholars in print. It is impossible to verify how accurate these objectified readings compared to the readings in action, which left no trace. In theory one can speculate on the numerous possibilities in reading new meanings into the text, but without objectification, there is no way of knowing the mind of the reader. This is the problem with de Certeau's approach, which privileges the reader over the text, a reversal of the structuralist position. The protocols of reading and the textual strategies inscribed in the paratext by the authors and publishers need to be considered in order to understand the constraints imposed by the text on the ways it could be read. In brief, the points of intervention occupied by the authors and publishers and the discursive strategies deployed in the paratext cannot be left outside the semantic field of the book.

## Decline of the Government School System

The vitality of an ideology both as a political tool and as a discourse/ knowledge depends on institutional support in its reproduction. The government school system was one of the institutions that helped to maintain the validity of the Cheng-Zhu exposition on the Confucian canon.[24] The Ming government had set up a system of schools throughout the empire at the county, prefectural, and metropolitan levels to provide training to holders of the lowest degree. Government students were given stipends and were required to receive instructions from educational officials and were tested periodically. The school system helped to strengthen the position of the Cheng-Zhu exposition on the Confucian Classics until the mid-fifteenth century, when training at government schools deteriorated.

The quality of government students declined in part because of the lowering of the quality of government instructors at prefectural and county schools from the mid-fifteenth century on. In the early Ming, the government filled teaching positions at prefectural and county schools by appointing a number of distinguished holders of the *juren* degree who failed the metropolitan examination as secondary graduates. It became a standard policy that the "second class" (*yibang*) graduates were appointed as government instructors at prefectural (*jiaoshou*), county (*jiao-yu*), and department schools (*xuezheng*). There was great resistance to the choice of educational appointments among the "second class" graduates because the career track of government instructor was secondary to that of the regular metropolitan graduates. The government had been strict in enforcing such a policy until the mid-fifteenth century. Despite the general resistance to this option, some second class graduates were willing to accept positions as instructors at government schools because they were allowed to continue to compete in the metropolitan examination.[25] But after the *Zhengtong* reign (1436–49), the *yibang juren* were no longer allowed to take the palace examination as *jinshi* and were designated as educational officials, hence closing the avenue to career trajectories of the metropolitan graduates.

Educational officials at the prefectural and county schools suffered further loss in prestige and status when the government recruited mostly "presented students" (*gongsheng*) as instructors since the Jingtai (1450–56) reign.[26] Tribute students, usually advanced in year, were chosen from government students who had taken the state examination for an extended period of time without passing higher examinations at the provincial and metropolitan levels. It had become customary to appoint tribute students as instructors ever since.[27] By 1453, the inferior qualifications of the tribute students appointed as government instructors had already caused alarm.[28] The lower qualifications of government instructors contributed to the lack of respect for educational officials, and corruption was widespread among them. Regular officials treated them like slaves.[29] Geng Dingxiang (1524–96), a follower of Wang Gen (1483–1540), recalled that he had seen six to seven new instructors at the government school during his ten-year stay. Every one of them demanded bribes from their students in the form of gifts. They prostrated before students from wealthy and powerful families and harassed students from poor families, who often incurred debts as a result of extraction by instructors at the schools.[30]

The decline in the quality and prestige of the government instructors can also be seen in the banning of government school instructors from serving as examiners at the metropolitan examination from 1454 onward.[31] There was growing attack on the inferior qualifications of government instructors, and increasingly officials in the capital with *jinshi* degrees were appointed as examiners at provincial examinations. By the end of the Jiajing (1522–66) period, the number of government school instructors appointed as provincial examiners had fallen into insignificance.[32]

The decline in government schools was also a result of deteriorating financial support from the government. Government schools initially were endowed with land (*xuetian*) to provide support for students. By the late Jiajing and early Wanli periods, most schools had lost their land to poor recordkeeping, mismanagement, and local magnates and powerful gentry. Officials who wanted to restore the quality of support often had to struggle against local elites in order to regain the land that had been appropriated. For example, several officials, including Yang Tingyun and Zhang Nai, had strove to restore and reendow land to the Songjiang prefectural school.[33]

The growing popularity of "public lecturing" (*jiangxue*) and the proliferation of private academies has been explained in terms of the pervasive influence of Wang Yangming (1472–1529) and the efforts of his large following in propagating his teachings. But other factors contributing to the dramatic increase in interest in building private academies from the Jiajing period onward include both the dysfunction of the government school system and the increase in educational opportunities.[34] Except for those assemblies attending the lectures by popular lecturers like Wang Gen and his disciple, Luo Rufang, most who flocked to public lectures were examinees. The strong interest or response to the "public lecture" movement spearheaded by Wang Yangming and his followers could be explained in terms of the examinees' growing frustration with the inferior training received at government schools and the unbearable level of competition as well as the heightened concern over unfair monitoring of the civil service examinations.

Zhang Juzheng's (1525–82) antipathy for private academies and itinerant lecturers contributed to the gradual decline of the lecture movement in the 1570s. The political struggle of the Donglin Academy in the early seventeenth century further hastened the demise of the lecture movement.[35] But the fading of the appeal of the lecture movement was not so much evidence of the success of political oppression as it was the emergence of a new arena that changed the rules of the game of power. To a considerable extent, the gradual recession of energies in building private academies was hastened by the extensively felt impact of commercial publishing from the mid-Wanli reign onward. At about the time when the public lecture movement and the construction of private academies began to wane, commercial publishing began to grow greater in importance in the preparation of examinees and the control over success at the civil service examination.[36] The lack of an imperial policy over the control of printing allowed the commercial market to create a competitive environment in which writers and critics were encouraged to publish their personal readings of the canons. A battle over entrance into the officialdom was to be fought in a new arena, the publishing world, which no one could afford to eschew.

### The Cheng-Zhu Orthodoxy and the Sishu Daquan

Although the Yuan emperor designated Zhu Xi's commentaries on the Four Books as the official texts for the civil service examinations in 1315, the Daoxue school's rendition of the Confucian heritage did not become state orthodoxy until the Ming. The role of the civil service examination in recruiting Chinese officials under the Yuan was inconsequential.[37] The Cheng-Zhu *Daoxue* Confucianism became orthodoxy in the Yongle reign (1403–24) when Zhu Xi's commentaries were designated the official texts for the civil service examinations, through which all officials were to be recruited ever since.[38] Commissioned by the Yongle emperor, the compilation of the *Sishu daquan* (Complete compendium on the Four Books) and *Xingli daquan* (Complete compendium on nature and principle) contributed to further consolidation of the Cheng-Zhu *Daoxue* Confucianism as the official orthodoxy.[39] Together with the *Complete Compendium on the Five Classics*, these texts were given to government schools, constituting the core texts of the Confucian canon.[40] Examinees had since depended on the *Sishu daquan* in their preparation for the examination, until the Wanli period.

In *Rudiments païens*, Jean-Francois Lyotard said: "To arrest the meanings of words once and for all, that is what Terror wants."[41] Indeed, the promulgation of the commentaries by Zhu Xi as the official rendering of the Four Books was meant to freeze the meaning of the canonical texts, imposing a government-sanctioned reading of the Four Books, turning the semantic field of the book into a communication circuit. This "frozen meaning," or in de Certeau's words, "orthodox literality," depended on institutional support.[42] The freezing of meanings of the Four Books was achieved primarily through the administration of the civil service examination. Candidates who "invented" new readings breaching the protocol of the communication circuit of the official texts would be rejected. Success at the examination required reproduction of the official voice. The success in fixing the meaning, however, depended on the effective administration of the civil service examination and the control of factors that intervened in the administration of the examination and the training of the examinees.

While mastery of the Four Books needed hard work, it was not a formidable task. But to show one's understanding is "better" than others while not in blatant deviation from the imperial position is a mind-boggling undertaking. Differentiating one's own essay from others inevitably lies in the use of literary strategies that involved both form and content. To provide a "new" exposition of the Four Books while appearing to be within the parameters of rectitude was the greatest challenge for all candidates. The search for "new" ideas to render the Classics helped to create a great demand for commentaries on the Four Books from the mid-Wanli period onward. For this reason, for advanced examinees at the provincial and metropolitan levels, the use of commentaries on the Four Books became critical. Commercial study aids written for the Four Books were in great demand as well as in abundant supply.[43] Some even reached foreign lands, including Japan.[44] The unprecedented explosion of commentaries in this period changed the ways the literati prepared for the civil examinations.

## Commercial Publishing and Commentaries on the Four Books

In the early Ming, examinees read examination aids such as *Jinghua richao* (Daily notes at the capital), *Yuanliu zhilun* (The best discourse on origins), and commentaries written by Yuan scholars.[45] Xie Duo (1435–1510) already recommended the government to crack down on commercial publishers that produced these examination aids.[46] Commercially produced commentaries on the Four Books were written and published primarily for helping candidates to pass examinations. Since commentaries were inexpensive, all candidates, with perhaps a few exceptions, likely read this particular type of examination aid. Their degree of familiarity with these texts might have been much greater than their knowledge of the writings of eminent thinkers such as Wang Yangming and Chan Ruoshui (1466–1560). Furthermore, since these writings were primarily concerned for success, candidates must keep abreast of current intellectual trends that influenced the examiners. The commentaries can therefore be used as possible indices for change in the intellectual climate.

Zhu Xi's exposition of the Confucian doctrine remained largely unchallenged until Wang Yangming.[47] Despite his prominence both as a great official and a scholar, Wang's influence did not make a significant impact on the civil service examinations during the Jiajing period. Before the Wanli reign, there were only a few commentaries written by Ming writers on the Four Books. Commercial publishers were more interested in reprinting the official *Complete Compendium on the Four Books (Sishu daquan)* by Hu Guang than putting out new commentaries. In addition to the official edition, there were at least seven different publishers that reprinted the *Complete Compendium*.[48] Despite the availability of the *Complete Compendium* to government students, from the late fifteenth century onward several commentaries on the Four Books written by scholars became popular references for examinees. Three commentaries—the *Sishu mengyin* (Introduction to the Four Books for beginners) by Cai Qing (1453–1508), and later Chen Chen's (1477–1545) *Sishu qianshuo* (The Four Books made easy), and Lin Xiyuan's (ca. 1480–ca. 1560) *Sishu cunyi* (Questions about the Four Books)—had been popular among examination candidates until the end of the sixteenth century.[49] Despite minor differences, these three commentaries espoused primarily Zhu Xi's expositions.[50]

The situation began to change, and rather drastically, in the mid-Wanli period. Beginning with the 1590s, commercial publishers printed commentaries in growing numbers and multiple formats. The majority of extant commentaries on the Four Books published in the Ming were dated after 1572. Nine of the seventy-two commentaries reviewed for this chapter have no dates. Of the sixty-three titles with datable prefaces, only two were published before the Wanli period.[51] This dramatic increase in the number of commentaries on the Four Books was part of the general boom of commercial publishing in the late Ming.[52] Of the seventy-two commentaries, none was a reprint of Hu Guang's *Complete Compendium*. There were only two other extant ones published in the 1580s that were based on the commentaries of Cai Qing and Lin Xiyuan.[53] The majority of them were newly compiled or new compilations of existing editions first published after the 1590s. In fact, a survey of other lists of commentaries on the Four Books yielded a total of 163 Ming imprints, of which 131 titles were published during or after the Wanli reign.[54]

## The Ministry of Rites and Commentaries

The proliferation of new commentaries obviously had great impact on the examinees and their performances in the examinations. The Ministry of Rites, responsible for organizing and monitoring the civil service examination, was in constant vigil about examinees' compliance with Zhu Xi's exposition of the Four Books. Ministers of rites would issue warnings against accepting nonconforming readings by examiners. For example, in the first year of the Jiajing reign, a bureau secretary (*zhushi*) in the Ministry of Rites denounced deviations and criticism of Zhu Xi's commentaries.[55] From that time onward, the Ministry of Rites issued several warnings to examiners at the provincial examinations against accepting answers deviating from the Cheng-Zhu orthodoxy. But it is not evident that the Ministry of Rites was able to enforce the policy.

The situation became more alarming from the mid-Wanli period onward. Several ministers of rites sought to correct the situation without much success. Troubled by the spreading practice, Shen Li (1531–1615), the minister of rites early in the mid-1580s, recommended a crackdown on improper writing styles and references to heterodox ideas such as Buddhism, Daoism, and the Hundred Schools.[56] Shen specifically put the blame on examination aids printed by commercial publishers.[57] Similar warning was issued by other ministers of rites, including Yu Jideng (1544–1600).[58] But the warnings had fallen on deaf ears. To exercise the authority of the ministry, no essays by the graduates were published from the 1600 metropolitan examination. Only the model essays by examiners were included. In the preface, Feng Qi (1559–1603), minister of rites, criticized the widespread deviation from Zhu Xi's exposition on the Four Books.[59] He was so disturbed by the practice of citing Buddhist and Daoist texts as authority in criticizing Confucian texts that in 1602 he recommended burning printing blocks of the "new expositions." Feng himself complained that previous order by the government to burn "heterodox" texts were not carried out by local officials.[60] Four years later, another minister of rites, Li Tingji, continued to criticize the trend of presenting "new expositions" and the common practice of citing Buddhist and heterodox texts in examination essays. He promised to screen essays passed by local examiners and disqualified any who violated the official standards set by the Ministry of Rites.[61] Ironically, some commentaries bore his name as the commentator.[62] One commentary printed by a Fujian publisher for elementary level students bears his name as the author and also lists Shen Li, minister of rites, as one of the proofreaders.[63]

It is not possible to document how the reading of these commentaries prompted the examinees to produce answers that invited the censure of the Ministry of Rites. But authors of these commentaries were also readers of this genre of examination aids. The large number of critics and commentators undoubtedly introduced new ways to render the Classics to the examinees.

During the late-Wanli reign, examination essays hardly conformed to the official interpretation.[64] Many followed the trend of advancing "new expositions" in order to distinguish themselves.[65] Candidates made extensive use of Buddhist texts in their answers.[66] Gu Menglin, a member of the Restoration Society, lamented that since the 1590s, students taking the civil service examinations favored new interpretations and simplicity. The *Complete Compendium on the Four Books* (*Sishu daquan*) was abandoned for its details and banality.[67] Previously popular commentaries by Ming scholars also lost their appeal. Gu observed that by the late 1620s even the works by Chen Chen and Lin Xiyuan and the *Complete Compendium* were not available at the bookstores because commercial publishers no longer reprinted them for lack of demand.[68] As mentioned above, the commentaries by Chen and Lin primarily follow Zhu Xi's exposition. Gu and his friend Yang Yi strove to revive the Cheng-Zhu rendition of the Four Books.[69]

While the printing of commentaries conforming to Zhu Xi's exposition declined, commentaries offering different interpretations proliferated rapidly. Printers and professional writers began to play a much greater role in shaping the examinations through their control of the printing of examination aids. They decided what books, and hence whose interpretations, would be published. There was no monopoly of production and distribution of books. Competition contributed to the outpouring of even more "new expositions" (*xinshuo*).

In the absence of institutional control over the publishers or a rigorous censorship system that required the submission of books for review before publication, mere warnings from the Ministry of Rites failed to correct the problem.[70] Although many publishers continued to offer new expositions, they did not ignore the government order completely. They employed a variety of tactics to forestall government sanctions.

The tactics were deployed primarily in the paratext of the book. Some publishers stated in prefaces, as token acts of compliance with government policy, that they would exclude any expositions that criticized or contradicted Zhu Xi's views. But some writers resorted to a tactic that would allow them to include new ideas without risking the danger of being accused of violating the government policy. The author of *Sishu weiyan* (Subtle words of the Four Books), for example, remarked in the preface that new expositions would be included only for the purpose of exposing their mistakes. By including "mistakes" as one of the comments, he allowed the reader to review the new ideas. The reader could choose to ignore the author's caveat at his own risk.[71] This tactic would provide the author, or more precisely the publisher, the editors, and the proofreaders, with a safeguard in case they were accused of promoting heterodox readings of the Confucian texts.

Another tactic attests to the ingenious creativity and caution of the publishers and compilers of commentaries. They included new expositions that had been accepted by previous examiners. For example, the author of *Liaofan Yuan xiansheng Sishu shanzheng* (Corrected and purged edition of the Four Books by Mr. Yuan Huang) provided a list of new expositions that were at odds with Zhu Xi's commentary but were accepted by previous examiners. This tactic of appealing to precedents of practice had the advantage of avoiding culpability for insinuating heterodox interpretations.[72] The outcome was the same: they encouraged discordance with the official interpretation and promoted differences. The commentaries themselves testify to the possibility of disparate interpretations, hence undermining the authority of the Cheng-Zhu orthodoxy endorsed by the imperial government.

*Expansion of Paratexts: Titles, Editorial Principles,*
*References, and Proofreaders*

Many of the commercial commentaries can be identified by the format that divides the page into two, or sometimes three, registers. The two-register format features an "illustration above and text below" (*shangtu xiawen*) and is used in most novels and dramas produced by Jianyang publishers. Many put the main text of the Four Books and Zhu Xi's commentaries in the bottom section. The top section was generally reserved for the critic's main points, often called "purports of the chapters and verses" (*zhangzhi*).[73] There were many commercially produced commentaries that did not use the sectional format but can be identified by explicit and implicit reference to the civil service examination in the prefaces, "editorial principles" (*fanli*), or references (see Figure 3.1, page 112). Some explicitly stated that the texts were written for examinees.[74] Others included instructions for writing the "eight-legged" style.[75]

Publishers played an indirect role in undermining the authority of the official commentaries. Through various paratextual devices, the publishers, editors, and authors contributed to the promotion of interests in creativity and difference. Those who have dealt with publishers know that choosing the title of a book is often the result of a compromise, and sometimes a battle with the publisher. For the publisher, the title of a book plays a very important function in capturing the attention of buyers. As Leo Hoek explains, the title is "a set of linguistic signs . . . that may appear at the head of a text to designate it, to indicate its subject matter as a whole, and to entice the targeted public."[76] The title of the commentaries provides important information on the marketing strategies of the publishers. As Genette has observed, all three functions—designating, thematic or descriptive (information on subject matter), and targeted public—are not fulfilled at the same time.[77] This observation is useful in helping us to identify books that were intended to target a wide readership among the examinees. Some phrases in titles are clearly chosen to play no function other than tempting buyers, thus differentiating commercially produced commentaries from those published by private scholars.

Facing keen competition, publishers of commentaries sought to use the title to differentiate his product from competitors. Many titles on the title page are preceded by phrases meaning "newly carved"; others are preceded by *dingjuan*, or "best carved."[78] Regardless of whether the book was actually published for the first time, a title including one of these phrases claims to carry new information or ideas about the Four Books.

In addition to phrases that denote a new edition, many commentaries bear the names of "new ideas" (*xinyi*) or "subjective meanings" (*zhuyi*).[79]

To give just a few examples: Qian Zhaoyang's *Sishu huijie xinyi* (New meanings through comprehensive exposition of the Four Books), Dong Qichang's *Sishu xinyi* (New meanings of the Four Books),[80] Zhu Chang-chun's *Sishu zhuyi xinde jie* (Personal understanding of the meanings of the Four Books), and Guo Wei's *Sishu Zhuyi baocang* (Treasury of meanings of the Four Books).

Another paratextual strategy used by publishers was to include information about the qualifications of the contributors in the titles. Both official and nonofficial titles of contributors are used. Titles like *Hanlin*, *taishi* (grand historian), *huiyuan*, or *huikui* (first place at the metropolitan examination) were meant to underscore the quality of the contributors who were successful exemplars.[81] What is noteworthy is that the official titles of the contributors whose names were designated as the authors were eliminated on the first page of the chapters. Authors who were officials were simply listed with the same title as the compiler or the editor as "Mr." and "Elder" (*xiansheng* and *fu*). In *Dingjin Shui'an Tang taishi Sishu mai*, the title identifies the author Tang Binyin as a "grand historian" (*taishi*), a Hanlin scholar. But on the first page, he was only listed as a "*fu*" from the county of Xuancheng.[82] Many publishers were content to list simply the authors or editors as "Mr."[83]

The depreciation of official titles of authors suggests the growing sense that intellectual authority was not the monopoly of scholars sanctioned by the imperial government. In his preface to the *Sishu jiebo bian* (Liberation from the constraints on the Four Books) of 1617, the compiler Zhong Tianyuan criticized the recent enforcement by the Ministry of Rites that commanded compliance with Zhu Xi's commentary. Zhong conceded that examinees' recent abandonment of Zhu Xi's commentary as a matter of principle was ill-considered. But those who sought solution in banning new interpretations and accepting only those who reproduced Zhu's views were no less misguided. "Truth essentially belongs to the public [*li ben tianxia gong ye*]. Why insist on the need to be in accord with Zhu Xi's [view]?"[84]

As *minggong*, or "reputable masters," gained status as the arbiters of literary taste and intellectual achievement, the inclusion of "discourses of reputable masters" (*minggong yilun*) were deemed an important quality of the book. Another title that was beginning to gain popularity was *caizi* (men of intelligence). A commentary compiled by the professional editor Guo Wei, simply called *Xinjuan liu caizi Sishu xingren yu* (New edition of the enlightening words on the Four Books by six men of intelligence); the six men of intelligence were Ge Yanliang, Zhang Nai, Zou Zhilin, Zhao Mingyang, Qiu Zhaolin, and Zhou Zongjian. This title became a new ideal of literati, as Jin Shengtan selected a group of texts—Sima Qian's *Shiji* (The historian's records), *Zhuangzi*, Qu Yuan's *Lisau* (Encountering sorrow), Du Fu's *Poetry*, *Shuihu zhuan* (Romance of the water margin), and *Xixiangji* (Romance of the western chamber)—with his own comments and called them "Books of the men of intelligence" (*caizi shu*).

The readings of an intelligent literati were extended beyond the conventional purview of Classics, history, and poetry to new genres such as novels and drama. The choice of nonofficial titles for commentator and editors of these commentaries clearly reflected the emergence of the literary authority of scholars regardless of their position. Even though it was still a common practice among publishers to use official titles, many preferred to use "Mr." (*xiansheng*) or "famous masters" (*minggong*). These choices certainly were made by the publishers.[85]

Publishers also inserted a list of references in the beginning of the commentary. Many lists run to several hundreds of titles. A popular commentary by Shen Shouzheng includes a list of 226 titles.[86] The commentary by Tang Binyin lists 214 references.[87] When scholastic studies (*kao*) were in fashion from the 1620s on, the list ran even longer. In *Sishu kaobei* (A scholarly study of the Four Books), a commentary attributed to Zhang Pu, titles of references took up thirty-one pages![88] A variation of this practice was the inclusion of authors, instead of the titles of references. *Sishu weiyan* (Subtle words of the Four Books) boasted a list of 236 authors of titles.[89] A commentary by the professional writer Xu Fenpeng listed 561 scholars as sources from whom ideas were drawn, of which 414 were from the Ming dynasty and thirty-seven were Buddhists and Daoists.[90] The reference list provided a new space for the production of reputation for contemporary writers.

The paratext of commercial books of most genres continued to expand as editors included lists of ever-growing number of contributors as proofreaders. Some even listed women as proofreaders. In the collected writings of Zhuo Fazhi, printed in Nanjing in the mid-1630s, there are 128 proofreaders, including eight young ladies (*guixiu*) and eighteen Buddhists. The list reads like a who's who in the late-Ming literary circles.[91]

This general practice was evident in the genre of commentaries. *Sishu qianbai nian yan* (Hundred and thousand years of viewing the Four Books), for example, lists seventy-six persons as proofreaders (*canyue*) and thirteen as compilers (*jigao*).[92] Another listed fifty-two proofreaders from the Jiangnan area.[93] Gu Menglin published a commentary entitled *Sishu shuoyue* (Concise exposition on the Four Books), in which was listed fifty-three proofreaders as his disciples.[94] A commentary published in Nanjing listed ninety-six proofreaders, among them were famous masters such as Ai Nanying, Chen Jitai, and Zhang Shichun. The list in *Sishu yeshi yuan chugao* (Draft of reading from the Garden of Multiple Truth on the Four Books) includes 108 proofreaders.[95] Chen Zushou of Suzhou in a commentary unabashedly entitled *Examination Writings on the Four Books* (*Sishu fumo*) had listed as proofreaders the names of forty-nine friends and sixty-eight disciples.[96] Feng Menglong listed eighty-one persons as proofreaders for his study guide for the Zuo commentary on *Chunqiu*.[97]

The expansion of the list of proofreaders served at least two purposes. To the publisher, the long list was evidence of the author's qualifications, who was presented as an influential scholar with a large following of disciples and admiring friends. From the perspective of those who were listed regardless of their actual participation, the list served to "publicize" them as scholars. The reputation of these proofreaders was generated in the expanding paratextual space, which the publishing industries had contributed to create.

Paratext that can be easily identified as selling strategies of publishers included specific methods of reading and writing for the examination. Commercial publishers offered detailed advice on how to read the commentary, the Four Books, and the accentuation markers in the "editorial principles" (*fanli*). "Editorial principles" increased from several on one page (block page) to a long list that ran to several pages in a commentary on the Four Books (1594).[98] Yuan Huang's *Liaofan Yuan xiansheng Sishu shanzheng jian shuyi* (Commentary on the Four Books edited and commented by Mr. Yuan Huang) provides more than eight pages of "editorial principles" to the reader. In an extreme case, a compendium of comments compiled by Xu Fenpeng offered the reader seventeen pages of "editorial principles."[99]

Commercially produced commentaries often included clear statements regarding the purpose of providing help to students in the "editorial principles" section. In *Sishu mai* (The Pulse of the Four Books), a commentary with Tang Binyin as the author, there are six pages of editorial principles. The first one explains why it is call "pulse": "Each chapter has its own pulse. [The reader] has to look for where it begins and where it ends. So does each section. [The reader] needs to see both the connections and transitions between sections. Each sentence has its pulse. [The reader] is advised to look for the word on which the sentence is anchored."[100] The author is unequivocally giving advice to the examinees on how to read the Four Books as a tightly organized body of ideas. This reading method is not just any general method of reading but the specific manner in which the examinee needed to learn in order to understand the organization of the text.

Commentaries were published by private scholars that were not expressly targeted at examinees but could still be republished as such by appending methods of reading and writing for the examination. The monk Hanshan Deqing published his commentaries on the *Great Learning* and the *Doctrine of the Mean*.[101] These two commentaries were republished by a publisher who appended one thirty-eight–page section on the skills of writing, and on how best to prepare for and perform at the examinations.[102] By adding this paratext, the publisher repackaged Hanshan Deqing's originally private commentary into a commercial product. The comments by a Buddhist monk on the Confucian Four Books now entered the market of examination aids. Simply by appending the section to a Buddhist commentary, the publisher surreptitiously contributed to subverting the official ideology that Zhu Xi sought to establish in his commentary, driving the wedge deeper into the originally porous boundary between Buddhist and Confucian heterodoxy and orthodoxy.

Commentaries targeting beginner examinees would even provide methods of writing "eight-legged" essays. A commentary attributed to Zhang Pu provided a list of the standard procedures for answering questions in the examination.[103] Others included general principles for writing the examination essay. A commentary attributed to Tang Binyin had a section called *"Lunwen zongzhi"* (Major points of writing). One piece of advice for the examinee was to focus on the major points and structure of the essay rather than on the trivial mistakes or imperfections. It also reminded the examinee to spend some time on understanding the main point of the examination question before answering it.[104]

Commercial publishers took pains to fashion the commentary in such a way as to provide a model question and answer format to the reader. The first editorial principle in Guo Wei's *Huang Ming bai fangjia wenda* (Questions and answers by one hundred specialists of the Ming dynasty) speaks directly to the examinees. "Which literatus attained a high position in government without studying the Four Books? . . . [In this compendium] I compile various expositions, selecting those that are in agreement with the true meanings of the Four Books. I put them in the question and answer format so that the students can use them as a guide."[105] Commentaries targeting examinees would include questions that emulated examination questions (*niti*).[106]

In fact, some commentaries were published shortly before an examination with predictions of possible questions. The compilers of a commentary included a section called, "List of suggested questions for the first session of the examination for 1615 and 1616" (*Beini mouchen jichu dati biaomu*).[107] The commentary was clearly aimed at examinees preparing to take the provincial examination in 1615 and the metropolitan examination in Beijing the following year. This commentary must have been published shortly before 1615 and would have been widely available in bookstores, and even from book peddlers, before the examination, when candidates streamed into the provincial seats and the capital.

## PARATEXT AND MULTIPLE READINGS OF THE CANON

In various ways, commentators challenged and undermined Zhu Xi's interpretation of the Four Books. Publishers used a wide range of markers to highlight different aspects of the text. To indicate the main ideas of a paragraph or section, publishers used markers such as *mizhi* (secret thesis), *tiyan* (main point),[108] *biaozong* (highlighting the main idea), or *dianyan* (pointing out the focus).[109] Many commentaries have markers to show new ideas. There are a great variety of different names used to draw attention to new expositions. *Sishu yan* (Interpreting the Four Books), for example, used a *biaoxin* (underlining new ideas) marker to highlight the ideas of famous masters.[110] In another commentary, *can xinjie* (new exposition for reference) markers were inserted in the upper register.[111] Many commentaries with two- or three-register formats used the upper register to list the "new ideas" (*xinyi*).[112] The ideas of famous masters often differ from those of Zhu Xi. But even before the reader began reading the comments, he would first encounter the commentator's or editor's statements of purpose and their general approach to the text in the editorial principles or reading guides.

## Dissenting Commentaries

As mentioned above, most of the commentaries printed in the first quarter of the seventeenth century had dispensed with the commentaries by Zhu Xi and other Song and early Ming scholars. They were initially peritexts that had taken on a separate existence of their own. There are two possible explanations. Commentaries without the commentaries of Zhu Xi were meant to be texts targeted at more advanced students who already had committed to memory the text of the Four Books and Zhu's commentaries. It also assumed the possession of an edition of the Four Books and Zhu Xi's commentaries, and hence there was no need to reproduce them. The omission of the text of the Four Books and Zhu Xi's commentaries made them cheaper and faster to publish.

In this type of commentary, little information was provided to clarify pronunciations and meanings. The authors expressed no interest in philological and historical accuracy. One typical method of compilation used in these commercial commentaries was to list under each chapter and verse the "general interpretations" (*dayi*) by other reputable commentators.[113] Whereas the works by Cai Qing, Chen Chen, and Lin Xiyuan were commentaries espousing Zhu Xi's expositions, the new commentaries took great liberty in advancing new explanations that were often at odds with Zhu's views. The editorial principles of many commentaries displayed new ways of understanding the Classical texts. In Zhang Zhenyuan's *Sishu shuotong* (Discourse on the lineage of the Four Books), one editorial principle openly declared, "New names and truth [are heard] every day, [the editors] dare not adhere to their personal view for fear of confounding the great truth."[114] Many disagreed with Zhu Xi in rendering *Daxue* (great learning) as the stage of learning that followed "primary learning" (*xiaoxue*).[115] The author of *Sishu tingyue* (Understanding the Four Books through listening to the moon) explained *mingde* (illustrious virtue) in terms of Wang Yangming's "inner knowledge of the good" (*liangzhi*).[116]

Most commentators explain their approach to understanding the Four Books in paratext, especially in the preface and the "editorial principles." *Sishu shuocong* (Collection of expositions on the Four Books) by Shen Shouzheng was a popular commentary. In the editorial principles, Shen referred to the proliferation of commentaries that offered a dazzling variety of expositions on the Four Books that criticized and challenged Zhu Xi's reading of the texts. He argued that "talents arise in every generation with infinite creativity. We cannot dismiss their works based on the person." Creativity for Shen could be found in nonofficial history, stories, and fictions.[117]

*Multiple Expositions, Pluralistic Readings,*
*and Autonomy of the Reader*

This general emphasis on "new" or "subjective" readings of the Four Books should not be taken as evidence of the pervasive influence of Wang Yangming's teachings. They were in fact primarily the result of attempts of the compilers and the printers to offer multiple explications to the wide reading public of examinees, and Wang Yangming was but one of many Ming scholars that were gaining popularity. In the paratext of many commentaries, the compilers praised Ming scholars for their contribution to the unraveling of the true meanings of the Four Books. Often, Ming scholars were regarded as having attained greater achievement than the Song *Daoxue* scholars. In seventeen pages of an editorial principles section of a compendium, Xu Fenpeng explained why he had included more ideas of Ming scholars than those of Song *Daoxue* scholars. It was primarily because scholars in the Ming had made great strides in illuminating the Classical texts.[118] The predominance of Ming scholars in these commentaries unequivocally points to the present-oriented approach to the interpretation of the Confucian canon. The ancients like Zhu Xi were no longer granted deference when it came to unraveling the meaning of the Confucian text.

As will be shown below, some commentaries provided the reader with a wide range of possible expositions on the text. The references in these new commentaries were rarely philological, nor historical, in nature, but were "encyclopedic" in scope. The purpose of citation was not for the illumination of the textual meanings of the Four Books, but for providing new ways of reading the texts. Commentaries and annotations with accurate philological information would be of little utility to the authors, who were interested in providing the students with as many new and outlandish interpretations as possible. For example, in the *Sishu shuocong*, Shen Shou-cheng listed 226 works in the bibliography, which included the works by Li Zhi (1527–1602), Wang Gen (1483–1541), Wang Ji (1498–1583), Zhou Rudeng (1547–1629), and Yang Qiyuan (1547–1599). He made it clear that his references included a great variety of genres outside the Confucian Classics: novels, unofficial histories, and even Buddhist text such as *Chuandeng lu* (Records of transmitting the lamp) and *Hongming ji* (Anthology for spreading the illuminating truth).

In most cases there was no attempt on the part of the compiler to explain the differences and similarities between various comments on the same text. One author explained that the reader would benefit from contrasting views and subtly different opinions.[119] Many reputable authors of these commentaries were quoted as authorities; for example, *Xinjuan liu caizi Sishu shengren yu* (Newly printed awakening statements by six talented scholars on the Four Books) and *Guo Zhuyuan xiansheng huiji shi taishi Sishu zhuyi baocang* (Treasury of the Four Books from ten official historians compiled by Mr. Guo Zhuyuan [Wei]). Many of these reputable commentators had been professional writers before they became officials. The growing emphasis on the interpretations by contemporary scholars was also evident in other compendia of commentaries that often included scores of writers of the Ming period.[120] This inclusive approach can be explained more in terms of the *intention* of the editors and printers to attract more readers than an intellectual commitment to pluralism. Or in fact, it is likely that many of the published commentaries could have been simply the study notes of the compilers and commentators, many of whom were still examinees taking higher levels of examinations.[121] In any case, the mere listing of different interpretations and additional information would change the way the examinees prepared for the examination. In some commentaries, the compiler did provide his view of the correct exposition. In *Sishu gangjian* (An examination of the outline of the Four Books), for example, a boxed marker with the word "verdict" (*duan*) was used to underscore the compiler's preference.[122]

Readers responded differently to the text. Some could be puzzled and frustrated by the different views and excess of information; but others might find it useful to select, take notes, and come to an understanding that makes the most sense to them. It behooved the intelligent and industrious examinees to mull over plausible and reasonable expositions.

How did this new paratextual change (that, is the listing of different readings of the Four Books) affect the way the examinees read and understand the Four Books? A few speculations can be made to suggest how the commentaries might have affected the examinees. By simply listing a large number of different expositions, commercial printers made it clear to the reader that there was no absolutely correct interpretation of the text. As many commentators and compilers explained in the paratext, the text can be read differently and from different perspectives. The presence and positive recognition of differences in interpretation would encourage an open attitude toward the Confucian Classics. However, the divergent views forced the intelligent reader to make his own choice if he was to make a coherent understanding of the text. The choices presented to the intelligent reader underscore the autonomy of the reader in choosing and even creating his own reading of the canonical text. This does not mean that the majority of the literati would be trained to think independently. Even if, as Gu Yanwu and Huang Zongxi charged, commercial printing contributed to further emphasis on rote learning, the encyclopedic format of the late-Wanli commentaries nonetheless expanded the interpretive possibilities of the Classics. To be familiar with, and to entertain, different views of a text is not only acceptable but a normal and healthy attitude of a scholar.

## New Commentaries and Intellectual Trends

These commentaries, however, present some difficulties in establishing authorship because forgeries and false attributions were common. As Zhang Pu, the leader of the Restoration Society, had witnessed, bookstores in the cities were filled with all sorts of examination aids attributed to renowned scholars and high officials. In fact, more than ten different anthologies of essays were attributed to Zhang Pu himself.[123] The famed painter Dong Qichang (1555–1636) found that many collections of model examination essays bearing his name as the author had circulated widely in Beijing.[124] It is difficult to establish authorship of individual texts, hence risky in any attempt to treat these works as sources for ideas of individual scholars. In many cases false attribution can be documented. It is nonetheless unwise to dismiss all as marketing strategies of commercial printers (see Chapter 3). While false attribution was not uncommon, actual involvement of reputable authors in the production of commentaries was extensive. Many commentaries were authored by reputable masters themselves. Authorship is not the issue here; these works taken as a whole would yield valuable information about the range of interpretations offered to anonymous candidates.

## Wang Yangming and His Disciples

Among the several trends evident in the commercially produced commentaries was the growing popularity of the teachings of Wang Yangming and his disciples such as Wang Ji and Wang Gen. Wang Yangming's new teachings were already well known among the gentry during the Jiajing reign. When Ouyang De served as the director of studies at the Imperial Academy (*Guozijian siye*) in 1527, he held public lectures on Wang Yangming's teachings.[125] Wang's teachings gained greater popularity when Xu Jie (1503–1583), a disciple and exponent, became a grand secretary in 1552. The tablet of Wang Yangming was approved by imperial order to be inducted into the Confucian temple in 1573.[126] Wang's ideas began to appear in examination essays.[127]

If students were not interested in attending public lectures in which new teachings were often popularized, candidates would still come to know Wang Yangming's new teachings through commentaries on the Four Books.[128] The popularity of the ideas of Wang Yangming and his disciple such as Wang Ji was on the rise and it aroused criticism from exponents of the orthodox view of Zhu Xi. A commentary published in the late 1570s took aim at Wang Yangming's idea that *liangzhi* (innate knowledge of the good) is spontaneous.[129] Even by the 1590s, some writers continued to endorse Zhu Xi's view and criticized Wang's idea of the unity of

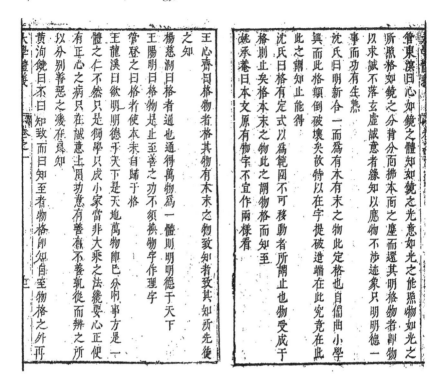

Figure 4.1: Folio from *Daxue tiyi*, a section in *Sishu tiyi* compiled by Shen Yan. Reproduced by permission of the National Archives of Japan.

the mind and principle.[130] But many commentaries published after the 1590s were particularly enthusiastic in promoting Wang's teaching of *liangzhi*.[131] Some even included Wang Yangming's polemical view that Zhu Xi in his last years regretted his mistake and agreed with his critic Lu Jiuyuan.[132] Others continued to reiterate Wang's rejection of Zhu Xi's "supplementary section" on "investigation of things" (*gewu buzhuan*).[133] What needs to be underscored, however, is that Wang Yangming did not command the highest regard among the many professional critics. He was but one of many authorities from the perspective of both the compilers and the readers. Figure 4.1 shows a folio page where a number of opinions are listed for the term *gewu* (investigation of things). Comments are from the commentator himself Shen Yan and a number of other scholars such as Guan Zhidao, Wang Gen, Wang Ji, and Yao Shunmu (Cheng'an).

## Daoism, Buddhism, and Syncretism

Another trend was the popular practice of explicating the Confucian texts in Daoist and Buddhist terms. One of the prefaces to Yao Wenwei's *Sishu wen* (Hearsay about the Four Books) told the reader that the author did not really understand the Four Books until he immersed himself in Buddhism and the writings of Laozi and Zhuangzi. In his own preface, Yao referred to himself as a *jushi* (lay Buddhist).[134] Yao actually passed his metropolitan examination in 1592.[135] This information about the Buddhist leanings of the commentator unequivocally identifies the commentary as a nonconforming exposition on the Four Books. The author of *Sishu shuocheng* (Explaining the truths of the Four Books) went so far as to dismiss scholarly commentaries and annotations (*zhushu*) as obstacles to the understanding of the Four Books.[136]

Guo Wei was the author and compiler of at least five extant commentaries on the Four Books.[137] His *Sishu zhuyi baocang* (Treasury of meanings for the Four Books) provided the readers only with the general opinions of the ten expositors who had no interest in philology. For example, one of the expositors gives a new twist to the meaning of the famous phrase from the *Analects*, "*xue er shi xi zhi, bu yi le hu*" (Does it not give one great pleasure to practice regularly as one learns!). He first quotes from *Laozi* the phrase *jue xue wu you* (when one abandons learning, one will have no worry), and followed by saying that "*shixi*" means the unity of effort and substance (*gongfu he benti*). Because of this unity one can speak of "rejoice" (*le*) immediately, and one does not have to wait until one has learned thoroughly to feel "rejoiced" (*budai xishu er hou le*).[138] The phrase from the *Analects* is quite straightforward and does not require much explanation. But in the hands of the commentator, it had become more complex and was brought to bear on the currently popular ideas of *gongfu* (effort) and *benti* (substance) in *Daoxue* learning.

With the quotation of *Laozi*'s phrase, the stress on learning in the *Analects* was in fact challenged and subverted. Laozi regarded learning as the major source of corruption in respect to human nature and individuality. Laozi's phrase unequivocally said that happiness comes from abandoning learning. This idea simply contradicts Confucius's idea of rejoicing in one's devotion to learning.

Many commentaries employed Chan Buddhist terminology. *Sishu shuosheng* (Residual meanings of the Four Books), printed in the 1610s, bristled with Buddhist ideas.[139] In another commentary, *Sishu wuxue wanyang bian* (My personal learning of the profound meaning of the Four Books), the Buddhist comparison of the mind to a lamp was used to explain the term "*mingde*" (illustrious virtues) in the *Great Learning*.[140] A commentary published in 1620 explicitly stated in the preface that it was through Buddhism that the author came to understand Confucian teachings.[141] This is reminiscent of Wang Ji's statement that "what Buddha taught is fundamentally the great path of us Confucians."[142] Many others explained in the paratext that insights from Buddhist and non-Confucian texts would be included.[143] This willingness to look to Buddhist, Daoist, and "heterodox" texts for new ideas was congenial to the various syncretic movements examined in many works on the intellectual development of the late-Ming period.[144] Printing and commercial publishing did not create syncretic movements, but they facilitated and popularized specific forms of religious practice, such as the recording of merits and demerits (*gongguoge*).[145] Publishers and writers played an important role in "publicizing" the syncretic approach to the Confucian canon.

## Hundred Schools and Han Scholarship

The quest for new ideas also led many writers to return to high antiquity for inspiration. Some relished in drawing on the texts by the "Hundred Schools of philosophers" (*zhuzi*).[146] Commercial printers had made these works widely available since the rise of the Archaist (*guwen*) school under the leadership of the Seven Early Masters (*Qian qizi*) since the mid-Jiajing and the early Wanli periods. The Former Seven Masters' interest in emulating the writing style of Han and pre-Han works had prompted the reprinting of the works by the "Hundred Schools of philosophers." The literary importance attached to these "Archaic texts" continued to animate the Seven Later Masters who dominated the literary circle in the late Jiajing and early Wanli periods.[147] These Han and pre-Han texts were not consulted by the Archaic writers such as Li Panlong (1514–70) and Wang Shizhen (1526–90) initially for inspiration in producing new interpretation of the Four Books. They easily found their way into the commentaries printed in the late-Wanli period, as these widely available printed texts were culled by commentators on the Four Books for new ideas.

The forgotten antiquity suddenly became a rich source for new ideas. In 1595 Chen Yumo (1548–1618) published *Jingyan zhizhi* (Insignificant meanings of the Classics), which included twenty-four chapters on the "names and things" (*mingwu*) in the Four Books. As a common practice of late-Ming publishing, these twenty-four chapters were also published separately as the *Sishu mingwu beikao* (Reference for the names and articles of the Four Books). Under each entry was listed a number of references. Among the work cited was a large number of exegeses by Han scholars, including *Erya* (Approach to elegance), *Fengsu tong* (Comprehensive record of customs), *Chunqiu fanlu* (The Radiant dew of the *Spring and Autumn Annals*), *Baihu tongde lun* (Comprehensive discourse of the White Tiger Hall). The citations often differed from and even contradicted one another. For example, under the entry of *xin* (mind-and-heart), one finds different passages, including the characters "*xin*," from the above books.[148] No attempt was made to reconcile or decide on the correct one. It provided philological information but offered no scholarly judgment. It is more like a dictionary of terms than a critical study, as the title "*beikao*" suggests. It is no surprise that Chen's work was criticized by the reviewer of the *Siku quanshu* (Complete library of the four treasuries) for making no attempt to come to terms with Han scholarship.[149]

In *Sishu zheng* (Corroborating the Four Books) *Erya*, *Shuowen* (On writing), *Baihu tong*, even the new text Classics *Hanshi waizhuan* (Han's outer commentary on the *Book of Songs*), and "apocryphal texts" of the Western Han period (206 B.C.–A.D. 9) were extensively quoted.[150] Xiang Yu's *Sishu renwu leihan* (Classified persons and things of the Four Books) and Xu Fenpeng's *Zuanding Sishu gujin daquan* (Complete compendia of the past and present commentaries on the Four Books) showed similar interest in Han exegeses.[151] Both works, however, like Chen's book, were not scholarly studies devoted to an accurate explanation of the persons, names, and things in the Four Books. They likewise showed no preference for a particular exegetical tradition nor did they make any effort in ironing out differences. Neither Han nor Song exegetical works were given privileged treatment.

In these works, Han philology was not used as a weapon against Song scholarship as it would be in the evidential scholarship of many Qing scholars in the eighteenth and nineteenth centuries.[152] That these ancient

Qin and Han texts were available for allegorical uses was in turn attributable to the publisher's efforts in reprinting them. If taken out of context, these extensive citations of pre-Han and Han texts could be taken as evidence for the beginnings of the philological movement that was to prevail in the mid-eighteenth century.[153] Nonetheless, the expansion of commercial publishing in the sixteenth and seventeenth centuries undoubtedly contributed to the reprinting of rare Han editions and to the printing of manuscripts.[154]

## Commentaries and Wanli Politics

Reading is an act of creating meanings, and writing commentary on a text itself constitutes an actualization of a person's specific reading. These books offered infinite opportunities for commentators to make the passages in the text relevant to contemporary issues. Indeed, there are numerous innovative and ingenious renderings of these texts that were written testimonies to the commentators' interest in political issues of the late-Ming period.

The Wanli emperor was notorious for many abuses and failures that were condemned by Confucian discourse on rulership. The dispatching of eunuchs as tax commissioners from the 1590s through the 1610s was universally condemned by government officials who belonged to the regular bureaucracy, whose members went through the ordeal of the civil examinations. The tax commissioners were censured as personal agents of the emperor, seeking to extract wealth from the people for the emperor's personal dissipation.

The legitimacy of rulers managing wealth through taxation was often addressed in the commentaries published in the period. In many commentaries, there was an increasing clarity in the distinction between imperial interests as private (*si*) and the subject's interests as public (*gong*). The conventional equation of government interests with the "public" and those of the subject with "private" was reversed. "Public justice" (*gong-ping*) in the distribution of wealth became the major issue in the maintenance of order. The final section of *Great Learning* explains how moral cultivation enables a ruler to manage the government of a state and finally to "pacify the realm" (*ping tianxia*). The specific virtue a ruler should aim to acquire is the *jieju zhi dao* (the way of being the model). The term "*jieju*" in the *Great Learning* refers to the model behavior of the ruler, who needs to be consistent in his dealings with his officials. The emphasis is on the effect of the ruler's conduct on the morality of the people. To illustrate this point, the canonical text continues to quote from the *Book of Odes*. The quote underscored the point that the virtue (*de*) of the ruler was the foundation of a state. Only with virtue can the ruler attract people to his side, and thus the ruler should set his mind on virtue, not wealth. If the ruler set his mind on getting rich over the pursuit of virtue, he would set a bad example for the people, who would then abandon themselves to the scrambling for wealth. Consequent upon the avarice of the ruler, the people would take leave and the state would disintegrate. The section concludes with the warning that the appointment of rapacious officials (*ju-lian zhi chen*) who pursued wealth relentlessly would bring disaster to the state.

In Zhu Xi's commentary, the proper attitude toward wealth and virtue was only one example of the model behavior of the ruler.[155] Many Yuan commentaries explain *jieju* in terms of the need to appoint virtuous officials while avoiding "mean people," thereby ensuring virtue over profit.[156] While this exposition was still current, many commentaries shifted the focus of their explanation to the role of the emperor in managing wealth and in ensuring economic justice as the public goal of government.

Shi Fenglai (1563–1642) won first place at the metropolitan examination in the spring of 1607, and a commentary with his name as the author was published later that year in Nanjing.[157] Commenting on the section on "bringing peace to the realm," the author pointed out that appointment of officials (*yongren*) and management of wealth (*licai*) were the two fundamental tasks of the way of modeling (*jieju*). And these two tasks were crucial to the fulfillment of the subject's moral obligations, such as filial piety and fraternal caring. But he argued that current commentators were mistaken in treating "appointment of officials" and "management of wealth" as two separate issues. In his reading, the ability to manage wealth was the criterion in the appointment of officials. The conventional emphasis on the morality of officials was replaced by a priority given to the ability of officials to manage wealth in a just manner.[158] Shi's concern for economic justice was particularly noteworthy in his reading of the phrase "*ping tianxia,*" which was rendered as "making [people] in all corners under the realm equal (*gege junju*)." It should be noted that in Shi's commentary the "*ping*" was not explained in terms of its conventional sense of "pacification" and the restoration of order. Instead, it was economic equality and justice that was underscored in the exposition. Shi further explains, "*The Great Learning*'s advice for the ruler is to 'disperse wealth' [*sancai*]. But the term '*sancai*' does not require the ruler to pass out his own wealth; it simply means that the ruler only takes what is proper and does not extract more than the [legal] rate [*zhishi qu qi dedang, er buwei ewai zhi zheng*]." Shi called this "public justice" (*gongping*) in contrast with "the monopoly of wealth" by the emperor (*zhuanli*).[159]

It bears noting that an outright criticism of the emperor was seething beneath the lines of the following explanation by another commentator:

> There is one person who desires to take advantage [of others], concerned only with his own interests and disregarded others. Consequently, others are not able to fulfill their wishes, and this is injustice! How much worse when he, occupying the emperor's throne, wielding absolute power over authority and fortune, indulges himself in the pursuit of his own profit! How can he bring peace/justice to the realm (*keyi ping tianxia hu*)? . . . Discourse on the consequences of the concentration and distribution of wealth will inevitably lead to the issue concerning the possession and loss of the Mandate of Heaven. The Mandate of Heaven lies nowhere but in the people's heart.[160]

This remark by Yao Shunmu (1543–1627) was included in Zhu Mingliang's compendium of commentaries published around 1594. It could be easily construed as a critique of the Wanli emperor, even if unintended. The connection explicitly highlighted between justice in taxation and the rise and fall of dynastic regimes was forcefully articulated. This exposition on the passages about the emperor's handling of wealth was adopted by other compilers of commentaries.[161]

The emperor was not regarded as the source of wealth, and he was rebuked implicitly for taking more than he deserved. Yao's remarks can be read out of context and into any specific social context involving the imperial government and taxation. Examinees reading these comments could hardly miss the striking similarities between the criticism of the ruler in the commentary and the outlandish pillaging activities of the eunuchs authorized by the Wanli emperor to extract extra taxes from the people. In 1597 an official in the Ministry of Justice submitted a memorial criticizing the Wanli emperor for allowing greedy "mean people" to set up "imperial shops" (*huangdian*). He quoted precisely those passages from the *Great Learning* that spoke against the ruler monopolizing wealth and its dire consequence of dispersing the subject as a result of the concentration of wealth in the hands of the emperor.[162] One hardly needed insinuation to see the relevance of the comment to the current issue of improper management of wealth by the Wanli emperor. In the spring of 1606, people in Yunnan resisted and killed eunuch tax commissioner Yang Rong.[163] Not only was there popular resistance to extra taxation extracted by the eunuch tax commissioners, some local officials also challenged their authority and refused to cooperate. A magistrate in Shenxi was brought to Beijing for trial for his refusal to comply with the eunuch's wishes.[164]

A commentary by Wang Najian (known by his popular name Guantao), *Sishu jiaxun* (Family instructions of the Four Books), was frequently cited by other commentators. In the passage on "the great way to create wealth," Guantao made some comments that explicitly made *licai* (wealth management) the most important of all the ruler's duties. He said, "Wealth should not be accumulated, and cannot be accumulated [by the ruler] . . . even the teaching of the *jieju* is not specifically made for wealth management. Nonetheless, wealth management is the most important [duty of the ruler]. . . . This is public justice and the correct way in creating wealth [*gongping zhengda zhi dao*]."[165] The conventional role of teaching the subject morality was no longer the major duty of the emperor. In contrast, in the words of some commentators, the emperor himself was the source of moral degeneration, the major cause of chaos.

In *Sishu mai* (Pulse of the Four Books, 1615), Tang Binyin (referred often to as Tang Shui'an) discussed the ruler's attitude toward wealth and elaborated on the consequence of the ruler's failure to serve as a model for his subject (*buneng jieju zhi shi*). "From morning till night, [the ruler] has his mind set on making profit, reversing the priorities between wealth and virtue, and competing with his subject for wealth. . . . When [the ruler] despoils the subject of their wealth, how could the subject do otherwise but struggle against the ruler's depredation? Therefore, the subject's struggle for more wealth actually was provoked by the ruler."[166] This view that political chaos originated in abuse and misuse of power by the ruler was common among commentators of the *Romance of the Water Margin*.[167] When the Wanli emperor sent eunuchs to set up taxing stations in all the major cities, readers were reminded of such comments on the rapacity of the ruler. Many degree holders were involved in resistance against eunuchs.

In elaborating on the point against monopolizing profit by the ruler (*zhuanli*), a commentator changed "the ruler" (*jun*) to *guan* (officials). "Not to engage in monopolizing profit-making by the officials is the way to benefit both the ruler and the subject."[168] The change expanded the target of criticism beyond the emperor and the avaricious ministers. It was an indictment against the entire bureaucracy, including the clerks and runners. Su Jun (better known as Su Zixi), whose commentary was popular even among commentators, elaborated on the phrase "*sheng cai you dadao*" (there is a great way to generate wealth). Since the Chinese language did not provide a qualifying subject for wealth, Su specifically explained that "to generate wealth" referred to the wealth of the people, not the wealth of the imperial state (*fei sheng guojia zhi cai, sheng minjian zhi cai ye*).[169]

The above examples clearly convey a sense that the commentators did not explain the meaning of the *Great Learning* in terms of its original intention, or "literal meaning." No examinees would mistake the comments as simply scholarly exposition. These comments constituted a new configuration of the basic duties of a government and the emperor. The primary goal and responsibility of a government lied in its ability to manage wealth properly. As it was unequivocally stated in the commentary by Chen Dingsheng, "For to bring peace to the realm under heaven depends solely on wealth. How can one dismisses wealth as a trivial concern!"[170] Indeed, the importance of commercial wealth, both in economic life and literary representation, was registered in these commentaries. In his com-

ment on the role of wealth in society, Xu Changji compared wealth to
blood that needed to be circulated. When wealth was accumulated and
stopped from circulating, problems would ensue.[171] This specific comment on the need to circulate or distribute wealth rather than accumulat-
ing it in private treasuries of the imperial family or wealthy families attested to the creativity of the commentators as readers, who actualized
their invented meanings outside the "literal" meaning sanctioned by the
imperial government.

Another example of subverting and appropriating official ideology was
unequivocally revealed in a comment on the distinction between "great
learning" and "lesser learning." Guo Wei (known as Guo Zhuyuan), the
compiler of *Sishu zhuyi baocang*, pointed out that the word "great" in
*Great Learning* is the opposite of "mean people" (*xiaoren*), who were
mentioned at the end of the chapter. "To illuminate one's own illustrious
virtue (*mingde*) is the great skill of the great men (*daren*). To accumulate
wealth through exploitation is the trivial calculation of the mean
people."[172] He was no longer discussing great learning as an advanced
level of learning following the completion of the primarily learning. The
procedural distinction was turned into a dichotomy of behavior of the
moral and the immoral!

Radical ideas and criticism of misrule and abuses of imperial power by
the emperor were freely circulated in the commentaries. The publishing
industry, by producing a large number of examination aids, contributed
to the destabilization of the official ideology and to the creation of new
discursive spaces for challenging the imperial government's authority
over the interpretation of the canonical texts. The modes in which official
ideology was challenged were created by the newly and vastly expanded
discursive space in the paratext, the threshold of interpretation. The
"packaging" of a commentary with ever longer titles, growing numbers
of editorial principles and prefaces, and longer lists of references, as well
as proofreaders, helped to expand the semantic field of the book by creating multiple points of intervention where commentators and critics
came to challenge and negotiate the meaning of the Confucian canon. The
compendium format of listing comments by different scholars visually
disrupted the floating eyes of the reader, forcing him to pause, to ponder
the differences between comments, and finally to come to terms with them

or be left baffled. Either way, the production of meaning no longer took place in the official edition of the *Sishu daquan*. A new materialized text, packaged with paratext that multiplied the points of intervention, rendered ineffective the circuit of communication the civil service examination sought to impose on the semantic field of the Confucian canon.

# 5
# Public Authority, Literary Critics, and Organizational Power

The impact of commercial publishing on the examination field was extensive and profound. In addition to the challenge to the official exposition on the Four Books posted by commercial commentaries, the expanding book market facilitated the shifting of literary authority from officials to professional writers and critics. These men of letters became the arbiters of literary taste and excellence. The explosion of publishing since the Wanli period not only expanded the semantic field of the Confucian classics, but also increased the number of literary critics whose authority came to rival that of the examiners. Commercial publishing in the sixteenth and early seventeenth centuries gradually became a major factor in the creation of authority over literary taste. The Ministry of Rites found it difficult to control the examination field as examinees were overcome with a deluge of conventional and new examination aids on the Four Books and the model of examination essays. The stylistic requirement of the "eight-legged" essay was not insulated from the competing models of literary excellence promoted by critics (*xuanshou*), many of whom were examinees seeking to influence the examiners' literary taste through edit-

ing and critiquing examination essays. Since the mid-Wanli period, examinees seeking to assume positions as critics of examination essays came
to recognize the power of organization in defining the criteria of success
at the civil examinations. The growing adoption of organized forms of
study groups among examinees culminated in the founding of the Restoration Society (Fushe), which signaled the growing autonomy of the field
of cultural production, on the one hand, and the emergence of the publishing world as a major arena where professional writers battled for the
authority to arbitrate competing models of literary excellence and divergent renderings of the Confucian canon, on the other.

## The Economics and Politics of Literary Production

David Perkins—in his recent book *Is Literary History Possible?*—reflects
on the crisis in literary studies in Anglo-European literature.[1] Anglo-European literary critics must decide what kinds of literary works and whose
works should be included when writing a literary history. It is no longer
a problem of who is better among the writers of the same genre. Nor is it
a problem of which works are representative of certain literary trends.
The problem lies deeper. The canon together with its poetics and history,
have been called into question amid the assaults and challenges from various methodological and perspective positions: deconstructionism, cultural materialism, postcolonialism, gender and ethnic studies, new historicism as well as various forms of postmodernisms. Those who are obligated to teach students the best models of literature in English and
American studies find themselves in the thick of the battle in this crisis. In
a recent anthology of essays by leading scholars in the field of English and
American studies, editors Stephen Greenblatt and Giles Gunn pungently
point out that "there [has] always been change, conflict, and diversity in
[their] profession, but until recently, professional differences rarely called
into question the cohesiveness of the field as a whole." The anthology represents a concerted effort to remedy the situation, seeking to redraw the
boundaries of literary studies "without pretending that the field can be
comprehended within a single, cohesive frame."[2] But without a common
frame of reference in terms of methodological and perspective positions,
the boundary, however it is redrawn, will lack an intellectual justification,
betraying nothing but the encyclopedic nature of the anthology. The at-

tempt is more bibliographical and disciplinary than an intellectual remedy of the crisis. It lends no help to answering the question that beleaguers these literary critics—Is literary history possible?

This question and the current crisis in Anglo-European literary studies raise the fundamental question about *value* in aesthetics. How do we define value in literature, and by the same token, art? How do we explain the *change* in the valuation of literary styles and standards? The question is how to avoid mistaking a congeries of literary styles and genres as an inevitable evolution or continuous development in a certain society as an essential representation of its *culture* in literary production. Rather, one must examine change to a considerable degree as what Bourdieu calls "symbolic struggles," which refers to the struggle among dominant groups over the imposition of specific styles on other groups in various fields of cultural production. Dominant groups in any given society strive to become the *arbiter elegantium*, or the "taste maker."[3] Any history of literary style and artistic preference is therefore incomplete without an investigation of how nondiscursive factors like printing determined how and who become the taste makers. For Bourdieu,

> the History of the [literary and artistic] field arises from the struggle between the established figures and the young challengers. The aging of authors, schools, and works is far from being the product of a mechanical, chronological slide into the past; it results from the struggle between those who have made their mark (fait date— "make an epoch") who are fighting to persist; and those who cannot make their own mark without pushing into the past those who have an interest in stopping the clock, eternalizing the present stage of things.[4]

By underscoring the struggle over the authority to define style or taste, Bourdieu draws attention to the fact that change in literary style cannot be studied as a history independent of the power relation among social groups. Bourdieu's empirical data came from modern Europe. What he analyzes are practices of a bourgeoisie society where the market had contributed to the "autonomization of the intellectual and artistic fields," which are fields of cultural production.[5] Since Bourdieu's study of modern Europe is not undertaken in any historicist and Eurocentric schemes, his analytical concepts can be applied to the study of practice in late-Ming China. The expansion of the market for cultural goods and services—the process of commodification of *wen*—had produced a similar effect, that is, the increase in the level of autonomy of the field of cultural production, resulting in the production of authority over literary taste in the literary field. Writers holding positions in the literary field came to challenge and negotiate the hierarchy of styles imposed by the imperial government through the civil service examination system.

A history of literary tastes needs to take into account the change in the structure of the field of cultural production, as well as its relation with the field of power. It is the history of the creation and destruction, the rise and fall of positions, in these two fields and the change in their relationship. Taste in art, whether material, literary, or performative, is socially produced and yet in Bourdieu's words, "it is the area par excellence of the denial of the social."[6] The discourse produced by exponents of specific literary styles does not explain how the producers themselves got to the positions in the field of cultural production.

In China, the social conditions, including various practices and institutions, that structured the field of cultural production underwent significant change in the sixteenth and seventeen centuries. Commercial publishing gradually created new positions for cultural production in the economic field; those who came to occupy these new positions were empowered to contest the authority of the officials who set standards of literary excellence as examiners. In short, commercial publishing created new practices that came to weaken the government's control over the standard of literary excellence through the civil service examination. This is a major structural difference one has to bear in mind when attempting comparative studies of literary change in China and Europe.

### Imperial Court and the Literary History of the Ming

The study of literary history, especially the rise and fall of different "schools of literary style" (*wenpai*) in late imperial China has been dominated by the use of two conventional labels of "literary entities": relative aesthetic quality and ideological values. Many have attempted to document and explain the "historical" origins of literary schools of poetry and prose such as the Fugu pai (Restoring Antiquity school), the Gong'an school, the Jinling school, and the Tang-Song school in terms of "dissatisfaction" with the "problems" (*liubi*) of the dominant school at any given time. Little attention has been paid to the enormous role played by the civil service examination and commercial publishing in the literary history of the Ming-Qing period.[7]

Since the early Ming, throughout most of the sixteenth century, political power and the authority over standards of literary excellence were coterminous. The imperial state and its promotion of the Cheng-Zhu orthodoxy had been important in the shaping of the practice and discourse of literary criticism in Ming China until the 1590s.[8] Throughout this period, various literary styles competed with and succeeded one another as models for literary styles in poetry and prose, the two major genres mastered by members of the literati. The different groups of writers that produced poetics and models of literary styles invariably occupied positions in the imperial government. Through their positions in political offices, these writers created and promoted literary standards and models for aspirants of political office to emulate.

### From the Hanlin Academy to the Six Ministries

The Taige style that "flourished" in the early Ming was primarily the style of high officials at the center of the Ming court. It refers to poetry and prose writings of the metropolitan graduates who were appointed as "bachelors" (*Shuji shi*) to the Hanlin Academy.[9] Officials from the Hanlin Academy had better opportunities of rising high in the bureaucratic ladder. The leaders of the Taige style, such as Yang Shiqi (1365–1444), Yang Rong (1371–1440), and Yang Pu (1372–1446), received appointment in the Grand Secretariat (Neige), whose secretaries were major advisors to emperors in their deliberation over important government policy and issues.[10] The authority in defining literary excellence inhabited the same space of political authority in the center of the imperial system.

Advocates of the Taige style produced pastiche of the prose styles of Song writers Ouyang Xiu and Zeng Gong.[11] The influence of the Taige style clearly indicates that in the early Ming it was the most powerful and prestigious group of officials at the center of the imperial court, setting the standard of literary excellence and defining the goals of literary creation.[12] That examiners were chosen from among members of the Hanlin Academy explains how the Taige literary style was able to reproduce itself through the civil service examination.[13]

In this early period many officials who entered the core of the imperial court—the Grand Secretariat and the Hanlin Academy—were natives of Ji'an, Jiangxi.[14] A number of natives from Taihe who were high officials served as chief examiners for the metropolitan examinations. Yang Shiqi, in particular, was instrumental in helping men from Taihe to gain ascendancy in the central government.[15] His exceptionally long tenure—over twenty years—as a grand secretary provided unprecedented opportunity for natives of Taihe and Ji'an.[16] During the early and mid-Ming dynasty, Ji'an boasted the largest number of *jinshi* and *juren*.[17] A contemporary hyperbole meant to ridicule the exceptionally large presence of Jiangxi men bespeaks the actual power of Jiangxi men in the central government: "Most of the Hanlin scholars were from Ji'an, half of the officials in court are from Jiangxi."[18]

The unity of political power, with authority over setting standard of literary excellence, continued throughout most of the fifteenth century. But from the early sixteenth century onward, the literary authority of the Hanlin academicians was increasingly challenged and subsequently replaced by literary critics without Hanlin backgrounds. A group of officials who came to be called the "Former Seven Masters" of the Archaic school began exerting influence on the discourse and practice of writing. They were active in the early sixteenth century. The leaders of this group represented the beginning of the long process of the gradual decline of the control over literary standards by the imperial government. Only three had been members of the Hanlin Academy. Li Mengyang (1472–1529) and He Jingming (1483–1521) were simply officials in the Six Ministries with a reputation in literary writing.[19] The Latter Seven Masters centered around Wang Shizhen (1526–1590) and Li Panlong (1514–1570). Wang served in the Ministry of Justice and two other officials from the same ministry were among the Latter Seven Masters. The leaders in these two groups were colleagues in the central government. None had the honor of being appointed at the Hanlin Academy.

The poetics of the leaders of the Former Seven Masters called for the "restoration of antiquity" *(fugu)*. They jettisoned as models poetry written after the late Tang and prose writings after the Han *(wen bi Qin-Han,*

*shi bi sheng Tang*).[20] In poetry, Li underscored the formalistic requirements of rhythmical patterns and an ancient style of versification (*gediao*). Li and others actually modeled their poetry on the *Book of Odes*
in matters of verse structure and rhythmical patterns.[21] Li Mengyang criticized the Taige poets for imitating Song poetry and was not satisfied with
Song *Daoxue* scholars' view of poetry, which stressed moral principles
(*li*). For him, "there are incidents that violate *li* but there is no sound not
based on *qing* [feelings]."[22] The expression of feelings or emotion played
no role in rationalistic poetry. Song *Daoxue* scholars focused on the "constant principle" (*li*) so much so that they neglected the vitality and dy-
namic expression of human emotion. By restricting the purpose of poetry
to didacticism, Song moralistic poetry gave no role to "feelings" (*qing*)
and lacked thematic diversity. It is important not to confuse criticism of
Song poetry with an ideological rejection of the Cheng-Zhu orthodoxy of
the Ming government. Li's criticism was leveled primarily from the perspective of writing poetry. He did not reject the "principles" of Confucian
ethics as such, nor did he question the political center's importance in
maintaining the moral order.

The literary criticism of poetry writing from the late Jiajing (1522–66)
to the mid-Wanli periods was dominated by models promoted by the Latter Seven Masters. The poetic creation and reputation of Li Panlong
(1514–1570) and Wang Shizhen (1526–1590) were a corollary of leisure
provided by their official positions. After Li became an official in 1544,
he devoted himself to poetry and poetics.[23]

The Latter Seven Masters continued to look to antiquity for models of
literary writings.[24] For them, prose writings after Han and poetry after
the late Tang were inferior. Wang Shizhen stressed the rhythmical patterns
and style of ancient poetry and was contemptuous of Song poetry.[25] But
in his later years, like Li Panlong, Wang Shizhen came to appreciate the
expressionism of the literary theory of his rivals—leaders of the Tang-
Song school prose.[26] Despite this change, they were opposed to using spontaneous and contemporary expressions. Li Panlong criticized vernacular-
ism in poetry writing.[27] Similarly, Wang Shizhen applied his archaic style
to his drama criticism. He continued to stress refined diction and the didactic function of drama.[28]

The foremost critic of the Former and Latter Seven Masters was prose writer Tang Shunzhi, who upheld Tang and Song writers as models for imitation. Tang belonged to the group "Eight Talented Masters" (*ba caizi*) and the Tang-Song school of prose. They were Tang Shunzhi (1507–1560), Chen Shu (1508–1540), Wang Shenzhong (1509–1559), Zhao Shichun (1509–1567), Xiong Guo, Ren Han, Li Kaixian (1502–1568), and Lü Gao (1505–1557).[29] Tang in his later years came under the influence of Wang Yangming's disciple, Wang Ji (1498–1583). He opposed poetics that stressed strict rules.[30] Tang criticized the Former and Latter Seven Masters for following models that were too remote from the present.[31] His poetics does not stress versification and diction.[32] He advocated "natural or original color" (*bense*) as a new criterion for evaluating literary excellence. Tang said: "poetry and prose are simply the reflection of one's heart and mind." *Bense* refers to the genuine *qing* the writer expressed in his work. It also refers to the unadorned, simple, easy to understand language, a language of the Tang-Song period that was closer to the Classical style of the Ming. This idea of *bense* implied several things: genuine *qing*, a simple language that can effectively communicate such emotions to the reader with no literary competence cultivated by a classical education. Heavy allusions, rigid rules, and reading protocols were obstacles. The Tang-Song school broke away from the Archaic school's perimeter of stylistic and rhythmical patterns by moving literary models down the time scale to the Tang and Song periods. In the poetics of Tang Shunzhi, the strands of expressionism and simplicity converged to demand the employment of new literary forms that would overcome the generic restrictions of poetry and prose.

Despite the insistence on simplicity and contemporary language, Tang Shunzhi still embraced the didactic function of literary writings. The Tang-Song school not only made a strong defense of the moral teachings of the Song *Daoxue* scholars, they also argued that their poetry should be the models of poetry.[33] Their poetics represented a vigorous effort in defending the Cheng-Zhu orthodoxy of the imperial state. Tang himself was a *jinshi* and entered the Hanlin Academy in 1533 only in his twenties.[34] All the exponents of the Tang-Song school, except Tang, earned their *jinshi* degree in either 1526 or 1529. But only three had served at the Hanlin Academy.[35] In other words, the literary critics were predominantly officials while they were influential writers. The occupation of positions in the imperial bureaucracy was still an important qualification of these arbiters of literary taste.

## Growing Importance of Publishing in the Production of Literary Reputation

The reputation of the Former Seven Masters was restricted to the official circles, and was not created via the reprint of their writings in anthologies, a growing important genre of commercial publication since the Wanli period. A brief survey of the publishing records of the two leaders of the Former Seven Masters provides a glimpse into the relationship between literary creation and commercial publishing in the early and mid-sixteenth century. The records of extant publications of Li Mengyang suggests the relative insignificance of editorial and publishing activities in Li's literary activities. He did not edit or anthologize other author's writings. Commercial publishing hardly played any role in his literary and economic life. In Wang Zhongmin's *Zhongguo shanbenshu tiyao* (Annotated catalog of Chinese rare books, hereafter *ZGSBS*), ten titles are listed under his name. Of those works, six are different editions of his own writings published posthumously; two works are by the Tang poet Meng Jiao, published by the publisher Ling Mengchu, who was listed as a commentator. The last two titles are likely false attributions, which were nonetheless published posthumously by Ling Mengchu. Only one collection of poetry by Yang Yiqing (1454–1530), published in the Jiajing period, listed him as one of the two who commented on and punctuated (*pingdian*) the book; he was listed as a disciple of Yang.[36]

Du Xinfu's *Mingdai banke zonglu* (hereafter *MDBKZL*), a catalog of extant Ming editions, lists more titles with Li Mengyang as the author. But the anthologies of his poetry and prose were edited by subsequent writers.[37] Li Mengyang's reputation came about posthumously by efforts of admirers such as Wang Shizhen and other authors in the Wanli period. There is a similar pattern in another catalog of Chinese rare books. The *Taiwan gongcang shanben shumu renming soyin* (*TWGCSB*), a union catalog of extant "good books," lists forty-three imprints under Li's name. Of these, all but one are different editions of his own writings and poetry.[38]

The reputation and influence of He Jingming is even less evident in print. In *ZGSBS*, there are seven titles bearing his name; six are different editions of his personal writings. They were all published by disciples and friends after his death.[39] *TWGCSB* listed twenty-eight books in fifteen titles under his name. All except three are collections of his poems and essays. None of the three is an anthology of essays or poetry.[40] While the relatively large number of titles listed under Li and He testify to their reputations and to the popularity of their writings, they also unequivocally bespeak their lack of extensive involvement in editing, anthologizing, critiquing, and commenting, activities that characterized the experience of the majority of the writers from the Wanli period on.

What distinguished the Latter Seven Masters from the Former Seven Masters was the increasing dependence on printed text as a major means for disseminating their writings and poetics. The Latter Seven Masters were active promoting their poetics, but their effect was not widely felt among the examinees until after Wang Shizhen retired from office. While in retirement in Taicang, through his personal influence and prolific production, Wang promoted the poetics of the Latter Seven Masters, who came to exert great influence on examinees in the south.

The Latter Seven Masters increasingly depended on printed text for the spread of their influence. Li Panlong worked very closely with at least two publishers: Xu Dianqing and Xu Ziyu.[41] Through mail, he sent them manuscripts, corrections, and changes.[42] Comparing the table of contents with actual selections, he pointed out to Xu Dianqing that a poem had been excised but the title was not deleted accordingly.[43] He disliked the title change Xu made to one of his poems.[44] Xu Dianqing was also involved in proofreading for his publications.[45] Except for one, most of the publications appeared to be his own poems and essays, which had been written in the company of Wang Shizhen.[46]

Li Panlong and Wang Shizhen worked closely in promoting the publication of their own works and those they held in high regard.[47] Wang wrote the preface for the collected writings of Zong Chen, one of the Latter Seven Masters.[48] Li had been collecting poetry for an anthology entitled *Gujin shi shan* (Selection of poetry across time), which covered the period from ancient time down to the Ming. He later had a change of mind. For some reason he did not want to include poems written by Ming writers.[49] That decision might have been prompted by his view that no poetry after the Tang was worthy.

This anthology appears to be the only work that he had attempted. There are several extant anthologies of poetry listing Li as the author. Of the nine anthologies of poetry bearing Li Panlong as the editor, eight were published posthumously in the Wanli period. They were attributed to him after his name became well known in the south.[50] Even though commercial publishing was not important to Li's career as a poet, his reputation was disseminated posthumously through printed anthologies. However, they were all published after the mid-Wanli reign with comments by famous critics such as Zhong Xing and Tan Yuanchun.[51]

The growing importance of commercial publishing in the production of literary reputation can be discerned in Wang Shizhen's publications. As Ai Nanying had observed, young literati did not have to study or practice writing. All they did was keep a copy of Wang Shizhen's *Yanzhou shanren sibu gao* (The Quadruplets of mountain man of Yanzhou). "When they needed to produce a literary piece in social occasions, they just cut and paste from what they had committed to memory of Wang's writing. And all their writings appeared to be rich and elegant. But under scrutiny they were nothing but products of a hackneyed formula."[52] That this widespread practice of appropriating Wang's poetry was possible is because of the wide circulation of his works. Wang's book was published in the 1570s by two commercial publishing houses, Shijingtang and Shidetang in Nanjing.[53] Wang Shizhen, despite being a powerful retired official with the resources to publish his own writings, was willing to have his works published by commercial publishers. At a time when anyone with resources could publish his own work, using a commercial publisher took on new meanings. Commercial publishers would not pay to publish a book that did not sell. Wang Shizhen became a popular name that publishers often chose to misonymize their books.[54]

*Commercial Publishing and* Shishang *Writers*

It is useful to examine the differences in the relationships among groups of writers, the imperial government, and commercial publishing. The relationship of writers with the imperial state can be measured in many dif-

*Table 5.1*

Average Age of *Shishang* Writers Obtaining *Jinshi*
Degrees and Life Spans Thereafter

| NAME | YEAR EARNING DEGREE* | AGE ATTAINING JINSHI/JUREN | YEARS THEREAFTER |
|---|---|---|---|
| Chen Jitai (1567–1641) | 1634 | 67 | 7 |
| Chen Zilong (1608–1647) | 1637 | 29 | 10 |
| Fang Yingxiang (1562?–1628) | 1616 | 54 | 12 |
| Huang Ruheng (1558–1626) | 1598 | 40 | 28 |
| Qiu Zhaolin (1572–1629) | 1610 | 38 | 19 |
| Zhang Pu (1602–1641) | 1631 | 29 | 10 |
| Zhong Xing (1574–1625 | 1610 | 36 | 15 |
| Zhou Zhong (d. 1645) | 1639 | — | 6 |
| Ai Nanying 1583–1646) | 1624 JR | 41 | 22 |
| Li Zhi (1527–1602) | 1552 JR | 25 | 50 |
| Tan Yuanchun (d. 1637) | 1627 JR | — | 10 |
| Xu Fuyuan (1599–1665) | 1642 JR | 43 | 23 |
| Average | | 40.2** | 17.6, 13.3*** |

*JR = *juren*; dates without JR are *jinshi* degree; **Average excluding Zhou Zhong and Tan Yuanchun; ***Average excluding the last four who only attained the *juren* degree.

ferent ways. One important indicator is the amount of time the writer had served or could serve in the government, that is, the amount of time they were able to take positions in the political field. This can be measured by the average age at graduation from the metropolitan examination and the number of years left after graduation.

The average age of the Former Seven Masters at graduation from the metropolitan examination was twenty-three.[55] They were born in the early Ming when competition was much less acute, and the population had not increased substantially. The average age of the Tang-Song Masters was twenty-two, and for the Latter Seven Masters, excluding Xie Jin and Liang Youyu, twenty-seven, indicating the growing competitiveness of the civil service examination.[56] The average number of years after graduation from the metropolitan examination for the Former Seven Masters was 32.2. Excluding Xu Jingqing, whose term was exceptionally short, the average rises to 36.6 years after obtaining the *jinshi* degree. For the Latter

*Table 5.2*

Comparison of the Average Ages of the Four Groups of Literary
Leaders Obtaining Higher Degrees and Life Spans Thereafter

| | AGE ATTAINING *JINSHI* | YEARS THEREAFTER |
|---|---|---|
| Former Seven Masters | 22.3 | 32.2 |
| Tang-Song Masters | 22 | 38.1 |
| Latter Seven Masters | 27 | 30 |
| *Shishang* writers | 41.8* | 13.3 |

*Excluding all the *juren* in Table 5.1.

Seven Masters, the average number of years after their metropolitan graduation is thirty; for the Tang Song Masters, thirty-four.[57]

In contrast, the average age at obtaining the metropolitan degree for
the professional group, the *shishang* writers, who were active during the
last fifty years of the Ming dynasty, was 40.2 (see Table 5.1). The average
remaining life span in this group after becoming *jinshi* is 13.3, which is
only one-third that of the Tang-Song Masters and less than 50 percent
that of the Former Seven Masters (see Table 5.2). Since the Wanli period,
leaders in the literary circles took up positions in the economic field for
periods in excess of those they eventually occupied in the imperial government. Their career trajectories fell mostly in the field of cultural production, rather than in the political field. Many had to "manage their living" (*zhisheng*) by assuming positions in the economic field through a
great variety of work: tutoring, operating a publishing business, hiring
out to publishers, providing literary services to merchants, gentry, and
officials. Their literary production was intimately linked with the market
of commercial publishing.

The growing importance of the publishing market in generating and
sustaining reputations of writers is documented in Tables 5.3–5.8, which
list extant publications with the names of the leaders of the different
schools included in *MDBKZL*. In addition to writers from the Former
Seven Masters, Latter Seven Masters, the Tang-Song Eight Masters, the
Gong'an school, and the Jinglin school, two authors without any literary

## Table 5.3
### Generic Distribution of Publications Bearing the Names of the Leading Literary Figures

| NAME | CL | FB | H | HP | WK | EC | AW | AP | NO | DR | OT | TOTAL | NUMBER OF GENRES |
|---|---|---|---|---|---|---|---|---|---|---|---|---|---|
| Li Mengyang | 0 | 0 | 0 | 0 | 9 | 0 | 0 | 0 | 0 | 0 | 0 | 9 | 1 |
| Li Panglong | 0 | 0 | 0 | 0 | 4 | 0 | 0 | 4 | 0 | 0 | 0 | 8 | 2 |
| Tang Shunzhi | 0 | 0 | 7 | 0 | 5 | 0 | 2 | 0 | 0 | 0 | 5 | 19 | 4 |
| Wang Shizhen | 0 | 0 | 1 | 0 | 5 | 1 | 0 | 0 | 0 | 0 | 9 | 16 | 4 |
| Li Zhi | 1 | 1 | 2 | 1 | 12 | 0 | 1 | 2 | 5 | 12 | 5 | 42 | 10 |
| Chen Jiru | 0 | 0 | 0 | 1 | 4 | 1 | 2 | 1 | 1 | 5 | 5 | 20 | 8 |
| Yuan Hongdao | 1 | 0 | 1 | 0 | 6 | 0 | 2 | 1 | 0 | 0 | 1 | 12 | 6 |
| Zhong Xing | 3 | 2 | 2 | 0 | 4 | 0 | 3 | 2 | 1 | 1 | 4 | 22 | 9 |

SOURCE for Tables 5.1–8: *MDBKZL*
CL=classics; FB=Four Books; H=history; HP=hundred philosophers; WK=personal works, including collection of personal writings and literary and scholarly works; EC=editing other writer's personal writings (*wenji*); AW=anthology of prose; AP=anthology of poetry; NO= novels, stories; DR=drama; OT=others, including memorials, almanacs.


## Table 5.4
### Types of Labor by Leading Literary Figures in Publications

| NAME | ZZ | BJ | PP | JYD | TOTAL | NUMBER OF ROLES |
|---|---|---|---|---|---|---|
| Li Mengyang | 9 | 0 | 0 | 0 | 9 | 1 |
| Li Panglong | 4 | 4 | 0 | 0 | 8 | 2 |
| Tang Shunzhi | 9 | 7 | 3 | 0 | 19 | 3 |
| Wang Shizhen | 11 | 5 | 0 | 0 | 16 | 2 |
| Li Zhi | 12 | 8 | 22 | 0 | 42 | 3 |
| Chen Jiru | 4 | 5 | 10 | 1 | 20 | 4 |
| Yuan Hongdao | 7 | 5 | 1 | 0 | 13 | 3 |
| Zhong Xing | 4 | 9 | 8 | 0 | 21 | 3 |

ZZ=authored (*zhu, zuan*); BJ=edited, compiled (*bian, ji, xuan*); PP=critique, comment (*piping, pidian, pingdian, zhu*); JYD=proofread (*jiao, jian, yue, ding, jianding*).

*Table 5.5*

Number of Titles, Genres, and Roles of the Leading Literary Figures

| NAME | TITLES | GENRES | ROLES |
|------|--------|--------|-------|
| Li Mengyang | 9 | 1 | 1 |
| Li Panlong | 8 | 2 | 2 |
| Tang Shunzhi | 19 | 4 | 3 |
| Wang Shizhen | 16 | 4 | 2 |
| Li Zhi | 42 | 10 | 3 |
| Chen Jiru | 20 | 8 | 4 |
| Yuan Hongdao | 12 | 6 | 3 |
| Zhong Xing | 22 | 9 | 3 |

affiliations are included. Li Zhi and Chen Jiru are included for their indisputable popularity in the late Ming.

By the late Jiajing reign, around the 1550s, literary leaders such as Tang Shunzhi and Wang Shizhen became increasingly involved in publishing, especially in the capacity as editor and compiler.[58] From the mid-sixteenth century onward, all the leading literary figures, from Li Zhi to Yuan Hongdao to Zhong Xing, had not only published their own works, but were also involved in editing, compiling, and critiquing works in a greater variety of genres (see Tables 5.3–5.5). The numbers of works of these writers are both underreported and exaggerated. They are not the complete listing of extant imprints and there are misonymized works. Nevertheless, as in the cases discussed in Chapter 3, there is no question that most of the authors had been involved in editing, compiling, critiquing, and anthologizing. Similar pattern of practice can be seen among a number of popular authors who were not specifically affiliated with the literary schools (see Table 5.6). Their reputations also fueled false attributions by commercial publishers who believed that they were powerful and skilful enough to avoid legal and financial consequences. These writers depended much less on influence generated by personal networking than did the literary leaders in the early Ming through the mid-Jiajing period.

No book listed Wang Shizhen as a critic or commentator (*piping*) (see Table 5.4). Nor is there any imprint in the genres of novel and drama that

Table 5.6

Roles by Other Popular Authors Listed in Publications

| NAME | ZZ | BJ | PP | JYD | TOTAL | NUMBER OF ROLES |
|---|---|---|---|---|---|---|
| Chen Renxi | 10 | 4 | 0 | 0 | 14 | 2 |
| Jiao Hong | 8 | 11 | 3 | 0 | 22 | 3 |
| Li Tingji | 3 | 2 | 4 | 0 | 9 | 3 |
| Tang Xianzu | 14 | 1 | 5 | 0 | 20 | 3 |
| Tu Long | 9 | 2 | 2 | 1 | 14 | 4 |
| Xu Wei | 5 | 0 | 8 | 0 | 13 | 2 |
| Zhang Pu | 1 | 2 | 0 | 0 | 3 | 2 |

ZZ=authored (*zhu, zuan*); BJ=edited, compiled (*bian, ji, xuan*); PP=critique, comment (*piping, pidian, pingdian, zhu*); JYD=proofread (*jiao, jian, yue, ding, jianding*).

bears the name of Tang Shunzhi or Wang Shizhen.[59] Wang's powerful connection with the officialdom and his local influence in Suzhou were effective deterrents for commercial publishers looking for a famous master to name a ghostwriter's work. It might also be a result of his reputation for not being interested in writing and publishing his comments on books that he read. However, Xu Wei and Tang Xianzu, perhaps the most talented playwrights in the Ming, and another playwright, Tu Long, were primarily listed as critics and commentators in the category of plays (see Table 5.6). No imprint lists them as contributors to the genres of Classics, the Four Books, and history (see Tables 5.7–5.8).

While misonymity was common in late-Ming commercial publishing, proving falsification is a serious matter. It appears that publishers did not randomly pick a famous master and attach his name to their books. They were mostly well informed of the special talents of specific authors and carefully decided whose name to put in different genres because they knew that the informed readers were not gullible to buy an obvious misonymous book that a reputable master had no interest and reputation for writing. The fact that Li Mengyang was not appropriated as a commentator like Li Zhi or Chen Jiru also suggests that commercial publishing in the late Ming was not a lawless jungle where one could pirate and misonymize freely without concern for consequences. Publishers and authors

*Table 5.7*

Generic Distribution of Publications Bearing the Names
of Other Popular Authors

| NAME | CL | FB | H | HP | WK | EC | AW | AP | NO | DR | OT | NUMBER OF GENRES |
|------|----|----|----|----|----|----|----|----|----|----|----|------------------|
| Chen Renxi | 1 | 1 | 1 | 1 | 2 | 0 | 1 | 0 | 0 | 1 | 1 | 8 |
| Jiao Hong | 1 | 0 | 3 | 4 | 3 | 1 | 1 | 0 | 0 | 0 | 10 | 7 |
| Li Tingji | 0 | 1 | 5 | 0 | 1 | 0 | 1 | 1 | 0 | 1 | 3 | 7 |
| Tang Xianzu | 0 | 0 | 0 | 0 | 5 | 1 | 0 | 1 | 0 | 13 | 1 | 5 |
| Tu Long | 0 | 0 | 0 | 0 | 7 | 1 | 1 | 0 | 1 | 1 | 2 | 6 |
| Xu Wei | 0 | 0 | 0 | 2 | 4 | 2 | 0 | 0 | 1 | 4 | 0 | 5 |
| Zhang Pu | 1 | 0 | 0 | 0 | 0 | 1 | 0 | 0 | 0 | 0 | 1 | 3 |

CL=classics; FB=Four Books; H=history; HP=hundred philosophers; WK=personal works, including collection of personal writings and literary and scholarly works; EC=editing other writer's personal writings (*wenji*); AW=anthology of prose; AP=anthology of poetry; NO= novels, stories; DR=drama; OT=others, including memorials, almanacs.

*Table 5.8*

Number of Titles, Genres, and Roles of Other Popular Authors

| NAME | TITLES | GENRES | ROLES |
|------|--------|--------|-------|
| Chen Renxi | 14 | 8 | 2 |
| Jiao Hong | 22 | 7 | 3 |
| Li Tingji | 9 | 7 | 3 |
| Tang Xianzu | 20 | 5 | 3 |
| Tu Long | 14 | 6 | 4 |
| Xu Wei | 13 | 5 | 2 |
| Zhang Pu | 3 | 3 | 2 |

did seek out and were able to track down and punish the transgressors (see Chapter 3). If publishers decided to misonymize a book to a famous writer, they had to make a plausible case by selecting the appropriate author in the genre in which the book would be recognized. This was one of the principles based on the diversity of readership that came to structure the field of cultural production.

Authors who were most "prolific," both in terms of actual production and in attribution by commercial publishers, were those whose names appeared in a wide spectrum of genres. Li Panlong had only publications in anthologies of poetry. That his specialty was poetry was not an adequate explanation because Zhong Xing was also a celebrated poet and critic, but his publications spanned a wide range of genres. Chen Jiru and Li Zhi were also celebrated poets. To be sure, few authors were able to attain the popularity of Chen and Li. The limited data shows that not one title of the thirty-five listed under Tang Shunzhi and Wang Shizhen was a novel or play (see Table 5.3).[60] Wang was heralded as a leader in prose and poetry as well as for his broad interests, which were reflected in the titles in the category "Other."[61] Tang was well known for his interest in history, statecraft, and prose. He has seven imprints in the history category and two anthologies of prose. An exhaustive survey may yield a few even in the categories of novels and plays, but the fact remained that misonymity was a practice regulated by the principles of the book market. The reputation of a writer was first established by the recognition of his name in the market, and the marketability of his name resulted in misonymization.

From the exponents of the Taige style to the Former and Latter Seven Masters and the Eight Talented Masters, there was a gradual shift of the power bases of the critics from the center of the imperial court—the Grand Secretariat and the Hanlin Academy—to the Six Ministries. Despite this outward movement of the leading literary critics from the Hanlin Academy to the bureaucracy at large, these literary critics were still in varying degrees involved in political struggles at the imperial court. The Former Seven Masters, for example, were active opponents of the powerful eunuch Liu Jin (d. 1510). Their struggle against Liu was an important factor in establishing their identity as a literary-political group. The Latter Seven Masters were also caught in the thick of a power struggle against Yan Song (1480–1565). To a significant degree, the reputation of these writers was still derived from the worth of their moral qualities as upright officials. In this sense, both the Former and Latter Seven Masters were held in esteem as model officials, who by contingency were great poets. The worth of their writings in part was derived from the moral value of their conduct in the political field.

Despite differences in the styles between the Tang-Song advocates and the Latter Seven Masters, their poetics were produced primarily to serve the literary and ideological needs of the imperial state and its clientele—the officials and gentry. Li Mengyang's idea of "authentic poetry [coming] from the common people" did not lead to a call for integrating the wide range of life experiences and local dialects of the common people into the themes and style of poetry writing. In other words, the poetics of the Former and Latter Seven Masters and the "Eight Talented Masters" were produced by members of the imperial officialdom who had common experiences in careers, a relative strong bond to the imperial government in terms of duration of career service, with an audience being primarily the examinees and fellow officials.

For the Fugu movement (Restoration of Antiquity), the Former Seven Masters, and the Latter Seven Masters, the temporal point of reference for writing skill was antiquity. Even with the decline of the Hanlin Academy as the center of literary authority, the poetics of poetry and prose of the period between the 1480s and the 1590s continued to evolve around the imperial center; the influential core exponents belonged to the group with strong government service backgrounds. These literary critics were already established in the political field before their works exerted influence on "admirers." But the boom of commercial publishing contributed to the creation of a new generation of literary critics who were struggling to enter the imperial officialdom through the examination system. Many literati had acquired reputations as commentators of the Confucian canon, or as excellent writers, or as great poets before passing, if they did, the higher level of examinations. Empowered by the reputation they garnered in the commercial market, examinees who had not graduated at the provincial and metropolitan levels gradually came to challenge the examiners in defining literary excellence at the examinations. Through publications, they came to make a name for themselves in literary history.

## PUBLISHING AND EXAMINATION SUCCESS

The boom of commercial publishing not only provided a wide range of examination aids to help candidates prepare for the examinations, it also provided them with a new means of publicizing their own work in order to attract the attention of the examiners. In the late sixteenth century, it had become customary for provincial and metropolitan graduates to publish the essays from their successful examinations as gifts for friends and relatives.[62] Some of the most talented became editors and critics for commercial publishers who produced examination aids. They did so in part to make ends meet, and in part to help themselves succeed at the examinations. Critics such as Ai Nanying, Chen Jitai, and Zhou Zhong (d. 1645) had published their own examination essays before they worked as critics for publishers. Printing—both private and commercial—was critical to the production of literary reputation for examinees and literary critics. The growing importance of commercial publishing contributed to the further shift of the locus of literary authority from the political field to the market of books, prying loose the imperial government's control over literary production.

## Official Models of Examination Essays

The Ming government took an active interest in controlling the prose style, which was a major criteria in selecting candidates at the civil examinations. Reproducing the literary taste upheld by examiners had been the goal of examinees until the late sixteenth century and the early decades of the seventeenth century. All examinees had to struggle with the same dilemma—how to show compliance with the official style, both in style and in exposition, while distinguishing oneself among tens of thousands of examinees at the various levels of examination. Since the Song, various measures adopted by the imperial government to prevent cheating had significantly reduced collusion between examinees and examiners.[63] The use of symbols in place of the names of examinees, and the requirement of copying the answers by clerks, had effectively prevented any attempt to reveal the identities of the examinees. However, these measures could not suppress the style or peculiar choice of words and expressions by each examinee. By knowing the location or "ward" (*fang*) where an examinee took his examination, an examiner could identify a candidate by his peculiar style.[64]

Examinees were required to answer questions on the Four Books in the "eight-legged" (*bagu*) style, a highly structured essay in eight parts.[65] Because of this official requirement of style, these essays were also called "regulated expositions" (*zhiyi*[a] or *zhiyi*[b]) or "eight-legged essays" (*baguwen*). The imperial government published records of metropolitan and provincial examinations regularly. Initially, examinees did not have knowledge of the questions because the government publication of examination results, *Huishi lu* (Records of the metropolitan examination), included only the names of the examiners, prefaces, and the names of the graduates. Beginning in 1385, the questions of the three sessions and a few examination essays were included.[66] But these were "model essays" (*chengwen*) either by examiners or by graduates after heavy editing by the examiners. In the early 1530s, officials attempted to print essays by metropolitan graduates without examiners' editing. Xia Yan (1482–1548), the Minister of Rites, however, objected to this practice and argued that unedited essays by the graduates could not be used as models. He recommended following the current practice of printing only the graduates' essays after revisions by the examiners themselves.[67]

The editing of successful essays served an important function. It ensured that published essays of graduates upheld official standards of excellence. Editing eliminated inappropriate style, quotations, and ideas. This policy was challenged again in the Wanli period. After 1585, in addition to the model essays of examiners, edited essays by successful examinees were included as models.[68] The formats of government examination records were similar even though there was no single format promulgated by the Ministry of Rites as the standard for all provincial records.[69] It was standard for government records to select only one essay from the graduates in each category in the three sessions.[70] Therefore, not even the top three graduates would have all their essays published in the official examination records. The models remained relatively few from the perspective of the examinees.

*Commercial Anthologies of Examination Essays*

In the first quarter of the sixteenth century, commercial anthologies of essays from examinations (*mojuan*) were rare.[71] Before the Longqing (1567–1572) and Wanli periods, there were few printed anthologies except the official examination records. Li Xu (1506–93) recalled that when he was studying for the examinations, there were no printed exercises by examinees. Peddlers selling books would carry twenty to thirty handwritten copies of examination essay exercises to his home for sale at 0.002 to 0.003 tael per essay. Even when Tang Shunzhi earned his metropolitan degree in 1529, his essays were published by a relative, rather than by a commercial publisher prior to his graduation. Similarly, when Xue Yingqi graduated from the metropolitan examination in 1535, his essays were published jointly by his disciple and Li Xu. No commercial publishers printed examination essays, even by the top graduates (*zhuangyuan*) such as Tang and Xue.[72]

In the mid-sixteenth century, commercial publishers began publishing different types of anthologies of examination essays. Gui Youguang (1506–1571) was among a few who were involved in making private selections of examination essays before he even passed the metropolitan examination in 1565. He selected essays and published them as anthologies of model essays.[73] However, he simply selected essays from several recent *Records of Provincial Examinations* (*Xiangshi lu*) and *Huishi lu* as well as essays by graduates of provincial examinations. Unlike later anthologies, the essays were not selected solely from one examination. Besides, the anthologies included only a few scores of essays. Gui also edited anthologies of treatises on policy issues by examinees.[74]

Anthologies of examination essays became the most popular examination aid because they provided ready-made answers to examination questions. And more important, they allowed the examinees to keep abreast of the intellectual as well as stylistic trends that might influence the examiners. It had become a common strategy for examinees to select three to four hundred model answers for memorization, which would generally cover the range of questions at the civil service examination.[75]

From the Wanli period onward, commercial publishers produced a growing number of anthologies of essays by graduates with comments, not by the original examiners but by professional critics, many of whom were already provincial graduates seeking to pass the metropolitan examination. The publication of these essays opened up a forum for examinees and editors to challenge the criteria and judgment of the examiners. More than just a few of the essays by the top graduates were printed; hundreds and later thousands of essays were brought before the eyes of the reader for scrutiny. Unlike the "model essays" written or revised by examiners, these essays were not modified.

By the 1590s, printed model essays filled the shelves of bookstores.[76] Records of examinations printed by the government were overshadowed by commercially produced anthologies in both quantity and popularity. They were too numerous for examinees to read all of them.[77] With the proliferation of various forms of anthologies and collections, examination essays had become a genre to be distinguished from other types of writings. It was perhaps the type of book that most bookstores kept in large supply both in copies and in varieties.[78] In the voluminous anthology of essays written in the Ming, the *Ming wen hai* (Sea of essays of the Ming dynasty), Huang Zongxi devoted eight juan to prefaces written to anthologies of examination essays.[79]

*Types of Anthologies*

There was a great variety of formats in which examination essays were anthologized in printed editions. In the early 1600s there were at least five types of anthologies of examination essays. The first type was essays written by examiners as models for examinees (*chengwen*).[80] Essays on the Four Books by examinees were called *mojuan* (paper in black ink). By the 1620s, for each metropolitan examination there were several hundred different selections of *mojuan* essays by the metropolitan graduates. The third type was essays on the Classics by successful candidates at the metropolitan examinations, called "essays from the wards" (*fanggao*).[81] The fourth type of collection was called *chuanggao* (exercises under the window [of the studio]).[82] Many examinees published their exercise essays and writings in order to publicize their names. The fifth type, "essays of literary society" (*shegao*), was a new anthology published by literary societies. It included the exercises of their members and was meant to advertise the talents of their members. This type of anthology arose as examinees sought to combine the power of publishing and organization in their attempt to pass the examinations in the 1620s.[83]

After the appearance of anthologies of essays on the Four Books, commercial publishers published anthologies of essays on the Five Classics sometime between 1592 and 1595. While every candidate was required to answer the same set of questions on the Four Books, each could choose to specialize on just one of the Five Classics. For the purpose of management and grading, examinees were divided into different "wards" (*fang*), and each of the Classics would have a different number of wards depending on the total number of examinees choosing the particular classic. The scope of inclusion for this type of anthology was coterminous with the number of examinees in the "same ward" (*tongfang*).[84] These anthologies were called *fangxuan* (selection from the wards).[85]

In addition to single examination anthologies, there were anthologies of essays from multiple examinations. The first anthology that included essays from examinations held in different years was compiled by a Hangzhou writer, Qian Gu, in 1580.[86] It became a common type of anthology by the early decades of the 1600s. An example is an anthology edited by Ai Nanying entitled *Bake fangxuan* (Selected examination essays from eight examinations). It anthologizes essays from eight examinations, covering the period from 1607 to 1628.[87] There were also anthologies including essays for the entire dynasty. The *Huangchao like Sishu mojuan pingzhuan* (a critical anthology of examination essays on the Four Books from the present dynasty) is an anthology for the entire Ming dynasty, including examination essays by renowned scholars and critics who eventually passed the metropolitan examinations. Authors include famous critics such as Qiu Zhaolin, Zhong Xing, Tang Binyin, and Huang Ruheng, and noted officials and thinkers such as Gu Xiancheng, Zhao Nanxing, Wang Ji, Yang Qiyuan, and Feng Mengzhen. Zhang Pu, leader of the Restoration Society, had edited similar anthologies.[88]

New ways of anthologizing continued to be invented by publishers and critics. By the 1600s, there was a special format of anthology that included essays from the provincial examination in the fall and the essays from the metropolitan examination in Beijing in the following spring. Zhang Pu had edited an anthology of examination essays for the provincial examination of 1627.[89] After the metropolitan examination was completed in the spring of 1628, he edited another anthology, which included essays from the 1627 examination. This is understandable because the majority of those whose essays were praised by the editor would not pass the metropolitan examination. And there were those who passed the metropolitan examination whose essays were not included in the early anthology. As Zhang Pu explained in his preface to the new anthology for both 1627 and 1628 examinations, "Those who edit model essays must include essays from both the fall and spring examinations . . . so that those left out can be included and those not included in other anthologies can be preserved."[90]

This format had become one of the more popular anthologies because it provided a sort of "history" of the practice of examinations. These types of anthologies provide examples of questions that had been asked in recent examinations. Examinees could then speculate on the possible questions that might be asked in the upcoming examination.

The selection and printing of these anthologies offered the professional critics the opportunity to make their own comments. Despite difference in format, these anthologies still endorsed the judgment of the examiners. Most "damaging" to the authority of the examiners was the publication of essays by those who failed the examination. Examination essays that were accepted at both the provincial and metropolitan levels were sent to the Ministry of Rites for review and recording.[91] The essays of those who failed were discarded. It is not clear when commercial publishers began publishing the essays of those who failed. Commercial publishers offered to pay 0.2 to 0.3 tael for the essays of those who failed at both levels.[92] They were then turned over to the critics for comments before printing. The editor-cum-critic became an alternative examiner, offering his own judgment on the literary performance of the examinees.

## Paratext and the Critic's Authority

The proliferation of various types of anthologies of examination essays on the Four Books and the Five Classics did not just provide more models to the candidates, it opened up a new discursive space for the examinees-cum-writers to challenge the judgment of the official examiners. The critics and editors had become the taste makers, *arbiter elegantium*.[93] In their hands, commercial publishing had invested the authority to arbitrate among different literary styles. They were catapulted into positions of authority in the literary field by commercial publishing. Pierre Bourdieu has argued that the "definition of culture" or "judgment of taste" is a result of the incessant struggle among factions of the dominant class. Occupation of these positions in the literary field allowed the critics of examination essays, as Bourdieu would argue,

> to define the legitimate principle of domination, between economic, educational or social capital, social powers whose specific efficacy

may be compounded by specifically symbolic efficacy, that is, the authority conferred by being recognized, mandated by collective belief.[94]

The authority of critics was recognized by readers of anthologies of examination essays. With the growing recognition of the critics' authority in arbitrating the quality of the examination essays, inclusion of one's essays in their anthologies became "public" evidence of excellence. The merits of examinees were publicly recognized by critics and editors. When the son of Zhang Juzheng took the metropolitan examination, his henchmen took the trouble to have a professional critic comment on his exercises.[95] To have one's essays selected by renowned editors was regarded as an honor, an achievement outside the institution of the civil service examination.[96] As made clear in a drama produced in the late 1620s, what defined a "famed literatus" (*mingshi*) was the selection of his essays in anthologies by critics (*ji you xuanke, bi shi zhi ming zhi shi*).[97]

The authority of the critics of anthologies was recognized by examinees. At the end of each examination, candidates sought out critics and sent them their essays for comments and inclusion. When Chen Jitai was in Beijing after the examination, he received a letter from Chen Zilong informing him that he would edit an anthology for the recent examination. Before Chen Jitai announced the news, more than three hundred examinees had already arrived at his door with their essays. Chen, himself a reputable critic, was serving as the liaison collecting the essays from the examinees in Beijing.[98]

There was a common way to use the critic's reputation to publicize the examinee's talents. Even if one's essays were not selected, one could still publish his own essays. To lend credit to one's own collection, examinees sought to include a preface by a famous critic or a "reputable master." Among the prefaces written by Li Mengyang and Li Panlong, there were no prefaces written for examination essays by candidates who were still trying to pass the provincial and metropolitan examinations.[99]

In contrast, Zhong Xing was approached by many examinees requesting prefaces for their works.[100] Ai Nanying never passed the metropolitan examination but close to fifty prefaces to the anthologies of individual candidates are included in his collected writings.[101] His friend Chen

Jitai, another critic from Jiangxi, had written more than thirty prefaces for anthologies of examination essays by individual examinees; so did Zhang Pu.[102] Tang Binyin was a reputable master in critiquing examinations and furnishing new comments on the Four Books. In his collection of personal writings he included no fewer than sixty prefaces and *tici* (remarks on the title) written for anthologies of examination essays. Most of them were the collection of one single examinee.[103] Fang Yingxiang (1561–1628) had published numerous examination essays with commercial publishers. His friend planned to compile a new anthology from them. Fang wrote a letter to Qian Qianyi (1582–1664) to request a preface for the anthology.[104] Included in the collected writings of Huang Ruheng were more than sixty prefaces written for anthologies of examination essays, of which more than twenty-five were collections by individual literati. Huang was the senior among the generation of critics who were active during the period 1600 to 1620. He wrote prefaces for other critics such as Shen Shouzheng, Qiu Zhaolin (1572–1629), and Fang Yingxiang.[105]

The remarks by Ai Nanying on the authority of professional critics are revealing with regard to the impact on the practice of the civil service examination. Ai had observed that two other critics—Zhou Zhong and Zhang Pu—were not able to impose their literary view on examinees in their own districts. But the latter could not afford not to read the critical anthologies edited by Zhou and Zhang. Inclusion in their anthologies was regarded as public recognition of literary achievement. Failure to have one's essays included was a tragic experience. Ai clearly was aware of the enormous influence critics like himself were able to exert on the process of the civil service examination through anthologizing and commenting on examination essays, a power he compared to that of the emperor.[106] The authority of the critics over literary excellence constituted an autonomous tribunal that official examiners had to come to terms with.

Once the critic's status was established as a competing or superior judge, the reputation of critics became a symbolic capital that examinees struggled to attain. Examinees who were critics had a better chance of passing the examination. To distinguish oneself, an examinee had to strike out a niche in the commercial publishing market as a critical editor. Li Zhongyi from Fujian, who had written commentary on the Four Books, was a critical editor while he was struggling to pass the provincial examination. His "public" reputation helped him pass the provincial examination.[107]

With the general recognition of the "power" of the critic, those examinees from wealthy families who would not have to live off working for commercial publishers chose to publish anthologies of examination essays. The case of Zhou Zhong was a good example. Zhou came from the most illustrious and wealthy family in Jinsha. As a talented writer, he distinguished himself as an emerging leader among the critics in Jiangnan since the early 1620s.[108] Despite an iota of evidence from bibliographies of Ming-edition books, Zhou was unmistakably involved in editing and critiquing examination essays as a professional critic.[109]

CRITICS AND COMMERCIAL PUBLISHING

Commercial publishing played a major role in the creation of professional critics of examination essays, as indicated by a group of critics from Zhejiang, Jiangxi, and Nanzhili who were active between 1590 and the 1630s. They overlapped to a certain extent, and many of them were friends.

Shen Shouzheng, a native of Hangzhou, had authored a popular commentary on the Four Books entitled *Sishuo shuocong*, which had become a frequently cited title in late-Ming commentaries. He passed the provincial examination in 1603 but was not successful at the metropolitan examination. Like most examinees, Shen had published several collections of his own examination essays.[110] To support his family and his sustained quest for the highest degree, he depended on tutoring and working for publishers and patrons. Like many other literati, he often had to take loans.[111] He had been involved in editing anthologies of examination essays of graduates and he specialized in the *Book of Odes* for the sessions on the Five Classics. In 1613, more than six hundred essays by examinees on the *Book of Odes* were sent to him by mail. He selected one-third with his comments for publication.[112] Shen befriended other critics from whom he requested prefaces. Huang Ruheng was one notable example.[113] In 1616, despondent at the prospect of success at the metropolitan examination, Shen finally decided to take up the position of instructor at a government school in the Huangyan county.[114]

Huang Ruheng, also from Hangzhou, published his own collection of examination exercises as early as 1588 while seeking to pass the provincial examination.[115] He had compiled a commentary on the Four Books entitled *Sishu quanzhi* (Themes in commentaries on the Four Books).[116] He had long been involved in editing anthologies for both single and multiple examinations. Of these, some were compiled from already published anthologies of collections.[117] He was also involved in the editing of the new type of anthology, including essays from the provincial examination and the metropolitan examination in the following spring; these include those held in 1609–10, 1612–13, and 1615–16.[118] What is noteworthy is that these anthologies were edited after he graduated from the metropolitan examination in 1598. In addition to these comprehensive anthologies, he also edited the essays of his own students who graduated in 1610 and 1613.[119] Like all other critics, he received essays from examinees and students via mail.[120]

The most popular critics of examination essays from Jiangxi in the 1610s through the 1630s were Ai Nanying, Chen Jitai, Qiu Zhaolin, and Luo Wanzao.[121] Qiu Zhaolin's anthologies of examination essays were commonly found on the desks of students.[122] He was listed as compiler for many anthologies published by commercial publishers in Nanjing and Jiangyang.[123] Qiu also edited a commentary on the *Book of Changes* that could have been used in his family for examination. It was published in Nanjing in the Chongzhen reign (1628–44). He had gotten the endorsement of Tang Binyin, who was the examiner who passed him at the metropolitan examination in 1610.[124] Tang was listed as having reviewed it (*jianding*).[125] Tang Binyin, a native of Xuancheng, Nanzhili, was also a reputable master of examination essays known more by the name of his studio, *Shui'an* (Studio of slumber).[126] Tang was among the most frequently quoted writer in commentaries on the Four Books (see Chapter 4). He had published anthologies of his own examination essays and had been involved in selecting and commenting on examination essays.[127] Like other reputable masters, he had written many prefaces for examinees' personal collections of essays.[128] Tang also edited the collected writings of his fellow native, the playwright Mei Dingzuo.[129] An anthology of writings selected from various histories was published by a Jianyang publisher (1604) with Tang listed as the editor.[130]

Jiangxi critics such as Chen Jitai and Ai Nanying had all edited and cri-

tiqued essays for a single examination.[131] Ai Nanying was one of the renowned critics of examination essays in the 1620s and 1630s. He had edited and commented on examinations for 1628, 1630, 1631, 1634, and
1635.[132]

A writer conventionally classified as a member of the Tang-Song style
of "ancient prose," he earned his *shengyuan* degree in 1600. Ai resented
the experience of taking the civil service examination; after close to
twenty years of repeated attempts, he passed the provincial examination
in 1619.[133] But he never passed the metropolitan examination. Like Chen
Jitai, he enjoyed a wide reputation as a critic of examination essays. He began his critiquing of examination essays no later than 1615.[134] Every time
he finished his metropolitan examination and returned south in dejection,
he would stay in Nanjing for a few months to work for commercial publishers.[135] As his reputation grew, publishers would personally greet him as
he traveled back from Beijing. In 1630, when Ai was going south, a Nanjing publisher greeted him in Wuhu, presenting to him the essays from the
1630 examination.[136] While working mostly as an independent critic, he
also collaborated with other writers in compiling anthologies.[137]

Critics often were at odds with the preference of commercial publishers who had their eyes on profit and speedy production. Ai Nanying often
compromised his ideas with those of the publishers. When he published
two anthologies of essays entitled *Jinwen ding* (Ultimate selection of contemporary writings) and *Jinwen dai* (Anticipated writings of contemporary writings) covering multiple examinations, his selection covered a
much wider temporal scope. Ai was unequivocally attempting to create
an anthology of essays that met his criteria of excellence. He treated it as
a serious scholarly undertaking. However, his publisher was only interested in including essays from recent examinations from 1608 through
1628, for the obvious reason that examinees were indifferent to truly out-
standing essays of all times. The conflict in intention was resolved in the
triumph of the publisher, who promised to append those essays before
1608 to the two anthologies. Ai recommended another critic, Wu Zhongsheng, to comment on the appended essays. But in his attempt to publish
the books speedily, the publisher chose to cut Wu's comments as well as
the appendix. Those excised essays and comments were appended to anthologies of the essays from the 1631 and 1634 examinations.[138]

This complex process of negotiation between the critic's choice and the publisher's concern for timely publication against competitors exemplifies the authority of the professional critics in literary criticism, on the one hand, and the constraints of commercial publishing imposed on the field of cultural production and the examination field, on the other. Commercial publishing fostered competition among critics who sought to impose their own views on their readers. To win over the readers, the critic could not help but to disparage his competitors. The diatribes among critics themselves contributed further to the elevation of status of the critic as the arbiter of literary excellence. In a letter to Chen Dingsheng, Wu Yingji blamed the critics (*pingxuan zhe*) for not discovering the "spirit of the ancients" (*guren zhi jingshen*). He singled out for criticism, for their respective roles in "burying" the "spirit of the ancients," the poetry critic Zhong Xing, the examination essay critic Zhang Nai, and the ancient prose critic Mao Kun: "They have comments and annotations for every word and every sentence. They underline and punctuate [*quandian*] every section and paragraph. They claim by so doing, they would provide methods and models for subsequent generations. People do not know that they distort the ancients and misguide the new generation."[139]

This criticism of professional critics by Wu Yingji, himself a critic and an active member of the Restoration Society, reveals how the critics sought to carve out a new space for themselves in assuming the authority over prose writing against previous and contemporary writers. But unlike the Former and Latter Seven Masters, these *shishang* writers were struggling examinees, speaking as masters of prose who were able to explain and teach the methods, the strengths, and weaknesses of writings.

Wu Yingji's criticism of Zhong Xing, Zhang Nai, and Mao Kun represents clearly the self-proclaimed and important roles of the critics in setting the trends in literary fashion. However, it also reflected the eclipse of the authority of officials by that of the critics whose reputation was derived from the publishing market.

### Critics against Examiners

According to Chen Jitai, before the Longqing reign, predictions of the place where the first place graduates at the metropolitan and palace examinations were always accurate. This was because commercial printing of examination aids had not yet expanded.[140] Chen suggested that the wider circulation of examination aids and the dependence on memorizing model essays helped students from areas that lacked scholarly tradition to be more competitive. Examinees from the Jiangnan area could no longer monopolize success at the examinations. His explanation undoubtedly oversimplified the complex ways in which publishing changed the ways the examinees prepared for the examination and the process of selecting graduates. He nonetheless underscored the important role of publishing in the politics of cultural production and distribution of political resources in the late Ming. Many examinees vied for the authority over literary excellence offered by commercial publishing. Printing provided a powerful means to express disagreement and grievances of the examinees. It invited the reading public to comment and judge the examiners' grading practices. Through printing, the review process of the examination system was forced opened and the examiners were made responsible for their grading and hence the distribution of privilege to enter the officialdom. Publication of examination essays had the same effect of those anthologies by individual examinees who were struggling to pass higher examinations. The praise garnered by examinees from authors of prefaces often conveyed the sense that something was wrong with a system that continued to fail such talented writers.

Growing discontent with the selection of graduates by examiners was widespread among examinees. The critics were particularly strident in their criticism of inconsistent application of literary standards and of the periodic proclamation by the Ministry of Rites concerning its intention to rectify the literary style of the examinees. Critics were not only aware of their newly gained authority over literary taste, but also fervent in defending their positions against government control over literary styles. In Chapter 4, we have seen how the Ministry of Rites' attempt to police the ideological content of the examination essays met with resistance. Many critics were skeptical and critical of government endeavor at imposing rigid standard on literary style.

Huang Ruheng, one of the early critics of examination essays, who had already established his reputation in the mid-Wanli reign, had observed the interplay of various factors in the determination of literary standards. In the preface to an anthology, which combines examination essays from the 1609 and 1610 examinations, he notes that "it is difficult to rectify literary style because neither the examinees nor the examiners are able to set the standard. In addition, publishers who treat writings as commodities added to the confusion by displaying a wide array of dazzling styles." After the ebbing of emotion and with the passage of time, the critic with impartiality is able to make his judgment based on reason and the examination question. It was only then when "literary authority" was exercised (*wenzhang zhi quan shen yi*), contended Huang.[141]

Many critics considered the attempts by the Ministry of Rites to impose strict rules on literary style a mistake. Critics saw regulations over style objectionable for both practical and intellectual reasons. In his preface to an anthology of examination essays, Tang Binyin explained the difficulty in selecting essays. He noted the discrepancy in the criterion with which the critics and the examiners made their choices.[142] In a similar vein, Qiu Zhaolin pointed out that what the Ministry of Rites publicly endorsed as the correct style was not enforced by examiners who preferred essays written in different styles.[143] Examinees were confused by the conflicting criteria adopted by the Ministry of Rites and individual examiners who did not always follow the directives of the ministry. Qiu, however, had a deeper concern about government attempts to regulate literary production.

In the preface to a 1610 anthology of examination essays, Qiu publicly criticized officials in the ministry who called for "rectifying the literary style" (*zhengwenti*). For Qiu, "nothing remains the same without the creation of novelty; no rules are inherited to the point of not giving rise to new ones" (*wu wugu er buxin, fa wu yin er buchuang*). Literary styles, he stressed, invariably differed with the passage of time. Each generation had its own style. Even examination essays during the different imperial reigns under the Ming saw changes with the succession of generations of writers. He traced the inevitable differences to the "spirits, strengths, talents, and characters" (*shen, qi, cai, pin*) of the writers.[144] In a word, it was the differences in the literary and moral qualities of the writers that rendered it impossible and futile to regulate literary style.

Zhong Xing, as a critic of poetry and prose, shared the views of his fellow critics. He was also hailed as the founder of the Jinglin school, the name of his native place. He condemned those officials who sought to "rectify the literary style" of examinees as circumscribing the talents of the literati. In his advice to his friends who assumed the duties as educational officers in the provincial government, he urged them to look for the learning, the truth, the strengths, the talents, feelings, spirits, and goals of the students. Rigid rules of literary form were of no use in education.[145]

Compared with earlier generations of literary critics such as the Former and Latter Seven Masters, and even the Tang-Song Eight Masters, critics such as Qiu, Zhong, Huang, and the Yuan brothers from Gong'an did not uphold a specific literary model for emulation. They invariably put a high premium on the need to appreciate diversity in style rooted in the differences in artistic, moral, and personal qualities of the individual writer. It is common knowledge that Tang Xianzu, Yuan Hongdao, and Zhong Xing all advocated the centrality of individuality or *"xingling"* in literary production, be it poetry or prose. They all repudiated compliance with rigid rules concerning content and form in literary production.[146] But the leaders of the Restoration Society, such as Zhang Pu and Chen Zilong, were exponents of the Qin Han writings. Their rival Ai Nanying opted for the Tang-Song style. Competition in the literary public sphere fueled rivalry and jealousy. The important point, however, is not what particular literary style the critics promoted, nor whose poetics was superior. What is significant is the challenge their poetics posed to the authority of officials and examiners who sought to impose an official standard on all examinees. It was the literary styles of these critics and writers, not those of the examiners or high officials, that the examinees regarded as the judge of literary taste and excellence. The arbitration of literary taste battled itself out in the literary public sphere populated by professional critics whose authority commanded the respect of the community of readers at large.

As pointed out above, examiners at the metropolitan examinations had been printing their own essays as models for examinees for each examination. By the 1620s as pressure from critics and the publishing industries continued to mount, examiners were afraid to edit essays of the graduates as models. In the wake of the metropolitan examination of 1625, the examiners simply did away with the practice of using their essays as models. The model essays selected were all by the metropolitan graduates. It was adopted by examiners at the provincial examination in 1627.[147] By the 1630s, the critics had nullified the authority of the examiners by publishing anthologies of model essays, including essays by members of literary societies, personal exercises of individual examinees, and the essays by graduates. In a preface to an anthology of model essays by examiners and successful examinees in the 1630 examination, Zeng Yi noted that "today anthologies of essays published by literary societies and individual examinees competed with those written by examiners and successful candidates."[148] By including essays of examinees who failed the examination, the professional writers publicly called into question the justice in the process of selecting graduates by the imperial government.

LITERARY SOCIETIES AND EXAMINATION SUCCESS

By the 1620s, publishing, professional critics, and the civil service examination began to become an inseparable nexus of activities in the field of cultural production. Examinees in the last fifty years of the Ming dynasty could not avoid publishing their writings, be they poetry, eight-legged essays on the Four Books and the Five Classics, or treatises on policy questions. As Chen Jitai made clear, the examinees published their poetry for review by the examiners, a preview before the actual test at the examination.[149] Glancing through the "collected writings" (*wenji*) of the late-Ming period, one cannot but be struck by the large number of prefaces written for examination exercises, especially the eight-legged style essays.[150] But publishing, especially private publications were inexpensive and accessible to almost all the examinees. Printing one's own writings as a private publication was no longer sufficient to distinguish oneself from the myriad examinees. Attempts to increase one's chance of success at the examination contributed to the strategy of combining the power of publishing and organization—the formation of study groups and literary organizations.

Before the Ming, examinees formed literary societies (*wenshe*) in order to better prepare themselves for the civil service examination.[151] The enormous importance and the intensity of the competition had prompted many candidates to engage in drilling exercises emulating the examination process. Candidates rehearsed the whole process of an examination, down to every detail, as if the candidates were actually taking the examinations.

Before the Wanli period, the famous literary societies were mostly poetry clubs organized by officials interested in writing and critiquing poetry. The Latter Seven Masters met at the White Cloud legislature (Baiyun lou), where the office of the Ministry of Punishment was located. Famous poetry clubs or literary societies before the Wanli period were founded by officials; membership reflected their close ties to the imperial state. The names of the clubs and societies were less important than the leaders. They were therefore referred to more by the names or persons, rather than by the abstract names of the associations. Most members were already officials. The reputation of these literary societies was derived from members who were already occupants of positions in the political field. The significance of their literary achievement was derivative and secondary. This was in accord with the relationship between the political field and the field of cultural production. The authority over literary taste was still firmly in the hands of those who occupied positions in the political field. In contrast, the literary societies that began to receive recognition were founded by examinees in the late-Wanli period. They were founded by candidates who were still outside the political field or at the most tenuously linked to the political field through the degree system.

The trend of turning study groups into literary societies that published their own exercises was in part the result of a brief period of tightening of the granting of *shengyuan* status. The number of *shengyuan* increased to such an alarming degree that in the Jiajing period, there were attempts to enforce a quota system. In 1532, a government decree ordered the reduction of the number of *shengyuan*. It was revoked because a censor submitted a memorial against it. Then in 1575, Zhang Juzheng ordered another reduction of *shengyuan* degrees. Smaller quotas meant even more competition.

Study groups or poetry clubs were common practice among literati in the Ming. Lu Shiyi traced the better-known literary societies in Suzhou to the founding of the *Yi she* by Duke Gu Wenkuang. Gui Youguang (1506–1571) later founded the Northern and Southern Societies (*Nanbei e she*).[152] Forming study groups was a common practice not confined to the

Lower Yangtze region. Examinees in Fujian also formed study groups in order to rehearse for the examinations. The famous official Li Tingji recalled when he was only twelve years old, he formed a study group with a few friends to prepare for the examinations.[153] Study groups formed by examinees lasted as long as the members remained unsuccessful. Once they passed the metropolitan examinations, the groups would cease to exist, since members would have to take up official positions away from home.

While forming study groups had been quite common before the 1590s, creating an organized society with a name was mostly a practice found in Nanzhili and Zhejiang. Zhong Xing from Hubei intimated that when he was a *shengyuan* during the period from 1591 to 1603, he did not know about literary societies.[154] Sun Kuang (1542–1613) related that most of the examinees in Yuyao, Zhejiang, had formed literary societies by the time he returned from Liaoning, possibly in the mid-1590s. Like other examinees, the members of a Changsongge (Pavilion of tall pines) society invited him to serve as editor and critic. He selected for publication more than fifty essays by its members.[155] Yuyao was one of the counties with the highest concentration of literati; before the 1590s, examinees did not regard literary societies as necessarily useful in preparing for the examination. They remained mostly small and exclusive in membership. An example was a society founded by Hao Jing (1558–1639) and Li Weizhen (1547–1626) to prepare for examinations in the late 1580s; it was a small group of five to six people.[156]

Many study groups that called themselves a "society" did not even have a name. They were simply referred to by the number of members. In Suzhou there were the "Ten persons society," "Six persons society," and "Eighteen persons society."[157] These "nameless" literary societies did not need a name to differentiate themselves from others for they were founded primarily as private groups to prepare for the examination. They had no public presence in terms of organization.[158]

*Literary Societies in the Tianqi Reign*

Before the 1620s, study groups that were organized into literary societies tended to be exclusive in membership. Most literary societies were intended to distinguish their members from other competing members in the same area. Membership hardly signaled prestige since they were exclusive and mostly restricted to close friends or relatives. Consequently, membership tended to be small, from three to a dozen. For example, the Foshui shanfang was organized by examinees from Changshu county; membership was no more than nine.

The Southern Society (Nanshe) was founded by examinees in Anhui with a small membership. Later one of its leaders, Wu Yingji, formed a new society with a Suzhou examinee, Xu Mingshi, calling it Kuangshe (Support Society). The initial membership of Kuangshe remained small.[159] Members of a Yunzanshe (Society of High Aspiration) in Kunshan asked Zhang Pu to write a preface for their anthology. Its membership appears to be restrictive.[160]

In Hangzhou, there was the Xiaochushe, organized around 1609 by the Yan brothers: Yan Tiaoyu, Yan Wushun, and Yan Chi. The family group was later expanded to become the Dushushe (Study Society) in 1627 and its membership was still restricted to about twenty-four.[161] Its active members include Wen Qixiang, the Yan brothers, and others.[162] Both Wen and Yan studied with Fang Yingxiang, a renowned critics from Shenxi.[163] The group was relatively small like most other societies before the late 1620s. The mentor and his disciples collaborated in editing and writing comments on books. For example, each of them edited and proofread a chapter in a commentary on *Zhuangzi*.[164] As a professional critic himself, Wen Qixiang had commented on other books and had edited anthologies of examination essays.[165] Other literary societies in Zhejiang remained small in membership.[166] In 1624, the Yingshe (Response Society), founded by Zhang Pu, had only thirteen members.[167]

The renowned critic from Jiangxi, Chen Jitai, was a member of the Ziyunshe (Purple Cloud Society), which met in a Buddhist temple. Other members included Ai Nanying, Luo Wanzu, Zhang Shichun, and Qiu Zhaolin. All were well-known critics from Jiangxi. Other literary societies in Jiangxi sought prefaces from them for their publications.[168] Examinees in Kaifeng, Henan, also began to organize into literary societies in 1624. The founding of the Haijinshe (Society of the Sea of Gold) the following year prompted other examinees in Henan to do likewise.[169]

During the late 1620s, the membership of literary societies in some areas appeared to have grown from small groups to several scores. For example, Feng Menglong, Yao Ximeng, Wen Zhenmeng, Qian Qianyi, Shen Yan, Wen Tiren, and Zhu Guozhen were leading members of the Yunshe (Rhyme Society), first organized sometime around 1620; it had grown to at least eighty-eight members.[170] In Songjiang, membership of the Jishe (Society of Hope) in the beginning was restricted to only six examinees.[171] By 1632, its membership had grown to more than one hundred.[172] The growth in membership size of literary societies was the result of the recognition of the literary authority of the critics and the need to form translocal societies.

*Publishing and the Power of Networking*

Small study groups eventually began to take advantage of the power of publishing to advance their fortune in the state examinations.[173] There were at least two trends: first, examinees sought to publish their exercises collectively as the work of the society, called *shegao*, in addition to publishing works under an individual examinee's own name.[174] Members of the same society were included as coreaders or coeditors or as authors of prefaces. They were called "friends of the same society" (*sheyou, shedi,* or *shemeng*).[175] Membership in a literary society became a symbol of literary excellence.

The second trend involved the formation of translocal communities of examinees since the mid-Wanli period. The involvement of members of literary societies in publishing made possible the creation of a community of critics that transcended boundaries of administrative districts. Xu Shipu recalled that during the 1560s, "The literati did not make networks and there were no commercial publications [of examination essays]. Literary meetings were restricted to kinsmen and students from the same neighborhood." But in the Wanli period, like other examinees, Xu began to communicate with examinees from other prefectures. They commented on one another's work. In a few years, "examinees from north and south were all connected and came to a 'great consensus' [*datong*]." Xu's explanation of why the authority over literary excellence at the examination had shifted from the government to the people below is revealing.

> The examiners make their selection based on the distinction between good and bad essays, making clear the evidence for their scholarly excellence. Then the "literary authority" [*wenzhang zhi*

*quan*] would remain in the hands of the examiners, and the examinees would be contented to study in order to meet the good standards. But when the selection is inappropriate and the criteria of right and wrong, good and bad, are no longer regarded by the examinees as justified, the literary authority will lie below.[176]

The ability of the examinees to "usurp" the authority of the examiners lay in the public authority they created by means of publishing their essays as a group as well as the reputation of the leaders as critics in the world of commercial publishing. As a leading critic in Hangzhou, Wen Qixiang was a leader of the Study Society (Dushushe). Examinees in Hangzhou and Zhejiang were anxious to have their writings critiqued by him.[177] Wen was either the sole owner or an associate of the publishing house called Dushufang, which had published at least sixteen books, including some by Chen Jiru.[178]

Members of Yingshe such as Chen Zilong and Gu Menglin also had ventured into publishing. Chen Zilong was a critic of poetry and examination essays. He compiled and published the voluminous compendium of essays on statecraft, the *Huang Ming jingshi wenbian* under his studio Pinglutang. And Gu Menglin published his own works such as *Sishu shuoyue* (Concise exposition on the Four Books) and *Shijing shuoyue* (Concise exposition on the *Book of Odes*) in his Lianjiju publishing house.[179] Gu clearly intended to gain reputation through these examination aids. But neither Gu nor Chen seems to operate a publishing house on a scale like Wen Qixiang's Dushufang in Hangzhou. The boundary between commercial and private publishing could hardly be drawn at a small scale.

Many leaders of literary circles clearly intended to use the organizational power of literary societies and their own reputation to enhance their chances of success at the examinations. In a preface to a collection of poetry published by Gu Menglin, Yang Yi, Zhang Shichun, and Zhang Cai, Chen Jitai argued that they organized societies to promote their skills in prose writing and poetry. Their poetry was published and disseminated so that they could be reviewed and chosen by examiners.[180]

Literary societies organized in the 1620s showed marked differences from previous ones. These groups were no longer examinees holding their private meetings in small groups. Many of their leaders were editors and critics who were well known outside their home counties. The anthologies of examination essays that they edited and critiqued were sold in bookstores and by book merchants throughout the empire. These examinees-cum-critics recognized the reputation commercial publishing had generated as important symbolic capital with which they came to build networks reaching beyond their local communities. Publicity produced in print enabled them to form larger and more powerful societies. Critics from the Suzhou area took the lead in this direction.

## The Dominance of Suzhou Critics

Examinees who had established themselves as reputable critics had to compete on two fronts: at the examination hall and in commercial publishing. The differences in their literary tastes became a polemics with important implications. The battle over literary style might carry with it practical consequences of success at the examination. Stories of rivalries among critics came to fill the pages of the literary history of the late sixteenth and early seventeenth century.

By the mid-Wanli period, around the 1590s, Suzhou had clearly emerged as the center of culture, exerting a dominant influence in the literary field. Suzhou with Nanjing were the two centers of the literary market in the Jiangnan region, with a high concentration of professional writers.[181] Located at the nexus of the most commercialized region of the empire and positioned in a transportation hub, and with its flourishing publishing industry and book trade Suzhou offered its local critics unmatched advantages over rivals from other parts of the empire.

According to Sun Kuang, examination essays by individual writers from Yuyao, Zhejiang, were widely read and regarded during the early Jiajing reign.[182] But by the late sixteenth century, it was no longer the case. Suzhou critics had become eminent arbiters of literary excellence, overshadowing critics from other regions. Critics from other localities could find their reputation surge with endorsing acclaim from Suzhou critics. A case in point was Chen Jitai. Chen's examination essays were not only widely circulated among examinees from Jiangxi but also highly regarded outside Jiangxi. But it was not until Zhou Zhong, a leading critic in Suzhou, included his essays in his anthologies that Chen achieved national acclaim.[183] It is true that Ai Nanying, Chen Jitai, Qiu Zhaolin, Luo Wanzu, and Zhang Shichun from Jiangxi had achieved reputations as critics. But they were hired by publishers in Suzhou or Nanjing. Their reputation would be greatly restricted had they not published with Suzhou or Nanjing publishers.

Despite his bitter rivalry with Suzhou critics, Ai Nanying could not but concede that "presently nowhere is more voluminous in the production of critical anthologies than Suzhou." Not only did Suzhou publishers turn out the largest number of anthologies of examination essays, but the critics from Suzhou became the leaders in the circle of professional critics. Ai compared Suzhou with his hometown in Jiangxi and offered an explanation for the cultural power of Suzhou. Unlike Suzhou, his hometown Dongxiang, in Jiangxi, was off the major routes of trade and communication. Mail was far less convenient, and consequently the delivery of essays via mail took longer and was unreliable. Commercial publishers who competed to issue critical anthologies were on strict schedules. Without the help of friends and teachers, it was an extremely exacting task to complete selection and comments within a short period of time.[184]

Suzhou critics had a strong sense of local identity. They considered themselves leaders of local literary communities. Zhou Zhong, for example, was particularly conscious of the power of his selection and put it to use in order to create publicity for examinees from Suzhou. As Zhang Pu boasted in a preface to an anthology of examination essays, "There are many who achieved their reputation by virtue of the promotion by Jiesheng [Zhou Zhong]."[185] Other Suzhou critics, such as Zhang Pu and Yang Tingshu, publicly promoted Suzhou examinees in their prefaces to anthologies of examination essays.[186] However, Zhou Zhong was also committed to promoting worthy examinees from other provinces, and Chen Jitai was but one example.[187]

Since the mid-1620s, Zhou Zhong, Zhang Pu, Yang Tingshu, and Yang Yi were all involved in editing various kinds of anthologies from single or multiple examinations to those by members of literary societies.[188] They specialized in their chosen Classics: Yang Yi and Gu Menglin were responsible for editing an anthology for essays on the *Book of Odes*; Zhang Pu for the *Book of Changes*; Zhou Zhong and his brother for the *Spring and Autumn Annals*; and Yang Tingshu for the *Book of Documents*.[189] In addition to anthologies of essays on the Four Books, they edited anthologies on historical essays and treatises on statecraft.[190]

The reasons for the dominance of Suzhou critics in the production of anthologies of examination essays were many. The bloodline of publishers was access to manuscripts. Publishers could depend on advertisements in the paratext of their books (see Chapter 2). But speedy delivery of essays from the two capitals and the provincial cities depended on good transportation. A network of connections was also crucial to critics and publishers. Soliciting and receiving essays from examinees all over the empire was essential to producing nonprovincial anthologies. In 1626, when Zhang Pu planned to compile a new anthology of essays on the *Book of Changes*, he solicited essays from friends and leading critics from other areas. He wrote to Chen Jitai and other literati in Jiangxi. Chen served as a collecting agent for him.[191] To claim a status of imperial scale and impartiality for their selections, critics like Zhang Pu had to maintain a network of examinees who were leaders in various local literary communities.[192]

## Collaboration and Rivalry

The relationship between critics could be one of collaboration, but it could also be bitter rivalry. Zhou Zhong and Zhang Pu advocated the use of the Classics in illuminating the Four Books. In his anthology of examination essays from the 1621–22 examinations, Zhou Zhong began urging examinees to read the Four Books in relation to the Classics. For them Classical scholarship was the foundation of learning.[193] They upheld the prose of the Qin Han periods as models. In the beginning, Ai Nanying appeared to be on good terms with Zhou. As late as 1624, he was communicating with him on reaching a consensus on the selection of essays. But they had difficulty reaching a common ground on literary models. His preference was the prose of the Tang-Song Masters, whereas Zhou promoted those of the Qin and Han.[194] Ai was upset by the praise Zhou heaped on Chen Jitai, who modeled himself after the excessive embellishment and parallelism of the Eastern Han. Ai sent Zhou letters to register his discontent with Zhou's selection and comments.[195]

Ai became increasingly impatient with Zhou Zhong as well as with other critics who looked to Zhou for leadership. "Nowhere publishes more anthologies of examination essays than Suzhou. But in my view, they are not anthologies of examination essays [by all examinees] but publications of literary societies."[196] Ai considered himself a disinterested critic who looked for the best essays regardless of the examinees' geographic origins. He accused the critics in Suzhou of partisanship, of appropriating the anthologies as tools for publicity. Their selections reflected not so much an impartial judgment of quality as a partisan collection of essays. For Ai, Suzhou critics were hardly contented to select the best examinees in their critical anthologies. They were in actuality seeking to further the chances of success for members of literary societies to which they belonged.

In Ai's writings there was clearly a sense of pride and bitterness over the domination of critics from Suzhou in the publishing industry of examination aids. In the wake of the 1628 examination, there were numerous anthologies, including many by members of the Yingshe, such as Zhang Pu, Ma Shiqi, and Song Fengxiang.[197] Ai published his own anthology, in which he criticized Zhang Pu and his followers for emulating only the literary style and diction, rather than the spirit, of the Classics.[198]

As Ai Nanying was involved in a debate and rivalry with Suzhou critics, being on good terms with critics outside Suzhou, he turned to critics from other areas for support. He appeared to be a good friend of Wen Qixiang, a critic of examination essays who operated a publishing business in Hangzhou.[199] Both Ai and Wen had compiled anthologies for the metropolitan examination of 1631. Ai spent the summer in Nanjing and completed the selection and comments for the anthology. He wrote a letter to Wen urging him to be rigorous in making his selection and not to use Buddhist and Daoist expressions in his comments. The main objective of the letter was actually an attempt to orchestrate a concerted effort to create a consensus between the two in order to counteract the Suzhou critics' selections. Ai suggested that Wen withhold publication of his anthology until his first anthology was published, thereby allowing Wen to exclude those essays Ai had criticized. Ai then put off his second anthology until he saw Wen's anthology. He would then include those in the second anthology that Wen had praised but had been excluded in his first anthology. By their collaboration, a "public opinion" (*tianxia zhi gongyan*) about the best prose style would be created.[200] Ai Nanying however was not able to compete with Suzhou critics such as Zhang Pu and Zhou Zhong because they eventually took the lead in fashioning a kind of "united front" of all the critics in their attempt to challenge the judgment of government examiners.

ALLIANCE OF LITERARY CRITICS:
THE RESTORATION SOCIETY (FUSHE)

The organization of local examinees into literary societies was an attempt to formulate public opinion on the best examiners at the local level based on administrative division. The Yuzhang Society in Jiangxi, for example, selected one examinee as the "director" (*jijiu*) for each prefecture. These examinees designated as directors were selected by examiners with only a few exceptions.[201] The organization of the examinees into literary societies, with their own process of selecting the best candidates, exerted pressure on official examiners, who would face considerable opposition from an organized group of examinees; this pressure remained local.

The proliferation of literary societies in the early decades of the seventeenth century cumulated in the founding of an alliance called the Restoration Society (Fushe) based in Suzhou in 1630. It marked the turning point in the development of the organizations of examinees. While locally based literary societies had some success in pressuring examiners into passing their leaders at the local level, candidates were still at the mercy of examiners who were vulnerable to bribery and pressure from high officials. The founding of the Restoration Society marked the appearance of an empirewide literary organization aiming at influencing the examiners in their selection of candidates at higher levels of examinations.

The Restoration Society that attained unprecedented reputation and power formed as a result of its merging with the Yingshe (Response Society). It was initially organized by Wu Zeng and Sun Chun. It aroused hostility from members of the Yingshe (Response Society), founded by Zhang Pu, Zhang Cai, Zhou Zhong, Yang Yi, and Gu Menglin. Some time in 1627 under the leadership of Zhang Pu and Zhou Zhong, the Response Society doubled its initial membership of thirteen by including critics from outside the Suzhou region.[202] The new society was simply called the Expanded Response Society (Guang Yingshe).[203]

With the effort of Zhang Pu, the two societies eventually merged under the name of the Restoration Society. After the merge, Wu and Sun sought to expand further its membership to include more examinees from outside the Suzhou region. Wu provided the money for Sun to travel extensively to recruit members. He sought out those examinees with reputations and were already organized into literary societies.[204] They included the Kuang-she in Nanzhili, Duanshe (Society of Rectitude) in Henan, Yishe (Society of the District) in Shangdong, Zhishe (Substance Society) in Huangzhou, Jishe (Society of Hope) in Jiangsu, and Chaoshe (Progress Society) and Zhuangshe (Dignity Society) in Zhejiang.[205] Members of these societies were invited to attend an organizational meeting in 1629.[206]

In the fall of 1630 when seventy-five hundred candidates convened in Nanjing for the provincial examination, Zhang Pu called a meeting of members of the Restoration Society to decide on the regulations and curriculum.[207] When the examination results were posted, many of its members graduated, including Yang Tingshu, Zhang Pu, Chen Zilong, Wu Weiye, and Wu Changshi. They were among the thirty members of the Restoration Society who passed the provincial examination. The total number of graduates who belonged to the Restoration Society amounts to 20 percent of the 150 *juren* degrees granted in that examination in Nanjing. The next spring, at the metropolitan examination held in Beijing, members of the Restoration Society continued to boast a spectacular success rate in graduating, with sixty-two, 18 percent of the total 347 *jinshi* of that year.[208] Not only did Zhang Pu take second place, his student Wu Weiye moved on to receive the first place.[209] Such a success rate for members of the same literary society convinced many of the need to join the Restoration Society or to form their own society. Success in the examination was impossible without first becoming a member of a well-publicized literary organization, unless one resorted to blatant bribery.

After Zhang Pu graduated in 1631, Zhou Zhong took charge of the editing of publications of the Restoration Society.[210] When it published essays of its members in 1632, they chose the title *Guobiao*, meaning "models of the state."[211] The anthology was unprecedented in including more than twenty-five hundred essays by more than seven hundred candidates from all over the empire. They were listed not by society membership, but by administrative units, beginning with province, prefecture, and county. For regions with higher concentrations of examinees, such as Nanzhili, Zhejiang, and Jiangxi, members were listed under their respective counties. For provinces with only one or half a dozen examinees, such as Sichuan, Shenxi, and Guizhou, no prefecture or county were listed. A chief (*zhang*) was chosen for each county or prefecture to be the leader and liaison for communication. For example, Zhang Pu was listed first in the Taichang district; Yang Tingshu headed the group of twelve in Wu county; Yang Yi was ranked ahead of his twelve fellow candidates from Changshu county; Xia Yunyi headed the Songjiang group; and Chen Zilong for Qingpu county. Zhou Zhong ranked number one under the Zhenjiang prefecture. The Huating group was headed by Zhou Lixun and Xu Fuyuan; Shen Shoumin was placed at the top for the Ningguo prefecture. Chen Jitai was listed under Fuzhou prefecture, Jiangxi. Other renowned critics such as Luo Wanzu and Zhang Shichun were also listed. Tan Yuanchun was listed in the front of the group from Jingling county, Huguang; Song Jideng headed the Laiyang county, Shandong.[212]

The Restoration Society was truly unprecedented in its scale of empire-wide association. The administrative units were simply a convenient way to present the candidates to examiners. It was by no means a principle endorsing the political authority of the Ming government. Each group had its own leaders who were selected locally through their literary reputation. The selection of leaders of local literary societies was not based on seniority nor family status, but on the individual leader's own literary skill and intellectual abilities. These abilities were proven by their roles as critics who had published anthologies. The fact that Zhang Pu was a son of a concubine and was poorly treated by his relatives testified to the truly meritocratic principle on which the Restoration Society was based.

The publication of the *Guobiao* anthology is significant in several ways. It was the formal publication of the huge organization of examinees and critics. It served as a public announcement of the consensus, the public opinion of the examinees with sample writings. The implications for the selection of graduates at the provincial and metropolitan examination were obvious to the examiners. The examinees themselves had already decided who deserved to pass the examination; they presented collectively to the examiners the names in the *Guobiao*. If those individuals were not among those who graduated, examinees would have reason to suspect corruption and fraud.

The *Guobiao* was just one, but a very special one, of many anthologies published in 1632. Its sale was such that commercial publishers from Fujian, Huguang, and Jiangxi offered to pay handsome amounts to reprint it.[213] After Zhang Pu and many members of the Restoration Society passed the provincial and metropolitan examinations, the power of organization was recognized by all examinees. Membership in the society became a hot commodity.[214] Even sons of powerful officials like Wen Yuren, the brother of Grand Secretary Wen Tiren, wanted to join. But he was not accepted.[215] Infuriated, he wrote and published a drama entitled "Green Hibiscus" (*Lü mudan*) to ridicule the Restoration Society.[216] Members of the Restoration Society were offended and complained to Zhang Pu and Zhang Cai. The Zhangs went to Zhejiang and had the education intendant, Li Yuankuan, ban the play; Li was also a member of the society. Li also ordered bookstores to destroy the play. They were able to indict member of the Wen family for writing the play.[217]

The success of the Restoration Society in the examination convinced examinees of the need to expand their membership. Lü Liuliang's brother organized a Chengshe (Pure Society) in 1639, admitting members from more than ten counties in Zhejiang.[218] In 1639, after the examination was over in Nanjing, Wu Yingji, Chen Zhenhui, Zhang Zilie, Mao Xiang, Huang Zongxi, Hou Fangyu, Gu Kao, and Fang Yizhi founded the *Guomen guangye she* (Expanded enterprise of the nation). The practice of organizing large literary societies continued in the early Qing as soon as the new government resumed holding examinations in the Jiangnan area.[219]

*Zhang Zilie and the New Commentary*

The widespread adoption of the organizational approach by the examinees-cum-critics accentuated the shift of authority in the field of cultural production from the imperial government to the literary public. It was the professional critics, not officials with literary talents, who were the arbiters of literary taste and exegetical positions. The popularity of the Restoration Society helped to promote the Qin Han style of prose. Championed by its leaders like Zhang Pu and Zhou Zhong in the examinations in 1637 and 1640, many examinees adopted such a style.[220]

The enormous market of examination aids supported and encouraged competition and rivalry among critics who panegyrized different literary models. Critics who found fault with the poetics of the leaders of the Restoration Society were able to find publishers to print their diatribes. In 1633 Ai Nanying edited several anthologies of examination essays. He criticized the various trends in recent styles in the examination essays: the Qin Han prose style, references to Buddhist ideas, colloquialisms, and deviations from the expositions of Cheng-Zhu.[221] He was the most ardent opponent of the poetics of Zhang Pu and Zhou Zhong. Zhang Zilie (b. 1597), a member of the Restoration Society and a native of Yiqun, Jiangxi, had been on good terms with Zhou Zhong and Zhang Pu. After he saw Ai Nanying's anthologies, he produced his own anthology, taking Ai to task on many issues.[222]

Zhang had a career trajectory similar to many other examinees. He went to study at the Imperial Academy in Nanjing in 1631 and remained there for more than ten years. In Nanjing, he made the acquaintance of other renowned critics, such as Zhou Zhong and Wu Yingji.[223] Zhang was a professional critic who selected and critiqued essays by successful examinees. He began working for publishers, editing anthologies of examination essays at both the provincial and metropolitan levels in 1633.[224] He had edited anthologies for examinations in 1633, 1636, 1637, 1640, and 1643.[225] In 1636, after another failure at the metropolitan examination, he did not have the needed money to travel back home. When friends such as Wu Yingji offered to provide him with one hundred taels, he refused. He hired himself out to a publisher and compiled a critical anthology on the *Book of Odes*.[226]

The Restoration Society in many ways signifies the organizational power of the literati through control of "public opinion" over the criteria of success in the civil service examination. Zhang had attained a reputation for his philological work on the *Complete Compendium of the Four Books* (*Sishu daquan*).[227] From 1638 through 1654, Zhang Zilie, his friends, and many supporting officials strove to convince the government to designate Zhang's commentary as the new official exposition on the Four Books. When he finished compiling the compendium in 1638, he and his friends at the academy orchestrated a campaign to recommend it to the government for adoption as the new official commentary. In 1639 a "public notice" or "petition" (*gongjie*) to print Zhang's commentary was submitted to the Imperial Academy in Nanjing by Yang Tingshu, Wu Yingqi, Chen Zhenhui, Shen Shoumin, all active critics, and several other degree holders to urge the publication of Zhang's commentary. It was submitted as a collective petition by all students at the academy.[228] Most of those whose names were listed on the petition were renowned critics of examination essays. The request was submitted by the Imperial Academy to the Ministry of Rites.[229] A barrage of letters and petitions were sent to individual officials, such as provincial educational intendants, magistrates, and provincial administration commissioners.[230] While waiting for a response from the government, a student of Zhang's offered to print the work with his own money. A Hangzhou publisher in Nanjing was in charge of carving the blocks and printing the copies. His friends Wu Yingqi, Zhou Biao, Fang Yizhi, and Shen Shoumin all contributed a preface to his commentary.[231]

It appears that the Ministry of Rites sought to avoid forwarding the petition to the emperor. The same group of students submitted "a second public notice" in 1640 to its promulgation as the official commentary.[232] It was referred to the Kiangxi provincial officials for deliberation because Zhang Zilie was a student from Jiangxi. The censorate of the Kiangxi circuit ordered Zhang to submit his manuscript for examination. The provincial surveillance commissioner of Kiangxi did not submit his recommendation to the Ministry of Rites until 1642. It was approved for submission to the emperor for review. Apparently the Ministry of Rites was not acting fast enough with its promulgation. Suspecting a deliberate delay on the part of the Ministry of Rites, the student leaders in the Imperial Academy submitted a third petition in the first month of 1644. Before the copying of the manuscript was completed for submission to the emperor, the Ming regime fell.[233]

Zhang's commentary was a great departure from the *Sishu daquan*, which enshrined Zhu Xi's exposition. Zhang abandoned Zhu Xi's division of the chapters into Classics and commentary. It had eliminated Zhu's supplementary section on "the investigation of things" (*gewu*).[234] The "correction" was based on the falsified Stele version of the *Great Learning* and Zheng Xiao's view. The treatise was restored as a chapter in the *Records of Rites*.[235] He quoted freely from Wang Yangming and included the falsified Stele version of the *Great Learning* in his commentary.[236] All these incidents showed the impact of commercial publishing, which made both authentic and falsified texts widely available.

Like others before him, Zhang Zilie's commentary represented only his personal opinion.[237] What distinguishes him from his predecessors, however, was the support he was able to mobilize and the manner in which he mobilized it. Being a critic of repute himself, he was able to mobilize other critics such as Wu Yingji and Shen Shoumin to support his exposition. The petition was no longer the opinion of an individual government student; it represented the public opinion of not only the government students at the Imperial Academy in Nanjing, but also the opinion of the association of critics, who were the arbiters of literary and intellectual excellence in the field of cultural production. All three of the petitions were called "public proclamations" (*gongjie*). Ironically, "*gong*" did not refer to the government, but to students and critics.

The organizational framework subtly but profoundly changed the politics of literary production and subsequently the politics of recruitment. On the one hand, the imperial government had come to terms with the newly emerged cultural authority created by the expansion of commercial publishing. And on the other, examinees seeking to enter the officialdom had to first carve out a niche in the publishing world in order to enhance their chances of success. Their experience lends new meaning to the phrase "publish or perish." They would have little to hang on to in the extremely competitive and turbulent sea of the examination. A reputation in the publishing world was a lifejacket with which they could hope to survive and finally gain entry into officialdom.

Unlike the Former and Latter Seven Masters, excluding Zhou Zhong, the majority of the critics and writers in the period from the 1590s through the 1640s did not pass the metropolitan examination until they reached the average age of 41.8, slightly better than the average *jinshi* in the Ming-Qing period. The average number of years after *jinshi* is only 13.3 years. This number contrasts strikingly with those of the three groups that came before them.

What is significant is the long span the late Ming critics spent in positions in the economic field, where they had to eke out livings on tutoring, editing and critiquing, and writing for patrons and publishers. By the

1620s even examinees from wealthy families such as Zhou Zhong had to first carve out a niche in the publishing market in order to establish a reputation for himself. Wealth and possession of other forms of power had to be first translated into "publicity" and subsequently public authority in the commercial publishing world. Publishing had become an integral part of both their economic and academic lives, a marked departure from the preceding generations of producers of poetics like the Three Yangs, the Former Seven Masters, the Tang-Song Masters, and the Latter Seven Masters. Such changes in the trajectory of careers for the renowned writers clearly shows the growing impact of commercial publishing on the practice of the civil service examination and the manner in which the imperial government recruited officials.

The formation of the Restoration Society was not possible without the prior extensive development of organized groups of examinees and the networking brought about by the publishing boom since the Wanli period. The formation of literary societies and the use of publishing to create cultural authority based on organized power enabled critics and authors to negotiate with the imperial government over the interpretation of the Confucian canons as well as the standard of literary excellence. The expansion of membership of literary societies was evidence for the general expansion of the literary public sphere that was outside kinship and the imperial government. It was one of many forms of voluntary organizations that were not initiated or supported by the government. It was the specific form of organization of the examinees, whose career trajectories traversed both the economic and the political fields, a practice that rendered the distinction between *shi* (literati) and *shang* (businessman) increasingly insignificant at both the personal and family levels.

# Conclusion: Printing and Literary Culture in Early Modern China

This study has examined the historical conjunction of two domains of practice—printing and literary production. The previous chapters have sought to achieve two goals: to demonstrate the specific impact of the expansion of printing in early modern China in the period 1550 to 1650; and to argue against the Eurocentric view that only movable-type printing was capable of producing "liberating" or "positive" change.

The impact of printing in general, and commercial publishing in particular, on Chinese society in this period was multiple: economic, social, cultural, and political. These impacts were not in one direction, nor monocausal. First, the expansion of commercial publishing meant that books and their technology contributed to the broader process of commercialization in the sixteenth and seventeenth centuries. The increase in book production created greater demand for the manufacturing and consumption of paper, ink, and wood, and for labor in writing, editing, compiling, carving, printing, binding, transporting, and marketing books. The low cost of book production and the simplicity and flexibility of woodblock printing allowed more people to seek their fortune in the publishing business. The lack of institutional control of printing also encouraged entrepreneurial merchants and literati to enter the publishing market, contributing to the unprecedented boom in commercial publishing. Greater number of books were sold, as Matteo Ricci had observed, at "ridiculously low prices." The rise into prominence of new publishing centers such as Suzhou, Nanjing, and Huzhou was indicative of the general expansion of commercial publishing in this period.

A major social impact of the expansion of commercial publishing was the restructuring of the relationship between the political and economic fields by virtue of the convergence of the career trajectories of the *shi* and *shang*. This impact was paradoxical—both supportive of and subversive to the imperial system. On the one hand, greater demand for literary and manufacturing labor created positions in the economic field, absorbing some of the supernumerary literati who were growing in greater number but were not able to get positions in the officialdom.[1] Intensified commodification of literary skill enabled the *shi* to assume the roles of *shang* as they took up roles in editing, compilation, writing, proofreading, and publishing. These income-generating positions in the publishing market enabled examinees to sustain their pursuit of success in the examinations. The longer the examinees spent their life span in the examination track, the stronger their commitment to the institution of the imperial state. Their ties with the imperial system were renewed periodically through their participation in the examination process. Ironically, by providing a "secondary" field to the examinees, where their de facto career trajectories fell, commercial publishing exerted a *cultural* pull away from the political center as the examinees, as professional literary producers, were obligated to meet the needs of the readers whose interests were much more diversified than those commanded by examinations and political careers.

The impact of the expansion of book production on the cultural field in general, and on the examination field in particular, was enormous. By producing an ever greater number of books and best-selling authors, the book market quietly eroded the authority of the imperial state in the field of cultural production. In the world of publishing, the imperial state no longer occupied the center position. The expansion of book production enabled the literary field to attain an unprecedented degree of autonomy, which came to challenge and rival the authority of the imperial state in cultural production. Such autonomy manifested itself in the authority nonofficial critics and writers wielded over literary taste and canonical exegesis. The expansion and growing autonomy of the literary public sphere comprising readers and literary associations was signaled by the dissociating references to the imperial government from the term "public" (*gong*). The imperial government could no longer represent or speak for the public. What was public (*gong*) would be decided by the spokesmen of the literary public sphere.

Through the publication of an ever increasing number of books, the book market produced best-selling critics and writers such as Li Zhi, Huang Ruheng, Chen Jiru, Sun Kuang, Zhong Xing, and Xu Fenpeng, whose authority was derived not from possession of positions in the political field, but from the literary public sphere that was increasingly structured by the market mechanism of commercial publishing. These best-selling critics and authors were no longer high officials, nor even officials, when they attained their reputations in the book market. By the 1620s, it was literary reputation that helped many examinees-cum-critics attain public offices.

In the examination field, critics and examinees were provided with reprinted or newly printed works that were not endorsed by the government. Private and commercial publishers had reprinted rare and non-canonical texts. Works of the Hundred Schools of Philosophy as well as commentaries and scholarly works by Han scholars were widely available. Armed with new ideas and information, critics freely crossed ideological boundaries, drawing upon a vast array of works they found in the expanding book market. Commercial publishers and their armies of critics and writers competed to offer examinees a wide array of textual aids for writing examination essays on the Four Books, the Five Classics, dynastic histories, and policy issues. New expositions on the Confucian canon profusely proffered in commentaries reduced the official commentary by Zhu Xi to just one of the many possible readings. Examinees could choose from numerous anthologies of commentaries, poetry, and prose with comments by famous critics who felt no obligation to conform to official standards in literary and ideological matters.

The impact of commercial publishing on the strategies for success pursued by examinees was more subtle. The rise of the authority of literary critics over that of official examiners drew examinees deeper into the book market. Commercial publishing had become crucial to success for examinees at higher levels. The growing sophistication in preparing for civil examinations by *shishang* families encouraged growing dependence on commercial examination aids that gathered information and model essays for examinees. The spread of methodical approaches to taking examinations was evidenced by the growing popularity of study groups and literary societies.

Reputation in the literary public sphere had become an important qualification for success for all examinees pursuing higher degrees. Wealth and power needed to be translated into and supplemented by reputation generated by reputation in the world of commercial publishing. The majority of the examinees sought to publish their own essays and to have their writings included in critical anthologies edited by famous critics. They joined literary societies that published the writings of their members for public review.

Examinees were not only required to be consumers of commercial publications for examinations, they needed to be producers if they were to be successful. They stood a better chance of success if they became critics and commentators themselves. Many became editors and critics for commercial publishers. These economic positions offered them authority and visibility in the public of letters.

Commercial publishing had changed the terms in which examinees competed. They had to compete for membership in literary societies and authoritative positions in commercial publishing before they entered the examination halls. The formation of an alliance of literary critics cumulating in the founding of the Restoration Society in the late 1620s registered the importance of both commercial publishing and the power of private organization in the pursuit of success in the examinations. Under the leadership of Zhang Pu, the Restoration Society came to exert an unprecedented influence on the result of the civil examinations and hence access to positions in the political field.

As commercial publishing came to intervene in the distribution process of political power, the pursuit of political privileges had become more tortuous and complicated for the *shishang* families. Being involved in commerce and trade, they nonetheless were better positioned to harness the

market forces of commercial publishing and use the power of private organizations to mobilize and translate public opinion into success at the
examinations. The examination field was but one of many sites where the
*shishang* appropriated and benefited from the effects of commercial publishing in this period.

## SYMBOLIC PRODUCTION
## OF *SHISHANG* CULTURE IN PARATEXT

The previous chapters have only sketched the impact of commercial publishing on cultural production as it pertains to the examination field.
There is still much terrain where commercial publishing had left profound
impressions. What was being expressed in the increasingly differentiated
reading public? If imperial ideology and culture no longer structured the
field of cultural production, were there any new ideologies emerging in
the world of print?

As book production expanded in this period in response to a wide
range of interests, the literary hierarchy and standards of the imperial
state were but some of many organizing principles that determined the
choices of the publishers. Books were produced to meet entertaining,
practical, and religious needs. Novels, plays, travel guides, and medical
and practical manuals provided much material and information to enhance the quality of life in an increasingly complex and commercial society in which a substantial number of its population depended on literacy
and books in their economic, social, and cultural capacities. These books
were written increasingly in an easy, plain, straightforward style of print
vernaculars. One general question concerning the impact of printing on
language arises. Expansion of commercial publishing did not contribute
to the rise of national vernaculars as it did in Europe.[2] But there are other
questions that are equally important that need to be raised. Did the growing market for entertaining and informative books written in various
styles of print vernaculars contribute to a growing discontent with the
Classical style of writing in which the Confucian Classics and the corpus
of dynastic histories and canonical literary works were written?

Thus, the previous chapters represent only a small, though very important, part of the larger process whereby an alternative literary culture

was being produced in print in the sixteenth and seventeenth centuries. The larger significance of the unprecedented autonomy manifested in the literary field needs to be placed in a broader context of the emergence of the *shishang* culture in this period.

The examinees-cum-writers were only one type of *shishang*—a growing group whose careers scattered in both the political and economic fields. The *practice* of pursuing a dual career or double status at the personal or family level was a common strategy for *shishang* families in the Jiangnan region, and those commercialized areas were intimately linked to the economically and culturally advanced part of the Ming empire. With practical interests in both education and commerce, the *shishang* elites began to negotiate on many fronts "a new cultural ideology" that no longer revolved around the imperial state. But this ideology did not find expression in systematic treatises and can be glimpsed and pieced together from the experience, desires, anxieties, and values left in the textual and paratextual space by the *shishang*. Such a detailed investigation of this complex alternative culture of the *shishang* is left to another study.[3]

## PRINTING IN CHINA AND EUROPE
## IN THE EARLY MODERN PERIOD

Printing—both movable type and woodblock—initiated profound but differential change in communication and cultural production. Contrary to the conventional view, which dichotomizes xylography and movable-type printing into "a primitive art" and "a modern technology," I argue that there are some similarities in practice between Chinese and European printing and publishing.

The misconception regarding the exaggerated difference between European movable-type printing and Chinese woodblock printing has its roots within the discourse on the history of European printing. One must reexamine the standard view that European printers had replaced block printing after the successful combination of the press and movable type by Gutenberg. That conception of "permanent rupture" or "technological breakthrough" allows scholars to represent movable type and block printing as two distinct technologies. Often narrated in a historicist mode, woodblock printing became the infancy phase in the evolution of printing in which Europe had moved beyond and China continued to be trapped. But in the sixteenth and seventeenth centuries, both printing methods—movable and block printing—were practiced in China and Western Europe.

Contrary to conventional accounts, woodblock printing continued to be used by European printers to produce iconic and textual elements—illustrations, title pages, page borders, initials, and extra-large letters.[4] A typical European printing shop in the sixteenth and seventeenth centuries included a block cutter whose duty was to produce all iconic elements, in exceptional sizes of fonts. Eisenstein points out that "even though block-print and letterpress may have originated as separate innovations and were initially used for diverse purposes . . . the two techniques soon became intertwined."[5] It is therefore more accurate to consider that woodblock printing had become integrated into the European printing shop, rather than replaced by the letterpress. Even though copper plates were used, their high cost throughout the early modern period continued to convince many publishers to use woodcuts.[6]

The shift to the movable-type method in printing text was a "logical" solution to printing European letters. But this does not mean that this "logic" applies exclusively to alphabetical languages. From the printer's viewpoint, recurrent scripts—be they European letters or Chinese characters—render movable types a "logical" solution. Nonetheless, the relatively larger number of distinct characters did favor the use of woodblocks if the other option for the printer was much more expensive metal types. But if movable types did not cost more and did not present problems in composing and organizing, there was no reason for Chinese printers to reject movable-type printing. Here it is primarily the economics of technology that determines the choice of printing method of a Chinese printer.[7]

As argued in Chapter 2, even though woodblock was the prevalent printing method in China in the sixteenth and seventeenth centuries, the use of movable type was growing. The high cost of making metal types had prompted Chinese printers to use wooden movable types. Though not as sturdy as woodblocks, wooden types were inexpensive to make and replace. The increase in the sizes and styles of fonts could be achieved by carving more wooden types without having to make new punches and to cast new types, as was the practice by European printers. More studies are needed regarding the extent to which movable type had been growing in popularity among Chinese publishing in the early modern period.

While the hand press could print faster than woodblocks, the significance of speed needs to be considered with other factors. The significance of the difference between xylography and movable types lies more in the economics of the operation of publishing houses under different sociopolitical conditions.

Publishers in Europe and China operated in very different economic and sociopolitical environments with varying constraints and options. Publishing was a much more risky business in Europe in terms of financial investment and security. European printers required higher levels of capital investment than their Chinese counterparts to establish a printing business in this period. The capital invested in types, presses, and expensive paper, which still depended on the supply of rag, made printing a business venture that was beyond the means of most people. Licensing systems and royalties not only increased the cost of production but also exerted a restricting effect on the expansion of the publishing industry.[8]

The movable-type method forced European publishers to print a larger run of editions to justify the labor and cost of composition. According to Febvre and Martin, the average size of European editions was between one thousand and fifteen hundred copies.[9] This range did not reflect the estimate of projected sales alone, but also the justification of the overhead cost. And this range might apply mostly to Latin books targeted at an international market. Nonetheless, European publishers were often stocked with many unsold copies. Many had to take their unsold copies to book fairs to sell to other booksellers who gathered in Lyons, Frankfurt, and Leipzig.[10] The international reach of the European book market, constituted of Latin readers, did provide an additional outlet for books that failed to attract domestic buyers. The need to print a relatively large number of books and the unexpected sales had prompted the development of practices that helped to provide capital. Beginning with the seventeenth century, publishers in England, the Netherlands, Italy, and France began using subscriptions to ensure sales and raise funds for the publisher.[11]

While the European book market was international in scope at the outset, with printers and publishers printing for both domestic and foreign readers, Chinese publishers operated primarily within the empire, despite the export of an unknown number of books to foreign countries such as Japan and Korea.[12] Chinese scholars of the book are struck by the relatively larger number of extant copies of European books from the sixteenth and seventeenth centuries. There are undoubtedly many reasons for this—better preservation in private and public libraries, or perhaps more durable rag paper. But extant late-Ming and early Qing editions printed on inexpensive Chinese bamboo paper appeared to be no less durable. One possible reason for the difference in the survival rate of European books and Chinese books, I submit, is that there were many more unsold copies that remained in the bookstores and inventories of European printers than books by their Chinese counterparts in the early modern period. The movable-type method not only required a much higher level of capital investment but also a larger cash flow to continue operation because of the frozen capital and the unrealized profit in unsold copies.

In contrast, publishing in China offered both woodblock and movable-type options. The low cost for wood carving and inexpensive paper rendered publishing a relatively low-risk business adventure. This did not mean most publishers became successful, but it did present fewer obstacles to entry into the publishing market. The simplicity and flexibility of woodblock printing allowed easy expansion and prompt adjustments to the changing demands of the market. As shown in the examples of Mei Dingzuo and Zang Maoxun (see Chapter 2), the size of the run of Chinese books could be easily adjusted to the availability of capital and changing demands. Expansion and speedy production could be easily achieved by simply enlisting the help of more carvers.[13] Even though it was common for both Chinese and European publishers to publish their work using printing presses and carvers in different locations, the coordination in the case of woodblock printing would present fewer problems than the European printing-press method. To print a text in different shops would require the European compositor to "cast off" his copy accurately—dividing the text into pages in advance. In contrast, the casting off of a Chinese text was completed with the writing of the "printer's copy," which already incorporated page division, page numbers, and all the justification. The Chinese carvers worked with a "galley," not a manuscript. The galley of a Chinese text could be easily distributed to different carvers, and in theory the printing could be done in a centralized or a diffused manner. The "atomistic" nature of woodblock printing was more adaptable to a highly competitive book market in the early modern period in China than in Western Europe.

As businessmen operating for profit, printers and publishers in Europe and China displayed many similarities: they minimized risk and increased profit by lowering the cost of production. Most publishers were conservative and watched the market carefully. Printing religious books and for a university audience were safe strategies for most European publishers.[14] Publishing for the examinees was an important survival strategy for most Chinese publishers. To cut cost or to obtain extra cash flow, Chinese and European publishers alike would reuse, rent, and trade woodblocks.[15]

Chinese and European publishers and printers also encountered different obstacles. There were two important factors that differentiated the level of risk for the European publishers—religious and political regulations—which in varying degrees influence their business in publishing.

When an ever increasing number of publishers freely entered the competitive book markets with minimal investment in China, the literary field in France and Britain had not assumed its autonomy and was still structured by feudal and religious institutions. First, the Roman Catholic Church and governments throughout Western Europe were concerned about the growing number of books and their threat to ecclesiastic and royal authority. Bulls were issued by the pope to condemn heretical books and their readers. Catalogs—lists of censored books—were promulgated. Since the printing of the first full index *Librorum Prohibitorum* in 1557 by Pope Paul IV, subsequent indices were promulgated by the church in 1564 and 1596. The constraining effect of the index was felt throughout Europe by printers and booksellers.[16] Printers and publishers were executed for publishing heretical books.[17]

The role of religion in structuring the book market in Western Europe was predominant. Nowhere was the effect more discernible than in the vexing and waning of publishing in Germany. Publishing in Germany developed rapidly in the early sixteenth century with the launch of the Protestant movement under Martin Luther.[18] Polemical works and illustrated broadsheets were produced profusely by the Protestants.[19] Reli-

gious strife was a major impetus in the expansion of publishing in the Reformation. But after the Thirty Years' War, the book trade, publishing,
and papermaking in Western Europe suffered immensely.[20]

The printing industry was strictly regulated by the printers' guild and
the government. As Daniel Roche points out, "From the sixteenth century
until the Revolution, censorship of speech and writing was official policy
in France."[21] The French government during this period issued regular or-
dinances regulating printers and booksellers. Publication without royal
permission was punishable by death.[22] The demand for "freedom of the
press" and freedom of expression would have been inconceivable without these government regulations and abuses. Knowledge and information was not freely disseminated because there was no freedom of the
press; rather, publishers had to purchase special privileges to publish from
the crown. In 1644 there were seventy-five printing offices in Paris, but
they were reduced to thirty-six by an edict in 1686.[23]

Given the low-cost operation, simplicity, and flexibility of woodblock
printing, one may venture to argue that the degree of importance printing held in Chinese society in the sixteenth and seventeenth centuries
equaled, if not exceeded, that in Europe. While new publishing centers
developed in many cities and cultural production as well as government
administration depended heavily on print in China in this period, printing in Britain was concentrated in London, outside of which was primarily a scribal society. The crown and its government did not have publishing facilities but commissioned publication of their documents to a small
number of licensed printers.[24] London printers were also regulated by the
Stationers' Company.[25] In 1615 there were only twenty-two printers in
London.[26] Until the lapsing of the Licensing Act in 1695, print was not
commonly used in everyday communication. "There were no printed
posters advertising estate or agriculture sales; there were no theatre bill
programmes, no newspapers, no printed handbills, bill headings, labels,
tickets, or other commercial pieces. There were no printed forms meant
to be completed by hand: no marriage certificates, printed indentures, or
receipts."[27] Since there were virtually no magazines or periodicals in England at the close of the seventeenth century, an independent, professional
class of writers had yet to emerge.[28]

Nor were the gentry and nobles disposed to commit their writings to print. It was a time when the attitude of the literate elites toward print was beginning to change. But the change in attitude did not spread fast enough to convince Shakespeare to publish his sonnets in his own name nor his plays during his life time.[29] Nor did printing bring much information about the political process to the reading public. Information about the government was rarely known to the public. Lists of members of the parliament were not published by commercial publishers until 1625—and these were just lists of names with titles.

In contrast, the Chinese government in the sixteenth and seventeenth centuries did not establish any regulations over the number of printers, nor did they regulate what they could print. There was no licensing system and no prepublication censorship. Except calendars and the history of the current dynasty, almost anything could be printed. The government occasionally issued warnings against using heterodox ideas to explain the Confucian classics in examination answers. To be sure, there was postpublication censorship. Despite isolated censorship after a book was banned, not until the late eighteenth century did Chinese publishers have much to worry about in terms of the political consequences of their publications, unless the publications dealt with politically sensitive issues or were prompted by political design.[30]

The Ming and early Qing government did not endorse one single religion. No church was there to police publications for heterodox ideas. Confucians, Buddhists, Daoists, and Christians were free to print and distribute their teachings. The *shishang* elite did not have to combat legal restrictions other than the arbitrary withholding of memorials and documents by the emperor. Their demand for transparency of the political process and the "right" of access to information was made in terms of public release of documents in the Government Gazette (*dibao*).[31]

Technology does not have a uniform impact on a society across time and space. This is the case because there is no abstract time and space for a technology to act upon. It is always a chronotype—a specific configuration of time and space—on which a technology makes its mark.[32] The impact, or nonimpact, of a technology does not depend exclusively on what it can do alone. The specific impact of printing—a technology of multiplying texts—cannot be understood if we consider only the technological advantage of printing in communication. It is not printing itself that determines how it will be used, but rather the specific attitudes of the group who came to use that technology as well as the ecological, economic, social, and political conditions under which a specific technology is developed, introduced, marketed, used, and resisted. These various factors also shaped the symbolic production of the technology itself.

APPENDIX I

# *Jiguge zhencang miben shumu*
# *A Catalog of Rare Books of the Best Collection*
# *of the Jiguge, by Mao Yi (1640–1713)*

| TITLE | PRICE (TAEL) | CE | PERIOD |
|---|---|---|---|
| *Guan pu* 冠譜 | 0.1 | 1 | Ming |
| *Kaogu xuefan* 考古學範 | 0.1 | 1 | Ming |
| *Liancheng yiyan* 樂城遺言 | 0.1 | 1 | Ming |
| *Sheshi suibi* 涉史隨筆 | 0.1 | 1 | Ming |
| *Dijing jingwu lue jingyao* 帝京景物略精要 | 0.2 | 1 | Ming |
| *Gengshen waishi* 庚申外史 | 0.2 | 1 | Ming |
| *Jinlin zaji* 涇林雜記 | 0.2 | 1 | Ming |
| *Nanjin jiwen lu* 南燼紀文錄 | 0.2 | 1 | Ming |
| *Pangjiu ting zaji* 旁秋亭雜記 | 0.2 | 1 | Ming |
| *Qidong yeyu shiyi* 齊東野語拾遺 | 0.2 | 1 | Ming |
| *Xiqian zhu* 西遷注 | 0.2 | 1 | Ming |
| *Xiwu liyu* 西吳里語 | 0.2 | 1 | Ming |
| *Yinzhai wenjian* 寅齋聞見 | 0.2 | 1 | Ming |
| *Bichou* 筆疇 | 0.3 | 1 | Ming |
| *Gaopo jiyi* 高坡紀異 | 0.3 | 1 | Ming |
| *Gujin zhu* 古今註 | 0.3 | 1 | Ming |
| *Qingxi xiabi* 清溪暇筆 | 0.3 | 1 | Ming |
| *Quanwen gong wenji* 權文公文集 | 0.3 | 1 | Ming |
| *Shuzhai laoxue congtan* 庶齋老學叢談 | 0.3 | 1 | Ming |
| *Luozi san xun* 羅子三訓 | 0.4 | 1 | Ming |
| *Nongtian yuhua* 農田餘話 | 0.4 | 1 | Ming |
| *Beichang zhike* 北窗炙課 | 0.5 | 1 | Ming |
| *Fujiao bian* 輔教編 | 0.5 | 1 | Yuan |
| *Kong Pingzhong tanyuan* 孔平仲談苑 | 0.6 | 1 | Ming |
| *Qishen lu, shiyi* 稽神錄(六卷)拾遺(一卷) | 0.6 | 2 | Ming |
| *Yutang jiahua* 玉堂嘉話 | 0.6 | 2 | Ming |
| *Hemo tushuo guizhong zhinan* 訶摩圖説規中指南 | 0.8 | 1 | Ming |
| *Tianwen yulixiangyi fu zhujie* 天文玉曆祥異賦註解 | 0.8 | 2 | Ming |
| *Tianwen xuanji yilan* 天文璇璣一覽 | 0.9 | 3 | Ming |
| *Bazi dangsheng shu* 八字當生數 | 1.0 | 1 | Ming |

| TITLE | PRICE (TAEL) | CE | PERIOD |
|---|---|---|---|
| *Chiwen dong bingfa* 赤文洞兵法 | 1.0 | 1 | Ming |
| *Dayi xuanji* 大易璇璣 | 1.0 | 1 | Yuan |
| *Jingqi ji* 精騎集 | 1.0 | 3 | Ming |
| *Sanshi chuxingzhi shijie mingti zhi* 三世出興志,世界名體志 | 1.0 | 1 | Song |
| *Shiyi* 識遺 | 1.0 | 2 | Ming |
| *Tianwen zhi Xingye zhinan Tianxiang fuhe* 天文志,星野指南,天象賦合 | 1.0 | 1 | Ming |
| *Yigui tongshu* 易卦通數 | 1.0 | 1 | Ming |
| *Youhuan jiwen* 遊宦紀聞 | 1.0 | 2 | Ming |
| *Jieyin lu biji* 芥隱錄筆記 | 1.2 | 1 | Song |
| *Lizi yiyin* 麗則遺音 | 1.2 | 1 | Yuan |
| *Pian yu ci* 片玉詞 | 1.2 | 2 | Yuan |
| *Wudang quanxiang qisheng shilu* 武當全相啓聖實錄 | 1.2 | 1 | Yuan |
| *Yangchun baixue* 陽春白雪 | 1.2 | 2 | Yuan |
| *Yuli tongzheng jing* 玉曆通政經 | 1.2 | 4 | Ming |
| *Guang zhuoyi ji* 廣卓異記 | 1.5 | 3 | Ming |
| *Dongguan yulun* 東觀餘論 | 1.6 | 4 | Ming |
| *Guixin zashi qianji houji bieji* 癸辛雜識前集後集別集 | 1.6 | 4 | Ming |
| *Hanjuan* 漢雋 | 1.6 | 4 | Yuan |
| *Rongzhai sanbi* 容齋三筆 (only 7–16 juan) | 1.6 | 4 | Song |
| *Shoujin zailan* 手鏡摘覽 | 1.6 | 2 | Ming |
| *Baihu tongde lun* 白虎通德論 | 1.8 | 3 | Yuan |
| *Shixue tiyao* 史學提要 | 1.8 | 3 | Yuan |
| *Baigong fengjian* 白公諷諫 | 2.0 | 1 | Song |
| *Dongjing menghua lu* 東京夢華錄 | 2.0 | 1 | Song |
| *Dushu fennian richeng* 讀書分年日程 | 2.0 | 2 | Yuan |
| *Guanwu bian* 觀物編 | 2.0 | 10 | Ming |
| *Huaxiang shou shen guangji qian hou er ji* 畫相搜神廣記前後二集 | 2.0 | 2 | Yuan |
| *Jinyang men shi* 津陽門詩 | 2.0 | 1 | Song |
| *Jiuwen zhengwu* 舊文證誤 | 2.0 | 1 | Song |
| *Ming chen shilue* 名臣事略 | 2.0 | 4 | Yuan |
| *Riyong juanji qimeng zonggui* 日用涓吉奇門總龜 | 2.0 | 2 | Yuan |
| *Shiyi jing wendui* 十一經問對 | 2.0 | 2 | Yuan |
| *Tangshi guchui* 唐詩鼓吹 | 2.0 | 4 | Yuan |
| *Yijia tushuo* 醫家圖說 | 2.0 | 1 | Song |
| *Baopu zi* 抱朴子 | 2.4 | 8 | Ming |
| *Jiaoming ji* 焦螟集 | 2.4 | 8 | Ming |
| *Qizha qingqian* 啓劄青錢 | 2.4 | 6 | Yuan |

| TITLE | PRICE (TAEL) | CE | PERIOD |
|---|---|---|---|
| *Shi jizhuan yishu* 詩集傳義疏 | 2.4 | 8 | Yuan |
| *Taiping heji jufang* 太平和劑局方 | 3.0 | 5 | Yuan |
| *Yanshu pinge lun* 演數品格論 | 3.0 | 3 | Ming |
| *Zuo keming yuefu* 左克明樂府 | 3.0 | 3 | Yuan |
| *Cefu yuangui* 冊府元龜 [only 249–54, 261–62, 276 juan] | 3.2 | 4 | Song |
| *Daode miyao* 道德祕要 | 3.2 | 16 | Ming |
| *Taiping yuefu* 太平樂府 | 3.2 | 4 | Yuan |
| *Benchao mengqiu* 本朝蒙求 | 4.0 | 2 | Song |
| *Bowu zhi* 博物志 | 4.0 | 1 | Song |
| *Han Changli waiji* 韓昌黎外集 | 4.0 | 2 | Song |
| *Jianzhai shiji* 簡齋詩集 | 4.0 | 4 | Song |
| *Moke kaogu tu* 墨刻考古圖 | 4.0 | 4 | Ming |
| *Zhouyi jianyi* 周易兼義 | 4.0 | 8 | Yuan |
| *Chaoshi yuanhou zonglun* 巢氏源候總論 | 4.8 | 8 | Yuan |
| *Wuzhi* 吳志 | 4.8 | 6 | Song |
| *Huanan zhenjing* 華南真經 | 5.0 | 5 | Song |
| *Liu gong yuezhang* 柳公樂章 | 5.0 | 5 | Song |
| *Jiangyin zhi* 江陰志 | 6.0 | 4 | Song |
| *Peiwei zhai wenji* 佩韋齋文集 | 6.0 | 4 | Song |
| *Siling shi* 四靈詩 | 6.0 | 3 | Song |
| *Tanliao ji yanmifang* 澹寮集驗祕方 | 6.0 | 10 | Yuan |
| *Wengong jiali* 文公家禮 | 6.0 | 4 | Song |
| *Yue zhuan weng gongci* 岳倦翁宮詞; *Shiping ci* 石屏詞; *Xu feimei wu ci* 徐棐梅屋詞 | 6.0 | 4 | Song |
| *Qin Huaihai ji* 秦淮海集 | 6.4 | 8 | Song |
| *Dexiao fang* 得效方 | 7.2 | 12 | Yuan |
| *Huajian ji* 花間集 | 8.0 | 4 | Song |
| *Liu Binke waiji* 劉賓客外集 | 8.0 | 4 | Song |
| *Lo Binwang ji* 駱賓王集 | 8.0 | 2 | Song |
| *Jijuan guwen yun hai* 集篆古文韻海 | 10.0 | 5 | Ming |
| *Sisheng bian* 四聲編 | 10.0 | 16 | Yuan |
| *Wei Suzhou ji* 韋蘇州集 | 10.0 | 5 | Song |
| *Xinji guwen sisheng yun* 新集古文四聲韻 | 10.0 | 5 | Ming |
| *Wujing zongyao qianji houji* 武經總要前集後集 | 12.0 | 40 | Ming |
| *Zhang Youshi wenji* 張右史文集 | 12.0 | 24 | Ming |
| *Zhongxu qianwen* 重續千文 | 12.0 | 2 | Song |
| *Zunjing yin bian* 尊經音辨 | 15.0 | 3 | Song |
| *Meng Dongye shiji* 孟東野詩集 | 16.0 | 4 | Song |
| *Tao Yuanming ji* 陶淵明集 | 16.0 | 2 | Song |
| *Liushu gu* 六書故 | 30.0 | 50 | Yuan |
| *Zhou Yigong quanji* 周益公全集 | 30.0 | 50 | Ming |

| TITLE | PRICE (TAEL) | CE | PERIOD |
|---|---|---|---|
| *Longkang shoujian* 龍龕手鑒 | 36.0 | 6 | Song |
| *Kongshi jiayu* 孔氏家語 | 50.0 | 5 | Song |
| *Songci yibai jia* 宋詞一百家* | 100.0 | | Ming |

*The poems of sixty poets were printed, and the poems of forty writers were copied by hand.

SOURCE: Mao Yi, *Jiguge shumu*, pp. 1–33.

# Books Bought by Pan Yunduan from 1586 to 1601

| TITLE | COST IN TAEL | DATE* |
|---|---|---|
| *Shi dajia wen* 十大家文 | 0.25 | 1586 |
| Two small books (Song edition) 宋版小書2種 | 0.5 | 1592 |
| Printed calligraphy (3 titles) 墨刻3種 | 0.6 | 1592 |
| *Liao shi* 遼史 | 0.8 | 1590 |
| *Lisao* 離騷 | 1.0 | 1590 |
| *Mingshan ji, Dili tongzong* 名山記，地理統宗 | 1.2 | 1586 |
| *Jijiu bian* (Song edition) 急就篇, 1 *ce* | 1.5 | 1587 |
| *Cizu* 辭藻 | 2.0 | 1586 |
| *Huayan jing* (Small Song edition) 宋刻小板華嚴經 | 2.0 | 1589 |
| *Huzhou beibian* 湖州裨編 | 2.3 | 1586 |
| *Huangting jing* 黃庭經 and 2 manuscript copies 及臨本二本 | 3.0 | 1590 |
| *Su (Shi?) wen* 蘇文 | 3.6 | 1597 |
| *Shizong shilu* 世宗實錄 | 4.0 | 1600 |
| *Tongjian* 通鑒 (Song edition, incomplete) 不全宋版 | 5.0 | 1592 |
| *Hanwen* (Song edition) 宋版韓文 | 5.0 | 1593 |
| *Liang Han shu* (1 copy) 兩漢書一部 | 6.0 | 1586 |
| *Bai Kong liutie* (Song edition, half) 白孔六貼，半部; | | |
|     *Tongjian* 通鑒, 1 copy | 8.0 | 1588 |
| *Zuozhuan* (Song edition) 宋刻左傳; *Jisheng bacui* 濟生拔粹 | 10.0 | 1590 |
| *Wenxuan* 文選, 1 copy | 35.0 | 1589 |
| *Tongjian* (Song edition) 宋刻通鑒, 160 *ce* | 80.0 | 1586 |
| *Hanshu* (Song edition) 宋版漢書 | 200.0 | 1591 |

SOURCE: *Yuhua tang riji.*
* The dates indicate the year when the transaction took place.

# Book Prices Listed by Shen Jin

| TITLE | COST | JUAN/CE | PUBLISHER | DATE |
|---|---|---|---|---|
| *Wanbao quanshu* 萬寶全書 | 0.1 | 34J? 37J? | | 1614? 1628? |
| *Xindiao wanqu changchun* 新調萬曲常春 | 0.12 | 3C? | Jin Gongtang 金拱塘 | 1572–1619 |
| *Helin yulu* 鶴林玉露 | 0.2 | 4C | | 1522–66* |
| *Ni Yunlin xiansheng shiji* 倪雲林先生詩集 | 0.2 | 7J/4C | Jinxi Chan Family 荊溪 蹇氏 | 1629* |
| *Xinjuan wuyan Tangshi huapu* 新雋五言唐詩畫譜 | 0.5 | 2C? | Huang Fengchi 黃鳳池 | 1572–1619 |
| *Xinjuan mei zhu lan ju si pu* 新雋梅竹蘭菊四譜 | 0.5 | 2J?/2C? | Huang Fengchi | 1572–1619 |
| *Qixiao liangfang* 奇效良方 | 0.7 | 1? | | 1522–66* |
| *Shiyu huapu* 詩餘畫譜 | 0.8 | 1C | Qingyin guan 清言館 | 1612–44 |
| *Yue lu yin* 月露音 | 0.8 | 4J/8C | Hangzhou, Li Ya 李衙 | 1572–1619 |
| *Nanfeng xiansheng Yuanfeng leigao* 南豐先生元豐類稿 | 0.8 | 51J/12C | ? | 1628–44 |
| *Wenxian tongkao* 文獻通考 | 0.9 | 349J/?C | | 1522–66* |
| *Lisao tu* 离騷圖 | 1.0 | ? | Tang Fu 湯復 | 1644 |
| *Xinbian shiwen leiju hanmo daquan* 新編事文類 聚翰墨大全 | 1.0 | 125J/?C | Fujian An-zhengtang Liu Shuangsong 安正堂 劉雙松 | 1611 |
| *Xinke Li-Yuan er xiansheng jingxuan Tangshi xunjie* 新刻李袁二先生精選 唐詩訓解 | 1.0 | 7J/4C | Jurentang Yu Xianke 居仁堂余獻何 | 1618 |
| *Guang jinshi yun fu* 廣金石韻府 | 1.0 | 5J/6C | Lian'an zhu-ren 蓮庵主人 | 1636 |
| *Song Wenwen shan xiansheng quanji* 宋文文山先生全集 | 1.0 | 21J/8C | Hangzhou, Zhong Yue 鍾越 | 1629* |

| TITLE | COST | JUAN/CE | PUBLISHER | DATE |
|---|---|---|---|---|
| *Kaogu zhengwen yinsou* 考古正文印藪 | 1.2 | 5J/?C | | 1589 |
| *Xuanhe jigu yinshi* 宣和集古印史 | 1.5 | 9J/8C | Lai Xingxue 來行學 | 1596 |
| *Liyue hebian* 禮樂合編 | 1.5 | 30J/16C | Huang Du 黃度 | 1633 |
| *Yonghuai tang guwen zheng ji* 永懷堂古文正集 | 2.0 | 10J/24C | Duan Jun-ding 段君定 | 1633 |
| *Xinke Zhong Pojing xian-sheng piping Fengshen yanyi* 新刻鍾敬伯批 評封神演義 | 2.0 | 20J/20C | Suzhou, Shu Wenyuan 舒文淵 | 1600s |
| *Yincun chuji* 印存初集 | 2.0 | 2J/2C | Hu Zhengyan 胡正言 | 1600s |
| *Da Ming Yitong zhi* 大明一統志 | 3.0 | 90J/16C | Fujian, 安正堂 Liu Shuang-song 劉雙松 | 1588 |
| *Xinbian gujin shiwen leiju* 新編古今事文類聚 | 3.0 | 170J/37C | Fujian, 安正堂 Liu Shuang-song 劉雙松 | 1607 |
| *Jigu yin zheng* 集古印正 | 3.0 | 6J/ 6C | Gan Yang 甘暘 | 1596 |
| *Han Wei Liuchao ershiyi mingjia ji* 漢魏六朝二十 一名家集 | 3.0 | 123J/?C | Huizhou, Wang Family 汪氏 | 1572–1644 |
| *Bencao* 本草 | 4.9 | ?J/10C | | 1522–66* |

SOURCE: Shen Jin, "Mingdai fangke tushu zhi liutong yu jiage" (Circulation and price of books at bookstores in the Ming dynasty). * Indicates time of purchase.

# Prices of Food, Utensils, and Miscellaneous Things, 1570s–1640s

| GOODS | UNIT | PRICE IN TAEL |
|---|---|---|
| Chicken | 1 | 0.034–0.05 |
| Pork | 1 catty | 0.02 |
| Beef | 1 catty | 0.015 |
| Lamb | 1 catty | 0.015–0.02 |
| Goose | 1 (big) | 0.2 |
| Fish | 1 catty | 0.02–0.05 |
| Laichee | 1 catty | 0.046–0.05 |
| Grapes | 1 catty | 0.05 |
| Peaches | 1 catty | 0.04 |
| Plums | 1 catty | 0.04 |
| Spinach | 1 catty | 0.15 |
| Mustard | 1 catty | 0.21 |
| Walnuts | 1 catty | 0.017 |
| Chestnuts | 1 catty | 0.018 |
| Winter melon | 1 | 0.1 |
| Sugar | 0.1 catty | 0.02 |
| Salt | 1 catty | 0.001[a] |
| Honey | 0.1 catty | 0.02 |
| Wine | 1 bottle | 0.05 |
| Chair | 1 | 0.4 |
| Tin winepot | 1 | 0.08 |
| Tin teapot | 1 | 0.14 |
| Rice bowl | 1 | 0.005 |
| Patterned plate | 1 | 0.066 |
| Knife | 1 | 0.02 |
| Chopsticks | 1 pair | 0.001–0.005 |
| Charcoal | 1 catty | 0.004 |
| Firewood | 1 catty | 0.007 |
| Umbrella | 1 | 0.13–1.5 |
| Folding fan | 1 | 0.2[b] |
| European eye glasses | 1 | 4.0–5.0[a] |

| GOODS | UNIT | PRICE IN TAEL |
|-------|------|---------------|
| Horse | 1 | 40.0[c] |
| Coffin | 1 | 3.0[d] |

SOURCE: Shen Bang, pp. 122–23, 141, 147–48, 151, 159, 170. [a]Prices in Shanghai from Ye Mengzhu, *Yueshi bian*, juan 7. [b]*Er xu Jinling suoshi*, 199b; [c]Zhang Yinyu, 1, p. 1110; [d] Zhou Hui, pp. 2412–13.

# Publications of Chen Renxi (1580–1634) in Different Capacities: Publisher, Editor, Commentator, Compiler, Proofreader

| DATE | TITLE | PUBLISHER |
|------|-------|-----------|
| 1615 | *Chen Baiyang ji* 陳白陽集 | YF |
| 1615 | *Shitian xiansheng ji* 石田先生集. | YF |
| 1618 | *Guwen qi shang* 古文奇賞 (WMY) | YY |
| 1620–44 | *Changuo ce qichao* 戰國策奇鈔 | |
| 1621 | *Xu Guwen qishang* 續古文奇賞 (WMY) | YY |
| 1621 | *Zangshu* 藏書 (WMY) | YF |
| 1621–27 | *Dongpo xiansheng shiji* 東坡先生詩集 | YF |
| 1621–27 | *Song Yuan tongjian* 宋元通鑒 | YF |
| 1623 | *Xu Zangshu* 續藏書 (WMY) | YF |
| 1624 | *Qishangzhai Guang wenyuan yinghua* 奇賞齋廣文苑英華 | QS |
| 1624 | *Sanxu Guwen qishang* 三續古文奇賞 (WMY) | YY |
| 1625 | *Liang Han qichao* 兩漢奇鈔 | |
| 1625 | *Mingwen qishang* 明文奇賞 (WMY) | YY |
| 1625 | *Sixu Guwen qishang* 四續古文奇賞 (WMY) | YY |
| 1625 | *Tongjian shiwen bianwu* 通鑒釋文辨誤 | |
| 1625 | *Zizhi tongjian* 資治通鑒, preface by Chen 1625 (WMY) | |
| 1626 | *Sanguo zhi* 三國志 (WMY) | YF |
| 1626 | *Zhuzi qi shang* 諸子奇賞 | |
| 1628 | *Jingshi ba bian leizuan* 經世八編類纂 | |
| 1628–44 | *Huang Ming shifa lu* 皇明世法錄 | |
| 1628–44 | *Xingli biaoti huiyao* 性理標題彙要 (WMY) | |
| 1629 | *Zizhi tongjian daquan* 資治通鑒大全 (WMY) | DH |
| 1632 | *Daxue yanyi bu* 大學衍義補 (WMY) | |
| 1632 | *Qian que ju leishu* 潛确居類書 (WMY) | |
| 1632 | *Yangshan zhi* 陽山志 | YF |
| 1633 | *Biao chengwen* 表程文, *Ce chengwen* 策程文 | BS |
| 1633 | *Huang Ming lun chengwen xuan* 皇明論程文選 | |
| 1633 | *Wumeng yuan ji* 無夢園集 | |
| 1634 | *Qishangzhai Guwen huibian* 奇賞齋古文彙編, This may be a reprint of 1625 edition by YY (WMY) | QS |
| 1634 | *Sishu beikao* 四書備考 | YF |

BOOKS WITHOUT DATES

*Yaofeng shanzhi* 堯峰山志
*Huang Ming er zu shisi zong zengpu biaoti pingduan shiji*
皇明二祖十四宗增補標題評斷實紀
Guoyu heping 國語合評
*Guoce heping* 國策合評
*Yipin yi han* 逸品繹函
*Wenpin dihan* 文品帝函
*Chen Mingqing ji* 陳名卿集
*Baichuan xuehai* 百川學海
*Xihan wending* 西漢文定
*Wen bianwu* 文辨誤
*Jingkou sanshan zhi* 京口三山志
*Xijing yijian lu* 義經易簡錄.
*Chen Mingqing xiansheng jingxuan gujin wentong* 陳明卿先生精選
古今文統

SOURCES: *MDBKZL*, 1.7a, 1.43b, 2.29a, 6.28a; *ZGSBS*, pp. 5, 45, 76–77, 91, 385, 441–42, 450, 519, 568–69; *ZGSBS*, *yibu*, p. 19; *SBSZ*, pp. 58–59, 144, 173, 187, 221, 229, 298–99, 349, 555–56; *TWGCSB*, 730–31; *WMSJK*, pp. 40–41; *TWGCSB*, 730; Shen Jin, p. 465; *SKJHS*, vol. 60, pp. 2–35.

Abbreviations: YF, Yuefantang; QS, Qishangzhai; YY, Youyoutang; DH, Dahuantang; BS, Baisongtang. WMY refers to the presence of a preface in Chen's *Wumengyuan ji* (Collected writings from the garden of no dream).

# A Chronological List of Commentaries on the
# Four Books Published in the Late Ming (HYX)

N.d.   Huang Qiyou 黃起有. *Xinke Huang taishi zuanji Sishu gangjian* 新刻黃 太史纂輯四書綱鑒.

N.d.   Li Tingji 李廷機. *Sishu dazhu cankao* 四書大註參考.

N.d.   Tang Binyin 湯賓尹. *Xinke Tang taishi yishou kechang tizhi* 新刻湯太史 擬授科場題旨天香閣說.

N.d.   Xiang Shengguo 項聲國 *Xiang huikui Sishu tingyue* 項會魁四書聽月.

N.d.   Xu Yan 徐牪. *Xinke Xu Jiuyi xiansheng Sishu fujue* 新刻徐九一先生四書 倍訣.

N.d.   Zhang Mingbi 張明弼. *Canbu Zou-Lu xinyin* 參補鄒魯心印集註.

N.d.   Zhang Pu 張溥. *Sishu yin* 四書引.

N.d.   Zhou Wende 周文德. *Simingju shanbu Sishu jiangyi shengxian xinjue* 四明居刪補四書講意聖賢心訣.

N.d.   Zhou Wende 周文德. *Sishu jiangyi cunshi* 四書講意存是.

1563   Xu Kuang 徐爌. *Sishu chuwen* 四書初問.

1568   Chen Chen 陳琛. *Lingyuan shanfang zhongding Sishu qianshuo* 靈源山 房重訂四書淺說, 1568.

1578   Huang Guangsheng 黃光昇. *Sishu jiwen* 四書紀聞.

1588   Liu Sicheng 劉思誠. *Sishu yizhuan sanyi* 四書翼傳三義.

1589   Xu Fenpeng 徐奮鵬. *Zhongke Sishu xubu bianmeng jiezhu* 四書續補便蒙 解註.

1590   Zhao Weixin 趙維新. *Ganshu lu* 感述錄.

1594   Zhu Mingliang 朱明良. *Xinqie Huang Ming bai mingjia Sishu lijie ji* 新鍥 皇明百名家四書理解集.

1596   *Sishu hezhu bian* 四書合註編 (no author).

1596   Wang Qiao 王樵. *Sishu shaowen bian* 四書紹聞編.

1597   Zou Yuanbiao 鄒元標. *Renwen shuitian jianyi* 仁文水田講義.

1600   Li Tingji 李廷機. *Xinjuan Hanlin Li Jiuwo xiansheng jiachuan Sishu wenlin guanzhi* 新鐫翰林李九我先生家傳四書文林貫旨.

1602   Xu Xie 許獬. Sishu chong Xi zhujie 四書崇熹註解.

1604   Ma Laiyuan 馬來遠. *Sishu zuisheng cang* 四書最勝藏.

1604   Tang Ru'e 唐汝諤. *Sishu weiyan* 四書微言.

1607   Yuan Huang 袁黃. *Xinke Liaofan Yuan xiansheng Sishu xuner sushuo* 新刻了凡袁先生四書訓兒俗說.

1610   Xu Fuyuan 許孚遠. *Sishu shu* 四書述.

1610 Xu Kuangyue 徐匡嶽. *Ruzong jiyao* 儒宗輯要.

1612 Ai Nanying 艾南英. *Ai Qianzi xiansheng shouzhu Sishu fahui jiejie* 艾千子先生手著四書發慧捷解.

1612 Qian Sule 錢肅樂. *Erke Qian Xisheng xiansheng shouzhu Sishu congxin* 二刻錢希聲先生手著四書從信.

1613 Qian Zhaoyang 錢肇陽. *Sishu huijie xinyi* 四書會解新意.

1613 Xu Fenpeng 徐奮鵬. *Bidongsheng xinwu* 筆洞生新悟.

1613 Zhu Changchun 朱長春. *Xinke Zhu Taifu xuan qi shanzhong shouer Sishu zhuyi xinde jie* 新刻朱太復玄栖山中授兒四書主意心得解.

1614 Zhu Wanlin 諸萬理. *Zhu Jiming Xili bian* 諸繼明析理編.

1615 Lin San 林散. *Sishu shusheng* 四書説剩.

1615 Shen Shouzheng 沈守正. *Sishu shuocong* 四書説叢.

1615 Tang Binyin 湯賓尹. *Shui'an Sishu mai* 睡庵四書脈.

1615 Wang Yu 王宇. *Sishu yeshiyuan chugao* 四書也是園初告.

1615 Yao Guangzuo 姚光祚. *Sishu wuxue wangyang bian* 四書吾學望洋編.

1615 Yuan Huang 袁黃. *Yuan xiansheng Sishu shanzheng jian shuyi* 袁先生四書刪正兼疏意.

1617 Hong Qichu 洪啓初. *Sishu yijian* 四書翼箋.

1617 Wang Najian 王納諫. Wang Guantao xiansheng *Sishu jiaxun* 王觀濤先生四書家訓.

1617 Yu Yingke 余應科. *Ke Qian Cao liang xiansheng Huang Ming bai fangjia wenda* 刻錢曹兩先生皇明百方家問答.

1617 Zhong Tianyuan 鍾天元. *Sishu jiebo bian* 四書解搏編.

1618 Guo Wei 郭偉. *Liu caizi Sishu xingren yu* 六才子四書醒人語.

1618 Ma Shiqi 馬世奇. *Dingjuan sanshi mingjia Sishu ji* 鼎鐫三十名家四書紀.

1618 Xu Fenpeng 徐奮鵬. *Sishu gujin daomai* 四書古今道脈.

1618 Zhou Yanru 周延儒. *Taishi Zhou Yusheng pingduan Siqi xinji guochao minggong zhuyigangmu bianduan* 太史周玉繩評斷四奇新輯國朝名公主意綱目辨斷.

1619 Huang Shijun 黃士俊. *Sishu yaojie* 四書要解.

1619 Xu Fenpeng 徐奮鵬. *Dingke Xu Bidong zengbu Shui'an Tang Taishi Sishumai jiangyi* 鼎刻徐筆洞增補庵湯太史四書脈講意.

1620 Yao Wenwei 姚文蔚. *Sishu wen* 四書聞.

1621 Ou Luoyang 區羅陽. *Ouzi Sishy yi* 區子四書翼.

1622 Li Hong 李竑. *Qiujizhai shuoshu* 求己齋説書.

1623 Zhang Zhenyuan 張振淵. *Shjing shanfang Sishu shuotong* 石鏡山房四書説統.

1623 Zhu Zhihan 朱之翰. *Xinjuan Sishu liyin* 新鐫四書理印.

1624 Guo Wei 郭偉. *Guo Zhuyuan xiansheng huiji shi taishi Sishu zhuyi baocang* 郭朱源先生彙輯十太史四書主意寶藏.

1624 Zhang Song 張嵩. *Sishu shuosheng* 四書説乘.

1626 Ma Shiqi 馬世奇. *Sishu dinglian* 四書鼎臠.

1626 Xu Fenpeng 徐奮鵬. *Bidong shanfang xinzhu zhixin lu* 筆洞山房新著知新錄.

1627 Wang Mengjian 王夢簡. *Sishu sheng* 四書徵.

1627  Wang Xianchen 王獻臣. *Sishu pidan* 四書闢旦.

1631  Zhang Yunluan 張雲鸞. *Sishu jingzheng lu* 四書經正錄.

1632  Xu Fenpeng 徐奮鵬. *Zuanding Sishu gujin daquan* 纂定四書古今大全.

1632  Zhang Pu 張溥. *Zhang Tianru xiansheng huiding Sishu hekao* 張天如先生彙訂四書合考.

1633  Chen Zhixi 陳智錫. *Sishu huizheng* 四書彙徵.

1633  Xiang Kun 項焜. *Sishu langhuan ji* 四書瑯嬛集.

1633  Yu Yingke 余應科. *Sishu qianbai nian yan* 四書千百年眼.

1634  Shen Shaofang 申紹芳. *Xinke Shen huikui jiachuan ke'er Sishu shunwen jiejie* 新刻申會魁家傳課兒四書順文捷解.

1637  Chen Zilong 陳子龍. *Shuoshu wenjian* 説書文箋.

1640  Gu Menglin 顧夢麟. *Sishu shuoyue* 四書説約.

1641   Xu Wenjin 徐文潽. *Sishu shengyan* 四書醒言.

1642  Zhang Pu 張溥. *Sishu kaobei* 四書考備.

1643  Wang Najian 王納諫. *Xinjuan Sishu yizhu jiangy* 新鐫四書翼註講意.

1644  Gu Menglin 顧夢麟. *Sishu shiyi jing tongkao* 四書十一經通考.

1644  Wu Dang 吳當. *Hedang Mengyin Cunyi dingjie* 合當四書蒙引存疑定解.

# Character List

Ai Nanying　艾南英

*ancha si*　按察司

*ba caizi*　八才子

*bagu*　八股

*baguwen*　八股文

*Baichuan shuzhi*　百川書志

*Baishi qiao zhen gao*　白石樵真稿

*baitailian*　白台連

*baiyang*　白楊

*Baiyun lou*　白雲樓

*bang zhi*　榜紙

*baomian zhi*　包麵紙

*baoren*　報人

Baoritang　寶日堂

*Beini mouchen jichu dati biaomu*　備擬卯辰急出大題標目

*beiwen*　碑文

*ben zhi*　本紙

*Bencao gangmu*　本草綱目

*bense*　本色

*bianding*　辨訂

*biao zhi*　表紙

*biaoxin*　標新

*biaozhi*　標旨

*Bidong sheng xinwu*　筆洞生新悟

*Bogu tu lu*　博古圖錄

*bubao*　不報

*budai xishu er hou le*　不待習熟而後樂

*bugan a si, yuan gong tong hao*　不敢阿私愿公同好

*buneng jieju zhi shi*　不能絜矩之失

*buzheng si*　布政司

*caizi*　才子

*caizishu*　才子書

*can*　參

*canbu*　參補

*canding*[a]　參定

*canding*[b]　參訂

*Canglang shihua*　滄浪詩話

*canyu*　參語

*canyue*　參閱

*canzheng*　參政

*cao*　槽

Cao Junyi　曹君義

*chadai po*　插帶婆

Changgengguan　長庚館

Changjue　常覺

Changshu　常熟

Changsongge　常松閣

Changxing　長興

Changzhou　長洲

Chaoshe　超社

*Chaoshi baowen tang shumu*　晁氏寶文堂書目

Chen Daila　陳大來

Chen Dingsheng　陳定生

Chen Jiru　陳繼儒

Chen Jitai　陳際泰

Chen Renxi　陳仁錫

Chen Shiye　陳士業

Chen Shu　陳束

Chen Yidian　陳懿典

Chen Yumo　陳禹謨

Chen Zhenhui　陳貞慧

Chen Zilong　陳子龍

Cheng Dayue　程大約

Cheng Fuxin　程復心

Chengshe　澄社

*Chengshi moyuan* 程氏墨苑

*chengwen* 程文

*chengwen zhi* 呈文紙

*chuanggao* 窗稿

*chuanqi* 傳奇

Chun'an 淳安

*chushi* 處士

Ciren si 慈仁寺

*congshu* 叢書

*congtan* 叢談

Cundetang 存德堂

Cunrentang 存仁堂

*da chengwen zhi* 大呈文紙

*da hongben zhi* 大紅本紙

*da hong zhi* 大紅紙

*Da zao gan* 打棗竿

*da ziqing zhi* 大瓷青紙

Dahuantang 大歡堂

*Dali si* 大理寺

Dantu 丹徒

*Danyuan conglu* 丹鉛總錄

Daojitang 道濟堂

*Daozong liushu* 道宗六書

*datong* 大同

*Datong li* 大統曆

*Daxue yanyi bu* 大學衍義補

*Daxue Zhangju* 大學章句

*dian* 點

*dianding* 點定

*dianshi* 典史

*dianyan* 點眼

*dibao* 邸報

*ding*[a] 定

*ding*[b] 訂

Ding Yunpeng 丁雲鵬

*dingjuan* 鼎鐫

Dong Qichang    董其昌

Dongxiang    東鄉

Du Linzheng    杜麟徵

*duan*    斷

Duanshe    端社

*Ducha yuan*    都察院

*dufa*    讀法

*dukan*    督刊

*duke*    督刻

*Dushu hou*    讀書後

*Dushu jing*    讀書鏡

*duxue nanji*    督學南畿

*duzi*    督梓

*fachao*    發抄

*fan li ren zhe jie shengren ye*    凡利人者皆聖人也

*fang*    房

Fang Yizhi    方以智

Fang Yulu    方于魯

Fang Yuxiu    方禹修

*fanggao*    房稿

*fangjian suben*    坊間俗板

*fangxuan*    房選

*fanke bijiu*    翻刻必究

*fanli*    凡例

*fei sheng guojia zhi cai, sheng minjian zhi cai ye*
    非生國家之財，生民間之財也

*fen*    分

*Fen zhuzi shumu*    分諸子書目

Feng Fang    豐坊

Feng Menglong    馮夢龍

*Fengshen yanyi*    封神演義

*fanli*    凡例

Foshui shanfang    拂水山房

*fu*    父 or 甫

*fu mu yi gong yu ren*    付木以公之於人

Fuchuntang    富春堂

*Fugu pai*　復古派

*fuku zhi cai*　府庫之財

Fuli　甫里

*Fushou quanshu*　福壽全書

Fushui　拂水

Fuzhou　撫州

*Gangjian tongyi*　綱鑑統一

*Ganying pian*　感應篇

*gao chi*　誥敕

*gediao*　格調

*gege junju*　各各均足

Geng Dingxiang　耿定向

*gewu buzhuan*　格物補傳

*gong*　公

*gong er bu zhi*　公而布之

*Gong qing juti panxing Sishu daquan bian di'er jie*
　　公請具題頒行四書大全辯第二揭

*Gong qing zixing Sishu daquan bian diyi jie*　公請梓行四書大全辯第一揭

*gong zhi hainei*　公之海內

*gong zhi tianxia*　公之天下

*Gong'an*　公安

*gongfu he benti*　功夫和本體

*gongguoge*　功過格

*gongjie*　公揭

*gonglun*　公論

*gonglun chu yu xuexiao*　公論出於學校

*gongping*　公平

*gongping zhengda zhi dao*　公平正大之道

*gongsheng*　貢生

*gongyi*　公議

*gou zhi*　扣紙

Gu Menglin　顧夢麟

Gu Qijing　顧起經

Gu Qilun　顧起綸

Gu Xiancheng　顧憲成

Gu Zhengyi　顧正誼

*Guan miji*　廣祕笈

Guan Zhidao　管志道

Guanglusi　光祿寺

Guangqitang　光啓堂

Guangyutang　光裕堂

Gui Youguang　歸有光

*Gujin shuke*　古今書刻

Guo Wei　郭偉

*Guobiao siji*　國表四集

*Guochao minggong hanzao*　國朝名公翰藻

*Guochao minggong jingji wenchao*　國朝名公經濟文鈔

*Guochao xianzheng lu*　國朝獻徵錄

Guomen guangye she　國門廣業社

*Guoshi jingjizhi*　國史經籍志

*Guoyu*　國語

*Guozijian siye*　國子監司業

*guren zhi jingshen*　古人之精神

*Gushi shishi*　顧氏詩史

*Gushi suo*　古詩所

Haijinshe　海金社

Hao Jing　郝敬

He Jingming　何景明

He Liangjun　何良俊

Hou Fangyu　侯方域

Hu Guang　湖廣

Hu Mao　胡貿

Hu Zhengyan　胡正言

Huancuitang　環翠堂

*Huang Ming guanke jingshi hongci xuji*　皇明館課經世宏詞續集

*Huang Ming jingshi wenbian*　皇明經世文編

*Huang Ming jinwen ding*　皇明今文定

*Huang Ming shifa lu*　皇明世法錄

Huang Ruheng (Zhengfu)　黃汝亨(貞父)

Huang Zongxi　黃宗羲

*Huangchao like Sishu mojuan pingxuan*　皇朝歷科四書墨卷評選

*huangdian*　皇店

*huanglian*   黃連

Huangyan   黃巖

Huangzhou   黃州

Huanhuxuan   玩虎軒

Huating   華亭

Hu-Guang   湖廣

*huiban*   毀版

*huiguan*   會館

*huikui*   會魁

*huiping*   彙評

*huishi lu*   會試錄

*huiyuan*   會元

*Hushang yulu*   湖上語錄

Huzhou   湖州

*ji*   輯

Ji'an   吉安

*jianding*   鑒定

*jiangti*   匠體

*jiangxue*   講學

Jiangyin   江陰

*jiangzhang*   講章

Jianluju   簡綠居

*jianzhi*   柬紙

*jiao*   校

Jiao Hong   焦竑

*jiaoding*   校訂

*jiaokan*   校刊

*jiaoshou*   教授

*jiaoyu*   校諭

*jiaoyue*   校閱

*jiaozi*   校梓

*jiatong*   家僮

Jiaxing   嘉興

*jie*   解

*Jie'an manbi*   戒庵漫筆

*jieju*   絜矩

*jieju zhi dao*  絜矩之道

*jigao*  輯稿

*Jiguge*  汲古閣

*Jiguge jiaoke shumu*  汲古閣校刻書目

*Jiguge zhencang miben shumu*  汲古閣珍藏秘本書目

*jijiu*  祭酒

*jimai*  寄賣

*Jin fanke Daoji tang shuji yuanshi*  禁翻刻道濟堂書籍原示

*Jin Ping Mei*  金瓶梅

*Jin wenxuan*  今文選

*jincheng zhi*  進呈紙

*Jinghua richao*  京華日抄

Jingling  竟陵

Jingming zhai she  靜明齋社

Jingshan cang  徑山藏

*Jingshi ba bian leizuan*  經世八編類纂

*Jingshi tongyan*  警世通言

*Jingu qiguan*  今古奇觀

*Jinlin xuji*  涇林續記

Jinsha  金沙

Jinshengju  近聖居

*Jinwen dai*  今文待

*Jinwen ding*  今文定

*jiping*  輯評

Jishe  機社

Jizhizhai  繼志齋

*jue xue wu you*  絕學無友

Jukuilou  聚奎樓

*julian zhi chen*  聚斂之臣

*jun*  君

*juren*  舉人

*jushi*  居士

*kaishu*  楷書

*kanhe zhi*  勘合紙

*kanzi jiang*  刊字匠

*kao*  考

*ke er gong zhi*　刻而公之

*keyi ping tianxia hu*　可以平天下乎

*kezi dian*　刻字店

*kezi jiang*　刻字匠

*kuang*[a]　眖

*kuang*[b]　狂

*Kuangfu zhi yan*　狂夫之言

Kuangshe　匡社

*Kuangyan*　狂言

Kuibitang　奎壁堂

Laiyang　萊陽

*lanwu wenji*　濫惡文集

*le*　樂

*li*　理

*li ben tianxia gong ye*　理本天下公也

Li Chao　李潮

Li Guangjin　李光縉

Li Kaixian　李開先

Li Mengyang　李夢陽

Li Rihua　李日華

Li Weizhen　李維楨

Li Yu　李漁

Li Yuankuan　黎元寬

Li Zhi　李贄

Li Zhuowu　李卓吾

*liangzhi*　良知

*lianqi zhi*　連七紙

*licai*　理財

*Lidai wenji*　歷代文紀

*Liechao shiji xiaozhuan*　列朝詩集小傳

*Lieguo zhi zhuan*　列國志傳

*Lienü zhuan*　列女傳

*liequ*　獵取

Lin Chao'en　林兆恩

*Lin jing zhiyue*　麟經指月

Linchuan　臨川

*ling* 綾

*Lisaotu* 離騷圖

Liu Yan 劉剡

*liubi* 流弊

*Lizi quanshu* 林子全書

Longtan 龍潭

Lu Guimeng 陸龜蒙

Lu Yunlong 陸雲龍

Lü Gao 呂高

Lü Yusheng 呂玉繩

*lunwen zongzhi* 論文宗旨

Luo Wanzao 羅萬藻

*Luqiu shishi ji* 鹿裘石室集

Macheng 麻城

*mai wen* 賣文

Mao Kun 茅坤

Mao Xiang 冒襄

Mao Yi 毛扆

*maobian zhi* 毛邊紙

Mei Dingzuo 梅鼎祚

Meigong 眉公

*Meihua shui* 梅花墅

*men shen* 門神

Meng Jiao 孟郊

*mian zhi* 綿紙

Min Qiji 閔齊伋

*Ming wen qi shang* 明文奇賞

Mingde shutang 明德書堂

*minggong* 名公

*minggong yilun* 名公議論

*mingshi* 名士

*mingwu* 名物

*mizhi* 秘旨

Moganzhai 墨感齋

*mojuan* 墨卷

*moli* 茉莉

Mou Yuanyi　茅元儀

Nanshe　南社

Nanbei er she　南北二社

Nanxun　南潯

*neige*　內閣

*niti*　擬題

*Nongzheng quanshu*　農政全書

Ou Luoyang　歐羅陽

*Oupoguan yuhua*　歐坡館餘話

Pan Jiuhua　潘九華

Pan Lei　潘耒

Pan Yunduan　潘允端

*pang zhi*　榜紙

Peng Bin　彭賓

Pi Rixiu　皮日休

*Piao jing*　嫖經

*pidian*　批點

*ping*　評

*ping tianxia*　平天下

Pingyuantang she　平遠堂社

*pingdian*　平點

*pinghua*　平話

Pinglu tang　平露堂

*pingxuan zhe*　評選者

*pingyue*　評閱

*Pipa ji*　琵琶記

*piping*　批評

*Pogu yezi*　博古葉子

*buzheng si*　布政司

Qian Qianyi　錢謙益

Qianshan　鉛山

*qing*　頃

Qiu Shun　邱橓

Qiu Zhaolin　丘兆麟

Qiushe　求社

Qizizhai　奇字齋

*qu*    趣

*quandian*    圈點

Ren Han    任瀚

*risan*    日傘

Rongyutang    容與堂

*Rucang*    儒藏

*Rulin Waishi*    儒林外史

*runbi*    潤筆

*sancai*    散財

*Sanjiao kaimi yanyi*    三教開迷演義

Santaiguan    三台館

*sengyou*    僧郵

*shan*    刪

*shanding*    刪定

*shang*    商

*shangtu xiawen*    上圖下文

*shanshu*    善書

*shanren*    山人

*shanzheng*    刪正

*shedi*    社弟

*shegao*    社稿

*shemeng*    社盟

Shen Guoyuan    沈國元

Shen Ji    沈幾

Shen Jing    沈璟

Shen Li    沈鯉

Shen Shoumin    沈壽民

Shen Yan    沈演

*shengcai you dadao*    生財有大道

*sheyou*    社友

Shi Fenglai    施鳳來

Shidetang    世德堂

*Shihuai*    史懷

*Shiji*    史記

*Shijing shuoyue*    詩經說約

Shijingtang    世經堂

*Shisan jing zhushu* 十三經注疏

*shishang* 士商

*shisi zhangbu* 市肆帳簿

*shiwen* 時文

*shixi* 時習

*shixue* 世學

Shizhuzhai 十竹齋

*shuajuan zhi* 刷卷紙

Shuanfengtang 雙峰堂

*shuayin jiang* 刷印匠

*shuchuan* 書船

*shuifu* 水夫

*Shuihu zhuan* 水滸傳

*shuji shi* 庶吉士

Shunchang 順昌

*shupo* 書帕

*shushou* 書手

*sibu* 四部

*sichu shumu* 嗣出書目

Sijiantang 師儉堂

Sili jian 司禮監

Sima Qian 司馬遷

*Sishu daquan* 四書大全

*Sishu quanzhi* 四書詮旨

*Sishu Shuotong* 四書說統

*Sishu shuoyue* 四書說約

*Sishu woxue wangyang bian* 四書吾學望洋編

*Sishu zhangtu tongkao* 四書章圖通考

*Sishu zhangtu zuanshi* 四書章圖纂釋

*Sishu zhixin* 四書知新

*Sishu Zhou Zhuang hejie* 四書周莊合解

Song Zhengbi 宋徵璧

*song zhuang zhi* 訟狀紙

Songjiang 松江

*suji* 蘇鬐

Su Jun (Zixi) 蘇濬 (紫溪)

Su Shi 蘇軾

*suyang* 蘇樣

*suyi* 蘇意

*suzuo* 蘇坐

Sun Chun 孫淳

Sun Kuang 孫爌

Su-Song dao 蘇松道

*suyi* 蘇意

*suzuo* 蘇坐

*Taigeti* 臺閣體

*tailian zhi* 臺連紙

*taishi* 太史

*Taixuan jing* 太玄經

Tan Youxia 譚友夏

Tan Yuanchun 譚元春

Tang Binyin 湯賓尹

Tang Chengye 湯承爍

Tang Fu 湯復

Tang Fuchun 唐富春

Tang Hezheng 唐鶴徵

*Tang Huiyuan jingxuan pidian Tang-Song mingxian celun wencui* 唐會元精選批點唐宋名賢策論文粹

*Tang Jinchuan bianzuan Zuoshi shimo* 唐荊川編纂左氏始末

*Tang leihan* 唐類函

Tang Liyao 唐鯉耀

Tang Ruxun 唐汝詢

*Tang Shi jie* 唐詩解

Tang Shunzhi 唐順之

*tianxia zhi gongyan* 天下之公言

*tici* 題詞

*tongfang* 同房

*tongxin* 童心

Tongzhou 通州

*tudi gong* 土地公

*waishi* 外史

Wan Shihe 萬士和

*Wanbao quanshu*　萬寶全書

*Wanshu zaji*　宛署雜記

Wang Baigu　王百穀

Wang Fengxiang　王鳳翔

Wang Gen　王艮

Wang Guanghua　汪光華

Wang Ji　王幾

Wang Jiusi　王九思

Wang Shenzhong　王慎中

Wang Shizhen　王世貞

Wang Tingna　王廷納

Wang Xianshan　王先善

Wang Xijue　王錫爵

Wanjuantang　萬卷堂

*wen bi Qin-Han, shi bi sheng Tang*　文必秦漢，詩必盛唐

Wen Qixiang　聞啓祥

Wen Tiren　溫體仁

Wen Yuren　溫育仁

Wen Zhenmeng　文震孟

Wenlinge　文林閣

*wenpai*　文派

*wenren*　文人

*wenshe*　文社

*Wenyuange shumu*　文淵閣書目

*wenzhang zhi quan*　文章之權

Wu De　吳德

Wu Guolun　吳國綸

*wu wugu er buxin, fa wuen er buchuang*　物無故而不新，法無因而不創

Wu Yingji　吳應箕

Wu Zeng　吳甑

Wu Zhenyuan　吳震元

Wu Zhongsheng　吳仲升

Wuhu　蕪湖

Wunian　無念

Wuxing　吳興

Wuying dian　武英殿

Xia Yan　夏言

Xia Yunyi　夏允彝

Xiang Shengguo　項聲國

Xiang Xu　項煜

*Xianqing nü shi*　閒情女肆

*xiansheng*　先生

Xiao Shaoqu　蕭少衢

Xiao Tenghong　蕭騰鴻

Xiao Tong　蕭統

*xiaopin*　小品

*xiaoshuo*　小説

*xiaoxue*　小學

*Xin jiaozhu guben Xixiang ji*　新校注古本西廂記

*Xinbian shiwen leiju hanmo daquan*　新編事文類聚翰墨大全

Xindu　新都

*Xingli daquan*　性理大全

*xingling*　性靈

*Xingshi hengyan*　醒世恆言

*Xingshi yinyuan zhuan*　醒世姻緣傳

*xingshu*　行書

*xingyi*　行移

*xinjuan*　新鐫

*Xinjuan Chen Meigong piping lieguo zhizhuan*　新鐫陳眉公批評列國志傳

*xinke*　新刻

*Xinke Zhong Bojing xiansheng piping Fengshen yanyi*
　　新刻鍾伯敬先生批評封神演義

*xinqie*　新鍥

*xinqin*　新鋟

*xinshuo*　新説

*xinyi*　新意

Xiong Guo　熊過

*Xiucai miyue*　秀才祕籥

*Xu Bidong xiansheng jingjuan wanbao quanshu*　徐筆洞先生精纂萬寶全書

Xu Boxing　徐燉與

Xu Dianqing　許殿卿

Xu Fenpeng　徐奮鵬 (筆洞)

Xu Fuyuan    徐孚遠

Xu Hongzu    徐弘祖

Xu Jie    徐階

Xu Shipu    徐世溥

Xu Xiangyun    徐象橒

Xu Yuangong    許元恭

Xu Zhi    徐智

Xu Zichang    許自昌

Xu Ziyu    徐子與

*xuan*    選

Xuancheng    宣城

*xuanshou*    選手

*xuan zhi*    宣紙

*xubian*    續編

*xue er shi xi zhi, bu yi le hu*    學而時習之不亦樂乎

*xuetian*    學田

*xuezheng*    學政

*Xuke Bidong xiansheng houwu*    續刻筆洞先生後悟

Yan Chi    嚴敕

Yan Jiugao    嚴九臯

Yan Song    嚴嵩

Yan Tiaoyu    嚴調御

Yan Wushun    嚴武順

Yang P'u    楊溥

Yang Rong    楊榮

Yang Shiqi    楊士奇

Yang Tingshu    楊廷樞

Yang Tingyun    楊廷筠

Yang Xiong    楊雄

Yang Yi    楊彞

*yanglian*    養廉

Yantai sizi    燕台十子

*Yanzhou shanren sibu gao*    弇州山人四部稿

*Yanzi jian*    燕子箋

Yao Wenwai    姚文蔚

Yao Ximeng    姚希孟

Yao Yuansu    姚元素

*yaoshu*    妖書

Ye Mengzhu    葉夢珠

Ye Tingguan    葉廷琯

Ye Zhou    葉晝

Yecheng she    冶城社

*Yeji*    野記

*yeshi*    野史

*yezi*    葉子

*yi gong xinshang*    以公欣賞

Yi she    邑社

*yi you xuanke, bi shi zhi ming zhi shi*    已有選刻必是知名之士

*yibang*    乙榜

*yilun*    議論

*Yimin zhuan*    逸民傳

Yingshe    應社

Yintian    應天

Yongfeng    永豐

*yongren*    用人

Youlong    遊龍

*youmin*    遊民

*Youyang shanren bianfeng ji*    酉陽山人編蓬集

Youyoutang    酉酉堂

Yu Jideng    余繼登

Yu Shanzhang    余羨章

Yu Yingqiu    余應虯

Yu yuan    豫園

*yuan gong tong hao*    願公同好

Yuan Hongdao    袁宏道

Yuan Jixian    袁繼咸

Yuan Wuya    袁無涯

Yuan Zongdao    袁宗道

*yuangao*    原稿

*Yuanliu zhilun*    源流至論

*Yuanqu xuan*    元曲選

*yue*    閱

Yuefantang　悅帆堂

Yuefeng　月峰

*Yuelu yin*　月露音

Yuequan yin she　月泉吟社

*yulan*　御覽

Yunzan she　雲簪社

*Yutai xinyong*　玉台新詠

Yuyao　餘姚

Yuzhang　豫章

Zang Maoxun　臧懋循

*zaoce zhi*　造冊紙

*zaju*　雜劇

Zhang Cai　張采

Zhang Juzheng　張居正

Zhang Mingbi　張明弼

Zhang Nai (Dongchu)　張鼐（洞初）

Zhang Pu　張溥

Zhang Shichun　章世純

Zhang Wujiu　張無咎

Zhang Yunluan　張雲鸞

Zhang Zhenyuan　張振淵

Zhang Zilie　張自烈

*zhangzhi*　章旨

Zhao Shichun　趙時春

*Zhe mei jian*　折梅箋

*zhen*　真

Zheng Banqiao　鄭板橋

*zheng shu fa*　徵書法

*zheng wenti*　正文體

Zheng Xuan　鄭瑄

*zhengbian*　正編

Zhenjiang　鎮江

*zhijia*　紙甲

Zhilianju　織廉居

*Zhinang*　智囊

*zhisheng*　治生

*zhishi qu qi dedang, er buwei ewai zhi zheng*   只是取其得當而不為額外之征

*zhiyi*[a]   制義

*zhiyi*[b]   制藝

*zhizhang*   紙帳

*zhong chengwen zhi*   中呈文紙

Zhong Xing   鍾惺

*zhongjia zhi*   中夾紙

Zhongshutang   種書堂

Zhongshu sheng   中書省

Zhongyitang   中一堂

Zhou Biao   周鑣

Zhou Lixun   周立勳

Zhou Rudeng   周汝登

Zhou Yinglin   周應廙

Zhou Zhong   周鐘

Zhou Zongjian   周宗建

*zhouben zhi*   奏本紙

Zhu Guozhen   朱國楨

Zhu Yunming   祝允明

*zhuang*   莊

Zhuang she   莊社

*zhuangyuan*   狀元

*zhuanli*   專利

Zhuo Fazhi   卓發之

*zhuqian*   朱鈐

*zhushi*   主事

*zhushu*   注疏

*zhuyi*   主意

*zhu zhi*   竹紙

*zhuzi*   諸子

*zhuzuo*   著作

*zi*   梓

*zi cheng zhi*   咨呈紙

*zi er gong zhi*   梓而公之

*zi yi gong shi*   梓以公世

*zi yi gong zhi hainei*   梓以公之海內

*zi yi gong zhi, yi ling tianxia zhi*　梓以公之，亦令天下知

*zifang*　咨訪

*Zihuibian*　字彙辨

*ziren*　梓人

*zixing*　梓行

Zixinzhai　自新齋

Ziyunshe　紫雲社

*Zizhi tongjian daquan*　資治通鑒大全

Zou Zhilin　鄒之麟

*zouben zhi*　奏本紙

*zuanding*　纂定

*zuanji*　纂輯

*zuocang qian*　坐艙錢

*zuojia*　作家

## Abbreviations for Libraries, Institutions, and Bibliographic Sources that Appear in Bibliography and Endnotes

| | |
|---|---|
| *BBCSJC* | *Baibu congshu jicheng* 百部叢書集成. Reprint. Taibei: Yiwen tushu, 1969. |
| BDT | Beijing daxue tushuguan (Beijing University Library) |
| *BJTS* | *Beijing tushuguan guji zhenben congkan* 北京圖書館古籍珍本叢刊. Beijing: Shumu wenxian chubanshe, 1987. |
| *BJTSGC* | *Beijing tushuguan cang zhenben nianpu congkan* 北京圖書館藏珍本年譜叢刊. Beijing: Beijing tushuguan, 1999. |
| *BJXS* | *Biji xiaoshuo daguan* 筆記小說大觀. Yangzhou: Jiangsu Guangling guji keyin she, 1983. |
| *BJXSDG* | *Biji xiaoshuo daguan* 筆記小說大觀. Taibei: Xinxing chubanshe, 1978–90. |
| BT | Beijing tushuguan (Beijing Library) |
| *CSJCCB* | *Congshu jicheng chubian* 叢書集成初編. Shanghai: Shangwu yinshuguan, 1936. |
| *CSJCSB* | *Congshu jicheng sanbian* 叢書集成三編. Taibei: Xin Wenfeng, 1996. |
| *CSJCXB* | *Congshu jicheng xubian* 叢書集成續編. Taibei: Xin wenfeng, 1989. |
| *DMB* | L. Carrington Goodrich, ed. *Dictionary of Ming Biography, 1368–1644*. New York: Columbia University Press, 1976. |
| *DMHD* | *Da Ming huidian* 大明會典. Taibei: Huawen shuju, 1964. |
| FD | Shanghai Fudan daxue tushuguan (Fudan University, Shanghai) |
| *FMLQJ* | Feng Menglong 馮夢龍. *Feng Menglong quanji* 馮夢龍全集. Ed. Wei Tongxian. Shanghai: Guji chubanshe, 1993. |
| *FSN* | Fu Sinian tushuguan (Academic Sinica, Taibei) |
| *GBXSCK* | *Guben xiaoshuo congkan* 古本小說叢刊. Zhonghua shuju, 1987. |

GBXSJC
:   *Guben xiaoshuo jicheng* 古本小説集成. Shanghai: Guji chubanshe, 1990.

HJAS
:   *Harvard Journal of Asiatic Studies*

HY
:   Hanxue yanjiu zhongxin 漢學研究中心 (Center for Chinese Studies, Taibei)

HYC
:   Harvard Yen-ching Library, United States

HYX
:   Xeroxed copy in Hanxue yanjiu zhongxin (Center for Chinese Studies, Taibei)

JAS
:   *Journal of Asian Studies*

LC
:   Library of Congress, United States

LDKS
:   *Lidai keshu gaikuang* 歷代刻書概況. Beijing: Yinshua gongye chubanshe, 1991.

LYQJ
:   Li Yu 李漁. *Li Yu Quanji* 李漁全集. 15 vols. Taibei: Chengwen chubanshe, 1970.

MDBHCK
:   *Mingdai banhua congkan* 明代版畫叢刊. Taibei: Guoli gugong bowuguan, 1988.

MDBKZL
:   Du Xinfu 杜信孚. *Mingdai banke zonglu* 明代版刻綜錄. Yangzhou: Jiangsu Guangling guji keyinshe, 1983.

MDDKL
:   *Mingdai dengke lu huibian* 明代登科錄彙編. Taibei: Xuesheng shuju, 1969.

MDSHJJ
:   *Mingdai shehui jingji shiliao xuanbian* 明代社會經濟史料選編. 2 vols. Fuzhou: Fujian remin chubanshe, 1981.

MDSJHK
:   *Mingdai shiji hui kan* 明代史籍彙刊. Vol. 25. Taibei: Xuesheng shuju, 1970.

MDSMTB
:   *Mingdai shumu ti ba congkan* 明代書目題跋叢刊. Beijing: Shumu wenxian chubanshe, 1994.

MDZJCK
:   Zhou Jinfu 周駿富, ed. *Mingdai zhuanji congkan* 明代傳記叢刊. Taibei: Mingwen shuju, 1991.

MGHF
:   *Meiguo Hafu daxue Yanjing tushuguan zhongwen shanben shu zhi* 美國哈佛大學哈佛燕京圖書館中文善本書(Annotated catalog of Chinese rare books in the Harvard Yen-ching Library). Comp. Shen Jin 沈津. Shanghai: Shanghai cishu chubanshe, 1999.

MJBSHB
:   *Ming ji bishi huibian* 明季稗史彙編. Shanghai: Shanghai tushu jicheng yinshuju, 1896.

MJSWB
:   Ming jingshi wenbian 明經世文編. Comp. Chen Zilong 陳子龍. Beijing: Zhonghua shuju, 1962.

| | |
|---|---|
| *MQJS* | *Ming-Qing Jiangsu wenren nianbiao* 明清文人年表. Comp. Zhang Huijian 張慧劍. Shanghai: Shanghai guji, 1986. |
| *MRZJ* | *Mingren zhuanji ziliao suoyin* 明人傳記資料索引. Taibei: Guoli zhongyan tushuguan, 1978. |
| *MS* | *Mingshi* 明史. 28 vols. Beijing: Zhonghua shuju, 1974. |
| *MWH* | *Ming Wenhai* 明文海. Comp. Huang Zongxi 黄宗羲. Beijing: Zhonghua shuju, 1987. |
| *MZYXJ* | Qian Qianyi 錢謙益. *Muzhai you xue ji* 牧齋有學集. *SBCK.* |
| *QDWZYD* | *Qingdai wenziyu dang* 清代文字獄檔. Shanghai: Shanghai shuchian, 1986. |
| *QKZQJ* | *Qiankun zhengqi ji* 乾坤正氣集. Taibei: Huanqiu shuju, 1966. |
| *SBBY* | *Sibu beiyao* 四部備要. Taibei: Zhonghua shuju, 1965. |
| *SBCK* | *Sibu congkan* 四部叢刊. Shanghai Hanfenlou, n.d. |
| *SBCKCB* | *Sibu congkan chubian* 四部叢刊初編. Taibei: Shangwu yinshuguan, 1967. |
| *SBSZ* | Qu Wanli 屈萬里. *Zhongwen shanben shuzhi* 中文善本書志, *Qu Wanli quanji* 屈萬里全集. Taibei: Lianjing, 1984. |
| *SBXQCK* | Wang Qiugui 王秋桂, ed. *Shanben xiqu congkan* 善本戲曲叢刊. Taibei: Xuesheng shuju, 1987. |
| *SKJHS* | *Sigu jinhui shu congkan* 四庫禁毀書叢刊. Beijing: Beijing chubanshe, 1997–2000. |
| *SKQS* | *Siku quanshu* 四庫全書. Taibei: Shangwu yinshuguan, 1986. |
| *SKQSZB* | *Siku quanshu zhenben* 四庫全書珍本. Taibei: Shangwu yinshuguan, 1979. |
| SKY | Zhongguo shehui kexueyuan, Lishi yanjiusuo 中國社會科學院歷史研究所 (Institute of History, Chinese Academy of Social Sciences, Beijing) |
| ST | Shanghai tushuguan 上海圖書館 (Shanghai Library) |
| *SWXHB* | *Siwuxie huibao* 思無邪彙寶. Taibei: Taiwan Encyclopedia Britannica, 1997. |
| *TWGCSB* | *Taiwan gongchang shanben shumu renming suoyin* 台灣公藏善本書目人名索引. Taibei: Guoli zhongyang tushuguan, 1972. |

| | |
|---|---|
| *TYBB* | Wang Zhongmin 王重民. *Zhongguo shanbenshu tiyao bubian* 中國善本書提要補編. Beijing: Shumu wenxian chubanshe, 1991. |
| *WMQJ* | Xu Shuofang 徐朔方. *Wan Ming qujia nianpu* 晚明曲家年譜. Hangzhou: Zhejiang guji chubanshe, 1993. |
| *XHLB* | *Xuehai leibian* 學海類編. Taibei: Yiwen yinshuguan, 1967. |
| *ZDCS* | *Zhaodai congshu* 昭代叢書. 4 vols. Shanghai: Guji chubanshe, 1990. |
| *ZGGDZX* | *Zhongguo gudai zhenxi ben xiaoshuo* 中國古代珍稀本小說. Shenyang: Chunfeng wenyi chubanshe, 1997. |
| *ZGGJBK* | *Zhongguo guji banke cidian* 中國古籍版刻辭典. Jinan: QiLu shushe, 1999. |
| *ZGGJSB* | *Zhongguo guji shanben shumu* 中國古籍善本書目. Vol. 1. Shanghai: Shanghai guji, 1989. |
| *ZGSBS* | Wang Zhongmin 王重民. *Zhongguo shanben shumu tiyao* 中國善本書目提要. Shanghai: Guji chubanshe, 1983. |
| *ZGSXCS* | *Zhongguo shixue congshu* 中國史學叢書. Taibei: Taiwan Xuesheng shuchu, 1965. |
| *ZT* | Zhongyang tushuguan (Central Library, Taibei) |

*Reference Matter*

# Notes

1. In this study, the terms "early modern China" and "late imperial China" are not incompatible. The "early modern" period of China here refers to the sixteenth and seventeenth centuries.

2. Ying-shi Yu is a pioneer in exploring the new development in Confucian thought as a result of what he calls the "interaction between the literati and the merchants" (*shishang hudong*) in the Ming–Qing period. Yu Ying-shi, "Shishang hudong." See also his earlier article on the "Spirit of merchants and Chinese religion," "Zhongguo jinshi." A few students of Ming literary studies have also foregrounded the merging of the *shi* and *shang* as a major social factor in the emergence of new literary thought. See Chen Jianhua, pp. 77–85, 325–39; Zheng Lihua, pp. 168–75.

3. The convergence of the literati and the merchants-businessmen is treated in greater details in my *Publishing, Literary Public, and Shishang Culture in Early Modern China*.

4. Detailed discussion of the relevance of the term "paratext" in this study will be given later.

5. For more on the impacts of print culture, see note 32 from this chapter.

6. To be sure, whether a reader will recognize the discursive significance endowed by various disciplines depends on his or her familiarity with academic discourses. But most scholars will recognize the idiomatic use of concepts such as capitalism, bourgeoisie, and Enlightenment.

7. Li Zhi, *Fenshu*, p. 227.

8. Ibid.

9. Ibid., pp. 30–31, 96–99.

10. De Bary, "Individualism," p. 188. For a similarly positive interpretation of Li Zhi's ideas, especially regarding the unity of nature (*ziran*) and socially shaped appetites (*chuanyi chifan*), as well as its connection with his advocacy of private interests, see Mizoguchi Yūzō, pp. 56–87.

11. De Bary, "Individualism," p. 214. For the historical context of Li's suicide and the reasons for his persecution, see Jin Jiang.

12. Ray Huang, p. 189. Despite his revisionist study of Li Zhi's persecution, Jin Jiang's view of the significance of Li Zhi is similar to that of Huang. See Jin Jiang, pp. 25–26.

13. Ray Huang, pp. 190, 221.

14. Ibid., p. 190. Carson Chang made a similar statement about the insignificance of Li Zhi's death and his victimization of a "custom-loving and conformist society." Quoted in de Bary, "Individualism," pp. 220–21.

15. Ray Huang, p. 221.

16. The term "West" used in this study does not refer to the totality of the life worlds of European countries or societies in practice but to the discursive construct as a homogenous megaunit of analysis in contrast with non-European societies called the "East." Even studies that rightly reject the dichotomization of cultural practices of European and non-European societies continued to use the terms "East" and "West" in the singular. See for example, Longxi Zhang.

17. Chakrabarty, pp. 31–32.

18. Ibid., p. 7.

19. For a discussion of the problems of this mode of history writing from the perspective of the politics of producing historical narratives of modern China, see Duara, ch. 1.

20. J. M. Blaut has crafted a concise critique of Eurocentric history—works that argue for the presence of unique conditions in Western Europe, be it race, culture, or geography that gave the "West" a permanent superiority vis-à-vis non-European communities. He underscores the importance of colonialism as a broader framework in which to understand how and why Europe was able to charge ahead with its exploitation of the colonies. See Blaut. But to argue that Western Europe was already on the rise in 1492 was to disregard the fact that during the period from 1500 through early 1800, Asia, especially China, was the center of a global economy. See Frank, chs. 1–2; Brook, *Confusion*, p. xvi.

21. Recent scholarship on China has moved beyond the dichotomized approach of "tradition" versus "modern," demonstrating change before European intrusion in the early nineteenth century. The use of "late imperial" for the long period from the Tang–Song transition to the Ming and Qing periods, however, only avoids the dichotomy between modern and tradition. It does not really solve the problem. The great convenience of the term "late imperial," however, simply enables one to suspend or delay the question. The continued use of the temporal marker "modern China" without problematizing the Eurocentric assumptions will minimize the significance of change before the nineteenth century. We need to give more attention to the embedded Eurocentric narratives in the studies of China. For a similar warning, see Duara, pp. 25–26.

22. De Certeau, *Writing History*, p. 218.

23. Referring to the impact of printing in China, William H. McNeill remarks: "Printing in China had helped consolidate and disseminate Confucian learning and had a thoroughly conservative effect on the country's society and literary culture. . . . In Europe, on the contrary, printing tended to disrupt older ways of life." See McNeill, p. 224.

24. Febvre and Martin, p. 75.

25. McLuhan, p. 152.

26. Eisenstein, p. 27n65.

27. For a similar view, see Mukerji, pp. 141–42.

28. The same argument is put forth in James Huffman's explanation for Japanese publishers' abandoning movable type method in the seventeenth century. It is well known that Toyotomi Hideyoshi printed books from copper movable types captured from Korea. And Ieyasu reportedly gave three hundred thousand pieces of wooden movable types to the Ashikaga family and had in possession two hundred thousand copper type cast in 1614. Despite the possession of, and its early experiment with, a new technology (movable type) by the shogunate, Huffman explains that "the complexity of the *kanji* [Chinese characters] used in Japanese writing and the aesthetic sterility of materials produced by interchangeable type fonts disturbed most Tokugawa–era printers, so after a few years they threw out the printing presses, just as they discarded the foreign guns and religions, and shifted back to the traditional slate and woodblock techniques." There is no question that the relatively large number of Chinese characters would present problems to printers. But the more important reason is not addressed. How economical was it to choose movable type over woodblock printing? How much more investment did a commercial printer need to set up a movable-type printing shop in comparison with a woodblock printing shop? The factors of cost and scale of economy are not addressed. Huffman, p. 20.

29. For a similar view, see Clair, p. 1.

30. In his study of the role of publishing in the creation of the public in modern Japan, James Huffman undertakes his analysis through a technological lens. See especially his discussion of the new conditions at the end of the Tokugawa period. Typical of the technological approach is his examination of literacy, schools, networks of disseminating information, a "desire" of farmers for information, new ideas and techniques, and merchants' need to know "prices in Osaka." Such analysis needs to take into consideration the fact that knowledge of prices and new techniques often is irrelevant if the merchants did not have the distribution network and the financial and supporting networks to transport goods on time to take advantage of the high prices in Osaka. New techniques and tech-

nology often were more expensive and less accessible to ordinary farmers. See Huffman, pp. 18–20.

31. For a recent broad survey of scholarship in European languages on the history of publishing in China, see Bussotti.

32. Pioneering works on the impact of print culture on Chinese society have begun to appear in greater number in recent years. The importance of printing to popular culture in Ming–Qing China is underscored in the collection of essays on popular culture edited by David Johnson, Andrew Nathan, and Evelyn Rawski. Oki Yasushi's study of the publishing world of Feng Menglong and the use of literature in political struggle and Patrick Hanan's marvelous examination of Li Yu both provide excellent insights into Jiangnan literati's involvement in commercial publishing and their roles as writers, editors, and publishers. Scholars in literature have contributed greatly to our understanding of the role of publishing in changing the practice of reading, different use of illustrations, as well as publishers' attempts to claim legitimacy for their professional activities. See Robert Hegel's study of audience and illustrations in novels; David Rolston on reading commentaries on novels; and Anne MacLaren, Ellen Widmer, Catherine Carlitz, on women, reading, publishing of story, novels, and drama. For studies of the special role of printing in religious practice, textual formation, and sacred sites, see Catherine Bell, Cynthia Brokaw, and Chun-fang Yu. Foremost in the examination of the specific impact of publishing on the practice and discourse on woman culture is the excellent work by Dorothy Ko, *Teachers of the Inner Chamber*. See also Widmer, "From Wang Duansha" and "Xiaoqing's Literary Legacy"; David Johnson, Andrew Nathan, and Evelyn Rawski, eds., *Popular Culture in Late Imperial China*; Rolston, *How to Read the Chinese Novel*; Hanan, *Invention of Li Yu*; Hegel, "Distinguishing Levels of Audience" and *Reading Illustrated Fiction in Late Imperial China*; MacLaren, "Popularizing the Romance of the Three Kingdoms" and "Ming Audiences and Vernacular Hermeneutics: The Uses of the Romance of the Three Kingdoms;" Oki, "Women in Feng Menglong's Mountain Songs" and "A Study of Printing Culture in the Jiangnan Region in the Late Ming Period." Carlitz, "Printing as Performance: Late Ming Literati Drama Publishing." For the role of printing in painting of scenes on porcelain, see Wenchin Hsu, *Fictional Scenes*. For printing and religion, see Bell, "Printing and Religion"; "A Precious Raft"; James Cahill, "Huang Shan"; Chun-fang Yu, "P'u-t'o Shan"; for studies of printing in the late Qing and the early twentieth century, see Joan Judge, *Print and Politics*; Catherine Yeh, "Reinventing Ritual"; "The Life Style"; Rudolf Wagner, "Ernest Major's Shenbaoguan"; and Leo Lee, *Shanghai Modern*.

33. Lucile Chia's excellent study of Jianyang publishing is an attempt to

enumerate the differences in the history of printing in China and Europe. She recognizes "the impact of printing in China has been as momentous as in Europe, but its story is quite different." Her discussion, however, does not engage the discourse on the role of printing in bringing about modern Europe. See Chia, "Printing for Profit," p. 6. A recent dissertation takes on the issue but ventures to explain why printing in China failed to act as an agent of change in contrast with Europe, an example of sinologistic narrative. See Ze, ch. 11.

34. Chartier, "Gutenberg Revisited," p. 9.

35. In his review of Peter Kornicki's study of the history of the book in Japan, Henry D. Smith II points out the mere furnishing of information by Kornicki on the book in Japan without situating his study in a larger framework will continue to put the experience of East Asia down as a "footnote in the narrative of the progress of Gutenberg's invention of global dominance." Henry D. Smith II, pp. 501–2.

36. Adrian Johns challenges the narrative of the invention of the movable-type method by Gutenberg, which has been the cornerstone of the metanarrative of the "printing revolution." As Johns reminds us, "The printing 'revolution' as we now know it is thus the product of a later, political revolution." Johns, ch. 5, esp. pp. 374–79.

37. Wong, Huters, and Yu, p. 5.

38. The concept of "field" is designed to replace categories rooted in various forms of subjectivism and objectivism. See Swartz, pp. 118–19.

39. Bourdieu and Wacquant, *An Invitation*, p. 97.

40. Ibid., p. 96.

41. Swartz, pp. 73–82.

42. Ibid., pp. 118–21.

43. Bourdieu, *The Field*, ch. 1.

44. John Sutherland calls this lack of interest in publishing history among literary critics "a hole at the centre of literary sociology." See Sutherland.

45. Genette, p. 12.

46. Genette does not underscore the subversive potential of paratext. But it is nonetheless implied in his theory of paratext as the threshold of interpretation.

47. It is still common to explain *gong* in terms of "official." See Judge, pp. 8–9.

48. See also Wan Shihe, "Fen zhuzi shumu," in *MWH* 479.5158.

49. Zhang Wenyan, preface.

50. Quoted in *MGHF*, p. 520.

51. Quoted in Ibid., p. 768.

52. Chen Jiru, *Meigong zazhu*, vol. 4, p. 1947.

53. Ibid., p. 1967.

54. In the preface of a popular examination aid by another Jianyang publisher, the author praised the publication of the book as "*gong zhi tianxia*" and in the "editorial rules" (*fanli*), the book is made "public within the seas" (*gong zhi hainei*). Similarly, Tang Binyin referred to the publication of an anthology of examination essays as "*gong zhu tianxia*" (making it public to the realm under heaven). In a preface written for an encyclopedia, Chen Renxi spoke of the publisher's effort "to publish for the world to see" (*zi yi gong shi*). A book in 1636 explained the reprinting of the book was his plan to "make it available to the public within the seas" (*zi yi gong zhi hainei*). Yuan Huang, *Sishu xun er sushuo*, preface; Tang Binyin, *Shui'an gao*, 5.18a–b; Shen Jin, "Mingdai fangke." See also *MGHF*, pp. 589, 786.

55. Chartier, *The Cultural Origins*, pp. 154–55.

56. Hai, p. 21.


CHAPTER 1

1. Trigault, p. 21.

2. S. Wells Williams, p. 477. Williams's account of China had exerted great influence in understanding China in America in the nineteenth century. A similar view on the extensive reach of printed books to the lowest strata in late-imperial China was echoed by James Legge. Legge wrote in a letter in 1849 when he was in Hong Kong: "In no country are books so cheap as in China, but we can make them cheaper than they ever have been." Like Williams, he was referring to the low price of books for the Chinese, not for foreigners like himself. Legge, p. 75; S. Wells Williams, p. 477.

3. Based on limited information on book prices, such as that by Arthur Smith, Idema concludes that literary novels were expensive and speculates that these novels and short stories had a very small circulation. See Idema, pp. lviii–lix; see also Ko, pp. 36–37; Shen Jin, "Mingdai fangke."

4. Zhang Xiumin and Han Qi, ch. 2.

5. There are several dates for the earliest example of printing in China. Some suggest that printing was invented before the Sui dynasty (581–617). Shi Jinbo and Yasin, p. 3. Most scholars trace the invention to the Tang, although they disagree by attributing it to the early or the mid-Tang. Li Zhizhong argues that printing was already invented in 636. Others who based their view exclusively on extant evidence date the origin of printing to 770 and 868, respectively. Li Zhizhong, "Tangdai," pp. 22–31; Carter, p. 41; Twitchett, pp. 13–16. For quotations

supporting the various views, see Cao Zhi, pp. 12–32; Shi Jinbo and Yasin, pp. 3–6. Zhang Xiumin, *Zhongguo yinshuashi*, pp. 20–22. For a general history of Chinese printing, see Tsien.

6. Li Zhizhong, "Songdai."

7. Cao Zhi, pp. 413–20.

8. The case of Song Minqiu (1019–1079) is indicative of the limited access to books that were either not printed or printed in small number. Song's personal collection of books was such that scholars would build houses next to his library in order to have access to his books. Zhu Bian, *Quwei jiuwen*, quoted in Lee, p. 415.

9. Li Zhizhong, "Songdai," pp. 69–70.

10. Zhang Xiumin, *Chung-kuo yinshua shi*, pp. 57–58.

11. Ibid., p. 59.

12. The number is based on Zhou Hongzu's *Gujin keshu* (Books printed in the past and present). Xiao Dongfa, "Jianyang," pp. 139–40; Ze, p. 131.

13. Cao Zhi, p. 365.

14. Lu Rong, p. 129.

15. Censorship began in France in 1547 with the Edict of Fontainebleau issued by Henry II. Louis XIV extended government control, refining methods of censorship as an attempt to regulate dissent. See Gough, p. 3. As soon as printing was introduced into England in the sixteenth century, the Tudor administrations had adopted measures to control its uses. The stationers company was but one of these institutions. Johns, pp. 189–90; Patterson, pp, 32-34.

16. Xu Xuemo, 2.9b–10a. For titles, see Shen Jin, pp. 341–42.

17. Publishing offices of the government such as the Ministry of Rites and the Imperial Academies in Beijing and Nanjing, had a modest record compared with private printers. The most important official printing office in Beijing was operated by the eunuchs under the Directorate of ceremonial (Sili jian). Zhang Xiumin, *Zhongguo yinshuashi*, pp. 340–42, 353–64, 390–402.

18. Ding Shen, p. 733; Edgren.

19. Books printed by the forty-three principalities numbered more than 430. Ye Dehui, 5.116–120. Zhang Xiumin, *Zhongguo yinshuashi*, p. 337; 402–45.

20. Lu Rong, pp. 128–29.

21. Zhang Xiumin, *Zhongguo yinshuashi*, p. 337.

22. For genealogies, see Taga, pp. 58–60; and Telford, pp. 41–43; for sectarian printed texts, see Overmeyer, p. 220, and Naquin, "The Transmission," pp. 256n2, 259.

23. McDermott.

24. Few take exception to the view that commercial publishing began to flourish since the Jiajing and Longqing periods. Ye Dehui, 1.3; K. T. Wu, p. 203; Oki, *Ming matsu*, pp. 185–86. The total number of extant titles included in the calculation of the rate is only 2,452. A catalog in the Qing lists 15,725 works by Ming authors. Zhong Xiumin, *Zhongguo yinshuashi*, p. 336. Genealogies are also excluded form this list.

For discussion of the publishing centers and detailed information about the publishing industry in the Ming, see Zhang Xiumin, *Zhongguo yinshuashi*, pp. 334–543. The rise of Huizhou painting was closely related to expansion of printing in the sixteenth century. Hiromitsu and Sabin, pp. 25–26.

25. It is a common view in European scholarship that movable type after its invention was not further developed and fell out of use until the nineteenth century when the Europeans brought their movable-type method to China. See Hind, p. 66.

26. K. T. Wu, pp. 212–20. See especially Zhang Xiumin and Han Qi.

27. Ibid., p. 203; Lust, p. 41.

28. Davis, pp. 139–41.

29. Zhu Guozhen, 17.7a.

30. Wang Chunyu, p. 148.

31. Chai E, juan 18.

32. Yuan Tongli, p. 1; Zhang Xiumin, *Zhongguo yinshuashi*, p. 527.

33. Zhang Dai (1591–1689) had a library of thirty thousand juan but few refer to him as one of the great book collectors in the late Ming. See Zhang Dai, 2.27.

34. Lin Qingzhang, *Mingdai*, p. 195.

35. Xu Boxing, p. 1625.

36. Zhang Xiumin, *Zhongguo yinshuashi*, p. 527.

37. *MWH*, vol. 3, p. 2355. For library sizes in Italy, France, and Britain in the sixteenth century, see Richardson, pp. 118–21; Febvre and Martin, pp. 263–64; Bühler, p. 19.

38. The rise of Huizhou painting was closely related to the expansion of publications with illustrations in the sixteenth century. See Kobayashi and Sabin, pp. 25–26. See also Hegel, *Reading*; Ko, ch. 1.

39. Lust, p. 37.

40. Ibid., pp. 40–46. With a short disruption during the Manchu conquest, the production of single prints revived and further developed a regional print style well into the late eighteenth century. Print shops operated in Suzhou and Nanjing as well as in new centers in Shangdong, Hebei, Sichuan. See Lust, ch. 2.

41. For a reprint of a 1640 woodblock print of a scene from *Romance of the West Chamber*, see Clunas, *Pictures*, p. 70.

42. David Johnson has cautioned against treating "the classically educated in Ming-Ch'ing times as a homogenous group." Johnson, pp. 61–62.

43. Li Ruiliang, p. 218.

44. Huang Zongxi, *Ming wenhai*, juan 307–14. See Chapters 4 and 5 for the two types of examination aids.

45. For the publication of topographical and institutional gazetteers, see Brook, *Geographical Sources*, pp. 3–19, 49–66. For mountain gazetteers, see Cahill, p. 272.

46. Brokaw, *The Ledgers*.

47. Li Yan, p. 361.

48. Widmer, "The Huanduzhai."

49. A hand-colored map of Ming China printed in 1555 is preserved in the Archivo General Indias, Seville, reprinted in Clunas, *Pictures*, p. 80. Another map drawn and printed by Cao Junyi in Nanjing in 1644 is in Philip Hu, p. 186.

50. For ritual manuals, such as Zhu Xi's *Family Rituals*, see Ebrey, pp. 176–83.

51. Chen Xuewen; for route books, see Brook, *Geographical Sources*, pp. 3–19.

52. Clunas, *Superfluous Things*.

53. For examples of tricks, see Zhang Yingyu, *Dupian xinshu*.

54. *ZGSBS*, p. 351.

55. Van Gulik, pp. 306–17, 324.

56. Wang Ermin, pp. 199–203.

57. Hegel, *Reading*, pp. 140–46; Carlitz.

58. *Pinghua* (tales told in plain language) printed in the Yuan was one type of printed books with illustrations. Mair, pp. 3–4.

59. See Hegel, *Reading*; Carlitz.

60. Hegel, *Reading*.

61. Lust, p. 41.

62. Yang Ye, pp. xxiii–xxvii. For a full range of categories grouped under *xiaopin*, see Lu Yunlong, *Huang Ming Shiliu jia*.

63. Li Ruiliang, pp. 215–16.

64. Xu Boxing, pp. 1731–34.

65. Lü Tiancheng, *Qupin* (Evaluative categories of songs); Qi Biaojia, *Qupin Jupin*.

66. See Oki, "Women."

67. Li Ruiliang, pp. 218–19.

68. For example, Gao Ru, pp. 1273–79; *Xuanlan zhai*, pp. 1533–37; Xu Boxing, pp. 1714–31.

69. Gao Ru, pp. 1264–66.

70. Carlitz.

71. Mote and Chu, p. 48.

72. Ibid., p. 169.

73. Ko, p. 49.

74. Van Der Stock, p. 60. The sizes of paper manufactured in Europe in the sixteenth and seventeenth centuries were invariably smaller than those made in China. Pan Jixing, *Zhongguo, Hanguo*, pp. 152–55.

75. Febvre and Martin, p. 32.

76. Ibid., p. 42.

77. Kernan, p. 59.

78. Ibid.

79. Febvre and Martin, p. 36.

80. Paper was only beginning to replace vellum as the material for the production of manuscripts in Europe in the first half of the fifteenth century. Bühler, p. 41.

81. Trigault, p. 16.

82. For a study of paper products before the Ming, see Pan Jixing, *Zhongguo zaozhi*, pp. 94–103, 110.

83. Zhang Xiumin, *Zhongguo yinshuashi*, pp. 538–39.

84. Lu Rong, p. 153.

85. Ye Dehui, 10.284.

86. Ritual paper was also a special paper product from Hangzhou. Shen Bang, pp. 192, 283. The production of this type of paper increased dramatically in the late Ming. Song Yingxing, pp. 327–28.

87. The common use of toilet paper is reflected in the frequent reference to it in late-Ming vernacular stories. See for example, Feng Menglong, *Xiaofu* (The depository of jokes), p. 80. The use of paper for toilet purposes can be traced back to the sixth century. Qian Cunxun, *Zaozhi*, pp. 159–60.

88. Toilet paper made in Hangzhou was particularly popular in the Ming court. See Jiang Zhaocheng, pp. 335–36.

89. *MDSHJJ*, p. 203.

90. Wuxian zhi, 29.37b, 39a–b. For a description of paper canopies, see Tu Long, 4.73.

91. *Nan Wu jiuhua lu*, 21.5b–6a.

92. *MDSHJJ*, vol. 2, p. 299.

93. Wang Shizhen, *Fengan yuhua*, p. 566.

94. Gui Youguang, 7.3.

95. Li Yu, *LYQJ*, vol. 5, p. 2258.

96. *Guwang yan*, vol. 2, 4.462; Tu Long.

97. Zhang Xiumin, *Zhongguo yinshuashi*, p. 538.

98. Li Yu, *Liwen ouji, LYQJ*, vol.6, pp. 2401–5.

99. For the contents of letter writings, see Feng Menglong, *Zhe mei jian*, pp. 1–12; Li Tingji, *Li Wenjie ji*, vol. 4, 27.12b.

100. Ye Changchi, 4.199.

101. Pan Jixing, *Zhongguo zaozhi*, pp. 110–11.

102. Tian Shengjin, pp. 88, 95, 210, 215, 269, 319, 320, 361.

103. Li Tingji, *Li Wenjie ji*, vol. 4, 27.12a–13b.

104. Other types of paper included *bailian* and *huanglian*. Li Tingji, *Li Wenjie ji*, vol. 4, 27.12b–13b.

105. Tian Shengjin, pp. 68, 83, 94, 210, 264, 315, 357, 396.

106. Pan Jixing, *Zhongguo zaozhi*, pp. 110–11; Xu Jianqing, pp. 135–37. For production of paper products in Hangzhou, Jiaxing, and Huzhou, see Jiang Zhaocheng, pp. 335–37.

107. Xu Jianqing, pp. 137–38.

108. *Zhongguo zuozhi shihua*, p. 169; Ye Xian'en, *Ming Qing Huizhou*, p. 101.

109. Song Yingxing, p. 325; Xu Jianqing, p. 135.

110. Zhang Xiumin, *Zhongguo yinshuashi*, p. 540.

111. Pan Jixing, *Zhongguo zaozhi*, p. 111.

112. Han Dacheng, *Mingdai chengshi*, p. 331.

113. The size of paper mills varied. Compared with those in Qianshan, paper mills in southern Shenxi appear to be smaller in scale. There the number of workers at each paper mill varied from forty to fifty to 120 to 150, and since it took four workers to operate production organized around a vat. This means an average of ten to thirty-five vats per paper mill. This figure is based on a reference made in the early nineteenth century. It was reported that small paper mills in southern Shenxi employed forty to fifty workers; larger mills employed more than one hundred. My estimation is based on forty to fifty as the smallest operational scale; and by doubling and tripling its scale, we get sizes of paper mills from forty to fifty, eighty to one hundred, and 120 to 150. See Pan Jixing, *Zhongguo zaozhi*, p. 109. For a description with illustrations and pictures of similar methods of paper making, see Dard Hunter, pp. 84–94.

114. Pan Jixing, *Zhongguo zaozhi*, p. 109.

115. Chen Xuewen, p. 174.

116. This information comes from a legal case that took place in the late eighteenth century. See Li Wenzhi, Wei Jinyu, and Jing Junjian, *Ming Qing shidai*, pp. 158–59. Chen Xuewen, p. 174.

117. Liu Renqing and Hu Yuxi, p. 78.

118. The use of water mills to produce paper paste could be dated back to the Song. See Pan Jixing, *Zhongguo zaozhi*, pp. 103–4.

119. Wang Shimao, *Minbu shu*, p. 2295.

120. Shen Defu, p. 26.

121. Pan Jixing, *Zhongguo zaozhi*, pp. 110.

122. In a record of expenses in 1657 in the management handbook of the Cheng lineage in Qimeng, Huizhou, there are references to the use of a great variety of paper. *Maobian* paper appeared to be already a very common type of paper for daily use. See Zhou Shaoquan and Zhaao Yaguang, pp. 100, 107, 114, 115, 121.

123. Xie Zhaozhi, 12.14b–15b (988–990).

124. Hu Yinglin, *Shaoshi shanfang bicong*, p. 57.

125. Xu Jianqing, p. 140. Suzhou's high quality paper for delivery to Beijing was stored in the Pufu Buddhist temple. See Qi Biaojia, *An Wu xi gao*, p. 534.

126. *Dupian xinshu*, 1.36a–b.

127. Hu Yinglin, *Shaoshi shanfang bicong*, p. 57.

128. This trend is based on information listed in bibliographies. See Li Qingzhi, p. 129.

129. Zhang Xiumin, *Zhongguo yinshuashi*, p. 540.

130. Ibid., p. 534. Experiences of British missionaries in Canton and Malacca in the early nineteenth century also confirmed that fifteen to twenty thousand copies could be printed from a woodblock before repair or new carving was needed. *LMSCWM*, South China, Incoming Correspondence, 1810, Dec. 28 (B1/F1/JD); Byrd, p. 10.

131. Hu Yinglin, *Shaoshi shanfang bicong*, p. 59.

132. The price of bamboo paper came from Ye Mengzhu, *Yue shi bian*. It might be a little high for prices in Shanghai in general were higher.

133. Weng, 35–39.

134. Wu Yingji, 12.10b–11b.

135. Huang Rubing, 14.43a, 14.44b–45a, 14.45b.

136. Li Xu, *Jie'an laoren manbi*, quoted in Yi Yingong, p. 267. The exchange rate between copper coins (*wen*) and silver (tael) varied from one tael to seven hundred coins to one tael to one thousand coins.

137. Here it is simply assumed a stable rate of one tael equal to one thousand *wen*.

138. Jiang Zhaocheng, pp. 203, 205–6.

139. The speed of carving depended on the level of skill of the carver. An average carver carved about one hundred characters a day for a Buddhist canon. *Litai keshu kaikuang*, pp. 558–59. According to the report by William Milne, a Scot missionary sent to Malacca, where he oversaw a printing shop, a good carver could cut 150 characters per day. Byrd, p. 10.

140. Yang Shengxin, p. 558.

141. For example, the cost for engraving a Buddhist scripture in the late Wanli period was approximately 0.05 tael of silver for one hundred characters. Yang Shengxin, pp. 565–66, 558–59.

142. Ye Dehui, p. 186. The exchange rate at that time was one tael to seven hundred copper coins (*wen*).

143. Ibid. I suspect that the twenty-four taels included the cost of woodblocks. If true, the cost for carving one hundred characters would be 0.03 tael.

144. Li Zhao'en, pp. 1240–41. Only 1,266 woodblocks were used in the edition. The remaining blocks could have been used for pamphlets or records of donors.

145. This information is included in several language learning texts compiled for students from the Liuqiu Islands who went to China in the seventeenth and eighteenth centuries. Books were among the regular items that students bought whenever they came to China. Raitoguchi Ritsuko, pp. 97–98, 130.

146. Qian Qianyi, *Muzhai youxue ji*, 46.12a.

147. Xie Zhaozhi, 13.20a.

148. Yuan Hongdao, *Ping hua zhai zalu*, 10a–b.

149. Ye Dehui, p. 196.

150. K. T. Wu, p. 244.

151. For example, he bought a hand-copied edition of *Yeji* for three taels. Mao told Pan Lei that he was willing to sell it for only two taels. Mao Yi, p. 17.

152. Ibid., pp. 16–17.

153. Ye Dehui, 6.166–71.

154. As a surveillance commissioner, Pan helped produce a woodblock edition of an album entitled *Di jain tu shuo* (The emperor's mirror, an illustrated discussion; 1573), which was conceived by Zhang Juzheng as a teaching text for the young Wanli emperor. See Murray.

155. *MQJS*, p. 309.

156. *MDBKZL*, 4.8b, 4.13a, 4.62b.

157. This book is either bound in eight or sixteen volumes. The copy in Princeton's Gest Oriental Library is bound in sixteen *ce*, whereas the one in Har-

vard Yen-ching Library is in eight *ce*. See *MGHF*, pp. 654–55; and *SBSZ*, pp. 438–39.

158. *Yuelu yin*, no. 6.

159. *Chen Pi Lieguo zhizhuan*, vol. 1, pp. 3, 121.

160. Xie Zhaozhi, 13.23b.

161. When Huang Zongxi went to survey the book collection of the Qi family in 1666, he did not even look at the examination aids and local gazetteers that were stored in two huge book shelves. Huang Zongxi, *Nanlei wending*, "Qianji," 2.19.

162. Wang Yu.

163. Li Tingji, *Sishu dazhu cankao*.

164. *MDBKZL*, 3.9b.

165. There was one episode in the *Jin Ping Mei* in which a merchant of silk from Huzhou gave a 10 percent discount to Simeng Qing. See ch. 33.

166. Ko, p. 36.

167. The Yuan style drama *zaju* was printed and sold to the audience no later than 1411. Wang Liqi, p. 14.

168. Shen Defu, p. 647.

169. Shen Jin, "Mingdai fangke."

170. Entertaining quarters in the late Ming provided lists and texts of dramas for customers. See for example *Cu Hulu*, p. 524.

171. Thus it was a small book printed from 16 blocks. *Li gong sheng ci ji ji yi shilu*, 6a–18b.

172. Shen Jin, "Mingdai fangke."

173. Zhang Anqi.

174. Rawski, *Education*, pp. 47–48.

175. Chen Jitai, the famous critic of examination essays, had to take up tutoring at the age of thirteen. Chen, 8.3a. See other examples of examinees and professional writers taking up tutoring in Chapter 3.

176. Li Xu, pp. 325–27.

177. Huang Zongxi, *HZXQJ*, p. 357.

178. Xie Zhaozhi, 10.32b.

179. After his retirement, He Liangjun resided in Nanjing. He complained about abuses in the acquisition of materials for the government by officials and subbureaucrats. For a fan priced at 0.2 tael, they could pay only half. He Liangjun, 12.3b.

180. In the drama *Yizhong yuan* by Li Yu, a young woman forged the calligraphy and painting of Dong Qichang and Chen Jiru. A fan with a falsified poem by Dong Qichang was sold at one tael. Li Yu, *Yizhong yuan*, 1.14a, 18b.

181. *Jin Ping Mei*, ch. 51.

182. Feng Menglong, *Xingshi hengyan*, p. 181.

183. *Jin Ping Mei*, ch. 9, p. 148.

184. Feng Menglong, *Xingshi tongyan*, 5, p. 451.

185. *Du pian xinshu*, p. 1282.

186. See for example the story of a daughter of an official sold to a brothel. Lu Yunlong, *Xingshi yan*, ch. 7, p. 353.

187. Feng Menglong, *Xingshi hengyan*, 3, p. 214; *Yugui hong*, 5, pp. 333–35.

188. *Xie Zhaozhi*, 15.30b.

189. Even though the market exchange rate between silver and rice might vary, the rate in Chun'an county was fixed at one tael per *shi*. According to the *Hua Yi yitong Da Ming guanzhi*, a magistrate's stipend was ninety *shi*. Quoted in Shen Jin, "Mingdai fangke."

190. This is the allowance for the Chun'an county. Hai, p. 128.

191. Ibid., pp. 48–49.

192. See for example Ye Mengzhu's praise for Peng Changyi, who became magistrate of Shanghai in 1644. Ye Mengzhu, *Yueshi bian*, pp. 371–72.

193. Zelin, pp. 137, 157, 159, 164.

194. As the right assistant censor in chief, Hai Rui tried to restrict the number of officials using the postal service in the Yingtian prefecture. Hai, pp. 266–68.

195. Huang Renyu, p. 503.

196. Wei Lin, "Ming guanchao," pp. 38–39.

197. Wu Han, "Mingdai di xin shihuan," p. 23.

198. Zhang Xiumin, *Zhongguo yinshuashi*, p. 337. Commercial publishers already printed a large number of examination aids in the Southern Song. Cherniack, pp. 80–82; Liu Xianguang, pp. 113–18.

199. Zhang Yingyu, p. 1271. Evelyn Rawski has shown that the salary of private tutors in the Qing ranged from five to eighty taels, with most falling in the twenty- to thirty-tael range. Rawski, *Education*, pp. 54–61. Alan Barr adds a few more examples from literature that confirms Rawski's findings. Barr, p. 66.

200. Wei Dazhong, p. 14.

201. Even though this is from the *Rulin waishi*, a work of the eighteenth century, the income of Mr. Ma was reasonable because he was a "reputable master" hired to comment on examination essays. Wu Jingzi, p. 142.

202. Li Xu, p. 16.

203. Ye Sheng, 1.3b.

204. Lu Rong, p. 189.

205. Zhong Xing, *Cuiyu ge*, 1b–2b.

206. Yu Ying-shih, "Shi-shang hudong," pp. 11–13.

207. Shen Zuan, *Jinshi congcan*, quoted in Xu Shuofang, vol. 1, p. 211.

208. Yang Xunji, 200.14a–b.

209. Preface by Zhang Taiding, in Chen Jiru, *Baishi qiao*. See also 1.2a, 1.33a–b, 1.37b.

210. Chen Jiru, *Baishi qiao*, 1.37b.

211. Clunas, *Superfluous Things*, p. 131.

212. *Zhaoshi bei*, p. 34. According to Hu Shi, this work was written in the early Kangxi period (1662–1722). The amount of eight taels appears to be high. But for an epitaph, that might still fall within the range of the emoluments in the seventeenth century.

213. Xu Wei, pp. 611–12. Zheng Banqiao (1693–1765) asked for three thousand taels for a painting of bamboo that was six feet tall. Fees for various literary services were also openly given to clients. Large calligraphy, six taels; medium-length calligraphy, four taels; short calligraphy, two taels; couplets, one tael; fan 0.5 tael. See Ye Tingguan, *Oupoguan yuhua*, quoted in Xu Jianrong, p. 136.

214. Chen Hongshou, pp. 122, 406–7, 409–18, 552.

215. Ibid., p. 553.

216. Ibid., pp. 58, 554.

217. A few days later, the son of another friend needed money to buy medication. Chen borrowed a tael from Mouqi; instead of paying him back, he painted a scroll for him. Ibid., p. 554.

218. According to Mao Qiling, more than several thousand painters throughout the empire depended on selling paintings attributed to Chen. This may be an exaggeration, but the fact was that his paintings were widely copied because of their great popularity. Chen Hongshou, p. 590.

219. Yang Xunji, 200.14a–b.

220. Li Yu, *Liweng wenji*, *LYQJ*, vol. 2, 5.60b–61a.

221. *MJSWB*, vol. 6, p. 4667.

222. Han Dacheng, *Mingdai chengshi*, p. 332.

223. Li Tingji, *Li Wenjie ji*, 27.22b.

224. Mi Chu Wiens has shown the decline in the relationship between the landlords and peasants in the sixteenth century. The relationship had changed from paternalistic to commercial as a result of market expansion. Landlords were giving less material benefits to the peasants. Wiens, pp. 8–9.

225. Fu Yiling, *Mingdai Jiangnan*, p. 83.

226. Li Tingji, *Li Wenjie ji*, 27.13a.

227. Hai, pp. 27–35.

228. For a detailed account of the various frauds of the clerks in Tongzhou, see Zhao Shiyu, "Mingdai fuxian," pp. 56–57.

229. He Liangjun, 13.8a–b.

230. Cai Guoliang, p. 259.

231. Tian Yiheng, 188.19a.

232. Zhang Dai, *Tao'an mengyi*, 5.67.

233. Ibid., 5.77.

234. It was common for women to take up weaving to supplement the family's income in the Lower Yangtze region. Pan Ming-te and Kenneth Pomeranz estimate that an adult woman and her nine-year-old daughter could add 11.73 taels to the family's income per year to a fairly poor peasant family. Pomeranz, p. 100.

235. *Jin Ping Mei*, ch. 12, p. 195.

236. Yang Xunji, 200.3a.

237. Lü K'un, p. 173.

238. The other was agricultural tools. Tang Wenji, "Mingchao," p. 23.

239. *DMHD*, 9.30b.

240. For example, books were very inexpensive for the very rich in Antwerp in the seventeenth century, but they were still very expensive for poor wage earners in the city. Correspondence with Johann Hanselaer. For discussion of the decline in real wage, see Allen.

CHAPTER 2

1. One is shocked to find that many widely read books on printing still perpetuate the erroneous view that woodblock printing was the only method known to the Chinese. For example, see Steinberg, p. 70. Though published in 1955, this book was revised in 1996.

2. Zhang Xiumin, *Zhongguo yinshuashi*, pp. 717–18.

3. Contrary to this view, the copper types used were cast, not carved. For a recent discussion, see Pan Jixing, *Zhongguo Hanguo*, pp. 92–95.

4. Febvre and Martin, p. 75.

5. The earliest extant copy of text printed with copper movable type dated to 1341–45. See Pan Jixing, *Zhongguo Hanguo*, pp. 86–88.

6. For discussion of the same advantages of block printing in Togukawa, Japan, see Kornicki, p. 138.

7. As the missionary William Milne had observed in Malacca in 1815, a single Chinese printer could perform all the specialized tasks involved in printing from a woodblock. Byrd, pp. 9–10.

8. This did not change much in the early nineteenth century. A respectable publishing house in London needed as much as two to five hundred pounds to begin. Warrington, p. 7; Kernan, pp. 55–56.

9. It was the same for movable-type printing shops in Europe. In 1528 a Parisian bookseller had a stock of 101,860 books; another had 263,696 books in 1545. Chartier, *The Cultural Uses*, p. 150. The bookstore of Juan de Janta in Burgos, a Spanish printer in the sixteenth century, had a stock of 15,827 volumes. Other Spanish bookstores in the same period also carried large inventories of books. Pettas, pp. 9–14. In sixteenth century Italy, booksellers also kept large stocks of books. A Milanese bookseller-publisher, Niccolò Gorgonzola, had 80,450 copies of 212 works. Richardson, p. 117.

10. I have more to say about this issue in the Conclusion.

11. There was a reason for the continued preference of woodblock illustrations even though copperplate engraving was being used by printers. Copperplate engraving cost more and took longer to produce. Woodcuts continued to be preferred for the simple economic reason—they were cheaper and faster to make. Steinberg, p. 16; Van der Stock, passim. For a catalog of books with woodcuts published in the sixteenth century, see *A Library of Woodcut Books of the Sixteenth Century*.

12. To give just one example, when the English bookseller and printer Henry Bynneman died in April 1583, his total stock of 19,125 copies were worth 76 percent of his entire property of 791 pounds, 12 shillings, 9d. Barnard and Bell, p. 8.

13. Nanjing, Hangzhou, and Suzhou were publishing centers in the sixteenth and seventeenth centuries. Beijing was more a center of book trade. However, it does not mean there were few carvers. On the contrary, there was a large number of carvers in Beijing. When Wen Tiren defended himself against the accusation of printing a book, he referred to the large number of carvers in Beijing. Jin Risheng, p. 445.

14. A person with several hundred taels went to a carver shop to hire a professional critic to edit an anthology of examination essays. Wu Jingzi, pp. 279–80.

15. According to Kong Shanren, the drama was based on "historical facts." The name of the bookseller Cai Yisuo is actually identical to a Jianyang publisher's. There is an extant collection of writings by a Wen Xiangfeng who earned his *jinshi* degree in 1610. It was published by Cai Yisuo of Jianyang. The Restoration Society was founded in 1629. Cai was clearly a real publisher operating in both Jianyang and Nanjing. The work is listed in *MDBKZL*, 6.24a. For similar examples of bookshop owners hiring critics to work on anthologies of examination essays, see Wu Jingzi, pp. 133–34.

16. Wu and Chen were both hired by publishers. Chen himself might also have been involved in publishing himself. See Wu Yingji, 15.8a–b.

17. The same Cai Yishuo and his hiring of Wu Yingji to edit and comment on examination essays was mentioned in another fictionalized history entitled *Qiaoshi tongsu yanyi* (Romance of a vernacular history related by a woodcutter historian) published in the late 1640s and early 1650s. *Qiaoshi tongsu yanyi*, p. 626.

18. It is not clear how many essays were included in the anthology. But for each examination, the number ranged between two and three hundred. Wu Jingzi, 29.287.

19. Febvre and Martin, pp. 136–38; Kernan, pp. 62–66.

20. Adrian Kempe and Herbert de Croock in Antwerp not only cut blocks, but also engaged in printing and selling books and prints. See Van Der Stock, pp. 366–67.

21. Edgren, p. 49.

22. For discussion of Tang's statecraft learning, see Elman, *Classicism*, pp. 76–83.

23. For a biography of Tang Shunzhi, see *DMB*, pp. 1252–56.

24. Tang Shunzhi, 13.23b–24b.

25. Ibid., 13.2b–24a.

26. An example of this is *Tang Jinchuan bianzuan Zuoshi shimo* (An account of the compilation of the *Zuo zhuan*), published by the Family School of the Tang in 1562. See *MGHF*, pp. 39–40.

27. Tang Shunzhi, 11.11b–12a; *SBSZ*, pp. 510–11.

28. *SBSZ*, p. 167.

29. The anthology *Selected Essays with Comments on Government Policies and Affairs by Tang-Song Notable Worthies* (*Tang Huiyuan jingxuan pidian Tang-Song mingxian celun wencui*) was printed in 1549. *SBSZ*, p. 511.

30. Xu Shuofang, vol. 3, p. 193.

31. Extant books with his name as author had no publishers. See *SBSZ*, p. 520.

32. Zang published a comprehensive anthology of poetry that included poems from the ancient period to those by Tang writers. He first published *Gu shisuo*. With the profit he made from selling the impression of that book, he published the second part, entitled *Tangshi suo*. Zang Maoxun, pp. 88.

33. Zang Maoxun, pp. 84–85.

34. Huang Zongxi, *HZXQJ*, p. 384;

35. *MQJS*, p. 303; *MGHF*, p. 583.

36. Li Yu was a commercial publisher who hired carvers to work in his

shop. One of his carvers went to Beijing looking for job. Li Yu recommended him to a high official as a private carver. Li Yu, *Liweng wenji, LYQJ*, vol. 1, 3.14a–b.

37. Publishers in early modern Europe could also speed up their process by parceling out sections of a book for both composition and printing. In order to do that, casting off of the page (calculating the actual number of words on the page) needed to be completed.

38. European publishers could also use more than one printing shop to produce a work. But they needed much more careful calculation and planning.

39. *MQJS*, pp. 160, 249, 289.

40. *MDBKZL*, "Juanshou," 4a.

41. See Denis Twitchett, *Printing*, p. 69; *MGHF*, pp. 609–10.

42. *MGHF*, p. 610.

43. The project did not see the light of day perhaps because of inadequate financing. *MQJS*, p. 501.

44. Zhang Xiumin, *Zhongguo yinshuashi*, pp. 683–86. According to Qian Cunxun, the type cast by the Hua family was an alloy of copper and tin. Qian Cunxu, *Zhongguo shuji*, p. 178.

45. Zhang Xiumin, *Zhongguo yinshuashi*, pp. 686–91.

46. Ibid., p. 695.

47. Ibid., pp. 678–82.

48. Xiao Dongfa, *Zhongguo*, pp. 343–44; Zhang Xiumin and Han Qi, ch. 2.

49. Zhang Xiumin, *Zhongguo yinshuashi*, pp. 701–2.

50. See Xu Xiaoman, table 3.

51. Zhang Xiumin, *Zhongguo yinshuashi*, pp. 710–14.

52. It seems that in both China and Japan in the seventeenth and eighteenth centuries, when a small number of copies were needed for a text, the wooden movable-type method was preferred. The run of imprints using wooden movable types was commonly one hundred or fewer; three hundred was the maximum. See Kornicki, pp. 158–62.

53. Xu Xiaoman.

54. This figure is based on Zhang Xiumin's study. According to Zhang, there are more than two thousand extant books printed from movable types. This figure does not include genealogies printed by movable types. See Zhang Xiumin and Han Qi, p. 106; Zhang Xiumin, *Zhongguo yinshuashi*, p. 307.

55. Hind, p. 66.

56. Ricci, p. 21.

57. For a description of the process of composition, see George Williams, *The Craft*, pp. 54–57.

58. Richardson, p. 22; Febvre and Martin, p. 131.

59. In woodblock printing, the proofreading was done before the blocks were carved.

60. Ricci, P. 21.

61. Gingerich, p. 58.

62. George Williams, p. 59. But according to Febvre and Martin, workers in Lyon had to print 3,350 sheets per day, 2,650 in Paris, and 3,050 to 3,373 per day in Frankfurt. These figures are not possible unless they are single sided impressions. However, the printers worked for fourteen hours a day, usually from 5 A.M. until 8 or 9 P.M. with only one hour for dinner. This figure clearly refers to single-side impressions. Febvre and Martin, p. 131; Richardson, p. 24; McKenzie, vol. 1, p. 134.

63. Steinberg, p. 137; Kernan, p. 55.

64. Van Der Stock, passim; see the catalog of a London book dealer, *Manuscripts*, passim.

65. Only with the improvement of wood engraving by Thomas Bewick in the nineteenth century were publishers able to print letter-press type side by side with images on woodblocks. Only then "image and text could be attractively and relevantly integrated on the page." See Hancher, p. 156.

66. For examples of prices of copperplates, see Van Der Stock, pp. 154–57.

67. In fact, end-grain wood engraving became the prevalent method in England as well as in France. Woodblock printing was the major method for printing illustrations in Europe in the eighteenth and nineteenth centuries. It was not replaced until the end of the nineteenth century. Jacob Kainen, pp. 188, 192.

68. *ZGGJBK*, p. 180.

69. *Ming-Qing shehui jingji*, pp. 81–84.

70. *DMHD*, 189.3b–5a.

71. *ZGGJBK*, p. 180.

72. *MGHF*, p. 821.

73. We do not have historical evidence for this, but Kong Shangren's *Peach Blossom Fan* mentions that lists of new books were posted in bookstores. Kong Shangren, pp. 184–85. Similarly, in *Rulin waishi*, we find similar scenes where titles of newly published examination aids were posted in bookstores. Wu Jingzi, p. 325.

74. Xiao Dongfa, "Jianyang," pp. 123–25.

75. Guo Wei, *Huang Ming*.

76. Zhang Zilie, *Sishu zhujia bian*, "Reading guidelines."

77. Wu Dang, preface.

78. Shen Zijin, p. 4.

79. Fang Yingxiang, *Qinglai ge*, 6.2a–3b.
80. Mair, p. 4.
81. Hegel, *Reading.*
82. Hu Yinglin, *Shaoshi shanfang bicong*, p. 58.
83. Li Yu, *Liweng ouji, LYQJ*, vol. 6, 4.90b.
84. The earliest printed solicitation for manuscripts in a book appeared in 1336 in an anthology of poetry. See Zhang Xiumin, *Zhongguo yinshuashi*, p. 325.
85. Chen Renxi, *Ming wen qi shang.*
86. Lu Yunlong, *Cuiyu ge.*
87. Ko, p. 63.
88. Xu Fenpeng, *Xu Bidong xiansheng.* See Wang Danchung's preface.
89. Wu Yingji, 17.9a.
90. Wu Jingzi, p. 144.
91. The study by Cynthia Brokaw provides rare information on book distribution and targeted regional markets of publishers in Sibao, Jianyang, in the Qing period. See her articles "Commercial Publishing" and "Bestsellers."
92. Pinglutang was also listed as the publisher of several other books: one by Chen's teacher Xu Guangqi, one by his friend Song Zhengbi, and six others that do not seem to target a wide audience. *MDBKZL*, 1.36a; *ZGGJSB*, p. 88.
93. Zhu Xizu, p. 120.
94. Chen Zilong, *Huang Ming*, "Fanli" by Song Zhengbi, p. 57.
95. See the comments written in the interlineal space in Cai Shishun, 1.1a.
96. Wu Jingzi, ch. 18, p. 178.
97. Hu Yinglin, *Shaoshi shanfang bicong*, p. 56.
98. Hu Yinglin, *Shaoshi shanfang leigao*, 116.9b; Chen Hongshou, pp. 32–33.
99. Chen Jitai, 1.1b.
100. Jian Jinsong, p. 144.
101. Xu Hongzu, p. 932.
102. Zhang Zilie, "Fanli," in *Sishu zhujia bian.*
103. Brokaw, "Reading."
104. Fang Xing, p. 161.
105. Mi Fei traveled with his books and paintings in boats. They were called "book and painting boats" (*shuhua chuan*). Mao Jin, *Haiyue zhilin*, p. 162.
106. Chen Xuewen, p. 379.
107. *QDWZYD*, vol. 2, p. 476.
108. The residence of Zhuang Tinglong in the industrial town Nanxun, in Huzhou, was frequently visited by book boats. Fan Hanwei, p. 333.
109. Li Yu mentioned that one of his friends was able to read one of his

new books by borrowing it from a book merchant operating on a boat. *LYQJ*, vol. 1, 3.55b–56a.

110. Yang Shen, 90.1a–b.

111. Wang Shizhen, *Gufuyu ting zalu*, 3.12a–b.

112. Ye Changchi, 2.113.

113. Zang Maoxun, pp. 85, 88.

114. Yang Shen, 90.1a–b.

115. See for example, Gui Youguang, vol. 1, 9.13a–b.

116. Li Rihua, *Weishuixuan*, p. 58.

117. Mao Jin, *Jiguge jiaoke shumu*, p. 867.

118. Zang Maoxun, pp. 84–85.

119. Zhang Xiumin, "Mingdai Nanjing," p. 78.

120. Zhang Xiumin, *Zhongguo yinshuashi*, pp. 378–83; see the various studies of Jianyang publishing by Chia.

121. Hu Yinglin, *Shaoshi shanfang bicong*, p. 57.

122. Zhou Lianggong, p. 8.

123. Hu Yinglin, *Shaoshi shanfang bicong*, p. 59.

124. Zhou Lianggong, pp. 43–44.

125. *MDBKZL*, 2.9a–b.

126. Ibid., 2.4a–6a.

127. Ibid., 3.10b–11a.

128. Ibid., 2.18a–b. The two books on *Zhuang zi* are also considered examination aids because from the 1590s onward, there was a trend in rendering the Four Books in terms of the ideas of the Hundred Schools. See Chapter 4 for discussion.

129. Ibid., 7.20a–21a.

130. Ibid., 7.13a–14b.

131. Edgren, pp. 16–22.

132. Hu Yinglin, *Shaoshi shanfang bicong*, p. 59.

133. Xie Zhaozhi, 13.21a.

134. Ibid., 13.21b.

135. *Ming-Qing shehui jingji*, p. 211.

136. Ibid., 3.33a–b.

137. Tang Binyin, *Shui'an gao*, 4.22b.

138. Zhong Xing, *Yinxiu xuan ji*, pp. 485, 619.

139. Mei Dingzuo, 10.19a–b.

140. Xie Zhaozhi, 13.21a.

141. Lü Liuliang, 2.30a–b.

142. Zhou Lianggong, p. 8.

143. Kong Shangren, p. 183.

144. The number of publishers in Nanjing identified by Chia doubles the number of the ninety-three publishers Zhang Xiumin lists in his book. See Chia, "Of Three Mountains Street"; Zhang Xiumin, *Zhongguo yinshuashi*, pp. 343–48.

145. Chia, "Of Three Mountains Street."

146. MDBKZL lists six books published by Guangyutang, four of them clearly on the Classics and the Four Books. Two books on the Hundred Schools can also be classified as examination aids. Since the mid-Wanli reign, there was a trend in interpreting the Classics in terms of the Hundred Schools. *MDBKZL*, 2.10a.

147. Ibid., 1.2b–3a.

148. Zhang Xiumin, "Mingdai Nanjing," p. 82.

149. *MDBKZL*, 1.11a–b.

150. Ibid., 1.38b–39a.

151. Ibid., 2.30a.

152. Li Yu, *Liweng ouji, LYQJ*, vol. 6, 4.89b–90b.

153. Wu Jingzi, p. 144.

154. Fan Jinmin, pp. 39–40.

155. Ibid., pp. 39–42.

156. Lü Zuoxie, "Ming-Qing shiqi," pp. 10–13; Santangelo, pp. 90–95.

157. Xie Zhaozhi, 15.

158. Wang Chunyu, p. 151.

159. Ibid.

160. Shi Xuan, 12b; Wang Chunyu, p. 151.

161. Xie Zhaozhi, 12.994–95.

162. *Huanxi yuanjia, SWXHB*, vol. 11, 23.771.

163. Qu Dajun, *Guangdong xinyu*, 16.

164. Shi Xuan, 14b.

165. Qian Xiyan, 3.21a. The term was also used in a vernacular novel. See *Xingshi yinyuan*, p. 83.

166. *Yi chun xiang zhi*, p. 116.

167. Qian Xiyan, 3.20b–21a.

168. Xue Gang, p. 326.

169. Wang Chunyu, pp. 147–48.

170. Ibid., p. 147.

171. Xu Shuofang, vol. 1, pp. 414–15. Shen Defu, 25.652.

172. Zhou Qirong, "Mingmo yinshua," pp. 299–300.

173. Ibid., p. 301; Zhai, pp. 242–45.

174. Zhou Qirong, "Mingmo yinshua," pp. 301–2; Carlitz, "The Social Uses."

175. All but one of the twenty-seven books listed in *MDBKZL* were published in the Wanli reign. *MDBKZL*, 2.45a–46a.

176. Hu Yinglin, *Shaoshi shanfang bicong*, p. 59.

177. Oertling, p. 168; Hegel, ch. 4.

178. Of 213 books carved by carvers from the Huang lineage, none was published before the Wanli period. Zhou Qirong, "Mingmo yinshua," pp. 302–3.

CHAPTER 3

1. Elman, "Social."

2. For strategies of families in the Song, see Hymes; for families in Tongcheng, see Beattie; and Chow, "Discourse."

3. Bourdieu, "The Production," in *Language*.

4. Ibid., p. 46–48.

5. Elman, " Social."

6. Even though there were many who sought to acquire the lowest degree in order to escape corvée, the effect would be similar. For discussion of the problem in Jiangxi, see Dardess, pp. 151–52.

7. There had long been criticism of the system as an unreliable method for recruiting good officials. See Nivison.

8. This is a history that has been amply documented. See the studies by Chaffee, Ho, Elman, and Bol.

9. Elman, *A Cultural History*, table 2.2, p. 653.

10. Ibid., pp. 157–58.

11. Chen Hongshou, p. 6.

12. Ai Nanying, 2.4a–8a.

13. Huang Yu, pp. 97–98. The experience was that of Wei Dazhong.

14. Ai Nanying, 2.8a; For similar complaints, see Yang Shicong, p. 93.

15. Ho, *The Ladder*, pp. 36–37.

16. Wu Zhihe, pp. 28–30. See Ma, "The Local Officials."

17. Guo Zizhang, 24.5b–6a.

18. Wu Yingji, 9.24b–25a.

19. The trip was by Fujian students in a novel published in the early Qing. They traveled from a county to the Zhangzhou prefecture to take the annual examination administered by the educational commissioner. Even though this novel

was set in the early Qing, the cost of travel would probably have been similar in the late Ming. See *Zhongxu meng*, p. 42.

20. *Zhang yingyu*, 2, pp. 1230–34.

21. For example of Yang Xinfang and Guo Xun, see Han Dacheng, *Mingdai chengshi*, pp. 564–65.

22. *Zhang yingyu*, 2, pp. 1230–34.

23. Huacun kan xing shizhe, 23a–b.

24. Zhou Hui, 2.81a–b.

25. Shen Shouzheng, "Shen wuhui xiansheng zhuan," *Xuetang ji*, 2b–3b, 5a. See the preface by Huang Ruheng, *Yulin ji*, 7.32b–33a. See also Chapter 4.

26. Wu Yingji, 9.25b–26b.

27. Wang Shizhen, *Gu bu gu lu*, 22a–b.

28. Chen Jitai, 13.19a–b.

29. Han Dacheng, "Mingdai gaolidai," pp. 530–51.

30. Yang Shicong, p. 8.

31. For an analysis of involvement of officials and examinees in commenting on the *Romance of the Three Kingdoms*, see McLaren, "Ming Audiences."

32. The Ming government did not increase the quota for the *jinshi* degree, and the bureaucracy did not expand to absorb the excessive number of examinees. There were an average of 290 successful candidates at the metropolitan examination from 1451 to 1505. The number rose only slightly to 330 in the period 1508–1643. See Ho, *The Ladder*, p. 189.

33. Peterson, p. 32.

34. Elman, "Social."

35. Zhang Fengyi only obtained the *juren* degree. His printed examination aides were entrusted to merchants for distribution. Xu Shuofang, vol. 1, p. 171.

36. Xiao Dongfa, "Jianyang," p. 125. For an example in the Qing, see Brokaw's discussion of the experience of Ma Yang-po's venture into publishing. Brokaw, "Bestsellers."

37. Zhang Pu, *Qiluzhai lunlue*, 2.24a–25a.

38. Xu Shuofang, vol. 1, 394–95.

39. Scholars have noted the expansion of education opportunities and functional literacy in the late Ming. Rawski, *Education*, pp. 11–16; Leung, pp. 381–84.

40. *MS*, 288.7588; Xu Shuofang, vol. 2, p. 309.

41. *MDBKZL*, 4.52a.

42. Shen Zuan, *Jinshi congcan*, quoted in Xu Shuofang, vol. 1, p. 211.

43. Zhang Fengyi, *Chushi tang ji*, 5.33a–34b; *SBSZ*, p. 486.

44. Xu Shuofang, vol. 3, p. 276.

45. Ibid., vol. 2, p. 456.

46. Ibid., p. 458.

47. Zang Maoxun, p. 88.

48. Febrve and Martin, pp. 159–63.

49. Kernan, pp. 28–35.

50. Bourdieu, *The Field*, p. 61.

51. For example, see the "Fanli," in Shen Shouzheng, *Xuetang ji.*

52. See for example, the bibliographical notes by Qu Wanli. *SBSZ*, pp. 511, 523, 531, 532, 536, 541, 544.

53. For example, *MGHF*, pp. 510, 520, 590; *SBSZ*, p. 351.

54. "Fanli," in Shen Shouzheng, *Xuetang ji.*

55. He referred to his professional activities by means of the metaphor of "chicken bones," which meant the small fees he charged to his patrons. Chen Jiru, *Chen Meigong*, 6.5.

56. Chen Jiru, *Baishi qiao*, 3.39b; Chen Menglian, p. 495.

57. Johnson never made a fortune from his writing. According to Kernan, his "generosity to other writers and to numerous poor friends and dependents constantly depleted his resources." Kernan, pp. 102–6.

58. Li Yu, *Yizhong yuan*, 2a–4a.

59. *Nan Wu jiuhua lu*, 21.7a.

60. Qiu Zhaolin, 11.46b–47b.

61. Tang Xianzu, vol. 2, p. 1365.

62. Ibid., pp. 1074–82. The several prefaces to examination essays included in his own collected writings do not contradict the idea that Tang Xianzu actually wrote many more prefaces for publishers.

63. Tang Shunzhi, 7.6a–b.

64. See for example, Tang Xianzu, p. 1539.

65. Xu wen chang, 26.17a–20a.

66. See for example Tang Xianzu, p. 1230.

67. Feng Menglong, *Gua zhi'er*, p. 258.

68. Feng Menglong, *Shange*, pp. 225–27.

69. See for example, *MDBKZL*, vol. 8, 5a–6a.

70. There was a book entitled *Chen Shanren ji* in Qi Chengye, p. 1042.

71. Ling Dizhi.

72. *SBSZ*, p. 474.

73. Tan Qian, *shing*, 46b.

74. Qian Xiyan, 3.23b–24a. *MQJS*, p. 377.

75. Zhong Xing, *Cuiyu ge*, 3.35a–b.

76. *SBSZ*, p. 545.

77. Ibid.

78. Zhong Xing, *Cuiyu ge*, 3.35a–b.

79. See for example a scene in *San she ji*, 1.7b. The characters in *San she ji* were based on historical personages.

80. Li Rihua did not depend on selling his expertise in collectibles for a living. But the range of his knowledge was shared by professional *shanren* who rendered their services to wealthy merchants and literati. For the range of collectibles traded through art merchants, see Li Rihua, *Weishuixuan*, pp. 27, 42–43, 46–47, 57, 60–62, 64–67, 74–75. For a discussion of connoisseurship as part of a layer discourse on the production of social distinction through consumption of material culture, see Clunas, *Superfluous Things*.

81. Li Rihua, pp. 21–22, 24–25, 35.

82. Xie Zhaozhi, 13.3a–b.

83. Sun Chengze, *Chunming*, 48.48b.

84. The phrase "write in order to live" was Voltaire's description of the writers of his time. Quoted in Chartier, *The Cultural Origins*, p. 58.

85. Qi Biaojia, *Qu pin*, pp. 40–41, 45, 53.

86. Xu Shuofang, vol. 2, p. 166.

87. Xu Wei, pp. 573, 640, 856, 1046, 1099.

88. Xu Shuofang, vol. 2, pp. 110, 120. For a biography of Hu, see *DMB*, pp. 631–38.

89. Xu Wei, pp. 430–37, 443–44, 449, 451–52, 522–28, 654–57, 881–85.

90. Ibid., pp. 284–85.

91. Shen Defu, 23.586–87.

92. Chen Jiru, *Chen Meigong*, 15.1.

93. Ibid., 15.1; Song Qifeng, p. 37.

94. Chen Jiru, *Chen Meigong*, 12.11, 12.17; *MQJS*, pp. 361, 375, 387, 432, 438.

95. Chen Jiru, *Chen Meigong*, 12.9.

96. Qian Qianyi, *Liechao shiji xiaozhuan*, *ding* section II. Quoted in Chen Wanyi, p. 101.

97. For example, in 1613 Chen Jiru wrote an essay on the endowment of land to the prefectural school in Songjiang. *Songjiang fuzhi*, 23.56b–59a.

98. Chen Menglian, *BJTSGC*, vol. 53, pp. 462–64.

99. Shen Defu, 25.636.

100. Oertling, pp. 168–69.

101. Kuo, pp. 182–83; Oertling, pp. 168–70.

102. See his poem. Chen Hongshou, pp. 62, 84, 122. Ann Burkus-Chasson has called into question the modern distinction between "professional" and

"amateur" in the case of painters like Chen. Indeed by the 1640s there was no so-cial identity or role clearly identified as "professional." The purely economic na-ture was often obscured in metaphorical expressions wherein those actions were intimated. See Burkus-Chasson.

103. Biographical essay by Mao Qiling in Chen Hongshou, p. 590.

104. Ibid., pp. 67–68.

105. Ibid., p. 552.

106. Ibid., p. 409, 397–407.

107. Oertling, pp. 168–70.

108. Chen Hongshou, p. 590.

109. Ibid., p. 590.

110. Ibid., p. 215.

111. Chen Jiru, *Baishi qiao*, 3.43b.

112. Genette, *Paratexts*, pp. 37–42.

113. The term *minggong* had already appeared in books printed in the Yuan dynasty. Zhang Xiumin, *Zhongguo yinshuashi*, p. 325.

114. *MDBKZL*, 1.25a, 3.18b, 4.74a, 6.35a, 7.13b, 7.15a; *SBSZ*, pp. 544, 546–47.

115. Johns, p. 33.

116. Li Rihua, *Weishuixuan riji*, 4.

117. Chen Jiru, *Yimin zhuan*.

118. Chen Jiru, *Chen Meigong*, 6.5.

119. Tang Xianzu, vol. 2, pp. 1080–81, 1500–1501.

120. Xu Shuofang, vol. 3, p. 444. The work was more than one hundred juan and was divided into dynastic parts. For extant copies, see *TWGCSB*, pp. 630–31.

121. Zhong Xing, *Cuiyu ge*, 1.43a–44a.

122. Zhong Xing, *Yinxiu xuan ji*, pp. 286–87.

123. Ibid., pp. 283–84.

124. Ibid., pp. 265–67.

125. Gu Menglin.

126. Ai Nanying, chs. 2–4; Zhong Xing, *Yinxiu xuan ji*, pp. 280–87; Zhang Pu, *Qiluzhai lunlue*, chs. 1–4; Chen Jitai, chs. 2–3.

127. Xu Shuofang, vol. 3, p. 437.

128. *ZGSBS*, p. 688.

129. Yu Yingqiu, *Sishu Yijing tujie*; Zhang Pu, *Sishu yin* and *Sishu kaobi*; Feng Mengzhen; Tang Ruxun, *Youyang shanren Bianfeng ji*, *SBSZ*, pp. 474, 479.

130. Yao Guangzuo.

131. *ZGSBS*, p. 305.

132. Xiao Dongfa, *Zhongguo*, p. 354.

133. Xu Fenpeng, *Xu Bidong xiansheng*, 80a–85a.

134. Ai Nanying, 2.4a.

135. Li Yu, *Liweng ouji*, *LYQJ*, vol. 6, 4.10b.

136. *MDBKZL*, 1.3b, 4.42b, 7.7a, 7.11a; *SBSZ*, 130, 523, 528; *MGHF*, p. 65.

137. See Tang Binyin, *Shui'an Sishu mai* (The pulse of the Four Books by Shui'an); also a later edition of the same book published by Yu Yingqiu, *Sishu mai jiangyi* (Discourse on the meaning of the pulse of the Four Books).

138. *MJSWB*, vol. 1.

139. The advertisement was written by Shen Guoyuan, who was listed as the proofreader. See Chen Renxi, *Ming wen qi shang*.

140. There were prefaces in the anthology dating to 1632 and 1633. It is clear that they were published originally as separate collections and were later reissued as an anthology. Lu Yunlong, *Huang Ming shiliu jia xiaopin*, p. 79.

141. There are titles like *Guochao minggong hanzao*, *Guochao minggong jingji wenchao*, and *Guochao minggon jingji hongci xuan*. *MDBKZL*, vol. 8, p. 26a.

142. Wang Xijue, *Huang Ming guanke*, p. 24.

143. *DMB*, pp. 1180, 1376–77.

144. See *SBSZ*, pp. 89–90, 461–62, 463, 540; Fang Yingxiang, *Xinjin Sishu xingren yu*; Zhou Wende, *Shanbu Sishu shengxian xinjue*; Xiang Xu, *Sishu renwu leihan*.

145. *TWGCSB*, pp. 749–52. The list of titles included in this catalog clearly is not comprehensive.

146. *Mingshi*, 217.5739–40.

147. *MDBKZL*, 7.11a, 21a.

148. See various titles in *SBSZ*, pp. 77, 89–90, 531.

149. *MDBKZL*, 7.20a–21b.

150. Tang Xianzu, vol. 2, p. 1322.

151. Lin San, *Sishu shuosheng*.

152. Zhou Wende, *Sishu shengxian xinjue*.

153. Feng Menglong, *Linjing zhiyue*, *FMLQJ*, vol. 1.

154. Ibid., pp. 1–6.

155. Gu Menglong, *Shijing shuoyue*, vol. 1, pp. 25–34. See Chapter 5 for a discussion of the intricate relationship between literary societies and publishing.

156. Zang Maoxun, pp. 51–52; Xu Shuofang, vol. 3, p. 466.

157. *ZGSBS*, p. 439.

158. Ibid.

159. Xu Shuofang, vol. 3, pp. 462, 468.

160. Zang Maoxun, pp. 85, 88.

161. A gazetteer of the Bailudong Academy was printed in the 1510s by the provincial commissioner of education of Jiangxi. The Education official of Nankang prefecture was listed as the "*duke.*" *ZGSBS*, p. 202. A county gazetteer was printed in the 1580s under the supervision of a county jailer or clerk (*dianshi*), who was listed as the "*duke.*" *TYBB*, p. 82.

162. *ZGSBS*, p. 582.

163. *TYBB*, p. 61.

164. Wu Mianxue was listed as proofreader and publisher, and Xu Zhi as supervisor of cutting in a commentary to the *Great Learning*. This text, however, appeared as part of a commentary on the Four Books, entitled *Sishu shiwen shilu*, compiled by Yang Wenkui. It was possible that the blocks first belonged to Wu Mianxue, who sold them to Yang. See Yang Wenkui, end of the *Great Learning* chapter, *Sishu shiwen shilu*.

165. According to Lucille Chia's list, Wu had published forty-six titles. See Chia, "Of Three Mountains Street." For the list of twenty-seven books published by Wu, see *MDBKZL*, 2.45a–46a.

166. There was another book published by a Huizhou native, Wu Congshan, who was listed as the "*duke.*" He was listed as the publisher from Xindu in *MDBKZL*, 2.45a.

167. *ZGSBS*, pp. 77, 393, 439; *MDBKZL*, 4.20b–21a.

168. Feng Menglong, *Xinke Gangjian tongyi*, p. 21.

169. Wang Xijue, *Huang Ming guanke*, p. 561.

170. Ibid., p. 532.

171. *SBSZ*, p. 574.

172. For example, the original publisher of the collected writings of Tang Shunzhi was from Zhejiang. He sold the blocks to a Nanjing publisher only two years after he carved them. Obviously, the less the blocks were used, the higher the price they would fetch. See *ZGSBS*, p. 608.

173. Chen Renxi, preface, *Wumengyuan ji*, p. 93.

174. Ibid., pp. 2–35.

175. *MS*, vol. 24, pp. 7394–95.

176. *MQJS*, p. 481; *MS*, vol. 24, pp. 7395.

177. See Appendix 5.

178. He published nine books under the Yuefantang house and two under Qishangzhai. See Appendix 5.

179. For example, Chen published *Guwen qishang* (In appreciation of amazing ancient prose), *Su wen qishang* (In appreciation of the amazing prose of Su Shi), *Ming wen qishang* (In appreciation of the amazing prose of the Ming dy-

nasty), and *Zhuzi qishang* (In appreciation of the amazing writings of the various schools). See *FMLQJ*, vol. 6, p. 2.

180. Preface, 1628. *SBSZ*, pp. 298–99.

181. *MDBKZL*, vol. 1, 1.7a. The other two works on statecraft were published after 1628. *Daxue yanyi bu* (1632) and *Huang Ming shifa lu* (1628–44), *SBSZ*, pp. 187, 22; *MDBKZL*, 6.27b–28a.

182. Chen Renxi, *Sishu jiangyi*, in *Wumengyuan ji*, pp. 710, 712, 750; *SBSZ*, pp. 58–9.

183. *MDBKZL*, 5.3a–4b; 1.38b–39a.

184. Ibid., 1.11a–b.

185. Ibid., 8.3b–4b.

186. For a discussion of Feng Menglong's three collections of short stories collectively known as the *Sanyan*, see Idema, pp. 30–56.

187. They are *Sishu zhiyue, Linjing zhiyue, Chunqiu hengku, Gangjian tongyi. FMLQJ*, vols. 6 and 8.

188. *FMLQJ*, vol. 6, p. 2; Hu Wanchuan, "Feng Menglong (Yu Fushe)," p. 98.

189. They are *Linjing zhiyue* and *Chunqiu hengfu. ZGSBS*, p. 30.

190. Hu Wanchuan, "Feng Menglong shengping," p. 39a.

191. Ibid., p. 41a.

192. *MDBKZL*, 6.27a.

193. Liu Zhizhong, p. 54.

194. Ibid., pp. 54–55.

195. Ibid., p. 55.

196. Qian Xiyan regarded the *Shuzhai manlu* as a forgery. Xu bought the book from Ye Zhou and then published it under his own name. It is clear that Xu bought the manuscript that Ye Zhou compiled as a publisher. He paid for Ye's service. See ibid., p. 62.

197. Ibid., pp. 56–57.

198. Ibid., p. 50.

199. Ibid., p. 55.

200. *MDBKZL*, 4.34b.

201. Liu Zhizhong, p. 50.

202. Ibid., pp. 54–57.

203. Xu Shuofang, vol. 3, pp. 517–20, 524.

204. See *MDBKZL*, 7.11a–b; and *TWGCSB*, p. 194.

205. Quoted in Gu Yanwu, *Rizhilu*, 18.29b–30a.

206. Sun Kuang, *Yuefeng xiansheng juye bian*, 3.112a–b, 3.117a–b.

207. Ibid., 3.61a–b, 3.66b.

208. Ibid., 3.109a–b.

209. Ibid., 3.109a, 3.112a.

210. Ibid., 3.117b, 3.119a.

211. Ibid., 3.61a–b.

212. Ibid., 3.120b.

213. Ibid., 3.14a. Sun Kuang, *Jin wenxuan*, preface, 1603. *TWGCSB*, p. 490.

214. Sun Kuang, *Yuefeng xiansheng juye cibian*, 3.31b–32b.

215. Ibid., 3.34a–b.

216. Ibid., 3.38b.

217. Sun Kuang, *Jin wenxuan*, preface by Tang is dated 1603.

218. Sun Kuang, *Jin wenxuan*.

219. *TWGCSB*, pp. 1081–82.

220. Zhong Xing, *Cuiyu ge*, 8.21a–b.

221. This work mostly included already published writings. It however included unpublished writings of Yuan. See the preface by Yang Ruji, in Yuan Hongdao, *Yuan Zhonglang quanji* (Ming edition).

222. Zhong Xing, *Yinxiu xuan ji*, pp. 468–69, 473, 481–86; Tan Yuanchun, p. 92, 119–21.

223. *ZGSBS*, p. 439.

224. Zhong Xing, *Yinxiu xuan ji*, p. 484; *ZGSBS*, p. 520.

225. Zhong Xing, *Cuiyu ge*, juan 1; *ZGSBS*, p. 520.

226. *MDBKZL*, 7.15b.

227. Xu Quangqi, p. 6.

228. *MDBKZL*, 7.22a.

229. The book entitled *Fushou quanshu* (The complete book of fortune and longevity) was reprinted from the blocks of a different book, *Zuo Fei an rizuan*, by Zheng Xuan. The blocks might have been sold to Jilianju which reprinted under its own name with Chen Jiru as the compiler. *SBSZ*, p. 302.

230. Xu Fenpeng, *Xu Bidong xiansheng*, 53a–b.

231. Three of his commentaries on the Four Books are extant. *Bidong sheng xinwu* (preface, 1613), *Xuke Bidong xiansheng houwu* (preface, 1613), and *Sishu zhixin* (preface, 1626).

232. He published a commentary on the popular play *The Western Chamber*. *MDBKZL*, 1.26a, 5.21b–22a.

233. *Xu Bidong xiansheng jingjuan wanbao quanshu*, quoted in Chen Xuewen, p. 241.

234. Xu Fenpeng, *Xuke*.

235. The publisher was Tianqi studio. There was a Tianqi studio in Nan-jing owned by Wang Fengxiang. *MDBKZL*, 2.10b, 1.25b.

236. *MDBKZL*, 1.26a.

237. Xu Fenpeng, "Zazhu zhuwen," in *Xu Bidong xiansheng*, 29a–b.

238. See his *Zuanding gujin sishu daquan, Sishu jinjianlu, ZGSBS*, p. 44. There are a few exceptions to Xu's rejection of prefaces by celebrated writers. An early Qing edition, a reprint of *Gujin zhitong*, includes a preface by Tang Xianzu, who came from the same province as Xu. See *ZGSBS*, p. 329. There is a preface by Jiao Hong in a commentary on the Four Books entitled *Sishu gujin daomai*, which was published by a Nanjing publisher, Guibitang.

239. Sun Kuang, *Yuefeng xiansheng juye cibian*, 3.19a.

240. Ray Huang, p. 199.

241. See his sense of helplessness in a letter to Jiao Hong about indirect de-pendence on the cultivation of relationships with officials and powerful elites. Li Zhi, *Xu Fenshu*, in *Fengshu*, p. 34.

242. Li Zhi, *Xu Fenshu*, p. 269.

243. Yuan Zongdao, *You ju pei lu*, p. 244.

244. Cui Wenyin argues that the comments in the Yuan Wuya edition were made by Ye Zhou. But the sources that he quotes clearly show that the edition Yuan Wuya brought to Ye for editing did include Li's own comments. See Cui, "Yuan Wuya." Besides, Li Zhi actually mentioned his commenting on the fiction in his *Xu Fenshu*. Li Zhi, *Fenshu*, p. 269; *Xu Fenshu*, pp. 34.

245. For discussion, see Plaks, pp. 513–17; and Rolston, *How to Read*, ap-pendix 2.

246. Li Zhi, *Xu Fenshu*, pp. 33, 39, 57, 59–60, 62–63.

247. Ibid., 33–34.

248. Li wrote essays on quotations from the Four Books. They were sent to Yuan Hongdao for comments. Many of these essays were included in his *Shuo-shu* (Expositions on the books). Li Zhi, *Fenshu*, pp. 47, 269–70; *Xu Fenshu*, pp. 33, 46.

249. Li Zhi, *Xu Fenshu*, p. 45.

250. *MDBKZL*, 5.26b.

251. Li Zhi, *Xu Fenshu*, pp. 59–60.

252. For example, a Shanxi merchant brought a letter to Yuan Hongdao informing him that a theft happened to his brother. Yuan Hongdao, *Yuan Zhong-lang quanji, Chidu*, p. 19. See also Xu Shuofang, vol. 3, p. 539.

253. Brook, "Communications," pp. 626–30.

254. Yuan Hongdao referred to such a communication network formed by traveling monks. They traveled between Danyang, Wujiang, and Suzhou. Yuan Hongdao, *Sabi tang ji*, 16.10a–b.

255. Yuan Hongdao, *Yuan Zhonglang quanji, wenchao*, p. 57.

256. Li Zhi, *Fenshu*, p. 268; *Xu Fenshu*, p. 34. Yuan Hongdao, *Yuan Zhonglang quanji, Chidu*, p. 68.

257. Li Zhi, *Xu Fenshu*, p. 45.

258. Li Zhi depended mostly on patronage by friends and followers. But he did not have enough to support the monks. Wunian had to make trips to Nanjing to teach and make connections. Li Zhi was uncomfortable with the situation but felt powerless to change it. *Xu Fenshu*, p. 34.

259. Jin Jiang has demonstrated convincingly that Li Zhi published his *Fenshu* in order to express his disagreement and anger with Geng Dingxiang. See Jin Jiang.

260. *MDBKZL*, 5.26b–27a.

261. See especially *Xu Fenshu*, p. 4.

262. *Guoshi jingjizhi* and *Guochao xianzheng lu. ZGSBS*, pp. 131, 215, 245.

263. For a study of Yuan's literary theory and his role as leader of the Gongan school, see Chou Chih-p'ing.

264. Yuang Hongdao, *Yuan Zhonglang quanji, Chidu*, pp. 2–7; Chou Chih-p'ing, pp. 93–94.

265. *MDBKZL*, 4.26a.

266. Yuang Hongdao, *Yuan Zhonglang quanji, Chidu*, p. 77; *MDBKZL*, 4.25b; *SBSZ*, pp. 475–77.

267. Yuang Hongdao, *Yuan Zhonglang quanji, Chidu*, p. 78.

268. Ibid., p. 16.

269. Ibid., p. 54.

270. Yuan Zhongdao, *Kexue zhai jin ji*, 2.190–91.

271. Chen Wanyi, pp. 117–28.

272. Genette, pp. 39–40.

273. Grafton, p. 8. For a general discussion of the various reasons why forgeries were made, see Chapter 1.

274. A case in point was the forgery of the Stele edition of *Great Learning* by Feng Fang. Feng was a well-known book collector and specialist in forgery who falsified *Great Learning on Stele* in order to prove that Wang Yangming's reconstruction of the *Old Text Great Learning* was correct. His text was printed as part of a collectanea *Qiuling xueshan* in 1568. Through the influence of the credulous

renowned scholar Zheng Xiao (1499–1566), it began to gain acceptance by the end of the Jiajing reign (1522–66). By the late Wanli reign, it was reprinted in many forms and accepted even by scholars such as Gu Xiancheng, Guan Zhidao, and Liu Zongzhou. See Li Jixiang, pp. 134–42.

275. *ZGSBS*, p. 384.

276. *Meigong xiansheng Wanxiangtang xiaopin*, in *MGHF*, p. 768. The ability of officials to trace a book to its publisher was also demonstrated in Li Tingji's effort to censor and destroy the printing blocks of a play written to ridicule Tu Long's homosexual involvement with an actor. See Shen Defu, p. 676.

277. For a detailed study of Lin Chao'en's teachings in the context of late-Ming religions, see Berling.

278. Lin Zhao'en, *Linzi quanji*, p. 1238.

279. For another case involving the tracing of a publisher and the destruction of blocks by officials, see Chapter 5.

280. Li Yu, *LYQJ*, vol. 1, 3.11a.

281. A rare document of government notice against book piracy is preserved in the paratext of a commentary by Zhang Zilie. In 1657 the Provincial Administration Commission issued a public notice against pirating Zhang's commentary, which was published by Daojitang. See "Jin fanke Daoji tang shuji yuanshi" in Zhang Zilie, *Sishu daquan bian*. See also Chapter 5 for further discussion on Zhang.

282. Rose, p. 242.

283. In France before 1566, there was no institutionalized censorship that required the submission of books for review prior to publication. When publishers submitted their books, they did so as "a voluntary act, initiated by the applicant for his own advantage. It did not form a part of any organized system of licensing." But in 1566, Charles IX decreed that no books should be published without permission. Only then "the separate identity of the privilege, as a commercial concession, was merged in that of a license to print." See Armstrong, p. 100. In England, the early history of copyright was not so much one of protecting the right of the author as a history of control, involving the stationers' trade regulation practices, the government's attempt to control anonymous controversial publications by requiring the identification of the author on the title page and the sanction against publication without the author's consent. See Rose, pp. 211–16.

284. Yuan Zhongdao, *Kexue zhai jinji*, p. 44.

285. Woodmansee, pp. 19–23.

CHAPTER 4

1. Elman, "Social."

2. Elman, *A Cultural History*, pp. 142, 147, 192–94, 295, 327, 362–63.

3. For an analysis of the tension between the imperial state and official families in the mid-Qianlong period (1736–95), see Man-cheong.

4. Foucault, *The Archaeology*, pp. 21–63. For a critique of Foucault's position, see de Certeau, *The Practice*, pp. 45–49.

5. Even though Elman points out that "civil service examinations were a cultural arena within which diverse political and social interests contested with each other and were balanced," his characterization of the civil service examination as a "cultural prison" works to undermine the importance of the struggle and tension between the literary elites and the imperial government by condemning everyone to the dungeon of traditional China. Elman, *A Cultural History*, p. xxiv.

6. The general effects of the broad socioeconomic changes on society constituted what I have called the "crisis of the Confucian order." Chow, *The Rise*, pp. 15–21. For general descriptions of the broad socioeconomic changes in the late Ming, see also Brokaw, *The Ledgers*, pp. 3–17; and Rawski, "Economic," pp. 3–16.

7. De Certeau, *The Practice*, pp. 45–49.

8. Ibid., pp. 48–49.

9. Ibid., p. 172.

10. De Certeau goes so far as to say that "a text has meaning only through its readers. The only context that de Certeau focuses on is the political, the power relationship between the readers and the producers of the texts. And the only constraints on the reader's creativity are located in the institutional control by the ruling elite. Therefore, de Certeau said, "The autonomy of the reader depends on a transformation of the social relationships that overdetermine his relation to texts." Ibid., pp. 170–73.

11. See McKenzie. For a summary of McKenzie's contribution to our understanding of the role of formal structures of the book, see Chartier, "Text," in *On the Edge*, pp. 81–89.

12. Genette, p. 3.

13. Ibid., p. 1.

14. Ibid., p. 2.

15. Ibid., pp. 10–11.

16. Ibid., p. 12.

17. By "tactics of practice," de Certeau refers to those everyday practice of reading, walking, talking, cooking, and dwelling. He does not specifically mention writing as an example of tactics for he has a personal bias against writing,

which he considers the technology of the modern ruling group. He argues that scripture/writing through the "clean-up" effects of "the techniques of diffusion," had "colonized and mythified" the "people's voice" (in other words, people versus the bourgeoise) by recent Western history. *The Practice*, p. xvii, p. 132.

18. Darnton, "What Is the History of the Book?" pp. 107–13.

19. This formulation takes issue with de Certeau, who gives almost complete autonomy to the reader. His theory of reading considers only two factors: the reader and the institutions that control the reading of texts, especially those on which the "cultural orthodoxy" rested. De Certeau, *The Practice*, p. 170.

20. Ibid., p. 174.

21. Ibid., pp. 170–72.

22. Wilson, p. 60.

23. Ibid., pp. 51–53.

24. Other institutions included the Confucian temple, construction of genealogies of Daoxue masters, and the compilation of anthologies. See Wilson.

25. Wu Zhihe, pp. 25–28.

26. Ibid., pp. 28–30.

27. Ibid., p. 29.

28. Zheng Xiao, *Jin yan*, 3.23a.

29. Zhang Xuan, 45.3770.

30. Ibid., 45.3770–71, 3780–81.

31. Wu Zhihe, pp. 139–40.

32. Ibid., pp. 140–48.

33. *Songjiang fuzhi*, 23.57b–62a.

34. Meskill, pp. 24–25; Ye Xian'en, pp. 136–37.

35. Qiu Zhaolin, 11.80a–b.

36. The rate of building new private academies declined in the Wanli period. Meskill, p. 139.

37. Thomas Wilson argues that it was more accurate to place the time when the Daoxue school became orthodoxy in the Ming, instead of in the Yuan. Wilson, pp. 47–59.

38. Ibid., p. 54.

39. For discussion of the role of the usurpation of power by the Yongle emperor in establishing the Cheng-Zhu Daoxue, see Elman, "The Formation."

40. Brook, "Edifying Knowledge," pp. 104–8.

41. Quoted in de Certeau, *The Practice*, p. 165.

42. Ibid., p. 171.

43. Song Jicheng, preface to *Sishu zhengyi*, quoted in Zhu Yizun, 259.9b–10a; See *Sishu qianbai nian yan*, "Fanli," 1a.

44. The son of Chen Jitai related that model essays written to prepare candidates for the civil service examination reached places overseas. Although this particular claim may be an invention of filial sentiment, a large number of examination aids did find their way to Japan. Oba Osamu, pp. 721–28. Chen's model essays were among the most popular. *Chishan ji*, 1.10b, in Chen Jitai, *Jiwu ji*.

45. As early as the eleventh century, printed examination aids had already aroused concern among officials. Liu Xiangguang, pp. 116, 124–26,

46. Zhang Xuan, 45.3b–4a.

47. Tu Wei-ming, 157–76. While arguing that Wang Yangming reformulated the "learning of the mind and heart," de Bary rejects the view that dichotomizes the differences between Zhu Xi and Wang Yangming into the School of Principle and the School of the Mind. See de Bary, *The Message*, pp. 79–87.

48. See *ZGGJSB*, vol. 3, 47a–48a.

49. Huang Zongxi, *Mingru xue'an, tse* 9, 46.27.

50. Zhu Yizun, *Jingyi kao*, 256.18a.

51. See Appendix 6 for the titles.

52. See Chia, "Of Three Mountains Street."

53. These two commentaries are *Xinkan liangjia cuiyi* (preface, 1583) and *Sishu Yizhuan sanyi* (preface, 1588). For the former, see *SBSZ*, p. 54. The latter includes the commentary of Chen Chen. See Appendix 6.

54. *ZGGJSB* shows that 141 imprints of commentaries on the Four Books were printed in the Ming, excluding thirteen official editions and reprints of Hu Guang's *Sishu daquan* and eighteen of Zhu Xi's own commentaries; five imprints were published in the Jiajing (1522–66) through the Longqing (1567–72) periods. Titles by Zhu Xi include *Sishu jizhu* and *Sishu huowen*. *ZGGJSB*, 3.42a–56a; *Nagoya-shi*, pp. 15–21. Added to this list are twenty-two different datable commentaries in the Magoya City Library, published during or after the Wanli reign.

55. *Tiaoli beikao*, "Libu," 1.2b–3a.

56. Shen Li submitted a memorial on eight major issues regarding education and the civil service examination sometime between 1584 and 1586. *Mingshi gao*, 96.6a–b.

57. Zhang Xuan, 44.12a–14a; *MS*, 217.5734.

58. *MS*, 216.5705.

59. See *MDDKL*, vol. 21, pp. 11605–725.

60. Sun Chengze, *Chunming*, 40.3a; Gu Yanwu, *Rizhilu*, 18.21b–22a; *DMB*, p. 444.

61. Li Tingji, *Li Wenjie ji*, 4.8b–9a, 4.11a–b.

62. To give just two examples: Li Tingji, *Sishu Wenlin guanzhi* (Unifying

themes of the literary world in the Four Books), a poorly printed commentary (see Appendix 6); and Li Tingji, *Sishu dazhu cankao* (Reference for the complete compendium of commentaries on the Four Books).

63. Li Tingji, *Sishu Wenlin guanzhi* (Unifying themes of the literary world in the Four Books). This is most likely an attribution to Li.

64. Qian Qianyi, *MZYXJ*, 19.17a–b.

65. Li Le, 5.72a–b.

66. Gu Yanwu, *Rizhilu*, 18.29a–b.

67. Gu Menglin, preface.

68. Ibid.

69. Qian Qianyi, *MZYXJ*, 19.17a. Yang Yi obviously had a large collection of books. His home was one of the most visited places in Changshu, Kiangsu. Ye Dehui, p. 192.

70. Compared to France in the eighteenth century, the Ming government did not develop any effective institutions of censorship outside the examination system. Publishers and printers were not required to register with the government; nor were books required to be sent to the magistrate office for review. For censorship in eighteenth-century France, see Roche.

71. Tang Ru'e, preface to *Sishu weiyan*.

72. Yuan Huang, *Liaofan*, "Fanli," 1a–5a.

73. See two-register commentaries by Yao Wenwei, Li Tingji, Zhuang Qimeng, Yang Wenkui, Yu Yingke, Yu Yingqiu, Yuang Huang, *Sishu xun er sushuo*; Tang Binyin, *Sishu mai jiangyi*; Xu Yan, Zhang Mingbi, Zhang Pu, *Sishu yin*, Zhou Wende, *Sishu jiangyi cunshi*. For three-register formats, see Li Tingji, *Sishu wenli guanzhi*; Qian Shule, Tang Binyin, Xu Xie, Zhou Wende's *Shanbu Sishu shengxian xinjue*. See Appendix 6.

74. See Yuan Huang, *Sishu shanzheng*; Zhang Song, *Sishu shuocheng*; Tang Binyin, *Sishu yenming jizhu* and *Tianxsiang ke shuo*; Zhou Wende, *Shanbu Sishu shengxian xinjue*; and Yu Yingke.

75. See for example, Li Tingjii, *Sishu Wenlin guanzhi*.

76. Quoted in Genette, p. 76.

77. Ibid., pp. 76, 89.

78. See the titles in Appendix 6.

79. Using "ideas" (*i*) in the title could be traced back to the Southern Song. Ye Dehui, 148–51.

80. The work by Dong Qichang (*Sibai*) was cited in the preface of another commentary by Tang Ru'e, *Sishu weiyan*.

81. See Appendix 6 for the titles.

82. Tang Binyin, *Dingjuan Shui'an Tang taishi Sishu mai*, "Great Learning," 1a. See Appendix 6.

83. See for example, Qian Jideng and Cao Xun, *Sishu qianbai nian yan*; Yuan Huang, *Liaofan Yuan xiansheng Sishu shanzheng jian shuyi*. See Appendix 6.

84. Zhong Tianyuan, preface to *Sishu jiebo bian*. See Appendix 6.

85. Other genres of books also used *minggong* in the title as an attraction. See titles in *MGHF*, pp. 571, 587, 592, 595, 680.

86. Shen Shouzheng, *Sishu shuocong*.

87. Tang Binyin, *Shui'an Sishu mai*.

88. Zhang Pu, *Sishu kaobei*.

89. Tang Ru'e, *Sishu weiyan*.

90. Xu Fenpeng, *Sishu gujin daomai*.

91. Among the reputable masters were Chen Jiru, Zhong Xing, Huang Ruheng, Tang Binyin, Dong Qichang, Tang Xianzu, Jiao Hong, Chen Jitai, Ai Nanying, Chen Renxi, Tan Youxia, and Wen Qixiang. Zhou Fazhi, *Luli ji*, pp. 295–96.

92. Yu Yingke.

93. Lin San, *Sishu shuosheng*.

94. Gu Menglin, *Sishu shuoyue*.

95. Wang Yu.

96. Chen Zushou.

97. Feng Menglong, *Linjing zhiyue*.

98. Zhu Mingliang.

99. Xu Fenpeng, "Fanli," in Sishu *gujin daomai*, 2a.

100. Tang Binyin, "Fanli," *Shui'an sishu mai*.

101. Hanshan Deqing, *Daxue gangmu jueyi* and *Zhongyong zhizhi*.

102. For example, the examinee is advised to work on the third question after completing the first. By reversing questions two and three, the examinee was able to deal with a common problem. The examinee would be exhausted by the time he got to the third question. To follow the regular sequence would give the examiner the impression that the quality of the answers decreases toward the end. However, the reversal would change that impression because the examiner would be thrilled to read the third answer, which was written immediately after the first. Even after reading through the second answer that had no spark, the examiner would be surprised by the quality of the third answer. "Xiucai miyue," Hanshan Deqing, *Daxue shu*, 2a–b. Even though this edition was published in the early Qing, the effect of paratext publishers adding to a text would be similar in the late Ming.

103. Zhang Nai, *Sishu yan*. There is a section on the formats or styles for writing the "eight-legged" essay in Li Tingji, *Sishu Wenlin guanzhi*.

104. Tang Binyin, *Tianxiangge shuo*, 3a–4b.

105. Guo Wei, "Fanli," *Huang Ming*, 8a.

106. See Zhang Nai, *Sishu yan*.

107. There was a preface by Qiu Zhaolin, who was active during 1610 as a famous writer of examination aids. The *maochen* years refers to years ending with *mao* and *chen*. Years with *mao* and *chen* were 1615, 1616, 1627, 1628, 1639, and 1640. According to Qiu's preface, *maochen* was likely 1615 and 1616. Tang Binyin, *Tianxiangge shuo*.

108. See Yu Yingke.

109. See Chen Zushou.

110. Zhang Nai, *Sishu yan*, "Fanli."

111. Zhou Wende, *Shanbu Sishu shengxian xinjue*.

112. See for example, Zhou Wende, *Shanbu Sishu shengxian xinjue* and *Sishu jiangyi cunshi*; Zhang Nai, *Sishu yan*; Huang Qiyou, *Sishu gangjian*.

113. See for example, Shen Ji, *Sishu tiyi*; Xu Fenpeng, *Sishu gujin daomai*; Xiang Shengguo, *Sishu tianyue*; Wang Najian's *Sishu yizhu*; Shen Shoucheng's *Sishu shuocong*; Tang Ru'e, *Sishu weiyan*.

114. Zhang Chenyuan, "Fanli," *Sishu shuotong*, 1b.

115. See for example, Yao Wenwei, "Daxue" in *Sishu wen*, 1.4a; Guo Wei, *Daxue* in *Sishu zhuyi baocang*, 5.1b; see Appendix 6.

116. Xiang Shengguo, 1a.

117. Shen Shouzheng, *Sishu shuocong*, "Editorial Principles." See Appendix 6.

118. Xu Fenpeng, "Fanli," in *Sishu gujin daomai*, 2a.

119. Zhou Wende, *Shanbu Sishu shenxian xinjue*, "Fanli," 2a.

120. Ma Shiqi, a member of the Restoration Society, was reputed to have compiled the commentaries by thirty famous writers in the *Dingjuan sanshi mingjia Sishu ji*. A work attributed to the famous scholar Jiao Hong, *Xinqie Huang-Ming baijia Sishu lijie ji*, claims to have included insightful comments from more than one hundred writers.

121. A manuscript of comments on the Four Books by Zhang Dai was discovered. It was perhaps ready for printing but was never printed. It comprised notes Zhang had taken when he was preparing for the examination. See the preface, Zhang Dai, *Sishu yu*, p. 1.

122. *Sishu gangjian*.

123. "Preface to the Complete Commentaries on the *Analects*," in Zhang Pu, *Qiluzhai lunlue*, 6.609. *Chih-kao* (Recent drafts), 1.117.

124. Dong Qichang, *Rongtai ji*, 2.11b.

125. Lin Liyue, *Mingdai*, pp. 134–35.

126. Hung-lam Chu, p. 68.

127. Ai Nanying, 1.28b.

128. One of the earliest references to Wang Yangming's *liangzhi* idea can be found in Xu Kuang, *Sishu chuwen* (First questions about the Four Books). See Appendix 6.

129. Huang Guangsheng, 1.28a. See Appendix 6.

130. Wang Qiao, *Sishu shaowenbian*, "Daxue," 40b, 70b–71a. See Appendix 6.

131. Shen Ji, *Sishu tiyi*, 1618, 1.5b, 1.24b, 1.30b–31a; Zhao Weixin, *Ganshu lu*, 2.15b–16a, 2.32b. Yao Wenwei, *Sishu wen*, Daxue, 7a–12b, 9a–10a. See Appendix 6.

132. Qian Zhaoyang, *Sishu huiyi xinjie*. This text was published between 1602 and 1613.

133. Yao Wenwei, *Sishu wen*, Daxue, 11a.

134. Preface by Liu Yikun, dated 1620, Yao Wenwei, *Sishu wen*.

135. *MRZJ*, p. 379.

136. Zhang Song, *Sishu shuosheng*, preface, 1624.

137. *Sishu zhijie zhinan*, 3.9b; *Xinke Yichou ke hua huiyuan Sishu zhuyi jinyu sui*; *Huang Ming bai fangjia wenda, Xinxie Huang Ming bai dajia zongyi Sishu zhengxin lu, Zengbu Guo Zhuyuan xiansheng huiji shi taishi Sishu zhuyi baocang*, 3.51b.

138. Guo Wei, *Sishu zhuyii baocang, Lunyu* 1.2a–b.

139. Lin San, 3.18b–19a, 3.46b–47a.

140. Yao Guangzuo, 1.11b.

141. Yao Wenwei, preface to *Sishu wen*.

142. Cited in Berling, p. 51.

143. Xu Fenpeng, "Fanli," in *Sishu gujin daomai* 6b; "Fanli," in Zhou Wende, *Sishu jiangyi shengxian xinjue*, 1a.

144. For the study of various strands of syncretism in the late Ming, see Araki, "Confucianism"; Chun-fang Yu, *The Renewal*; Berling; Edward Ch'ien, *Chiao Hung*.

145. See Brokaw's study of this form of religious practice in the late Ming. Brokaw, *The Ledgers*.

146. Zhang Zhenyuan, preface to *Sishu shuotong*.

147. Chen Jianhua, pp. 191–210, 266–89.

148. Chen Yumo, 1.11b–12a.

149. *Siku quanshu zongmu tiyao*, "Jingbu," 37.31 [765].

150. Wang Meng Chien, *Sishu cheng*.

151. Xiang Yu, a native of Wu county, Kiangsu. Tan Qian, *renji*, 7b. Xu Fenpeng, *Zuanding Sishu*, "Great Learning," 2.5a–6a, 2.64b–66b.

152. Chow, *The Rise*, chs. 6 and 7.

153. For a discussion of the differences between the interests in Han scholarship in the late Ming and the those in the mid-Qing, see Chow, "Writing for Success," p. 146; and Chow, *The Rise*, chs. 6 and 7.

154. As discussed in the last chapter, Sun Kuang's personal interest in printing works by Han scholars was but one example of the role of publishing in the growth and spread of interest in Han scholarly works and commentaries.

155. Zhu Xi, *Daxue zhangju*, pp. 6–7.

156. See for example, the various comments by Cheng Fuxin in Wang Xianshan's *Sishu zhangtu tongkao, Daxue Zhangju*, 43b–45a. This photocopy from the central library in Taiwan lists Liu Yan as its compiler. But on the first page of the *Daxue zhangju*, Cheng Fuxin and Wang Xianshan were listed as the authors. Wang's commentary was an expansion of Cheng's *Sishu zhangtu zuanxi*. See the title in the "Fanli."

157. Shi Fenglai, 1607 preface; *MRZJ*, p. 341.

158. Shi Fenglai, "Daxue," 26a–b. For an example of a conventional reading of this passage, see Cai Qing, p. 65.

159. Ibid., 29a–b, 31a–32a.

160. Zhu Mingliang, "Great Learning," 39a–b.

161. For example, see Ma Shiqi, *Sishu dinglian*, "Daxue," 10a–b; Shi Fenglai, "Daxue," 27a.

162. *WLDC*, vol. 2, pp. 1022–24.

163. Ibid., p. 1355.

164. Ibid., p. 1357.

165. Wang Najian, "Daxue," 31b–32a.

166. Tang Binyin, "Daxue," *Shui'an Sishu mai*, 20b–21a.

167. See Chow, *Printing and Shishang Culture in Early Modern China*, ch. 4.

168. Zhu Mingliang, "Daxue," 40b.

169. Quoted in Ma Shiqi, *Sishu dingluan*, 1.10a–b.

170. Chen Dingsheng, 1.23b.

171. Tang Ru'e, "Daxue," 19a.

172. Guo Wei, *Sishu zhuyi baocang*, 5.1b.


## CHAPTER 5

1. Perkins.

2. Greenblatt and Gunn, pp. 1–3.

3. Bourdieu, *Distinction*, see ch. 4, esp., pp. 244–55.

4. Bourdieu, *The Field*, p. 60.

5. Ibid., part I, "The Field of Cultural Production."

6. Bourdieu, *Distinction*, p. 13.

7. See for example, Chih-p'ing Chou's study of Yuan Hongdao. Liu Xiang-guang's study of the impact of printing on the literary style of examinees during the Song dynasty is among a very few exceptions.

8. For a discussion of how the Yongle emperor co-opted the Cheng-Zhu *Daoxue* learning into the imperial ideology through the civil service examination, see Elman, "The Formation."

9. Jian Jinsong, pp. 19–21.

10. Li Tianyou, pp. 66–67. For the careers of the Three Yangs, see Mote and Twitchett, pp. 284–88, 306–8; for Yang Shiqi, see Dardess, pp. 143–44, 179.

11. Chih-p'ing Chou, p. 9.

12. Jian Jinsong, pp. 39–52; Chen Jianhua, pp. 135–36.

13. Wang Shizhen, *Yanshan tang bieji*, juan 81–83.

14. Chen Jianhua, pp. 135–36. For discussion of natives from Taihe who rose to high official positions in the early Ming, see Dardess, pp. 173–89.

15. Yang Shiqi, Wang Zhi, and some other high-ranking officials from Taihe served as chief examiners in the metropolitan examinations held in 1412, 1415, 1421, 1427, 1433, 1436, 1439, and 1454. Dardess, p. 187.

16. Ibid., pp. 2–3, 175–79, 186–89.

17. Jian Jinsong, pp. 115–19.

18. Quoted in Chen Jianhua, p. 135.

19. Jian Jinsong, pp. 52–58. The other five of the Seven Masters were Bian Gong, Kang Hai, Wang Jiusi, Wang Tingxiang, and Xu Zhenqing. Only Kang, Wang Jiusi, and Wang Tingxiang had been members of the Hanlin Academy. *MS*, pp. 7346–55, 7384–85.

20. Chih-p'ing Chou, pp. 5–9.

21. Jian Jinsong, pp. 219–20.

22. Quoted in Zheng Lihua, p. 58.

23. Biographical essay by Wang Shizhen; see Li Panlong, p. 721.

24. The other five masters were Liang Yuyu, Xu Zhongxing, Zong Chen, Xie Zhen, and Wu Guolun.

25. Wang Yunxi and Gu Yisheng, pp. 477–84.

26. Ibid., pp. 483–84; Chih-p'ing Chou, pp. 12–14.

27. Li Panlong, juan 18, "*Sanyun lieya xu.*"

28. Chen Jianhua, pp. 412–20.

29. Ibid., p. 248.

30. Guo Shaoyu, pp. 308–9.

31. Chih-p'ing Chou, pp. 14–15.

32. Ibid., pp. 15–17.

33. Chen Jianhua, pp. 247–48.

34. Jian, p. 22.

35. Chen Jianhua, p. 248; *MS*, pp. 5422, 7367–68, 7370–71.

36. The other title was a gazetteer of an academy. *ZGSBS*, pp. 202, 497, 573, 579–80.

37. One anthology of poetry was edited and commented on by Yang Shen in 1544, and another anthology was printed in two colors by Min Qiji in the mid-Wanli period. Two imprints of selections of his writings were also published in the same period, both by celebrated authors—Feng Fang and Tang Binyin. *MDBKZL*, 2.15a, 2.22a, 4.46b, 4.52a, 2.8b, 4.52a, 5.16a, 5.49b.

38. The only exception was perhaps a collection of anecdotes published in the early Qing. *TWGCSB*, pp. 260–61.

39. The other one is a gazetteer of Shenxi. *ZGSBS*, pp. 201, 584–75; *MGHF*, p. 219.

40. In addition to the Shenxi gazetteer, there is a collection of miscellaneous reflections and a treatise on rites. *TWGCSB*, p. 318.

41. Li Panlong, pp. 672–78.

42. Ibid., p. 675.

43. Ibid.

44. Ibid., p. 676.

45. Ibid., p. 674.

46. Ibid., pp. 673, 695, 709.

47. Wang published the writings of Li Panlong, *Cangming xiansheng ji*, in 1567. There are at least three extant copies of this book. See *MDBKZL*, 1.22b.

48. Li Panlong, pp. 673–74.

49. Ibid., p. 694.

50. See *ZGSBS*, pp. 437, 460–61, 473.

51. *MGHF*, p. 539.

52. Ai Nanying, 5.25b–26a.

53. *ZGSBS*, p. 628. That there are at least eight extant copies of this work attests to the large number of copies and reprints in the Ming. See *MDBKZL*, 1.39a.

54. Wang was widely read and had written numerous works, including anecdotes of the Ming and biographical essays. *ZGSBS*, pp. 109–10, 131, 444–45.

55. Li Mengyang (1472–1529) earned his degree at twenty-one, He Jinming (1483–1521) at nineteen, Kang Hai (1475–1540) at twenty-seven, both Bian

Gong (1476–1532) and Gu Lin (1476–1545) at twenty, Wang Tingxiang (1474–1544) at twenty-eight, and Xu Zhenqing (1479–1511) at twenty-six.

56. The average age of the Tang-Song Masters was lower because of two who attained *jinshi* at the incredible age of seventeen. Tang Shunzhi (1507–60) and Chen Shu (1507–40) earned their degrees at twenty-two, Wang Shenzhong (1509–59) and Zhao Shichun (1509–67) at seventeen, Li Kaixian (1502–68) and Lu Gao (1505–57) at twenty-four, and Wang Jiusi (1468–1551) at twenty-eight.

57. The figure for the Tang-Song Masters is higher because they, in general, lived almost two decades after the generation of the Latter Seven Masters. The number is also distorted by the two (Chen Shu and Wang Shenzhong) exceptionally young ages of graduation at the metropolitan level and the comparable life terms thereafter.

58. For publications by Wang Shizhen, see Jiang Gongtao, pp. 61–80. Tang Shunzhi was one of the earliest writers to whom were attributed many anthologies of essays and treatises (see Chapter 3). In *TWGCSB*, there are twenty titles with Tang as either the author or editor. Excluding five that are either collections or anthologies of his own essays, he was listed as the editor of three anthologies of poetry and commentator of two histories. The *ZGSBS* lists six additional titles, including anthologies of essays attributed to his credit as editor. *ZGSBS*, pp. 100, 146, 231, 444, 445, 520.

59. Of the forty-nine Ming imprints listed in TWGCSB, there is only one novel and one drama. See pp. 57–60.

60. Yuan Hongdao also shows no title in the category of drama and novels. But another catalog does list some drama with Yuan as the commentator. See *MGHF*, pp. 782, 785.

61. Titles in the category "Other" include a great variety of genres: one book on painting, his notes *Fengzhou biji*, a biography of Wang Xijue's daughter (the controversial *Tanyang zi*), his voluminous *Yanzhou shiliao*, a collection of anecdotes about Su Shi, and a collection of anecdotes of the Tang period. *MDBKZL*, 4.21a, 4.40b, 4.53b, 5.39b, 3.3b, 6.17a, 7.2a.

62. Ye Mengzhu, *Yueshi bian*, p. 292.

63. For discussion of the various measures, see Chaffee, p. 51.

64. For examples of cases when examiners identified candidates by means of style, see Ai Nanying, 2.5b. For a discussion of more methods of cheating in the Ming and early Qing, see Elman, *A Cultural History*, pp. 196–98.

65. For a general discussion of the history and style of "eight-legged essay," see Elman, *A Cutural History*, pp. 380–99.

66. Wang Shizhen, *Gufuyu ting zalu*, 2.18b. Selections of essays by successful examinees were printed as early as the late fifteenth century. But the se-

lected essays for publication represented a small fraction of the total number of examination essays. In 1587, the Ministry of Rites was instructed to select and publish essays of metropolitan graduates from the beginning of the Ming dynasty through the early Jiajing period. Gu Yanwu, *Rizhilu*, 16.10a, 16.21a.

67. Sun Chengze, *Chunming*, 41.8a–b.

68. Xu Xuemo, 7.8b–9a.

69. A survey of the examination records shows clearly that there were no strict rules governing the selection of essays by the graduates. Essays by graduates who ranked behind the top three could be included. The essays by the top three were not included as a matter of principle in these government records. To give just two examples, in the 1585 metropolitan examination, the essay on the Four Books by the third-ranked graduate was not published. Nor was his essay on the *Book of Changes*, his chosen Classic, included. Instead the essay on the Four Books by a ninth-ranked graduate was selected. In the Zhejiang provincial examination of 1582, the essay on the Four Books by the third-ranked graduate was listed before the first-ranked graduate. The essay on the Four Books by the second-ranked was not included. Only his essay on the *Record of Rites* was included. *MDDKL*, vol. 20, pp. 11135–16; vol. 19, pp. 10505–62.

70. Yuan Jixian, for example, was ranked third and had only two of his essays selected to be included in the official records. See Yuan Jixian, p. 399.

71. Qian Qianyi, *MZYXJ*, juan 45, p. 447.

72. Zhao Jishi, 7.7a–b.

73. Gui Youguang, 5.10a.

74. It is not clear whether the essays by provincial graduates selected by Gui were taken from *Records of the Provincial Examination* or from those that were not included. Gui Youguang, 5.10a.

75. That was the advice given to an examinee by the examination essay specialist Fang Yingxiang. Fang Yingxiang, *Qinglai ge*, 3.7a–b.

76. Li Ao, p. 334.

77. Yuang Hongdao, *Shabi tang xuji*, p. 653.

78. The wide availability of anthologies of examination essays is evident in the novel *Guwang yan*, 4.474.

79. Huang Zongxi, *Ming wenhai*, juan 307–14.

80. The meaning of the term "*chengwen*" has undergone some change. For Zhang Cai, the terms "*cheng*" and "*mo*" were used loosely to refer to the model essays written by both the examiners and the examinees. Xie Guozhen, *Ming-Qing zhiji*, p. 139.

81. According to Shen Shouzheng, the publishing of the examination essays on the Classics began in 1583. Yang Yi put the publishing of the essays on the

Classics in 1592. These different dates may not be contradictory. Shen's date probably referred to the publishing of essays on some of the Five Classics, not on all of the Classics. Yang Yi perhaps refers to the publishing of essays on all Five Classics. Shen Shouzheng, *Xuetang ji*, 5.9a–b. Gu Yanwu, *Rizhilu*, 16.9b–10a.

82. The publication of exercises written by examinees in preparation for the examinations was rare in the early decades of the sixteenth century. It was a late-sixteenth century development.

83. Xie Guozhen, *Ming-Qing zhiji*, p. 119.

84. Cha Shenxing, 1.67b–68a.

85. Ai Nanying, 3.28a. See also Chen Jitai, 2.6a–7a.

86. Cha Shenxing, 1.67b.

87. Ai Nanying, 1.17a.

88. Ibid., 6.5a; Zhang Pu, *Qiluzhai lunlue*, 1.28a–b.

89. This title was actually edited by Zhang. *MDBKZL*, 4.53a. The renowned critic Huang Ruheng had edited such an anthology in 1609–10, incorporating examination essays from the provincial and metropolitan examinations. See Huang Ruheng, *Yulin ji*, 7.24b–25a.

90. Zhang Pu, *Qiluzhai lunlue*, 2.32a.

91. These duplicated essays were also called *mojuan* (black papers) to be distinguished from the *zhujuan* (red papers), those with examiners' markings and comments. Later in 1585 the problem of changing essays during the process of transcription prompted the Ministry of Rites to recommend sending both the "black papers" and the "red papers" to the ministry. Verification of correct transcription would be conducted in case a problem of fraud was reported. The recommendation was approved, and local officials were required to send both the "black papers" and the "red papers" to the ministry three days after the results were posted. See Wang Shizhen, *Yanshan tang bieji*, 83.18b–19a.

92. Ye Mengzhu, *Yueshi bian*, p. 294.

93. Bourdieu, *Distinction*, p. 255.

94. Ibid., p. 254.

95. Cai Shishun, 2.16b.

96. Ai Nanying, 3.29a.

97. *Lü Mudan chuanqi*, 2.22a. It is commonly believed that this drama was written by Wen Tiren's brother Wen Yuren who was rejected by leaders of the Restoration Society.

98. Chen Jitai, 2.7a.

99. See Li Panlong; and Li Mengyang. It is certainly possible that they had written prefaces for such anthologies but were excluded by editors of their writings. But this possible exclusion through editing, however, also applied to later

collections of writings. That collections of writings by later writers contained large numbers of this type of preface can be taken as evidence for the change in practice.

100. There are ten prefaces written for anthologies of examination essays, mostly by individual writers, including Tang's own. Zhong Xing, *Yinxiu xuan ji*, juan 18.

101. Ai Nanying, juan 1–4.

102. Chen Jitai, juan 2–4.

103. Tang Binyin, *Shui'an gao*, juan 2–6.

104. Fang yingxiang, *Qinglai ge*, 5.20b–21a.

105. Huang Ruheng, *Yulin ji*, juan 7.

106. Ai Nanying, 3.28a–29b.

107. Qian Qianyi, *MZYXJ*, juan 45, p. 448.

108. Lu Shiyi, pp. 172–73. Very few of Zhou Zhong's writings survive. One rare example is a critical anthology he edited in 1623. See Zhou Zhong.

109. Because of Zhou Zhong's disloyalty, hardly any of his writings and publications survived. But there are still several extant books he had compiled and commented on. See *Zuishi ju pingci mingshan ye Huang Ming xiaolun*, *Chilu zhai lunlue*, and *Chilu zhai wenji*, in *TWGCSB*, p. 360.

110. Shen Shouzheng, *Xuetang ji*, "Huang Ming douchayuan siwu Wuhui Shen gong mubiao," 5b.

111. Shen Shouzheng, *Xuetang ji*, "Shen wuhui xiansheng zhuan," 2b–3b.

112. Ibid., 5.9a–b.

113. See the preface by Huang Ruheng, *Yulin ji*, 7.32b–33a.

114. Shen Shouzheng, *Xuetang ji*, 1a–7b.

115. Huang Ruheng, *Yulin ji*, 7.47b–48a.

116. Ibid., 26.37a.

117. See his preface to the 1609–10 anthology. Ibid., 7.24b–25a.

118. Ibid., 7.24b–25a, 30.21b, 30.23a–b, 7.43a–44b, 7.51b–52a, 7.55b–56b.

119. Ibid., 7.40b–41a, 7.45b–46a.

120. Huang Ruheng received essays by examinees from afar. They wanted their essays included in his anthology. Ibid., 7.11b–a–13a, 7.51b–52a.

121. Despite the wide popularity of their critical anthologies at the time, few survive. This was consistent with the low survival rate of anthologies of examination essays compared to other genres. An anthology of examination essays entitled *Huang Ming jinwen ding* by Ai Nanying is in the Library of Beijing University. *ZGSBS*, p. 481.

122. Tang Binyin, *Shui'an gao*, 4.25b–26a.

123. One was published in Nanjing by Zheng Siming's Kuibitang with a

preface dated 1620, the other in 1614 by a Jianyang publisher. *MDBKZL*, 6.35a; *MGHF*, pp. 588, 592. The other one was probably published in Suzhou. Qiu Zhaolin was listed as a (*canbu*) in an anthology of examination essays entitled *Huang Ming wenjin* (1620), published by Xiao Shaoqu of Sijiantang. Yuan Hong-dao was listed as the primary editor (*xuan*) and Chen Jiru as one who identified the themes (*biaozhi*), Zhang Nai as the reader, Wu Congxian the expositor (*jieshi*), and Chen Wanyan the "chief commentator" (*huiping*). *ZGSBS*, p. 480.

124. Tang Binyin, *Shui'an gao*, 4.25b–26a.

125. *ZGSBS*, p. 5.

126. Tang Xianzu, p. 1335.

127. Tang Binyin, *Shui'an gao*, 3.1a–b, *juan* 4. *SBSZ*, p. 207.

128. Tang Binyin, *Shui'an gao*, 4.30a, 6.25a–b.

129. *ZGSBS*, p. 651.

130. *SBSZ*, p. 295.

131. Chen Jitai, 2.6a–b; Ai Nanying, 1.9a–16b, 1.20a–25a.

132. Ai Nanying, 1.12a–14a.

133. Ibid., 2.4a.

134. Wu Yingqi mentioned that the critiques of Ai Nanying focused on upholding essays that conformed to Zhu Xi's commentary. See Wu's comment in ibid., 1.11a.

135. Ibid., 1.12a, 3.28a, 6.5a.

136. Ibid., 1.12a.

137. He co-edited an anthology of examination essays with Wen Qixiang. See ibid., 6.6b–7a.

138. Ibid., 1.18a.

139. Wu Yingqi, 15.8a.

140. Chen Jitai, 1.1b.

141. Huang Ruheng, *Yulin ji*, 7.24a.

142. Tang Binyin, Shui'an gao, 3.1a–b.

143. Qiu Zhaolin, 3.43a–b.

144. Ibid., 12.50b–51a.

145. Zhong Xing, *Yinxiuxuan ji*, pp. 306, 475.

146. Chen Jianhua, pp. 424–33; Guo Shaoyu, pp. 363–89. For the discussion of the Gong'an school, see Chaves; Chih-p'ing Chou.

147. Sun Chengze, *Chunming*, 41.8a.

148. Huang Zongxi, *Ming wenhai*, vol. 3, 309.3192.

149. Chen Jitai, 2.9a.

150. See for example, Zhong Xing, *Xuiyin xuan ji*; Sun Kuang, *Yuefeng xiansheng juye bian*; Tang Binyin, *Shui'an gao*, juan 4.

151. Qian Qianyi mentioned a Yuequan yin she formed in the Yuan dynasty. *MZYXJ*, 84.881–882.

152. Lu Shiyi, p. 171.

153. Li Tingji, *Li Wenjie ji*, vol. 4, 21.32b.

154. Zhong Xing, *Xiuyin xuan ji*, p. 289.

155. Sun Kuang, *Yuefeng xiansheng juye bian*, 2.21a–22b.

156. Hao Jing, *Shancao tang ji*, preface by Li Weizhen, 7a.

157. *Nan Wu jiuhua lu*, 23.1a–3b.

158. There are vivid details of how literary groups rehearsed the examination in novels and plays. See for example Ruan Dacheng, *Lu mudang quanqi*, 1.13b–26a.

159. Xie Guozhen, *Ming-Qing zhiji*, p. 124.

160. Zhang Pu, *Qilu zhai lunlue*, 2.46a–b.

161. Xie Guozhen, *Ming-Qing zhiji*, pp. 177–80.

162. Huang Zongxi, *HZXQJ*, vol. 1, p. 376.

163. Fang Yingxiang, *Qinglai ge*, 6.18b.

164. The book has a preface by Chen Jiru dated 1626. Given the fact that they were friends of Chen Jiru, this preface should be authentic. *ZGSBS*, p. 238.

165. This collection of the examination essays by Shen Youzai also has a preface by Chen Jiru. *ZGSBS*, p. 327. See Ai Nanying's letter to Wen. Ai Nanying, 6.6b.

166. Xie Gouzhen, pp. 181–84.

167. Zhang Pu, *Qiluzhai lunlue*, 3.7a–8b.

168. See the prefaces written by Ai Nanying for the Yingshe and Ping Yuantangshe. Ai Nanying, 3.5a–b, 4.50a.

169. Zhou Lianggong, p. 7.

170. Jin Demen, pp. 282–83.

171. They were Xia Yunyi, Chen Zilong, Xu Fuyuan, Zhou Lixun, Peng Bin, and Du Linzheng. Xie Guozhen, *Ming-Qing zhiji*, p. 153.

172. Du Dengchun, p. 971.

173. Xie Guozhen, *Ming-Qing zhiji*, pp. 119–120; Ōkubo, pp. 164–65.

174. Chen Jitai, 2, 7a–8b, 2.9b; Atwell, pp. 337–38.

175. Huang Jingxing; Yu Yingqiu, *Sishu Yijing tujie*.

176. Huang Zongxi, *Ming wenhai*, vol. 3, p. 3230.

177. Qian Qianyi, *MZYXJ*, 54.21a–22b. He was listed as a critic of a collection of examination essays by a Hangzhou native. *ZGSBS*, p. 327.

178. *MDBKZL*, 6.10b, 8.9b–10a. Dushufang also published a commentary on the Four Books entitled *Sishu mingwu kao*, attributed to Chen Yumo. See

*A Catalog of Chinese Books in the Osaka City Library*, p. 20. See Chen's letter to Wen. Chen Jiru, *Baishi qiao*, "Letters," 3.54a–b.

179. See Chang Kang-I Sun; *MDBKZL*, 7.21b–22a.

180. Chen Jitai, 2.8b–9a, 3.7b; *Qishan ji*, 1.11a–b.

181. Zheng Lihua, p. 162.

182. Sun Kuang, *Yuefeng xiansheng juye bian*, 2.21a.

183. Zhang Pu, *Qiluzhai lunlue*, *Qiluzhai ji*, 1.24a–b; preface by Zhang Cai, in Chen Jitai.

184. Ai Nanying, 4.53a, 6.10a, 4.61b, 4.53a.

185. Zhang Pu, *Qiluzhai lunlue*, 1.24b.

186. Ibid., 1.24a–25b.

187. Ibid.

188. See the various prefaces by Zhang. Ibid., juan 1.

189. Ibid., 1.36a–37a, 2.1a–5a, 2.24a–25a.

190. Yang Yi and Gu Menglin coedited an anthology of essays on historical subjects. Zhang Pu edited an anthology of essays on current affairs and government policies. Ibid., 2.43a–45b, 2.36a–37a.

191. Ibid., 2.24a–25a, 5.21a–22a, 5.29a–b, 5.31a–b, 5.33a–34a.

192. Ibid., 2.24a–25a.

193. Zhang Pu referred to that anthology in his preface of 1618. Zhang Pu, Ibid., 2.29b.

194. Ai Nanying, 5.1a–2b.

195. Ibid., 5.1a–8a, 10a–12b.

196. Ibid., 6.10a.

197. Lu Shiyi, p. 177.

198. Ai Nanying, 1.9b–10a. For the two anthologies edited by Zhang Pu, see *Qiluzhai lunlue*, 2.26a–31a.

199. Wen published books for Chen Jiru. Chen Jiru, *Baishi qiao*, p. 498.

200. Ai Nanying, 6.6b–7a.

201. Xie Guozhen, *Ming-Qing zhiji*, p. 123.

202. Ibid.; Atwell, pp. 339–40.

203. Zhang Pu, *Qiluzhai lunlue*, 1.32a–35a.

204. Xie Guozhen, *Ming-Qing zhiji*, p. 130.

205. Lu Shiyi, p. 181.

206. Xie Guozhen, *Ming-Qing zhiji*, pp. 126–27.

207. Zhu Yizun, *Zhu Zhuzhai shihua*, p. 165.

208. Dennerline, p. 34; Elman, *A Cultural History*, pp. 210–11.

209. Lu Shiyi, p. 205

210. Zhou Zhong became *jinshi* in 1639; Chen Jitai became a *jinshi* in 1634 after many frustrating attempts.

211. Zhang Pu, *Qilu zhai ji*, 3.3a–4a.

212. Lu Shiyi, pp. 181–204.

213. Du Dengchun, p. 969.

214. Lu Shiyi, p. 205.

215. Zhu Xizu, p. 20.

216. Lu Shiyi, p. 208.

217. Later Wen Tiren criticized Li for his incompetence in evaluating examination of the *shengyuan*. Ibid., p. 216.

218. Lü Liuliang, 5.17a–b.

219. Huang Zongxi, *Sijiu lu* in *HZXQJ*, vol. 1, pp. 358–59; Xie Guozhen, *Ming-Qing zhiji*, pp. 158–62.

220. Chen Yidian, 1.32b.

221. Ai Nanying, 1.1a–8b.

222. Huang Zongxi, *HZXQJ*, p. 358–59.

223. *MQJS*, p. 502.

224. Zhang Zilie, *Jishan wenji*, 11.23a.

225. Ibid., 11.24a–26a.

226. Wu Yingji, 17.11a–b.

227. The 1636 preface to *Sishu zhushu daquan he zuan*, attributed to Zhang Pu, was not written for Zhang Zilie's *Sishu daquan bian* (A critique of the complete compendium of the Four Books). Zhang himself mentioned several critics who had written prefaces for his book: Wu Yingji, Fang Yizhi, and Shen Shoumin. Zhang Zilie, *Jishan Wenji*, 11.8b. It was apparently inserted either by the publisher or Zhang Zilie himself to enhance its credibility. Zhang Zilie, *Sishu daquan bian*.

228. Zhang Zilie, *Sishu daquan bian*, 10a–b.

229. "Gong qing zixing Sishu daquan bian diyi jie" (The First public request to print *A Critique of the Complete Compendium of the Four Books*) in Zhang Zilie, *Sishu daquan bian*.

230. See the list of documents in the "Account of the reprinting of the *Sishu daquan bian*," in Zhang Zilie, *Sishu daquan bian*.

231. Zhang Zilie, *Jishan wenji*, 11.8a–b.

232. "Gong qing juti panxing sishu daquan bian dier jie," *Complete Compendium of the Four Books* in Zhang Zilie, *Sishu daquan bian*.

233. Zhang Zilie, *Jishan wenji*, 11.8a–9a; *Sishu daquan bian*, 36a–39a.

234. Zhang Zilie, "Great Learning," *Sishu daquan bian*, 7b–8a.

235. Ibid., 14a–b.

236. Ibid., 6a–b.

237. In 1629 a student at the Imperial Academy submitted a commentary on the *Classic of Filial Piety* to the government and it was approved for official publication. "Gong qing juti panxing sishu daquan bian dier jie" (Second public request to promulgate *A Critique of the Complete Compendium of the Four Books*) in Zhang Zilie, *Sishu daquan bian*. In 1630, Zhang Yunluan, a *shenyuan* from Wuxi submitted his own commentary for review requesting it be adopted as the standard commentary for examinees. See Zhang Yunluan, preface, *Sishu jingzheng lu* (Record of correcting the *Four Books* based on the Classics).

## CONCLUSION

1. David Johnson has long pointed out that the literati was not a homogenous group. See Johnson, pp. 53–61.

2. Febvre and Martin, pp. 319–32; Benedict Anderson emphasizes in particular the impact of printing on the rise of national vernacular and national consciousness. Anderson, ch. 3.

3. Chow, *Printing and Shishang Culture*.

4. Elizabeth Eisenstein refers to the "significant role played by printed illustration in anatomy texts" and "how illustrating textbooks helped to guide scientific observation." Eisenstein, pp. 266–67, 485–86; Febvre and Martin, pp. 47–49, 277–78. See also the chapters by Tedeschi and Camille in Hindman. For the evidence of the continued importance of woodcut and block printing, see also Van Der Stock's study of image printing in Antwerp and the various studies of printing in the Renaissance in Tyson and Wagonheim. For the history of woodblock painting in fifteenth-century Europe, see Hind.

5. Eisenstein refers to the publishers' extensive practice of recycling illustrations and images cut on woodblocks. Eisenstein, pp. 54, 258–59.

6. Febvre and Martin, p. 92–93.

7. The explanation given in *The Coming of the Book* regarding China's failure to use movable types suffers from a lack of knowledge of the development of commercial publishing in the early modern period. Febvre and Martin, pp. 75–76.

8. This does not mean that there was no illegal publishing activities as revealed in Robert Darnton's study of the literary underground on Grub Street in eighteenth-century France. See Darnton, *The Literary Underground*.

9. Febvre and Martin, pp. 216–18.

10. Ibid., pp. 224–33; Clair, pp. 219–22.

11. Subscription was first launched in England in 1617 and the Netherlands in 1660. As a method for raising capital, it had obvious limitations. The cases in Venice of the eighteenth century suggest that subscribers were confident in successful or known works. Reprints were numerous among subscription publications. Waquet, pp. 78–83.

12. For the study of books imported into Japan, see Oba.

13. This does not mean that European printing was not capable of making adjustments to fluctuating demands. The seventeenth century, for example, witnessed in France the development of sharing printing presses by publishing houses. The gradual separation of printing and publishing enabled publishing offices to divide printing jobs among printing presses operated by different printers in response to tight schedules and increasing demands. Clair, p. 298.

14. Ibid., p. 295.

15. Febvre and Martin, pp. 93–4; This practice began early in the fifteenth century in Europe, see Tedeschi, 45–46.

16. The Tridentine index promulgated in 1654 was widely circulated. The 1596 index was promulgated by Pope Clement VIII. Clair, p. 158.

17. Ibid., p. 168. My comparison focuses on the presence of institutional censorship, not the actual effect of censorship, which is a topic of debate. According to Febvre and Martin, those who were persecuted in France were colporteurs, or occasionally small booksellers. Those "great printing dynasties that dominated the trade" had enough protection and resources to keep out of trouble. Febvre and Martin, pp. 310–12. Annabel Patterson, however, has argued that while a few were able to protect themselves from punishment, "if one reads the annals of censorship, this list rapidly becomes so long as to put their exceptionality in question." The list refers to the small number of high-profile cases of censorship, such as those of Bruno, Galileo, Sir John Hayward, and William Prynne. Patterson, pp. 29–30.

18. Febvre and Martin, pp. 287–95; Eisenstein, ch. 4.

19. See Andersson.

20. Clair, p. 274.

21. Roche, p. 3.

22. Clair, p. 291. For an analysis of the French Revolution from the perspective of the printers, publishers, and writers, who resented the restrictions and abuses of the literary system of the old regime, see Hesse.

23. Ibid.

24. France did not establish its own printing office, the Imprierir Royale, until 1631. Clair, p. 299.

25. Queen Mary granted a charter to printers and booksellers to establish

the Stationers' Company in 1557. But concern about the output of seditious pamphlets resulted in the Licensing Act of 1586, which limited the number of presses in London. Febvre and Martin, pp. 191–92.

26. Ibid.

27. Belanger, p. 6.

28. Since printing was restricted to the university towns of Oxford and Cambridge, few could earn a good living by exclusively writing literary works. Ibid., pp. 6, 22.

29. Davis, p. 139.

30. An example is the banning of the *Water Margin* after the outbreak of rebellions in the north. See Chow, *Printing and Shishang Culture*, ch. 4. There was no systematic censorship and concerted effort to police the publishing world until the eighteenth century. See Goodrich; and Guy.

31. For the issue of political transparency as it pertained to the demand for releasing memorials submitted to the emperor, see Chow, *Printing and Shishang Culture*, ch. 6.

32. "Chronotype" is a term Bakhtin borrows from mathematics in his attempt to develop a poetics of the novel. See "Forms of Time and of the Chronotype in the Novel," in Bakhtin, pp. 84–258.

# Bibliography

Ai Nanying 艾南英. *Tianyong zi ji* 天傭子集. Reprint of a Kangxi edition. Taibei: Yiwen yinshu guan, 1980.

Anderson, Benedict. *Imagined Communities: Reflections on the Origin and Spread of Nationalism.* London: Verso, 1991.

Andersson, Christiane. "Popular Imagery in German Reformation Broadsheets." In Gerald P. Tyson and Sylvia S. Wagonheim, eds., *Print and Culture in the Renaissance: Essays on the Advent of Printing in Europe.* Newark: University of Delaware Press, 1986.

Ariki, Kengo. "Confucianism and Buddhism in the Late Ming." In William Theodore de Bary, ed., *The Unfolding of Neo-Confucianism.* New York: Columbia University Press, 1975.

Armstrong, Elizabeth. *Before Copyright: The French Book Privilege System, 1498–1526.* Cambridge: Cambridge University Press, 1990.

Avis, Frederick C. "Miscellaneous Costs in Sixteenth-Century English Printing." *Gutenberg-Jahrbuch* (1976): 306–10.

Bakhtin, M. Mikail. *Dialogic Imagination: Four Essays.* Trans. by Caryl Emerson and Michael Holquist. Austin: University of Texas Press, 1981.

Barnard, John. "Some Features of the Stationers' Company and Its Stock in 1676/7." *Publishing History* 336 (1994): 38.

Barnard, John, and Maureen Bell. "The Inventory of Henry Bynneman (1583): A Preliminary Survey." *Publishing History* 29 (1991):5–46.

Barr, Alan. "Four Schoolmasters: Educational Issues in Li Hai-kuan's Lamp at the Crossroads." In Benjamin A. Elman and Alexander Woodside, eds. *Education and Society in Late Imperial China, 1600–1900,* pp. 50–75. Berkeley: University of California Press, 1994.

Beattie, Hilary J. *Land and Lineage in China: A Study of T'ung-ch'eng County, Anhwei in the Ming and Ch'ing Dynasties.* Cambridge: Cambridge University Press, 1979.

Belanger, Terry. "Publishers and Writers in Eighteenth-century England." In Isabel Rivers, ed., *Books and Their Readers in Eighteenth-Century England,* pp. 5–26. New York: St. Martin's Press, 1982.

Bell, Catherine. "'A Precious Raft to Save the World': The Interaction of Scriptural Traditions and Printing in a Chinese Morality Book." *Late Imperial China* 17, no. 1 (1996): 158–200.

———. "Printing and Religion in China: Some Evidence from the Taishang Ganying Bian." In *Journal of Chinese Religion* 20 (1992): 173–86.

Berling, Judith. *The Syncretic Religion of Lin Chao'en.* New York: Columbia University Press, 1980.

Black, Jeremy. *The English Press in the Eighteenth Century.* London: Croom Helm, 1987.

Blaut, J. M. *The Colonizer's Model of the World: Geographical Diffusionism and Eurocentric History.* New York: The Guilford Press, 1993.

Bloom, Irene, trans. and ed. *Knowledge Painfully Acquired: the K'un-chih chi by Lo Ch'in-shun.* New York: Columbia University Press, 1987.

Bol, Peter. *"This Culture of Ours": Intellectual Transitions in T'ang and Sung China.* Stanford: Stanford University Press, 1992.

Bourdieu, Pierre. *The Field of Cultural Production: Essays on Art and Literature.* Ed. Randal Johnson. New York: Columbia University Press, 1993.

———. *Distinction: A Social Critique of the Judgment of Taste.* Trans. Richard Nice. Cambridge, Mass.: Harvard University Press, 1984.

———. *Language and Symbolic Power.* Ed. John B. Thompson and trans. Gino Raymond and Matthew Adamson. Cambridge, Mass.: Harvard University Press, 1991.

———. *Outline of a Theory of Practice.* New York: University of Cambridge Press, 1977.

Bourdieu, Pierre, and Loïc J. D. Wacquant. *An Invitation to Reflexive Sociology.* Chicago: University of Chicago Press, 1992.

Brandauer, Frederick P. "The Emperor and the Star Spirits: A Mythological Reading of the Shuihu chuan." In idem and Chün-chieh Huang, eds., *Imperial Rulership and Cultural Change in Traditional China*, pp. 206–29. Seattle: University of Washington Press, 1994.

Brokaw, Cynthia. "The Commercial Publishing in Late Imperial China: The Zou and Ma Family Businesses of Sibao." *Late Imperial China* 17, no. 1 (1996).

———. *The Ledgers of Merit and Demerit: Social Change and Moral Order in Late Imperial China.* Princeton: Princeton University Press, 1991.

———. "Reading the Bestsellers from the Nineteenth Century: The Publications of Sibao." In idem and Kai-wing Chow, eds., *Printing and Book Culture in Late Imperial China.* Berkeley: University of California, forthcoming.

———, and Kai-wing Chow, eds. *Printing and Book Culture in Late Imperial China*. Berkeley: University of California Press, forthcoming.

Brook, Timothy. "Communication and Commerce." In Denis Twitchett and Frederick W. Mote, eds., *The Cambridge History of China, vol. 8. The Ming Dynasty, 1368–1644, Part 2*, pp. 579–707. Cambridge: Cambridge University Press, 1998.

———. *The Confusion of Pleasure: Commerce and Culture in Ming China*. Berkeley: University of California Press, 1998.

———. "Edifying Knowledge: The Building of School Libraries in Ming China." *Late Imperial China* 17, no. 1 (1996): 93–119.

———. *Geographical Sources of Ming-Qing History*. Ann Arbor: Center for Chinese Studies, University of Michigan, 1988.

Bühler, Curt. *The Fifteenth Century Book: The Scribes, the Printers, the Decorations*. Philadelphia: University of Pennsylvania Press, 1960.

Burkus-Chasson, Anne. "Elegant of Common Chen Hongshou's Birthday Presentation Pictures and his Professional Status." *Art Bulletin* 26, no. 2 (1994): 279–300.

Bussotti, Michela. "General Survey of the Latest Studies in Western Languages on the History of Publishing in China." *Revue bibliographique de sinologie* (1998): 53–68.

Byrd, Cecil K. *Early Printing in the Straits Settlements, 1806–1858*. Singapore: Singapore National Library, 1970.

Cahill, James. "Huang Shan Paintings as Pilgrimage Pictures." In Susan Naquin and Chun-fang Yu, eds., *Pilgrims and Sacred Sites in China*. Berkeley: University of California Press, 1992.

Cai Guoliang 蔡國梁. *Jin Ping Mei kaozheng yu janjiu* 金瓶梅考證與研究. Xi'an: Renmin chubanshe, 1984.

Cai Qing 蔡清. *Sishu mengyin* 四書蒙引. *SKQS*, vol. 206.

Cai Shishun 蔡士順. *Tongshi shanglun lu* 同時賞論錄. Preface 1633. *BJTS*, vol. 120.

Cao Zhi 曹之. *Zhongguo yinshuashu di qiyuan* 中國印刷術的起源. Wuchang: Wuhan daxue chubanshe, 1994.

Carlitz, Catherine. "Printing as Performance: Literati Playwright-Publishers of the Late Ming." In Cynthia Brokaw, ed., *Printing and Book Culture in Late Imperial China*. Berkeley: University of California Press, forthcoming.

———. "The Social Uses of Female Virtue in Late Ming Editions of Lienü Zhuan." *Late Imperial China* 12, no. 2 (1991): 117–48.

Carter, Thomas Francis. *The Invention of Printing in China and Its Spread*

*Westward*. Rev. L. Carrington Goodrich. New York: The Ronald Press Co., 1955.

Censer, Jack R., and Jeremy D. Popkin, eds. *Press and Politics in Pre-Revolutionary France*. Berkeley: University of California Press, 1987.

Chaffee, John. *The Thorny Gate of Learning in Sung China*. Albany: State University of New York Press, 1995.

Chai E 柴萼. *Fantian lu conglu* 梵天廬叢錄. Shanghai: Zhonghua shuju, 1925.

Chakrabarty, Dipesh. *Provincializing Europe: Postcolonial Thought and Historical Difference*. Princeton: Princeton University Press, 2000.

Chang, Kang-I Sun. *The Late Ming Poet Ch'en Tzu-lung: Crises of Love and Loyalty*. New Haven: Yale University Press, 1991.

———. "Ming and Qing Anthologies of Women's Poetry." In Ellen Widmer and idem, eds., *Writing Women in Late Imperial China*. Stanford: Stanford University Press, 1997.

Chartier, Roger. *The Cultural Origins of the French Revolution*. Trans. Lydia G. Cochrane. Durham, N.C.: Duke University Press, 1991.

———. *The Cutural Uses of Print in Early Modern France*. Trans. Lydia G. Cochrane. Princeton: Princeton University Press, 1987.

———. "Gutenberg Revisited from the East." *Late Imperial China* 17, no. 1 (1996): 1–9.

———. *On the Edge of the Cliff: History, Language, and Practices*. Trans. Lydia G. Cochrane. Baltimore: Johns Hopkins University Press, 1997.

———. "Texts, Printing, Readings." In Lynn Hunt, ed., *The New Cultural History*. Berkeley: University of California Press, 1989.

Chaves, Jonathan. "The Expression of Self in the Kung-an School: Non-Romantic Individualism." In Robert Hegel and Richard C. Hessney, eds., *Expressions of Self in Chinese Literature*. Pp. 123–50. New York: Columbia University Press, 1985.

Chen Baoliang 陳寶良. "Mingdai di she yu hui" 明代的社與會. *Lishi yangjiu* 歷史研究 no. 5 (1991): 140–55.

Chen Dachuan 陳大川. *Zhongguo zaozhi shu shengshuai shi* 中國造紙術盛衰史. Taibei: Zhongwai chubanshe, 1970.

Chen Hongshou 陳洪綬. *Chen Hongshou ji* 陳洪綬集. Hangzhou: Zhejiang guji chubanshe, 1994.

Chen Jianhua 陳建華. *Zhongguo Jiang-Zhe diqu shisi zhi shiqi shiji shehui yishi yu wenxue* 中國江浙地區十四至十七世紀社會意識與文學. Shanghai: Xuelin chubanshe, 1992.

Chen Jiru 陳繼儒. *Baishi qiao zhen gao* 白石樵真稿. 1636. SKJHS, vol. 66.

———. *Chen Meigong quanji* 陳眉公全集. Shanghai: Dadao shuju, 1935.

———. *Meigong xiansheng wanxiang tang xiaopin* 眉公先生晚香堂小品. Ming edition (HYC).

———. *Meigong zazhu* 眉公雜著. 4 vols. Taibei: Weiwen chubanshe, 1977.

———. *Wanxiang tang ji* 晚香堂集. Chongzhen edition. *SKJHS*, vol. 66.

———. *Yimin zhuan* 逸民傳. 1603. (BDT).

Chen Jitai 陳際泰. *Jiwu ji* 己吾集. Taibei: Weiwen shuju, 1977.

Chen Keng 陳鏗. "Cong Xingshi yinyuan kan Ming Qing zhiji di difang shishen" 從醒世姻緣看明清之際的地方士紳. *Ming-Qing Shi* 明清史, no. 12 (1984): 15–23.

Chen Menglian 陳夢蓮. *Meigong fujun nianpu* 眉公府君年譜. *BJTSGC*, vol. 53.

*Chen Pi Lieguo zhizhuan* 陳批列國志傳. *GBXSCK*, ser. 40, vols. 1–4. (Original in the National Archives of Japan.)

Chen Qinghao 陳慶浩 and Wang Qiugui 王秋桂, eds. *Siwuxie huibo* 思無邪匯寶. Taibei: Taiwan Daying baike, 1995.

Chen Que 陳確. *Chen Que ji* 陳確集. Beijing: Zhonghua shuju, 1979.

Chen Renxi. *Ming wen qi shang* 明文奇賞. Ming edition (SKY).

———. *Wumengyuan ji* 無夢園集. *SKJHS*, vol. 60.

Chen Tianding 陳天定. *Huiyan shanfang shuoshu* 慧眼山房説書 (HYX).

Chen Wanyi 陳萬益. *Wan Ming Xiaopin yu Ming ji wenren shenghuo* 晚明小品與明季文人生活. Taibei: Da'an chubanshe, 1988.

Chen Xuewen 陳學文. *Ming Qing shehui jingji shi yanjiu* 明清社會經濟史研究. Taibei: Daohe chubanshe, 1991.

Chen Yidian 陳懿典. *Chen Xueshi xiansheng ji* 陳學士先生集 (HYX).

Chen Zilong 陳子龍. *Chen Zhongyu gong quanji* 陳忠裕公全集. *QKZQJ*, vol. 30.

———. *Huang Ming Jingshi wen bian* 皇明經世文編. Beijing: Zhonghua shuju, 1962.

———. *Shuoshu wenjian* 説書文箋. Ming edition, preface 1637 (HYX).

Chen Zushou 陳組綬. *Sishu fumo* 四書副墨 (HYX).

Cheng Renqing 程任卿. *Sijuan quanshu* 絲絹全書. Reprint of a Wanli edition. *BJTS*, vol. 60.

Cheng, Yu-ying. "The Ethics of the Sphere Below (*Hsia*): The Life and Thought of Ho Hsin-yin." *Chinese Studies* 11, no. 1 (1993): 49–101.

———. *Wan Ming bei yiwang di sixiangjia: Luo Rufang shiwen shiji biannian* 晚明被遺忘的思想家：羅汝芳詩文事跡編年. Taibei: Guangwen shuju, 1995.

Cherniak, Susan. "Book Culture and Textual Transmission in Sung China." *Harvard Journal of Asiatic Studies* 54, no. 1 (1994): 5–125.

Chia, Lucille. "Of Three Mountains Street: The Commercial Publishers of Ming Nanjing." In Cynthia Brokaw and Kai-wing Chow, eds., *Printing and Book*

*Culture in Late Imperial China.* Berkeley: University of California Press, forthcoming.

————. "Printing for Profit: The Commercial Printers in Jianyang, Fujian (Song-Ming)." Ph.D. diss., Columbia University, 1996.

Ch'ien, Edward T. *Chiao Hung and the Restructuring of Neo-Confucianism in the Late Ming.* New York: Columbia University Press, 1986.

Chou, Chih-p'ing. *Yuan Hung-tao and the Kung-an School.* New York: Cambridge University Press, 1988.

Chow, Kai-wing. "Discourse, Examinations, and Local Elites: The Invention of the T'ung-ch'eng School in Ch'ing China." In Benjamin A. Elman and Alexander Woodside, eds., *Society and Education in Late Imperial China.* Berkeley: University of California Press, 1994.

————. (Zhou Qirong 周啓榮). "Mingmo yinshua yu Huizhou difang wenhua" 明末印刷與徽州地方文化 (Printing and Huizhou local culture in the late Ming). In Zhou Shaoquan 周紹泉 and Zhao Huafu 趙華富, eds., *Guoji Huixue xueshu taolun hui lunwenji* 國際徽學學術討論會論文集, pp. 299–305. Hefei: Anhui daxue chubanshe, 1995.

————. *Printing and Shishang Culture in Early Modern China.* Stanford: Stanford University Press, forthcoming.

————. *The Rise of Confucian Ritualism: Classics, Ethics, and Lineage Discourse in Late Imperial China.* Stanford: Stanford University Press, 1994.

————. "Writing for Success: Printing, Examinations, and Intellectual Change in Late Ming China." *Late Imperial China* 17, no. 1 (1996): 120–157.

Chu, Hung-lam. "The Debate over Recognition of Wang Yang-ming." *HJAS* 48, no. 1 (1988): 47–70.

Clair, Collin. *A History of European Printing.* London: Academic Press, 1976.

Clunas, Craig. *Pictures and Visuality in Early Modern China.* Princeton: Princeton University Press, 1997.

————. *Superfluous Things: Material Culture and Social Status in Early Modern China.* Urbana and Chicago: University of Illinois Press, 1991.

*Cu Hulu* 醋葫蘆. *GBXSCK*, ser. 8.

Cui Wenyin 崔文印. "Yuan Wuya kanben Shuihu Li Zhi ping bianwei" 袁無涯刊本水滸李贄評辨偽. *Zhonghua wenshi luncong* 中華文史論叢, no. 2 (1980): 311–17.

Dardess, John. *A Ming Society: T'aiho County, Kiangsi, in the Fourteenth to Seventeenth Centuries.* Berkeley: University of California Press, 1996.

Darnton, Robert. "History of Reading." In Peter Burke, eds., *New Perspectives on Historical Writing.* University Park: Pennsylvania State University Press, 1992.

————. *The Literary Underground of the Old Regime.* Cambridge, Mass.: Harvard University Press, 1982.

————. "What Is the History of the Book?" In idem, *The Kiss of the Lamourette: Reflections in Cultural History.* New York: W. W. Norton, 1990.

Davis, Lennard J. *Factual Fictions: The Origins of the English Novel.* Philadelphia: University of Pennsylvania Press, 1983.

de Bary, William Theodore. "Individualism and Humanitarianism in Late Ming Thought." In idem, ed., *Self and Society in Ming Thought*, pp. 188–247. New York: Columbia University Press, 1970.

————. *The Message of the Mind in Neo-Confucianism.* New York: Columbia University Press, 1989.

————. *Self and Society in Ming Thought.* New York: Columbia University Press, 1970.

De Certeau, Michel. *The Practice of Everyday Life.* Trans. Steven Rendall. Berkeley: University of California Press, 1984.

————. *The Writing of History.* Trans. Tom Conley. New York: Columbia University Press, 1988.

De Weerdt, Hilde. "Aspects of Song Intellectual Life: A Preliminary Inquiry into some Southern Song Encyclopedias." *Papers on Chinese History* (Harvard University) vol. 3 (spring 1994): 1–27.

Dennerline, Jerry. *The Chia-ting Loyalists: Confucian Leadership and Social Change in Seventeenth-Century China.* New Haven: Yale University Press, 1981.

Ding Shen 丁申. *Wulin cangshu lu* 武林藏書錄. *CSJCXB*, vol. 3.

Dong Qichang 董其昌. *Rongtai ji* 容臺集. 4 vols. Taibei: Guoli zhongyang tushuguan, 1968.

————. *Xuanshang zhai shumu* 玄賞齋書目. *MDSMTB*, vol. 2.

Du Dengchun 杜登春. *Sheshi shimo* 社事始末. *ZDCS*, vol. 2.

Du Xinfu 杜信孚. *Mingdai banke zonglu* 明代版刻綜錄. Yangzhou: Jiangsu guangling guzhi keyinshe, 1983.

————. "Mingmo chuban jianshi xiaokao" 明末出版簡史小考. *Chubanshi yanjiu* 出版史研究, no. 3 (1995): 173–80.

Duara, Prasenjit. *Rescuing History from the Nation: Questioning Narratives of Modern China.* Chicago: University of Chicago Press, 1995.

Ebrey, Patricia. *Confucianism and Family Rituals in Imperial China, 1400–1900.* Berkeley: University of California Press, 1991.

Edgren, Soren. "Southern Song Printing at Hangzhou." In *Museum of Far East Antiques Bulletin*, no. 61 (1989).

Eisenstein, Elizabeth. *The Printing Press as an Agent of Change: Communications and Cultural Transformations in Early-Modern Europe.* London: Cambridge University Press, 1979.

Elman, Benjamin A. *Classicism, Politics, and Kinship: The Ch'ang-chou School of New Text Confucianism in Late Imperial China.* Berkeley: University of California Press, 1990.

———. *A Cultural History of Civil Examinations in Late Imperial China.* Berkeley: University of California Press, 2000.

———. "The Formation of 'Dao Learning' as Imperial Ideology During the Early Ming Dynasty." In Theodore Huters, Bin Wong, and Pauline Yu, eds., *Culture and State in Chinese Society: Conventions, Accommodations, and Critiques.* Stanford: Stanford University Press, 1997.

———. *From Philosophy to Philology: Intellectual and Social Aspects of Change in Late Imperial China.* Cambridge, Mass.: Harvard University Press, 1984.

———. "Social, Political, and Cultural Reproduction in Civil Service Examination." *JAS* 50, no. 1 (1991): 7–28.

——— and Alexander Woodside, eds. *Education and Society in Late Imperial China, 1600–1900.* Berkeley: University of California Press, 1994.

*Er xu Jinling suoshi* 二續金陵瑣事. *BJXSDG*, ser. 16, vol. 4.

Fan Hanwei 范韓魏. *Fanshi ji sishi shi* 范氏記私史事. *ZGYSJC*, vol. 39.

Fan Jinmin 范金民. "Ming Qing shiqi huoyue yu Suzhou di weidi shangren" 明清時期活躍與蘇州的外地商人. *Zhongguo shehui jingjishi yanjiu* 中國社會經濟史研究, no. 4 (1989): 39–42.

Fan Lian 范濂. *Yunjian jumu chao* 雲間據目抄. *BJXSDG*, ser. 22. vol. 5.

Fang Bao 方苞. *Fang Bao ji* 方苞集. Shanghai: Guji chubanshe, 1983.

Fang Hao 方豪. "Wanli nianjian zhi gezhong jiage" 萬曆年間之各種價格. *Shihuo yuekan* 食貨月刊, new series, vol. 2, no.1 (1972): 18–20.

Fang Hanqi 方漢奇, ed. *Zhongguo xinwen shiye tongshi* 中國新聞事業通史. Vol. 1. Beijing: Zhongguo Renmin Daxue chubanshe, 1991.

Fang Xing 方行. *Ming Qing chubanye di ziben zhuyi mengya wenti qiantan* 明清出版業的資本主義萌芽淺談. *Pinghuai xuekan* 平淮學刊, no. 1 (1985): 159–65.

Fang Yingxiang 方應祥. *Qinglai ge chuji* 青來閣初集. *SKJHS*, vol. 40.

———. *Xinjuan Sishu xingren yu* 新鐫四書醒人語. Ming edition, preface 1618 (HYX).

Febvre, Lucien, and Henri-Jean Martin. *The Coming of the Book.* London: Verso, 1997.

Feng Menglong 馮夢龍. *Chunqiu hengku* 春秋衡庫. *FMLQJ*, vols. 3–4.

———. *Feng Menglong quanji* 馮夢龍全集. *FMLQJ*. 43 vols. Shanghai: Guji chubanshe, 1993.

———. *Gua zhi'er* 掛枝兒. *FMLQJ*, vol. 42.

———. *Jiaxin jishi* 甲辛紀事. *FMLQJ*, vol. 13.

———. *Linjing zhiyue* 麟經指月. *FMLQJ*, vols. 1–2.

———. *Shange* 山歌. *FMLQJ*, vol. 42.

———. *Xiaofu* 笑府. *FMLQJ*, vol. 41.

———. *Xin Pingyao zhuan* 新平妖傳. *FMLQJ*, vol. 29.

———. *Xinke Gangjian tongyi* 新刻綱鑒統一. *FMLQJ*, vols. 8-12.

———. *Xingshi hengyan* 醒世恆言. *GBXSCK*, ser. 30.

———. *Xingshi tongyan* 醒世通言. *GBXSCK*, ser. 32.

———. *Zhe mei jian* 折梅箋. *FMLQJ*, vol. 43.

Feng Mengzhen 馮夢禎. *Kuaixue tang ji* 快雪堂集. Ming edition, preface 1616 (SKJH).

Frank, Andre Gunder. *ReOrient: Global Economy in the Asian Age.* Berkeley: University of California Press, 1998.

Foucault, Michel. *The Care of the Self, The History of Sexuality.* Vol. 3. Trans. Rober Hurley. New York: Vintage Books, 1986.

Fu Shan 傅山. *Shuang hongkan ji* 霜紅龕集. Taibei: Hanhua wenhua, 1971.

Fu Yiling 傅衣凌. *Mingdai jiangnan shimin jingji shitian* 明代江南市民經濟試探. Taibei: Gufeng chubanshe, 1986.

———. *Ming-Qing shehui jingji shi lunwen ji* 明清社會經濟史論文集. Beijing: Renmin chubanshe, 1982.

Gallagher, Louis J., trans. *China in the Sixteenth Century: The Journals of Matthew Ricci: 1583–1610.* New York: Random House, 1953.

Gao Ru 高儒. *Baichuan shuzhi* 百川書目. *MDSMTB*.

Ge Gongzhen 戈公振. *Zhongguo bao xue shi* 中國報學史. Hong Kong: Taiping shuju, 1964.

Geiss, James. "The Chia-ching reign, 1522–1566." In Denis Twitchett and Frederick W. Mote, eds., *The Cambridge History of China, vol. 7. The Ming Dynasty, 1368–1644, pt. 1.* New York: University of Cambridge Press, 1988.

Genette, Gerard. *Paratexts: Thresholds of Interpretation.* Cambridge: Cambridge University Press, 1997.

Gernet, Jacques. *China and the Christian Impact.* Trans. Janet Lloyd. Cambridge: Cambridge University Press, 1985.

Gingerich, Owen. "Copernicus's De Revolutionus: An Example of Renaissance Scientific Printing." In Gerald P. Tyson and Sylvia S. Wagonheim, eds., *Print and Culture in the Renaissance: Essays on the Advent of Printing in Europe.* Newark: University of Delaware Press, 1986.

Goodrich, L. Carrington. *The Literary Inquisition of Ch'ien-lung.* Baltimore: Waverly Press, 1935.

Gough, Hugh. *The Newspaper Press in the French Revolution.* Chicago: Dorsey Press, 1988.

Grafton, Anthony. *Forgeries and Critics: Creativity and Duplicity in Western Scholarship.* Princeton: Princeton University Press, 1990.

Greenblatt, Stephen, and Giles Gunn, eds., *Redrawing the Boundaries: The Transformation of English and American Literary Studies.* New York: Modern Language Association, 1992.

Gu Menglin 顧夢麟. *Shijing shuoyue* 四書説約. Ming edition, preface 1640 (HYX).

———. *Sishu shuoyue* 詩經説約. Reprint of a Japanese edition of 1669. Taibei: Institute of Philosophy and Literature, Academic Sinica, 1996.

Gu Xiancheng 顧憲成. *Jingao zang gao* 涇皋藏稿. *SKQS*, vol. 1292.

Gu Yanwu 顧炎武. *Gu tinglin siwenji* 顧亭林詩文集. Beijing: Zhonghua shuju, 1959.

———. *Rizhilu jishi* 日知錄集釋. Ed. Huang Rucheng 黃汝成. 4 vols. *SBBY*.

———. *Tinglin wenji* 亭林文集. Beijing: Zhonghua shuju, 1983.

Gui Youguang 歸有光. *Zhenchuan wenji* 震川文集. *SBBY*.

Guo Shaoyu 郭紹虞. *Zhongguo wenxue shi* 中國文學史. Hong Kong: Hongzhi shudian, n.d.

Guo Wei 郭偉. *Huang Ming bai fangjia wenda* 皇明百方家問答. Preface 1617 (HYX).

———. *Sishu zhijie zhinan* 四書直解指南. Chongzhen edition. *MDBKZL*.

———. *Xinjuan liu caizi Sishu xingren yu* 新鐫六才子四書醒人語. Ming edition (HYX).

———. *Xinke yichou ke Hua huiyuan Sishu zhuyi jinyu sui* 新刻乙丑科華會元四書主意金玉髓. HYC.

———. *Zengbu Guo Zhuyuan xiansheng huiji shi taishi Sishu zhuyi baocang* 增補郭洙源先生匯輯十太史四書主意寶藏. Ming edition. *ZGGJBS*.

Guo Zhiqi 郭之奇. *Wanzaitang wenji* 宛在堂文集 (HYX).

Guo Zizhang 郭子章. *Qinglei gong yishu* 青螺公遺書 (FSN).

*Guwang yan* 姑妄言. *SWXHB*.

Guy, R. Kent. *The Emperor's Four Treasuries: Scholars and the State in the Late Ch'ien-lung Era.* Cambridge, Mass.: Harvard University Press, 1987.

*Guzhang juechen* 鼓掌絕塵. Ming edition, preface 1631. *GBXSCK*, ser. 11.

Habermas, Jürgen. *The Structural Transformation of the Public Sphere: An Inquiry into a Category of Bourgeois Society.* Trans. Thomas Burger, with Frederick Lawrence. Cambridge, Mass.: MIT Press, 1989.

Hai Rui 海瑞. *Hai Rui ji* 海瑞集. Beijing: Zhonghua shuju, 1962.

Han Dacheng 韓大城. *Mingdai chengshi yanjiu* 明代城市研究 (A study of cities in the Ming dynasty). Beijing: Zhongguo renmin daxue chubanshe, 1991.

———. "Mingdai gaolidai ziben di tedian ji qi zuoyong" 明代高利貸資本的特點 及其作用. *Mingshi janqiu luncong* 明史研究論叢, no. 4 (1991): 348–67.

———. "Mingdai shangpin jingzhi di fazhan yu ziben zhuyi di mengya" 明代商 品經濟的發展與資本主義的萌芽. In *Ming Qing shehui jingzhi xingtai di yanjiu* 明清社會經濟形態的研究, Shanghai renmin chubanshe, 1957.

Hanan, Patrick. *The Chinese Vernacular Story.* Cambridge, Mass.: Harvard University Press, 1981.

———. *The Invention of Li Yu.* Cambridge, Mass.: Harvard University Press, 1988.

Hancher, Michael. "Gazing at the Imperial Dictionary." *Book History* 1 (1998).

Hanselaer, Johan. "De prijs van antieke teksten, gedrukt door Plantijn." In M. De Schepper and F. De Nave, eds., *Ex officina Plantiniana. Studia in memoriam Christophori Plantini (ca. 1520–1589). De Gulden Passer* 66–67 (1988–89): 337–48.

Hanshan Deqing 憨山德清. *Daxue gangmu jueyi* 大學綱目決疑 and *Zhongyong zhizhi* 中庸直指 (HYX).

*Hanxue yanjiu zhongxin yinzhao haiwai icun guji shumu chubian* 漢學研究中心 影照海外佚存古籍書目初編. Taibei: Hanxue yanjiu zhongxin, 1990.

Hao Jing 郝敬. *Shancao tang ji* 山草堂集 (BT).

He Liangjun 何良俊. *Siyou zhai congshuo* 四友齋叢説. Beijing: Zhonghua shuju, 1959.

Hegel, Robert. *Reading Illustrated Fiction in Late Imperial China.* Stanford: Stanford University Press, 1997.

———. "Sui T'ang Yen-i and the Aesthetics of Seventeenth-Century Suchou Elite." In Andrew Plaks, ed., *Chinese Narrative: Critical and Theoretical Essays.* Princeton: Princeton University Press, 1977.

Heijdra, Martin. "The Socio-economic Development of Rural China during the Ming." In Denis Twitchett and Frederick W. Mote, eds., *The Cambridge History of China, vol. 7 The Ming Dynasty, 1368–1644, pt. 1.* New York: University of Cambridge Press, 1988.

Hess, Carla. "Economic Upheavals in Publishing." In Robert Darnton and Daniel Roche, eds., *Revolution in Print: The Press in France, 1775–1800.* Berkeley: University of California Press, 1989.

Hind, Arthur M. *A History of Woodcut with a Detailed Survey of Work Done in the Fifteenth Century.* 2 vols. New York: Dover Publications, 1963.

Hindman, Sandra, ed. *Printing the Written Word: The Social History of Books, circa 1450–1520.* Ithaca: Cornell University Press, 1991.

Ho, Ping-ti. *The Ladder of Social Success in Imperial China.* New York: Wiley and Sons, 1962.

Hu, Philip K., comp. and ed. *Visible Traces: Rare Books and Special collection from the National Library of China*. New York: Queens Borough Public Library; Beijing: National Library of China and Morning Glory Publishers, 2000.

Hu Wanchuan 胡萬川. "Feng Menglong ji Fushe renwu" 馮夢龍及復社人物. In *Feng Menglong jiqi zhuzuo* 馮夢龍及其著作. Taibei: Tianyi chubanshe, 1982.

———. "Feng Menglong shengping ji qi dui xiaoshuo di gongxian" 馮夢龍生平及其對小説的貢獻. M.A. thesis, Taiwan National University, 1973.

Hu Wenhuan 胡文煥. *Qun yin leixuan* 群音類選. 4 vols. Beijing: Zhonghua shuju, 1980.

Hu Yinglin 胡應麟. *Shaoshi shanfang bicong* 少室山房筆叢. Beijing: Zhonghua shuju, 1964.

———. *Shaoshi shanfang leigao* 少室山房類稿. *CSJCXB*, vol. 146.

Huacun kan xing shizhe 花村看行侍者. *Huacun tan wang* 花村談往. Taibei: Dahua yinshuguan, n.d.

*Huanxi yuanjia* 歡喜冤家. *SWXHB*, vols. 10–11.

*Huang chao like Sishu mojuan pingxuan* 皇朝歷科四書墨卷評選 (Examination essays on the *Four Books* in the Ming dynasty). Ming edition, preface 1625 (ZT).

Huang Jingxing 黃景星. *Sishu jie* 四書解 (HYX).

Huang Miantang 黃冕堂. *Mingshi guanjian* 明史管見. Taibei: Xuesheng shuju, 1985.

Huang, Philip. "'Public Sphere'/'Civil Society' in China? The Third Realm between State and Society." *Modern China* 19, no. 2 (1993): 216–40.

Huang, Ray. *1587: A Year of No Significance: The Ming Dynasty in Decline*. New Haven: Yale University Press, 1981.

Huang Renyu 黃仁宇. "Cong Sanyan kan wan Ming shangren" 從三言看晚明商人. In *Ming shi yanjiu luncong* 明史研究論叢, vol. 1. Taibei: Tali chubanshe, 1982.

Huang Rubing 黃儒炳. *Xu nanyong zhi* 續南雍志. 3 vols. Taibei: Weiwen tushu chubanshe, 1976.

Huang Ruheng 黃汝亭. *Sishu Zhou Zhuang hejie* 四書周莊合解 (HYC).

———. *Yulin ji* 寓林集. *SKJHS*, vol. 42.

Huang Ruiqing 黃瑞卿. "Mingdai zhong hou qi shiren qi xue jingshang zhi feng chutan" 明代中後期士人棄學經商之風初探. *Zhongguo shehui jingji shi yanjiu* 中國社會經濟史研究, no. 2 (1990): 33–39, 46.

Huang Yu 黃煜. *Bixue lu* 碧血錄. In *Donglin shimo* 東林始末. Shanghai: Zhongguo shudian, 1982.

Huang Zongxi 黃宗羲. *Huang Zongxi quanji* 黃宗羲全集. Hangzhou: Zhejiang guji chubanshe, 1985.

———. *Ming wenhai* 明文海. 5 vols. Beijing: Zhonghua shuju, 1987.

———. *Mingru xue'an* 明儒學案. Shanghai: Commercial Press, 1930.

Huffman, James. *Creating a Public: People and Press in Meiji Japan.* Honolulu: University of Hawaii Press, 1997.

———. *Nanlei wen ding, qianji, houji,* and *sanji* 南雷文定前集，後集，三集. *CSJCCB.*

Hunter, Dard. *Papermaking: The History and Technique of an Ancient Art.* New York: Dover Publications, 1974.

Hymes, Robert. "Marriage, Descent Groups, and the Localist Strategy in Sung and Yüan Fu-chou." In Patricia B. Ebrey and James L. Watson, eds., *Kinship Organization in Late Imperial China, 1400–1900.* Berkeley: University of California Press, 1986.

Idema, Wilt L. *Chinese Vernacular Fiction: The Formative Period.* Leiden: E. J. Brill, 1974.

Jian Jinsong 簡錦松. *Mingdai wenxue piping yanjiu* 明代文學批評研究. Taibei: Xuesheng shuju, 1989.

Jiang Gongtao 姜公韜. *Wang Yanzhou di shengping yu zhuzuo* 王弇州的生平與著作. Tabei: Taiwan daxue wenxueyuan, 1974.

Jiang, Jin. "Heresy and Persecution in Late Ming Society: Reinterpreting the Case of Li Zhi." *Late Imperial China* 22, no. 2 (2001): 1–34.

Jiang Zhaocheng 蔣兆成. *Ming Qing Hang Jia Hu jingjishi yanjiu* 明清杭嘉湖經濟史研究. Hangzhou: Hangzhou daxue chubanshe, 1994.

Jiao Hong 焦竑. *Tanyuan ji* 澹圓集. 1606. Reprint. Jinling congshu. 2nd ser. Taibei: Datong shuju, 1969.

———. *Tanyuan xuji* 澹圓續集. *CSJCXB,* vol. 187.

Jin Demen 金德門. "Feng Menglong sheji kao" 馮夢龍社籍考. *Zhonghua wenshi luncong* 中華文史論叢, no. 1 (1985): 281–84.

*Jin Ping Mei* 金瓶梅. Reprint of Wanli edition, n.d.

Jin Risheng 金日升. *Songtian lu bi* 頌天臚筆. Preface 1629. *SKJHS,* vol. 5.

Johns, Adrian. *The Nature of the Book: Print and Knowledge in the Making.* Chicago: University of Chicago Press, 1998.

Johnson, David. "Communication, Class, and Consciousness in Late Imperial China." In idem et al., eds., *Popular Culture in Late Imperial China.* Berkeley: University of California Press, 1985.

Johnson, David, Andrew Nathan, and Evelyn Rawski, eds. *Popular Culture in Late Imperial China.* Berkeley: University of California Press, 1985.

Judge, Joan. *Print and Politics: Shibao and the Culture of Reform in Late Qing China.* Stanford: Stanford University Press, 1996.

Kainen, Jacob. "Why Bewick Succeeded: A Note in the History of Wood Engraving." *Contributions from the Museum of History and Technology,* Bulletin 218 (1959): 186–201.

Kernan, Alvin. *Samuel Johnson and the Impact of Printing.* Princeton: Princeton University Press, 1989.

Ko, Dorothy. *Teachers of the Inner Chamber: Women and Culture in Seventeenth Century China.* Stanford: Stanford University Press, 1994.

Kobayashi, Hiromitsu, and Samantha Sabin. "The Great Age of Anhui Painting." In James Cahill, ed., *Shadows of Mt. Huang: Chinese Painting and Printing of the Anhui School,* 25–33. Berkeley: University Art Museum, 1981.

Kong Shangren 孔尚任. *Taohua shan* 桃花扇. Hong Kong: Hongzhi shudian, n.d.

Kornicki, Peter. *The Book in Japan: A Cultural History from the Beginnings to the Nineteenth Century.* Hononlulu: University of Hawaii Press, 2001.

Kuo, Jason chi-sheng. "Hui-chou Merchants as Art Patrons in the Late Sixteenth and Early Seventeenth Century." In Chu-tsing Li, ed., *Artists and Patrons: Some Social and Economic Aspects of Chinese Painting.* Seattle: University of Washington Press, 1989.

Kutcher, Norman. *Mourning in Late Imperial China: Filial Piety and the State.* New York: Cambridge University Press, 1999.

Lach, Donald. *Asia in the Making of Europe.* Vol 2. Chicago: University of Chicago Press, 1970.

Lee, Leo. *Shanghai Modern: The Flowering of a New Urban Culture in China, 1930–1945.* Cambridge, Mass.: Harvard University Press, 1999.

Lee, Thomas H. C. *Education in Traditional China: A History.* Leiden: E. J. Brill, 2000.

Legge, Helen Edith. *James Legge: Missionary and Scholar.* London: The Religious Tract Society, 1905.

Leung, Angela Ki Che. "Elementary Education in the Lower Yangtze Region in the Seventeenth and Eighteenth Centuries." In Benjamin A. Elman and Alexander Woodside, eds., *Education and Society in Late Imperial China, 1600–1900.* Berkeley: University of California Press, 1994.

*Li gong shengci ji ji yi shilu* 李公生祠紀義實錄 (HYX), n.d.

Li Jixiang 李紀祥. *Liang Song yilai Daxue gaiben zhi yanjiu* 兩宋以來大學改本之研究. Taibei: Xuesheng shuju, 1988.

Li Kaixian 李開先. *Li Kaixian ji* 李開先集. Beijing: Zhonghua shuju, 1959.

Li Le 李樂. *Jianwen zaji* 見聞雜紀. BJXSDG, ser. 44, vol. 8.

Li Mengyang 李夢陽. *Kongtong xiansheng ji* 空同先生集. Taibei: Weimin tushu, 1976.

Li Panlong 李攀龍. *Cangming xiansheng ji* 滄溟先生集. Taibei: Weimin tushu, 1976.

Li Qingzhi 李清志. *Gushu banben jianding yanjiu* 古書版本鑒定研究. Taibei: Wenshizhe chubanshe, 1986.

Li Rihua 李日華. *Weishui xuan riji* 味水軒日記. *BJTS*, vol. 20.

———. *Tianzhi tang ji* 恬致堂集. *SKJHS*, vol. 64.

Li Ruiliang 李瑞良. *Zhongguo muluxue shi* 中國目錄學史. Taipei: Wenjin chubanshe, 1993.

Li Sunzhi 李遜之. *Sanchao yeji* 三朝野記. *BJXSDG*, ser. 4, vol. 7.

Li Tan 李楨. *Donglin dangji kao* 東林黨籍考. *MDZJCK*, vol. 6.

Li Tianyou 李天佑. "Mingdai di neige" 明代的內閣. In *Ming Qing shi guoji xueshu taolunhui lunwenji* 明清史國際學術討論會論文集. Tianjin: Renmin chubanshe, 1982.

Li Tingji 李廷機. *Li Wenjie ji* 李文節集. 4 vols. Taibei: Wenhai chubanshe, 1970.

———. *Sishu dazhu cankao* 四書大註參考. Ming edition, Chunzhen (HYX).

Li, Wai-yee. *Enchantment and Disenchantment: Love and Illusion in Chinese Literature*. Princeton: Princeton University Press, 1993.

Li Wenzhi 李文治, Wei Jinyu 魏金玉, and Jing Junjian 經君健. *Ming Qing shidai di nongye ziben zhuyi mengya wenti* 明清時代的資本主義萌芽問題. Beijing: Zhongguo shehui kexue chubanshe, 1983.

Li Xu 李翊. *Jie'an laoren manbi* 戒庵老人漫筆. Beijing: Zhonghua shuju, 1982.

Li Yan 李儼. *Zhongguo shuxue dagang* 中國數學大綱. 2 vols. Beijing: Kexue chubanshe, 1958.

Li Yu 李漁. *Liweng ouji* 笠翁偶集, *Liweng wenji* 笠翁文集. *LYQJ*.

———. *Yizhong yuan* 意中緣. *LYQJ*, vol. 8.

Li Zhi 李贄. *Fenshu Xufenshu* 焚書·續焚書. Beijing: Zhongghua shuju, 1975.

———. *Cangshu* 藏書. Beijing: Zhonghua shuchu, 1959.

Li Zhizhong 李致忠. "Songdai keshu shulue" 宋代刻書述略. *LDKS*, pp. 46–89.

———. "Tangdai keshu kaolue" 唐代刻書述略. *LDKS*, pp. 22–45.

*Li Zhuowu piping zhongyi Shuihu zhuan* 李卓吾批評忠義水滸傳. Reprinted as *Ming Rongyu tang ke Shuihu zhuan* 明容與堂刻水滸傳. Shanghai: Renmin chubanshe, 1975.

*Lidai keshu gaikuang* 歷代刻書概況. Bejing: Yinshua gongye chubanshe, 1991.

Lin Liyue 林麗月. *Mingdai di guozi jiansheng* 明代的國子監生. Taibei: Shangwu yinshuguan, 1978.

Lin Qingzhang 林慶彰. *Mingdai kaojuxue yanjiu* 明代考據學研究. Taibei: Xuesheng shuju, 1986.

———. "Wan Ming jingxue di fuxing yundong 晚明經學的復興運動" in *Shumu jikan* 書目季刊 18, no. 3 (1984): 3-40.

Lin San 林散. Sishu shuosheng 四書説乘 (HYX).

Lin Zhao'en 林兆恩. *Linzi quanji* 林子全集. *BJTS*, vol. 63.

Lindenbaum, Peter. "Sidney's *Arcadia* as Cultural Monument and Proto-Novel." In Cedric C. Brown and Arthur F. Marotti, eds., *Texts and Cultural Change in Early Modern England*. Basingstoke and London: Macmillan, 1997.

Ling Dizhi 凌迪知, ed. *Guochao minggong hanzao* 國朝明公瀚藻. Preface 1582 (HYC).

Ling Mengchu 凌濛初. *Erke Pai'an jingqi* 二刻拍案驚奇. 4 vols. Preface 1632. *GBXSCK*, ser. 14.

Liu Jialin 劉家林. *Zhongguo xinwen tongshi* 中國新聞通史. 2 vols. Wuhan: Wuhan daxue chubanshe, 1995.

Liu, Kwang-ching. "Socioethics as Orthodoxy: A Perspective." In idem, ed., *Orthodoxy in Late Imperial China*. Berkeley: University of California Press, 1990.

Liu Liangming 劉良明. *Zhongguo xiaoshuo lilun piping shi* 中國小説理論批評史. Taibei: Hongye wenhua shiye, 1997.

Liu Renqing 柳仁慶 and Hu Yuxi 胡玉熹. "Woguo gu zhi di chubu yanjiu" 我國古紙的初步研究. *Wenwu* 文物 (1976): 74-79.

Liu Xiangguang 劉祥光. "Yinshua yu kaoshi: Songdai kaoshi yong cankaoshu chutan" 印刷與考試宋代考試用參考書初探. In *Zhuanbian yu dingxing: Songdai shehui wenhuashi xueshu taolunhui lunwenji* 轉變與定型：宋代社會文化史學術討論會論文集. Taibei: History Department, National University of Taiwan, 2000.

Liu Zhizhong 劉致中. "Xu Zichang jiashi shengping zhushu keshu kao" 許自昌家世生平著述刻書考. *Wenxian*, no. 2 (1992): 47-66.

Liu Zhongri 劉重日 et al. *Zhongguo shigao* 中國史稿. Vol. 6. Beijing: Renmin chubanshe, 1987.

*Liubu ji tiaoli fu duchayuan tiaoli* 六部及條例附都察院條例. Manuscript edition, Zhongshan dauxe tushuguan. Canton: Zhongshan University Library.

Lu Qian 盧前 et al. *Shulin zhanggu* 書林掌故. Hong Kong: Mengshi tushu, 1972.

Lu Rong 陸容. *Shuyuan zaji* 菽園雜記. Beijing: Zhonghua shuju, 1985.

Lu Shen 陸深. *Yanshan wenji* 儼山文集. 100 juan. Ming edition, 1551 (SKY).

———. *Kechang tiaoguan* 科場條貫. *BJXSDG*, ser. 18, vol. 3.

Lu Shiyi 陸世儀. *Fushe jilue* 復社紀略. In *Donglin shimo* 東林始末. Shanghai: Shanghai shudian, 1982.

Lu Yunlong 陸雲龍. *Cuiyu ge pingxuan shizui* 翠娛閣評選詩最. Ming edition, preface 1631 (FD).

————. *Huang Ming shiliu jia xiaopin* 皇明十六家小品. Reprint of Ming Chung-zhen edition. Beijing: Zhongguo tushuguan chubanshe, 1997.

————. *Wei Zhongxian xiaoshuo chijian shu* 魏忠賢小説斥奸書. ZGGDZX, vol. 5.

————. *Xingshi yan* 型世言. Reprint of Ming edition. Taibei: Institute of Chinese Philosophy and Literature, Academic Sinica, 1992.

Lü Kun 呂坤. *Shizheng lu* 實政錄. BJTS, vol. 48.

Lü Liuliang 呂留良. *Lü Wancun xiansheng wenji* 呂晚村先生文集. Taibei: Zhong-ding wenhua, 1967.

*Lü Mudan zhuanqi* 綠牡丹傳奇, *Quan Ming chuanqi* 全明傳奇, vol. 89. Taibei: Tianyi chubanshe, 1983.

Lü Tiancheng 呂天良. *Qupin* 曲品. MDSMTB, vol. 2.

Lü Zuoxie 呂作燮. "Ming Qing shiqi Suzhou di huiguan he gongso" 明清時期蘇州的會館和公所. *Zhongguo shehui jingzhi shi yanjiu* 中國社會經濟史研究, no. 2 (1984): 10–24.

Lust, John. *Chinese Popular Prints*. Leiden and New York: E. J. Brill, 1996.

Ma Shiqi 馬世奇. *Dingjuan sanshi mingjia huizuan Sishu ji* 鼎鐫三十名家彙纂四書紀. Ming edition, preface 1618 (HYX).

Ma, Tai-loi. "The Local Officials of Ming China, 1368–1644." *Oriens Extremeus* 22 (June 1975): 11–27.

Mair, Victor. *Painting and Performance: Chinese Picture Recitation and Its Indiana Genesis*. Honolulu: University of Hawaii Press, 1988.

Man-Cheong, Iona D. "Fair Fraud and Fraudulent Fairness: The 1761 Examination Case." *Late Imperial China* 18, no. 2 (1997): 51–85.

*Manuscripts, Incunables, Woodcut Books and Books from Early Presses*. London: Maggs Bros., 1920.

Mao Jin 毛晉. *Jiguge jiaoke shumu* 汲古閣校刻書目. MDSMTB.

————. *Haiyue zhilin* 海嶽志林. BJXS, vol. 7.

————. *Yinhu tiba* 隱湖題跋. CSJCXB, vol. 5.

Mao Yi 毛扆. *Jiguge zhencang miben shumu* 汲古閣珍藏秘本書目. CSJCCB.

Martin, Henri-Jean. *The History and Power of Writing*. Trans. Lydia G. Cochrane. Chicago: University of Chicago Press, 1994.

Maza, Sarah. *Private Lives and Public Affairs: The Causes Celebres of Prerevolutionary France*. Berkeley: University of California Press, 1993.

McDermott, Joseph. "The Ascendance of the Imprint in Late Imperial Chinese Culture." In Cynthia Brokaw and Kai-wing Chow, eds., *Print and Book Culture in Late Imperial China*. Berkeley: University of California Press, forthcoming.

McKenzie, D. F. *The Cambridge University Press, 1696–1712: A Bibliographical Study*. 2 vols. Cambridge: Cambridge University Press, 1966.

McLaren, Anne E. "Ming Audiences and Vernacular Hermeneutics: The Uses of the Romance of the Three Kingdoms." *T'oung Pao* 81 (1995): 51–80.

McLuhan, Marshall. *The Gutenberg Galaxy: The Making of Typographic Man*. Toronto: University of Toronto Press, 1962.

McNeill, William H. "World History and the Rise and Fall of the West." *Journal of World History* 9, no. 2 (1998): 215–36.

Mei Dingzuo 梅鼎祚. *Luqiu shishi ji* 鹿裘石室集. *SKJHS*, vol. 58.

Meng Pengxing 孟彭興. "Shiliu, shiqi shiji Jiangnan shehui zhi pibian ji wenren fanying" 十六十七世紀江南社會之丕變及文人反應. *Ming-Qing shi* 明清史, no. 5 (1998): 24–33.

Meng Sen 孟森. *Mingdai shi* 明代史. Taibei: Zhonghua congshu weiyuanhui, 1957.

Meskill, John. *Academies in Ming China: A Historical Essay*. Tuscon: University of Arizona Press, 1982.

Miao Changqi 繆昌期. *Congye tang cungao* 從野堂存稿. *CSJCXB*, vol. 147.

Milne, William. "Letter from Canton," 7 Feb. 1814 (London Missionary Society Archives, Incoming Correspondence, Morrison, B1/F3/JB), School of Oriental and African Studies.

*Ming-Qing shehui jingji xingtai di yanjiu* 明清社會經濟形態的研究. Shanghai: Shanghai renmin chubanshe, 1957.

*Ming-Qing Suzhou gongshangye beike ji* 明清蘇州工商業碑刻集. Shanghai: Jiangsu renmin chubanshe, 1981.

*Ming taixue jingji zhi* 明太學經籍志. *MDSMTB*.

*Mingshi* 明史. 28 vols. Beijing: Zhonghua shuju, 1974.

*Mingshi gao* 明詩稿. *MDZJCK*, vol. 96.

Mote, Frederick W., and Hung-lam Chu. *Calligraphy and the East Asian Book*. Ed. Howard L. Goodman. Boston: Shambhala, 1989.

Mote, Federick W., and Denis Twitchett, eds. *The Cambridge History of China: The Ming Dynasty, 1368–1644, Part 1*. New York: Cambridge University Press, 1988.

Mukerji, Chandra. *From Graven Images: Patterns of Modern Materialism*. New York: Columbia University Press, 1983.

Murray, Julia K. "Didactic Illustrations in Printed Books: Choice and Consequence." In Cynthia Brokaw and Kai-wing Chow, eds., *Printing and Book Culture in Late Imperial China*. Berkeley: University of California Press, forthcoming.

*Nagoya-shi Hosa bunko kanseki mokuroku* 名古屋市逢左淮籍目録. Nagoya: Nagoya kyoiku iinkai, 1975.

*Nan Wu jiuhua lu* 南吳舊話錄. Comp. Zhang Lie 蔣烈. Preface 1915.

Naquin, Susan, and Chun-fang Yu, eds. *Pilgrims and Sacred Sites in China*. Berkeley: University of California Press, 1992.

———. "The Transmission of White Lotus Sectarianism in Late Imperial China." In David Johnson, Andrew Nathan, Evelyn Rawski, eds., *Popular Culture in Late Imperial China*. Berkeley: University of California Press, 1985.

Nivison, David. "Protest against Conventions and Conventions of Protest." In Arthur Wright, ed., *The Confucian Persuasion*. Stanford: Stanford University Press, 1960.

Ōba Osamu 大庭修. (Edo jidai ni okeru) *Tōsen mochiwatashisho no kinkyū* (江戸時代における) 唐船持渡書の研究. Kansai Daigaku Tōzai Gakujutsu Kenkyūsho, 1967.

Oertling, Sewall, II. "Patronage in Anhui During The Wan-Li Period." In Chutsing Li, ed., *Artists and Patrons: Some Social and Economic Aspects of Chinese Painting*. Seattle: University of Washington Press, 1989.

Oki Yasushi. 大木康. *Ming matsu no hagu ne chishikini*. 明末のはぐれ知識人. Tokyo: Kodansa, 1995.

———. *Minmatsu Kōnan ni okeru shuppan banka no kenkyu* 明末江南における出版文化の研究 (A study of printing culture in the Jiangnan district in the Late Ming period). *Hiroshima University Bulletin of the Faculty of Letters* 50, special issue, no. 1 (1991).

Ōkubo Eiko 大久保英子. *Min-shin jidai shoin no kenkyū* 明清時代書院の研究 (A study of academies in the Ming-Qing period). Tokyo: Kobusho kankokai, 1976.

Pan Jixing 潘吉星. *Zhongguo Hanguo yu Ouzhou caoqi yinshuashu di bijiao* 中國、韓國與歐洲早期印刷術的比較. Beijing: Kexue chubanshe, 1997.

———. *Zhongguo zaozhi jishushi gao* 中國造紙技術史稿. Beijing: Wenwu chubanshe, 1979.

Pan, Ming-te. "Rural Credit in Ming-Qing Jiangnan and the Concept of Peasant Petty Commodity Production." *JAS* 55, no. 1 (1966): 94–117.

Patterson, Annabel. *Censorship and Interpretation: The Conditions of Writing and Reading in Early Modern England*. Madison: University of Wisconsin Press, 1984.

Perkins, David. *Is Literary History Possible?* Baltimore: Johns Hopkins University Press, 1992.

Peterson, Willard. *Bitter Gourd: Fang I-chih and the Impetus for Intellectual Change*. New Haven: Yale University Press, 1979.

Pettas, Willliam. "A Sixteenth-Century Spanish Bookstore: The Inventory of Juan de Junta." *Transactions of the American Philosophical Society* 85, pt. 1 (1995): 1–247.

Plaks, Andrew. *The Four Masterworks of the Ming Novel*. Princeton: Princeton University Press, 1987.

Pomeranz, Kenneth. *The Great Divergence: China, Europe, and the Making of the Modern World Economy*. Princeton, N.J.: Princeton University Press, 2000.

Qi Biaojia 祁彪佳. *An Wu xigao* 按吳檄稿. *BJTS*, vol. 48.

———. *Qupin Jupin* 曲品劇品. Taibei: Zhu Shangwen, 1960.

Qi Chengye 祁承業. *Tansheng tang cangshu mu* 澹生堂藏書目. *MDSMTB*.

Qian Cunxu 錢存訓. *Zaozhi yu yinshuai* 造紙與印刷. Taibei: Shangmu yinshu guan, 1995.

———. *Zhongguo shuji, zhi mo ji yinshuashi lunwenji* 中國書籍紙墨印刷史論文集. Hong Kong: Chinese University Press, 1992.

Qian Qianyi 錢謙益 (see also Tsien Tsuen-hsuin). *Liechao shiji xiaozhuan* 列朝詩集小傳. Taibei: Shijie shuju, 1961.

———. *Muzhai chu xue ji* 牧齋初學集. *SBCK, SBCKCB*.

———. *Muzhai youxue ji* 牧齋有學集. *SBCK, SBCKCB*.

Qian Xiyan 錢希言. *Xixia* 戲瑕. *BJXSDG*, ser. 17, vol. 2.

*Qingdai naifu keshu mulu tijie* 清代內府刻書目錄題解. Beijing: Zijincheng chubanshe, 1995.

Qiu Zhaolin 丘兆麟. *Yushu ting quanji* 玉書庭全集. Ming edition, 1632 (ST).

Qu Dajun 屈大均. *Guangdong xinyu* 廣東新語. Beijing: Zhonghua shuju, 1985.

Raitoguchi Ritsuko 賴戶口律子. *Liuqiu guanhua keben yanjiu* 琉球官話課本研究 (Study of the official language). Hong Kong: Institute of Chinese Culture, Chinese University, 1994.

Rawski, Evelyn S. "Economic and Social Foundations of Late Imperial Culture." In David Johnson, Andrew J. Nathan, and Evelyn S. Rawski, eds., *Popular Cutlure in Late Imperial China*. Berkeley: University of California Press, 1985.

———. *Education and Popular Literacy in Ch'ing China*. Ann Arbor: University of Michigan Press, 1979.

Ricci, Matthew. *China in the Sixteenth Century: The Journal of Matthew Ricci*. New York: Random House, 1953.

Richardson, Brian. *Printing, Writers, and Readers in Renaissance Italy*. Cambridge: Cambridge University Press, 1999.

Roche, Daniel. "Censorship and the Publishing Industry." In Robert Darnton, ed., *Revolution in Print: The Press in France, 1775–1800*. Berkeley: University of California Press, 1989.

Rolston, David, ed. *How to Read the Chinese Novel.* Princeton: Princeton University Press, 1990.

———. *Traditional Chinese Fiction and Fiction Commentary: Reading and Writing between the Lines.* Stanford: Stanford University Press, 1997.

Rose, Mark. The Author in Court: Pope v. Curll (1741)." In Martha Woodmansee and Peter Jaszi, eds., *The Construction of Authorship: Texual Appropriation in Law and Literature,* pp. 211–29. Durham: Duke University Press, 1994.

Ruan Dacheng 阮大誠. *Yanzi jian* 燕子箋. Hong Kong: Guang zhi shuju, n.d.

*San she ji* 三社記. *Quan Ming chuanqi* 全明傳奇. Taibei: Tianyi chubanshe, 1983.

Santangelo, Paolo. "Urban Society in Late Imperial Suzhou." In Linda Cooke Johnson, ed., *Cities of Jiangnan in Late Imperial China,* pp. 81–116. Albany: State University of New York Press, 1993.

Shen Bang 沈榜. *Yuanshu zaji* 宛署雜記. Bejing: Guji chubanshe, 1982.

Shen Defu 沈德符. *Wanli Yehuo bian* 萬歷野獲編. *BJXSDG,* ser. 15, vol. 6.

Shen Jin 沈津. "Mingdai fangke tushu zhi liutong yu jiage" 明代坊刻圖書之流通與價格 (Circulation and price of books at bookstores in the Ming dynasty). *Guojia tushuguan guankan,* no. 1 (June 1996): 101–18.

Shen Shaofang 申紹芳. *Xinke Shen huikui jiazhuan ke'er sishu shunwen jiejie* 新刻申會魁家傳課兒四書順文捷解 (HYX).

Shen Shouzheng 沈守正. *Sishu shuocong* 四書説叢 (HYX).

———. *Xuetang ji* 雪堂集. Ming edition, 1630 (ZT).

Shen Zijin 沈自晉. *Zhongding nan jiugong cipu* 重定南九宮詞譜. *SBXQCK,* vol. 1.

Shi Fenglai 施鳳來. *Xinke Shi huiyuan zhenzhuan Sishu zhuyi suijue chuanbi* 新刻施會元真傳四書主意髓橡覺筆. Preface 1607 (SKY).

Shi Jinbo 史金波 and Yasin Ashuri 雅森吾守爾. *Zhongguo huozi yinshuashu di faming he zaoqi zhuanbo* 中國活字印刷術的發明和早期轉播. Beijing: Shehui kexue wenxian chubanshe, 2000.

Shi Xuan 史玄. *Jiujing yishi* 舊京遺事. *BJXSDG,* ser. 9, vol. 8.

Smith, Henry D., II. "Japaneseness and the History of the Book." *Monumenta Nipponica* 53, no. 4 (1998): 499–514.

Song Qifeng 宋起鳳. *Bishuo* 稗説. *MSZLCK.*

Song Yingxing 宋應星. *Tiangong kaiwu* 天工開物. Hong Kong: Zhonghua shuju, 1978.

*Songjiang fuzhi* 松江府誌. Preface 1631 (HYX).

Steinberg, S. H. *Five Hundred Years of Printing.* Rev. John Trevitt. London: The British Library and Oak Knoll Press, 1996.

Su Jing 蘇精. *Ma Lixin yu zhongwen yinshua chuban* 馬禮遜與中文印刷出版. Taibei: Xuesheng shuju, 2000.

Sun Chengze 孫承澤. *Chunming meng yu lu* 春明夢餘錄. *SKQSZB*, ser. 6.

———. *Tianfu guangji* 天府廣記. Beijing: Beijing chubanshe, 1962.

Sun Kuang 孫爌. *Jin wenxuan* 今文選. Ming edition, preface 1603 (BT).

———. *Yuefeng xiansheng juye bian* 月峰先生居業次編. Ming edition, preface 1594 (ST).

———. *Yuefeng xiansheng juye cibian* 月峰先生居業編. Ming edition (ST).

Sutherland, John. "Publishing History: A Hole at the Centre of Literary Sociology." In Philippe Desan, Priscilla Parkurst Ferguson, and Wendy Griswold, eds., *Literature and Social Practice*, pp. 267–82. Chicago and London: University of Chicago Press, 1988.

Swartz, David. *Culture and Power: The Sociology of Pierre Bourdieu*. Chicago: University of Chicago Press, 1997.

Taga Akigorō 多賀秋五郎. *Sofu no kenkyū* 宗譜の研究. Tokyo: The Tokyo Bunko Publications, 1960.

Tan Qian 談遷. *Zaolin zazu* 棗林雜俎. *BJXSDG*, ser. 22, vol. 6.

Tang Binyin 湯賓尹. *Shui'an gao* 睡庵稿. Ming edition, preface 1610 (ZT).

———. *Shui'an Sishu mai* 睡庵四書脈. Ming edition, preface 1615 (HYX).

———. *Xinke Tang yishou kechang tizhi* 新刻湯太史擬授科場題旨. Ming edition, preface 1614 (HYX).

Tang Shunzhi 唐順之. *Jingchuan ji* 荊川集. *CSJCXB*, vol. 144.

Tang Wenji 唐文基. "Mingchao dui xingshang di guanli he zhengshui" 明朝對行商的管理和征稅. *Zhongguo shi yangjiu*, no. 3 (1982): 19–32.

Tang Xianzu 湯顯祖. *Tang Xianzu ji* 湯顯祖集. Beijing: Zhonghua shuju, 1962.

Tedeschi, Martha. "Publish and Perish: The Career of Lienhart Holle in Ulm." In Sandra Hindman, ed., *Printing the Written Word: The Social History of Books, circa 1450–1520*. Ithaca: Cornell University Press, 1991.

Telford, Ted. *Chinese Genealogies at the Genealogical Society of Utah: An Annotated Bibliography*. Taibei: Chengwen chubanshe, 1983.

Tian Yiheng 田藝衡. *Liu qing ri zha zhechao* 留青日扎摘鈔. *Jilu huibian, BBCSJC*.

*Tiaoli beikao* 條例備考. Ming Jiajing edition (HYX).

Trigault, Nicola, and Matteo Ricci. *China in the Sixteenth Century: The Journals of Matthew Ricci, 1583–1610*. Trans. Louis J. Gallagher. New York: Random House, 1953.

Tsien Tsuen-hsuin. *Paper and Printing*. In Joseph Needham, ed., *Science and Civilization in China*. Vol. 5, Chemistry and Chemical Technology, Part 1. New York: Cambridge University Press, 1985

Twitchett, Denis. *Printing and Publishing in Medieval China*. New York: Frederic C. Beil, 1983.

Twitchett, Denis, and Frederik W. Mote. *The Ming Dynasty, 1368–1644, Part 2. The Cambridge History of China.* New York: Cambridge University Press, 1998.

Tu Long 屠隆. *Kaopan yushi* 考槃餘事. CSJCCB, vol. 1559.

Tu, Wei-ming. *Neo-Confucian Thought in Action: Wang Yang-ming's Youth (1472–1529).* Berkeley: University of California Press, 1976.

Tyson, Gerald P., and Sylvia S. Tyson. *Print and Culture in the Renaissance: Essays on the Advent of Printing in Europe.* Newark: University of Delaware Press, 1986.

Van Der Stock, Jan. *Printing Images in Antwerp: The Introduction of Printmaking in a City, Fifteenth Century to 1585.* Trans. Beverly Jackson. Rotterdam: Sound and Vision Interactive Rotterdam, 1998.

Van Gulik, R. H. *Sexual Life in Ancient China.* Leiden: J. E. Brill, 1961.

Wagner, Rudolf. "Shenbaoguan zaoqi di shuji chuban (1872–1875)" 申報館早期的書籍出版, 1872–1875. In Chen Pingyuan et al. eds., *Wan Ming yu Wan Qing: Lishi chuancheng yu wenhua chuangxin* 晚明與明清歷史傳承與文化創新. Wuhan: Hubei jiaoyu chubanshe, 2002.

Wang Chunyu 王春瑜. "Mingdai shangye wenhua chutan" 明代商業文化初探. *Zhongguo shi yanjiu* 中國史研究, no. 4 (1992): 141–54.

Wang Ermin 王爾敏. *Ming Qing shidai shumin wenhua shenghuo* 明清時代庶民文化生活. Tabei: Academic Sinica, Institute of Modern History, 1996.

Wang Liqi 王利器. *Yuan Ming Qing sandai jinhui xiaoshuo xiqu shiliao* 元明清三代禁毀小説戲曲史料. Shanghai: Shanghai guji chubanshe, 1981.

Wang Shimao 王世懋. *Minbu shu* 閩部疏. CSJCCB.

Wang Shizhen 王世貞. *Yanshan tang bieji* 弇山堂別集. ZGSXCS.

Wang Shizhen 王士禎. *Fengan yuhua* 分甘餘話. CSJCXB, vol. 214.

———. *Gufuyuting zalu* 古夫于亭雜錄. CSJCXB, vol. 214.

Wang Xijue 王錫爵, ed. *Huang Ming guanke jingshi hongci xuji* 皇明館課經籍宏詞續集. SKJHS, vol. 92.

Wang Yu 王宇. *Sishu yeshiyuan chukao* 四書也是圍初告. Ming edition, preface 1615 (HYX).

Wang Yunxi 王運熙 and Gu Yisheng 顧易生. *Zhongguo wenxue piping shi* 中國文學批評史. Taibei: Wunan tushu chuban youxian gongsi, 1991.

Wang Zhongmin 王重民. *Zhongguo shanbenshu tiyao* 中國善本書提要. Shanghai: Shanghai guji chubanshe, 1983.

Waquet, Françoise. "Book Subscriptions in Early Eighteenth-century Italy." *Publishing History* 33 (1993): 77–88.

Warrington, Bernard. "The Bankruptcy of William Pickering in 1853: The Hazards of Publishing and Bookselling in the First Half of the Nineteenth Century." *Publishing History* 27 (1990): 5–25.

Wei Dazhong 魏大中. *Zangmi zhai ji* 藏密齋集. *SKJHS*, vol. 45.

Weng Tong-wen 翁同文. "Yinshushu duiyu shuji chengben di yinxiang" 印刷術對於書籍成本的影響. *Tsing-hua hsueh-pao* 清華學報 6, nos. 1–2 (1967): 35–40.

Widmer, Ellen. "The Epistolary World of Female Talent in Seventeenth-Century China." *Late Imperial China* 10, no. 2 (1989): 1–43.

———. "From Wang Duanshu to Yun Zhu: The Changing Face of Women's Book Culture in Qing China." In Cynthia Brokaw and Kai-wing Chow, eds., *Printing and Book Culture in Late Imperial China*. Berkeley: University of California Press, forthcoming.

———. "Huangduzhai of Hangzhou and Suzhou: A Study in Seventeenth-Century Publishing." *HJAS* 56, no. 1 (1996): 77–122.

———. "Xiaoqing's Literary Legacy and the Place of Women Writers in Late Imperial China." *Late Imperial China* 13, no. 1 (1992): 111–55.

Wiens, Mi Chu. "Lords and Peasants: The Sixteenth to the Eighteenth Century." *Modern China* 6, no. 1 (1980): 3–39.

Williams, George Walton. *The Craft of Printing and the Publications of Shakespeare's Works*. London: Folgers Books, 1985.

Williams, S. Wells. *The Middle Kingdom: A Survey of the Geography, Government, Education, Social Life, Arts, Religion, & etc., of the Chinese Empire and Its Inhabitants*. New York: John Wiley and Sons, Publishers, 1876.

Wilson, Thomas A. *Genealogy of the Way: The Construction and Uses of the Confucian Tradition in Late Imperial China*. Stanford: Stanford University Press, 1995.

Wong, Bin, Theodore Huters, and Pauline Yu. *Culture and State in Chinese History: Conventions, Accommodations, and Critiques*. Stanford: Stanford University Press, 1997.

Woodmansee, Martha. "On the Author Effect: Recovering Collectivity." In idem and Peter Jaszi, eds., *The Construction of Authorship: Textual Appropriation in Law and Literature*. Durham: Duke University Press, 1994.

Wu Han 吳晗. "Mingdai di xin shihuan jieji, shehuidi zhengzhidi wenhuadi guanxi jiqi shenghuo" 明代的新仕宦階級，社會的政治的文化的關係及其生活. *Mingshi yanjiu luncong* 明史研究論叢, no. 5 (1991): 1–68.

Wu Dang 吳當. *Hezuan sishu mengyin cunyi dingjie* 合纂四書蒙引存疑定解 (HY).

Wu Jingzi 吳敬梓. *Rulin waishi* 儒林外史. Hong Kong: Zhonghua shuju, 1972.

Wu, K. T. "Ming Printing and Printers." *Harvard Journal of Asiatic Studies* 7, no. 3 (1943): 203–60.

Wu Yingji 吳應箕. *Loushan tang ji* 樓山堂集. *Yueya tang congshu* 粵雅堂叢書.

Wu Zhihe 吳智和. *Mingdai di ruxue jiaoguan* 明代的儒學教官. Taibei: Xuesheng shuju, 1991.

Wuxian zhi 吳縣志. *Tianyi ge Mingdai fangzhi xuan kan xubian*. Preface 1642. Shanghai: Shanghai shudian, reprint.

Xiang Dingxuan 項鼎鉉. *Huhuan riji* 呼桓日記. *GJZBCK*, vol. 20.

Xiang Shengguo 項聲國. *Sishu ting yue* 四書聽月 (HYX).

Xiang Yu 項煜. *Sishu renwu leihan* 四書人物類涵. Mind edition (HYX).

Xiao Dongfa 肖東發, ed. "Jianyang Yu shi keshu kao" 建陽余氏刻書考. *LDKS*, pp. 90–146.

———. *Zhongguo bianji chubanshi* 中國編輯出版史. Shenyang: Liaoning jiaoyu chubanshe, 1996.

Xie Guozhen 謝國楨 *Ming-Qing zhiji dangshe yundong kao* 明清之際黨社運動考. Beijing: Zhonghua shuju, 1982.

Xie Zhaozhi 謝肇淛. *Wu Zazu* 五雜俎. Taibei: Xin Xing shuju, 1971.

*Xinbian shiwen leiyao qizha qingqian* 新編事文類要啟劄青錢. Tokyo: Nagasawa Kikuya 長澤規矩也 and Koten kenkyu kai 古典研究會, 1963.63.63

Xu Boxing 徐燉興. *Xushi jiazang shumu* 徐氏家藏書目. *MDSMTB*, vol. 2.

Xu Fenpeng 徐奮鵬. *Bidong sheng xinwu* 筆洞生新悟. Preface 1613 (HYX).

———. *Sishu gujin daomai* 古今道脈. Ming edition (HYX).

———. *Sishu zhixin* 四書知新. Preface 1626 (HYX).

———. *Xuke Bidong xiansheng houwu* 續刻筆洞先生後悟. Preface 1613 (HYX).

———. *Xu Bidong xiansheng shi'er bu wenji* 徐奮鵬先生十二部文集. Ming edition (BDT).

———. *Zuanding gujin sishu daquan* 纂定四書大全. Ming edition (HYX).

Xu Fuyuan 許孚遠. *Daxue kao* 大學考, *Daoxue shu* 大學述, *Daxue zhiyan* 大學支言, *Zhongyong shu* 中庸述, *Zhongyong zhiyan* 中庸支言, and *Lunyu shu* 論語述 (HYX).

Xu Guangqi 徐光啓. *Nongzheng quanshu jiaozu* 農政全書校注. Shanghai: Guji chubanshe, 1979.

Xu Hongzu 徐宏祖. *Xu Xiake youji* 徐霞客遊記. Taibei: Shijie shuju, 1970.

Xu Jianqing 徐建青. "Qingdai di zaozhi ye" 清代的造紙業. *Zhongguo shi yanjiu*, no. 3 (1997): 135–44.

Xu Jianrong 徐建融. *Mingdai shuhua jianding yu yishu shichang* 明代書畫鑒定與藝術市場. Shanghai: Shanghai shudian chubanshe, 1997.

Xu Shuofang 徐朔方. *Wan Ming Qujia nianpu* 晚明曲家年譜. 3 vols. Hangzhou: Zhejiang guji chubanshe, 1993.

Xu Wei 徐渭. *Xu Wenchang sanji* 徐文長三集. 4 vols. Taibei: Guoli zhongyang tushuguan, 1968.

———. *Xu Wei ji* 徐渭集. Beijing: Zhonghua shuju, 1983.

Xu Xiaoman 徐小蠻. "A Study of Printing Genealogies in Shanghai and Jiangsu-Zhejiang Area in the Qing Dynasty." In Cynthia Brokaw and Kai-wing Chow, eds., *Printing and Book Culture in Late Imperial China*. Berkeley: University of California Press, forthcoming.

Xu Xuemo 徐學謨. *Shimiao shi yu lu* 世廟識餘錄. Taibei: Guofeng.

Xu Zhaotai 徐肇臺. *Jiayi jizheng lu* 甲乙記政錄. *SKJHS*, vol. 6. chubanshe, 1965.

*Xuanlan zhai shumu* 玄覽齋書目. *MDSMTB*.

Xue Gang 薛岡. *Tianjue tang biyu* 天爵堂筆餘. *Mingshi yanjiu luncong*, no. 5 (1991): 322–56.

Yang Shen 楊慎. *Shaoshi shanfang leigao* 少室山房類稿. *CSJCXB*, vol. 146.

Yang Shengxin 楊繩信. "Lidai kegong gongjia chutan" 明代刻工工價初探. *LDKS*, pp. 553–67.

Yang Shicong 楊士聰. *Yutang huiji* 玉堂薈記. Taibei: Taiwan sheng zhengfu yin-shuai chang, 1968.

Yang Sichang 楊嗣昌. *Yang Wenruo xiansheng ji* 楊文弱先生集. *SKJHS*, vol. 69.

Yang Wenkui 楊文魁. *Sishu shiwen shilu* 四書事文實錄. Ming edition (HYX).

Yang Xunji 楊循吉. *Sutan* 蘇談. *Jilu huibian* 記錄彙編. *BBCSJC*.

Yao Guangzuo 姚光祚. *Sishu wuxue wangyang bian* 四書吾學望洋編. Ming edition, preface 1615 (HYX).

Ye Changchi 葉昌熾. *Cang shu jishi shi* 藏書紀事詩. Taibei: Shijie shuju, 1961.

Ye Dehui 葉德輝. *Shulin qing hua* 書林清話. Taibei: Shijie shuju, 1961.

Ye Mengzhu 葉夢珠. *Chungming mengyu lu* 春明夢餘錄. *SKQSZB*, vol. 224–38.

———. *Tianfu guangji* 天府廣記. Beijing: Bejing chubanshe, 1962.

———. Yueshi bian 閱世編. *Shanghai zhanggu congshu* 上海掌故叢書. Vol. 1. Taibei: Xuehai chubanshe, 1968.

Ye Sheng 葉盛. *Shuidong riji* 水東日記. *ZGSXCS*, vol. 25–26.

Ye Xian'en 葉顯恩. *Ming Qing Huizhou shehui yu tianpuzhi* 明清徽州農村社會與佃僕制. Huizhou: Renmin chubanshe, 1983.

Ye, Yang. *Vignettes from the Late Ming: A Hsiao-p'in Anthology*. Seattle: University of Washington Press, 1999.

Yeh, Catherine. "The Lifestyle of Four Wenren in Late Qing Shanghai." *HJAS* 57, no. 2 (1997): 419–70.

———. "Reinventing Ritual: Late Qing Handbooks for Proper Customer Behavior in Shanghai Courtesan Houses." *Late Imperial China* 19, no. 2 (1998): 1–63.

*Yi chun xiang zhi* 宜春香質. *SWXHB*, vol. 7.

Yin Yungong 尹韻公. *Zhongguo Mingdai xinwen chuanbo shi* 中國明代新聞傳播史. Chongqing: Chongqing chubanshe, 1990.

Yu, Chun-fang. "P'u-t'o Shan: Pilgrimage and the Creation of the Chinese Pota-laka." In Susan Naquin and Chun-fang Yu, eds. *Pilgrims and Sacred Sites in China*. Berkeley: University of California Press, 1992.

———. *The Renewal of Buddhism in China: Chu-hung and the Late Ming Synthesis*. New York: Columbia University Press, 1980.

Yu Yingke 余應科. *Qian Cao liang xiansheng Sishu qianbai nian yan* 錢曹兩先生四書千百年眼. Ming edition, preface 1633 (HYX).

Yu Yingqiu 余應虬. *Sishu mai jiangyi* 四書脈講意. Ming edition, 1619 (HYX).

———. *Sishu Yijing tujie* 四書翼經圖解. Ming edition (HYX).

Yu Ying-shih 余英時. "Shishang hudong yu ruxue zhuanxiang: Ming Qing she-huishi yu sixiangshi zhi yi mainxiang" 士商互動與儒學轉向:明清社會史與思想史之一面相. In Hao Yanping and Wei Xiumei, eds., *Jinshi zhongguo zhi zhuantong yu tuibian: Liu Guangjing yuanshi qishiwu sui zhushou lunwenji* 近世中國之傳統與蛻變:劉廣京院士七十五歲祝壽論文集. Taibei: Academic Sinica, 1999.

———. "Zhongguo jinshi zongjiao lunli yu shangren jingshen" 中國近世宗教倫理與商人精神. In *Zhongguo sixiang quantong di xiandai quanshi*. Taibei: Liangjing chubanshe, 1990.

Yuan Hongdao 袁宏道. *Ping hua zhai zalu* 瓶花齋雜錄. *XHLB*.

———. *Shabi tang xuji* 灑碧堂續集. *SKJHS*, vol. 67.

———. *Sabi tang ji* 灑碧堂集. *SKJHS*, vol. 67.

———. *Yuan Zhonglang quanji* 袁中郎全集. Ming edition, preface 1629 (BDT).

———. *Yuan Zhonglang quanji* 袁中郎全集. Shanghai: Shijie shuju, 1935.

Yuan Huang 袁黃. *Baodi zhengshu* 寶邸政書. In *Liaofan zazhu* 了凡雜著. *BJTS*, vol. 80.

———. *Liaofan Yuan xiansheng sishu shanzheng jian shuyi* 了凡袁先生四書刪正兼疏義(HYX).

———. *Sishu xun er sushuo* 四書訓兒俗說 (HYX).

Yuan Jixian 袁繼咸. *Liuliu tang ji* 六柳堂集. *SKJWS*, vol. 116.

Yuan Tongli 袁同禮. "Mingdai sijia cangshu gailue" 明代私家藏書概略. *Tushu-guan xue jikan* 圖書館學季刊, no. 2 (1926–37). Beijing: Zhonghua tushu-guan xiehui.

Yuan Yi 袁逸. "Mingdai yiqian shuji jiaoyi ji shujia kao" 明代以前書籍交易及書價考. *Zhejiang xuekan* 浙江學刊, no. 6 (1992): 174–78.

Yuan Zhongdao 袁中道. *Kexue zhai jinji* 珂雪齋近集. Shanghai: Shanghai shu-dian, 1983.

———. *You ju shi lu* 遊居柿錄. In *Yuan Xiaoxiu riji* 袁小脩日記. Taibei: Taibei shuju, 1956.

*Yuelu yin* 月露音. *MDBHCK*, no. 6.

*Yugui hong* 玉圭紅. *SWXHB*, vol. 4.

Zang Maoxun 臧懋循. *Fubaotang ji* 負苞堂集. Shanghai: Gudian wenxue chubanshe, 1958.

Ze, David Wei. "Printing as an Agent of Social Stability: The Social Organization of Book Production in China during the Song Dynasty." Ph.D. diss., Simon Fraser University, 1995.

Zelin, Madeleine. *The Magistrate's Tael: Rationalizing Fiscal Reform in Eighteenth Centruy Ch'ing China*. Berkeley: University of California Press, 1984.

Zha Duo 查鐸. *Chandao ji* 闡道集. Preface 1609 (SKY).

Zha Jizuo 查繼佐. *Zui wei lu* 罪惟錄. Hangzhou: Zhejiang Guji chubanshe, 1986.

Zha Shenxing 查慎行. *Renhai ji* 人海記. *CSJCXB*, vol. 214.

Zhai Tunjian 翟屯建. *Ming Qing shiqi Huizhou keshu jianshu* 明清時期徽州刻書簡述. *Wenxian* 文獻, no. 4 (1988): 242–51.

Zhang Anqi 張安奇. "Ming gaoben Yuhua tang riji zhong di jingji shiliao yanjiu" 明稿本《玉華堂日記》中的經濟史料研究. *Mingshi yanjiu luncong* 明史研究論叢, no. 5 (1991): 268–311.

Zhang Dai 張岱. *Sishu yu* 四書遇. Hangzhou: Zhejiang guji chubanshe, 1985.

———. *Tao'an meng yi* 陶庵夢憶. Taibei: Kaiming shudian, 1957.

Zhang Fengyi 張鳳翼. *Chushi tang ji* 處實堂集. Wanli edition (ZT).

———. *Juzhu shanfang ji* 句注山房集. *SKJHS*, vol. 70.

Zhang, Longxi. *Mighty Opposites: From Dichotomies to Differences in the Comparative Study of China*. Stanford: Stanford University Press, 1998.

Zhang Nai 張鼐. *Zhang Dongchu xiansheng xieyu yinmeng Sishu yan* 張洞初先生設喻引蒙四書演(HYX).

Zhang Pu 張溥. *Qiluzhai lunlue* 七錄齋論略. Taibei: Weiwen shuju, 1977.

———. *Sishu kaobei* 四書考備. Ming edition (HYX).

———. *Sishu yin* 四書印. Ming edition (HYX).

———. *Sishu zhushu daquan he zuan* 四書注疏大全合纂. Ming edition (HYX).

Zhang Wenyan 張文炎. *Guochao minggong jingji wenchao* 國朝名公經濟文鈔. *BJTS*, vol. 120.

Zhang Xiumin 張秀民. "Mingdai Nanjing di keshu" 明代南京的刻書. *Wenwu* 文物, no. 11 (1980): 78–83.

———. *Zhongguo yinshuashi* 中國印刷史. Shanghai: Renmin chubanshe, 1989.

Zhang Xiumin and Han Qi 韓琦. *Zhongguo huozi shi* 中國活字史. Beijing: Zhongguo shuji chubanshe, 1998.

Zhang Xuan 張萱. *Xiyuan jianwenlu* 西園見聞錄. *ZHWSCS*, ser. 5, vols. 1–8. Reprint of 1940 edition. Taibei: Huawen shuju, 1975.

Zhang Yingyu 張應俞. *Dupian xinshu* 杜騙新書. *GBXSCK*, ser. 35, vol. 3.

Zhang Yunluan 張雲鸞. *Sishu jingzheng lu* 四書經正錄 (HYX).

Zhang Zilie 張自烈. *Jishan wenji* 芑山文集. *CSJCXB*, vol. 188.

———. *Sishu daquan bian* 四書大全辨. Preface 1656 (HYX).

———. *Sishu zhujia bian* 四書諸家辯. Preface 1656 (HYX).

Zhao Jishi 趙吉士. *Ji Yuan ji suo ji* 寄園寄所寄. Wensheng shuju, 1911.

Zhao Lu 晁瑮. *Zhaoshi baowen tang shumu* 晁氏寶文堂書目. *MDSMTB*.

*Zhao shi bei* 照世盃. Taibei: Tianyi chubanshe, 1974.

Zhao Shiyu 趙世瑜. "Mingdai fuxian lidian shehui weihai" 明代府縣吏典社會危害. *Zhongguo shehui jingji shi yanjiu*, no. 4 (1988): 53–61.

Zheng Lihua 鄭利華. *Mingdai zhongqi wenxue yanjin yu chengshi xingtai* 明代中期文學演進與城市形態. Shanghai: Fudan daxue chubanshe, 1995.

Zheng Xiao 鄭曉. *Jin yan* 今言. *BJXSDG*, ser. 18, vol. 3.

*Zhong pi Shuihuzhuan* 鍾批水滸傳. *GBXSCK*, ser. 24, vol. 1-4.

Zhong Xing 鍾惺. *Cuiyu ge pingxuan Zhong bojing xiansheng heji* 翠娛閣評選鍾伯敬先生合集 (SKY).

———. *Yinxiu xuan ji* 隱秀軒集. Shanghai: Guji chubanshe, 1992.

———. *Shihuai* 史懷. Wanli edition (ZT).

Zhong Xing and Tan Yuanchun 譚元春, eds. *Gushigui* 古詩歸. Ming edition, preface 1617 (ZT).

*Zhongguo kaoshi zhidushi ziliao xuanbian* 中國考試制度史資料選編. Hefei, Anhui: Huangshan shushe, 1992.

*Zhongguo zuozhi shihua* 中國造紙史話. Taibei: Mingwen shuju, 1985.

*Zhongxu meng* 終須夢. *ZGGDZX*, vol. 4.

Zhou Dechang 周德昌. *Zhongguo jiaoyushi yanjiu* 中國教育史研究:明清分卷. Shanghai: Huadong sifan daxue, 1995.

Zhou Hongzu 周弘祖. *Gujin keshu* 古今書刻. *MDSMTB*, vol. 2.

Zhou Hui 周暉. *Xu Jinling suoshi* 續金陵瑣事. *BJXSDG*, ser. 16, vol. 4.

Zhou Lianggong 周亮工. *Shuying* 書影. Shanghai: Gudian wenxue chubanshe, 1957.

Zhou Qirong 周啓榮. See Chow, Kai-wing.

Zhou Shaoquan 周紹泉 and Zhao Yaguang 趙亞光, eds. *Doushan gong jiayi jiaozhu* 竇山公家議校注. Hefei: Huangshan shushe, 1993.

Zhou Wende 周文德. *Shanbu Sishu shengxian xinjue* 刪補四書聖賢心訣. Ming edition, (HYX).

———. *Sipengju Sishu shengxian xinjue* 四朋居四書聖賢心訣 (BT).

———. *Sishu jiangyi cunshi* 四書講義存是 (HYX).

Zhou Zhong 周鍾. *Zuishiju pingci mingshanye huang Ming xiaolun* 醉石居評次名山業皇明小論. Preface 1623 (SKY).

Zhu Guozhen 朱國楨. *Yongtong xsioa-pin* 涌潼小品. *BJXSDG*, ser. 22, vol. 7.

Zhu Mingliang 朱明良. *Huang Ming baijia sishu lijie ji* 皇明百家四書理解集. Ming edition, preface 1594 (HYX).

Zhu Xi 朱熹. *Daxue zhangju* 大學章句. In *Sishu Wujing Song Yuan ren zhu* 四書五經宋元人注. Beijing: Zhongguo shudian, 1985.

Zhu Xizu 朱希祖. *Ming ji shiliao tiba* 明季史料題跋. Beijing: Zhonghua shuju, 1961.

Zhu Yizun 朱彝尊. *Jingyi kao* 經義考. *SKQS*, vol. 680.

Zhuo Fazhi 卓發之. *Luli ji* 漉灕集. *SKJHS*, vol. 107.

# Index

Ai Nanying, 77, 94–5, 113, 114, 119, 144, 170, 199, 200, 208, 212, 214–15, 216–18, 222, 230–33, 237, 346*n*121, 347*n*134
Almanac, 44, 80, 82
American literature, 190
Analects, 179
Ancha si, 21
Anderson, Benedict, 351*n*2
Anonymity, 138
Anthology of examination essays, 24, 209–13, 235–37, 344*n*78; increase in 210–11, rarity of, 209–10. *See also* Examination aids
Antwerp, 28, 29, 325*n*20
Archaic (*guwen*) school,194, 196. *See also* Former Seven Masters; Latter Seven Masters
Astronomy, 21
Austra, 29
Author, best-selling, 243; naming, 111; reputation of, 111; titles of, 115, 168. *See also* Reputation; *Fu* (Mr.)
Authorship, 142. *See also Banquan*; Copyright

*Baichun shuzhi*, 26
*Baihu tong. See Baihu tongde lun*
*Baihu tongde lun*, 181
*Baijiaxing* (Hundred surnames), 46
Bakhtin, Mikhail, 353*n*32
Bailutong Academy, 327*n*161
*Banquan* (right to print) 141–42, 145, 332*n*283.
*Baoren* (reporter), 96
Beijing, 22, 61, 77, 80, 86, 121, 185
Beijing Library, 22
Bell, Catherine, 300*n*32
*Bense* (natural or original color), 196
*Benti* (essence), 179
Bewick, Thomas, 317*n*65
Bian Gong, 342*n*55
Bible, 70
Blaut, J.M., 298*n*20
*Bogu tu lu*, 108

Book, advertising of, 73, 231, 317*n*73, 326*n*139; binding, 45; as commodity, 38–9, 81; classification of, 26; credibility of, 111; collectors of, 23, 33; cost of 33–38; erotic, 25; from Jianyang, 42, 81; format of, 152; heretical, 250; Latin, 248; packaging of, 74–5; piracy, 75, 138–41; prices of, 19, 38–47, 54–55, 121; printed by movable types, 316*n*54; printed in Song, 20; printed in Tang, 20; tax on, 55; production, 22; standardization of, 27; survival rate of, 249; trade, 77–80; unsold copies of, 248. *See also* Booksellers; Bookshops; Page; Publishing
Book boats (*shuchuan*), 79, 318*n*105, 318*n*108, 318–19*n*109. *See also* Books
Book market, 87; expansion of, 2, 242. *See also* Commercial Publishing; Reading publics
*Book of Changes*, 99, 135, 230, 231, 344*n*69. *See also* Classics
*Book of Documents*, 230. *See also* Classics
*Book of Odes*, 183, 216, 228, 230–31, 237. *See also* Classics
Booksellers, 251, in Britain, 314*n*12; in Europe, 62; in Paris, 314*n*9; in Italy, 314*n*9; and stock of books, 314*n*12. *See also* Bookshops
Bookshops, 140, 176, 236, 317*n*73; in Nanjing, 83–84; in Suzhou; in temples, 83, 79
Bourdieu, Pierre, 11–12, 191–92, 213
Britain, 100, 103; gentry, 251; missionaries, 308*n*130; writers, 23
Broadsheets, 250
Brokaw, Cythnia, 300*n*32, 318*n*91
Bruno, 352*n*17
Brynneman, Henry, 314*n*12
Buddhism, 164, 179–80; Chan, 179–80; in examination essays, 232, 237; scriptures, 72, 165, 309*n*141; texts, 252. *See also* Monks; Temples

Cai Qing, 163, 173. *See also Sishu mengyin*

Official ideology. *See* Imperial Ideology
Oki Yasushi, 300*n*32
Onymity, 138. *See also* Anonymity;
Misonymity
Osaka, 299*n*301
Ouyang De, 177
Ouyang Xiu, 193
Oxford, 353*n*28

Page, casting off of, 316*n*37; composition
of, 63; format of, 25, 28, 152, 173;
number of characters in, 27, 37; sizes
of, 27
Painting, 108
Pan Jiuhua, 140
Pan Lei, 40
Pan Mingta, 313*n*234
Pan Yunduan, 41, 54
Paper, color, 30; cost in Europe, 28–29,
248; cost of, 28, 30; different uses of,
28–31; inexpensive, 249; from Korea,
32; prices of, 35; sizes in Europe,
306*n*74; types of, 34–5. *See also* Paper
products; Printing paper; Paper products
Paper mill, 30, 32, 307*n*113
Paper products, armor (*zhijia*), 31; boxes,
30; canopy (*zhizhang*), 30, 31; firecrackers, 30; flowers, 30–1; folding fans,
30, 46; lanterns, 30; posters, 30; ritual
paper, 30, 306*n*86; toilet paper, 30,
306*n*87, 306*n*88; wall paper, 31; window paper, 30; wrapping paper, 23, 35.
*See also* Printing paper; Writing paper
Paratext, 16, 17, 27, 59, 109–11, and au-
thority of critics, 213–16; concept of,
12–4; and multiple reading, 172; and
publicity, 119–20. *See also* Peritext;
Epitext
Paris, 70, 251*n*317*n*62
Patronage, 13, 100, 104, 135, 143–44,
146, 331*n*258
Pawnshop, 97
*Peach Blossom Fan*, 83. *See also* Kong
Shangren
Peritext, 3, 152, 157. *See also* Epitext;
Paratext
Perkin, David, 190
Pi Rixiu, 127
*Ping tianxia* (to pacify the realm), 182–84
*Pingdian* (comment and punctuate), 197,
203
Pinglutang, 77, 132, 228, 318*n*92. *See also*
Chen Zilong
*Pipa ji* 26, 82, 135
*Piping* (criticism), 197, 203

Play. *See* Drama
Playing cards, 109
Playwright, 63, 98, 103, 107, 125, 204.
*See also* Feng Menglong; Kong Shangren;
Mei Dingzuo; Shen Jing; Tang Xianzu;
Zang Maoxun; Zhang Fengyi
Poetics, 17. *See also* Poetry
Poetry, anthology of, 72, 198–99, 342*n*37;
club, 224; model of, 194–96; of the
Tang dynasty, 128
Political legitimacy, 182–86
Pomeranz, Kenneth, 313*n*234
Ponder, Robert, 70
Pope Paul IV, 250
Postmodernism, 190
Postal system, 136. *See also* Mail
Preface, as commodity, 103–4, 110; to
anthology of examination essays, 102–
3, 114; and networking, 112; increase
in number of, 114, 214–15; as paratext,
27; and print publicity, 133; sale of, 110
Primer, 46
Print publicity, 133, 138, 143; and proof-
readers, 169–70. *See also* Reputation
Printing, color, 25, 342*n*37; multicolor, 23;
origin of Chinese, 302*n*5; scale of production, 64–6, 71; speed of, 70. *See also*
European printing; Government, printing; Woodblock printing; Movable type
printing
Printing paper, 33, Bamboo paper (*zhuzi*),
29, 31, 32, 35; cotton paper (*mianzi*),
33; Korean paper, 32; Shunchang paper,
32. *See also* Maobian; Lianqi
Printing press, 70–1
"Printing revolution," 9, 301*n*36
Printing shops, 20, 304*n*40. *See also* Booksellers; Bookshops; Carvers; European
printers; Hangzhou publishers; Jianyang
publishers; Nanjing publishers; Suzhou
publishers
Printing supervisor (*dukan, duke, duzi*),
65, 121–22, 327*n*166
Prints, of Buddhist and Daoist deities, 24,
30; of scenes in novel and plays, 24; of
Protestants, 250
Private publishing, 20, 22, and commercial
publishing, 60, 62–3, 171, 228. *See also*
Publishing
Professional writers, 2, 51–2, 106–7;
authority of, 2, 189–90; cooperation
among, 128–31; income of, 141; indis-
tinguishable from amateur, 324–25*n*102;
specialization among, 123–38. *See also*
Critics; Shanren

Proofreaders, increase in number of,
119–20, 169–70; published names
of, 65
Prostitutes, 25, 48
Prynne, William, 352*n*17
Pseudonymity, 138
Public lecture movement (*Jiangxue*), 160
Public opinion (*gonglun, gongyi*), 15, 16,
232, 245. *See also* Gong
Public sphere, 15. *See also* Literary public
sphere
Publishers, acquisition of manuscripts,
75–77; book stock of European, 250;
branches, 84, 314*n*15; European, 141;
and literary society, 236; marketing
strategies, 166–73, 317*n*73; as patrons,
92, 96. *See also* Chen Renxi, Chen
Dalai; Feng Menglong; Jianyang publishers; Hangzhou publishers; Huizhou
publishers, Li Yu; Nanjing publishers,
Qizizhai; Suzhou publishers; Tang
Dazhen; Xu Zichang, Yu Shanzhang
Publishing, 1, 22, 66, 241–45 ; centers, 80;
and cultural production, 190–92; differentiation in, 27; and discursive space,
187–88; European and Chinese compared, 246–52; expansion of, 1–2, 22,
23, 89, 97; in Japan, 299*n*30; local orientation, 88; profit, 45; risk in European, 250; specialization in, 81, 84,
123–32, 125; standardization in, 27. *See
also* Carvers; Carving shops; European
printing; Publishers; Movable type printing; Woodblock printing

Qi Biaojia, 216, 107
Qi Chengye, 23, 26
Qian Chaoyang, 168
Qian Daxin, 128
Qian Qianyi, 38, 215, 227
*Qianzi wen*, 46
*Qing* (love, emotion), 195,196
Qishangzhai, 124. *See also* Chen Renxi
Qiu Shun, 46
Qiu Zhaolin
Qizhizhai, 64
Queen Mary, 352*n*25

Rag, 29. *See also* Paper
Rawski, Evelyn, 311*n*199
Reader, 154–55; autonomy of, 333*n*10;
and response, 176
Reading, guidelines (*dufa*), 73; protocols,
151–52, 157; pluralistic, 174–82;
publics, 15, 89, 92, 117, 123, 144; and

resistance, 151–54. *See also* Literary
public sphere
*Records of Rites*, 238, 344*n*69. *See also*
Classics
Religion, and books, 9; and publishing, 22,
252; in European publishing, 250–51
Ren Han, 196
Renaissance, 7
Reputable masters. *See Minggong*
Reputation, 197–207. *See also* Print
publicity
Ricci, Matteo, 19, 29, 69, 114, 242
*Rites of Zhou*, 129
Roche, Daniel, 251
Rome, 69
*Romance of the Lute. See Pipa ji*
*Romance of the Three Kingdoms.
See Sanguozhi yanyi*
*Romance of the Water Margin.
See Shuihuzhuan*
*Romance of the West Chamber.
See Xixiang ji*
Romanticism, 3
Rongyutang, 135. *See also* Yuan Wuya
Royalties, 248
*Rulin Waishi*, 62, 77, 317*n*73
*Runbi*, 49. *See also Maiwen*

*Sanguozhi yanyi*, 322*n*31
*Sanjiao kaimi yanyi*, 140
*Sanyi jiao* (Religion of Union of the Three
Teachings), 37, 140
*Sanzijing* 46
Semantic field of the book, 152, 154–56,
189. *See also* Reading
Seville, 305*n*49
Shakespeare, 252
Shandong, 47, 78
*Shang* (merchants/businessmen), 2, 98.
*See also Shishang*
*Shangtu xiawen*, 166
*Shanren*, 51, 104–9, 146
Shen Bang, 34
Shen Defu, 44
Shen Guoyuan, 75
Shen Jin, 73
Shen Jing, 42, 144
Shen Li, 164, 165
Shen Shixing, 114
Shen Shoumin, 235, 238, 239, 350*n*227
Shen Shouzheng, 96, 102, 169, 215, 216,
344*n*81
Shen Yan, 178
Shen Yiguan, 118
Shen Youzai, 348*n*164

Printed and bound by CPI Group (UK) Ltd, Croydon, CR0 4YY

09/06/2025

14685886-0001